THE MONSTROUS REGIMENT
OF WOMEN

The Monstrous Regiment of Women

Female Rulers in Early Modern Europe

Sharon L. Jansen

palgrave
macmillan

THE MONSTROUS REGIMENT OF WOMEN

First published 2002 by
PALGRAVE MACMILLAN™
175 Fifth Avenue, New York, N.Y. 10010 and
Houndmills, Basingstoke, Hampshire, England RG21 6XS.
Companies and representatives throughout the world.

PALGRAVE MACMILLAN is the global academic imprint of the
Palgrave Macmillan division of St. Martin's Press, LLC and of Palgrave Macmillan Ltd. Macmillan® is a registered trademark in the
United States, United Kingdom and other countries. Palgrave is a
registered trademark in the European Union and other countries.

ISBN 0-312-21341-7 hardback

Library of Congress Cataloging-in-Publication Data

Jansen, Sharon L., 1951–

    The monstrous regiment of women : female rulers in early mod-
ern Europe / Sharon L. Jansen.
        p. cm.
    Includes bibliographical references and index.
    ISBN 0-312-21341-7
    1. Women heads of state—Europe—Biography. 2. Queens—
Europe—Biography. 3. Europe—Kings and rulers—Biography.
4. Europe—Politics and goverment—1492-1648. 5. Europe—History—15th century. I. Title.

D226.7 .J36 2002
940.2'1'0922—dc21   2002025395

A catalogue record for this book is available from the British Library.

Design by Publishing Synthesis Ltd.

First edition: October 2002
10 9 8 7 6 5 4 3 2 1

Printed in the United States of America.

October 2002

For my mother, Helen Jean Jansen,
and my son, Kristian Jansen Jaech

CONTENTS

ACKNOWLEDGMENTS

Early in 1996, I spent several weeks at the British Library, still at its Great Russell Street location, reading the extreme, sometimes violent, arguments about female rule penned by John Knox, Jean Bodin, Robert Filmer, and Bishop Jacques Bossuet, among many others. As I called up manuscript volumes, paged through collections of letters, and slowly deciphered early printed books, all the while consulting a variety of reference books and modern historical studies, I moved back and forth between the Manuscripts Students' Room, the North Library, the North Library Reading Gallery, and the Main Reading Room. I would like to express my gratitude to the British Library for providing access to all of these resources. Staff members were always helpful, courteous, and efficient, even while they were in the midst of preparing for their move to a new location.

Once I returned home, I turned to librarian Laura Lewis for assistance. I would like to express my deepest appreciation to Laura, whose ability to locate and produce even the most obscure material in a timely fashion has made my work much easier.

For their efforts in bringing this book to print, I would like to thank Michael J. Flamini, senior editor, and Amanda Johnson, assistant editor, of the Scholarly and Reference Divison at St. Martin's Press, which produced this book under its Palgrave imprint.

On a more personal note, I am grateful to my dear friend Tom Campbell, who always calls just when I need him and who is always interested in the details.

A NOTE ON NAMES

I have tried to refer to the many women in this study by the name most familiar to English readers, even when this results in some inconsistencies. Thus, I use *Caterina* Sforza rather than "Catherine," though I refer to *Catherine* de' Medici rather than the Italian "Caterina." When the woman is less well known to English readers, I have retained the name reflecting her linguistic background, thus "Blanca," "Blanche," and "Bianca" all appear in these pages.

I have been much more consistent in my effort to retain women's original names and titles rather than adopting the names or titles they acquired through marriage. Thus I have preferred "Anne of France," for example, to the equally common "Anne of Beaujeu," and "Margaret of Austria" to "Margaret of Savoy."

The question of names does remain problematic, however, and I sincerely apologize for the inconsistencies or inconveniences that almost inevitably result from my decisions.

REDRAWING THE LINES OF POWER

To promote a woman to bear rule, superiority, dominion, or empire above any realm, nation, or city is repugnant to nature, contumely to God, a thing most contrarious to His revealed will and approved ordinance, and finally it is the subversion of good order, of all equity and justice.[1]

This uncompromising assessment of a woman's right to govern was made by the Protestant reformer John Knox. When Mary Tudor became queen of England in 1553, the succession of a woman to the throne horrified many, including Knox, who argued that any woman who presumed to "sit in the seat of God, that is, to teach, to judge, or to reign above a man" was "a monster in nature." Women were incapable of effective rule, for "nature . . . doth paint them forth to be weak, frail, impatient, feeble, and foolish, and experience hath declared them to be unconstant, variable, cruel, and lacking the spirit of counsel and regiment."

Knox published this blistering assessment of female rule, *The First Blast of the Trumpet Against the Monstrous Regiment of Women,* in 1558; his bitter indictment of "gynecocracy" was quickly followed in print by a series of pamphlets that echoed, expanded, disputed, and countered his argument that female rule was unnatural, unlawful, and contrary to scripture.[2] From Knox's point of view, the political situation could hardly seem worse. Not only had Mary Tudor succeeded to the throne of England, but Mary Stuart, wife of the dauphin of France, had become queen of Scotland, while *her* mother, Marie of Guise, was acting as regent in Scotland on Mary's behalf.

Unfortunately for Knox, though, the political situation could get worse, and did, almost immediately. When Mary Tudor died only a few months after the *Blast* appeared, her half-sister Elizabeth succeeded her as queen of England. In France, following the death of her husband Henry II, Catherine de' Medici attempted to become regent of France for her son, Francis II. Outmaneuvered in 1559, she succeeded a year later when Francis died and the dowager queen assumed the regency for her second son, Charles IX. Thus, by 1560, England, Scotland, and France were under the direct "regiment" of women.

When I began to think about making my own addition to the discussion of this "monstrous regiment," I wanted to write a series of biographical portraits of the remarkable women whose lives had inspired the debate, exploring the way each of these women achieved, maintained, and manipulated her position even as her right and her ability to do so were contested. I was at first uncertain about how to proceed. Aside from Mary and Elizabeth Tudor, Mary Stuart and her mother, and Catherine de' Medici, I knew of only two other women to include in my project: Margaret of Austria, regent of the Netherlands, and Jeanne d'Albret, the Protestant queen of Navarre, whose son had become Henry IV, king of France. Would it be possible, I wondered, to find enough female rulers to make a "series" of such profiles possible?

But the more I thought about my project, the more I came to see what had been there all along. These weren't the first powerful women in early modern Europe.[3] Any analysis of female rulers in the period should really begin by focusing on the lives of four formidable women who died early in the sixteenth century: Isabella of Spain (d. 1504), who inherited the throne of Castile; Lady Margaret Beaufort (d. 1509), who chose not to press her own claims to the English throne in order to promote the cause of her son, Henry Tudor; Caterina Sforza (d. 1509), who seized power in Imola and Forlì ostensibly to preserve it for her son, Ottaviano; and Anne of France (d. 1522), who acted as a shrewd and politically adept regent for her brother, Charles VIII. The careers of these powerful and successful women seemed to me to provide models for the women who were to follow in the next generation.

Still, as notable as they were, these weren't the only women to whom Mary Tudor or Catherine de' Medici could look for example. As I searched the indexes of political histories and biographies, I began to find the names of women about whom I knew little or nothing. Despite arguments like Knox's against female rule and despite the ordinary descent of political power from one man to another, it became clear to me that a whole range of "dynastic accidents" in early modern Europe had resulted in a surprising number of women ruling as queens or functioning as regents.[4] It became equally clear that the lives and political careers of these sixteenth-century queens were hardly without precedent.[5] Yet I could find little more than names at first. How many Isabellas of Aragon were there? Of Castile? Of Portugal? Were Charlotte of Savoy and Bona of Savoy related? If so, how?

How did Louise of Savoy fit in? Were Anne of France and Anne of Beaujeu the same woman? What about Marie of Guise and Marie of Lorraine? And why was all this so difficult for me to sort out? It was hard to find out much about these Isabellas, Annes, and Maries in traditional political history. In my effort to figure out who these women were and whether and how they were related, I began to focus on the family trees in the books I had in front of me. And that's when I began to notice what (or who) was missing.

In most of the family trees I looked at, one Henry or Charles followed another in succession, son after father, sometimes brother after brother, on occasion nephew after uncle, but all of them springing forth as if by spontaneous generation. I searched, sometimes in vain, for women; wives and mothers were simply absent from many of the genealogies appended to the histories and biographies I was reading. I think my favorite is a Valois "family tree" that charts four branches of the family over the course of nearly four hundred years.[6] It looks as if the line of Valois kings (from 1328 through 1547, anyway)—Philip VI, John II, Charles V, Charles VI, Charles VII, Louis XI, Charles VIII, Louis XII, Francis I—managed to do without any wives or mothers at all. Then again, maybe I like best the Habsburg genealogy that begins in the tenth century and, over the next five centuries, notes only four wives among nine generations of Habsburg descendants. At least according to this family tree, no Habsburg daughters were born between 950 and the mid-sixteenth century, when Eleanor and Mary show up on one branch.[7]

Meanwhile, in England, the five daughters of Edward III (r. 1327-77) are all too often lumped together at the end of the genealogical line as "daughters," but that at least is an improvement over the tables that chart the descendants of his sons without noting that he had any "daughters" at all.[8] I imagine that "issue," as it often appears on such family trees, could include insignificant males as well as females, but I am suspicious that "other issue" refers exclusively to daughters. I am almost afraid to think of what the disclaimer on one "short genealogical tree" might mean: "The irrelevant branches have been pruned."[9]

Of course not all the family trees I looked at omitted women. The "Kings and Queens of England" poster that is hanging right next to me as I type indicates the wives of Edwards I through III, Henry IV and V, Henry VII and Henry VIII (all six). But why isn't the wife of Henry VI included, especially since she was the strong and powerful Margaret of Anjou (Shakespeare's "tiger's heart wrapped in a woman's hide")? Edward IV and Richard III are also missing their wives, as are James V of Scotland and his grandson James VI, who becomes James I of England. Then again, to be absolutely fair, while Mary Tudor's husband (Philip II of Spain) is listed, Mary Stuart's husbands, all three of them (Francis, Darnley, Bothwell), are eliminated. Still, this version of the poster is a marked improvement over the previous edition, which left out the wives of Edwards I through III, Henry IV and V as well as Henry VI, and limited Henry VIII to only three of his six wives. If there are rules to determine when women are included and when they are omitted in such genealogies, I haven't been able to figure out what they are.

I must admit I took unexpected pleasure in some of the inconsistencies I found. The Oxford History of England's volume of *The Earlier Tudors* eliminates all six of Henry VIII's wives; while I am, in general, frustrated that so many women have disappeared from royal family trees, I was delighted to see that Henry's entire matrimonial career had been wiped out. Interestingly, his sisters Margaret and Mary are accompanied by their husbands, or at least some of them; Margaret has her first two, James IV of Scotland and Archibald, earl of Angus, while Mary has only her second, Charles, duke of Brandon—I don't know why she didn't get to keep her king, Louis XII of France. Henry, for whatever reason, hasn't been allowed to keep a single wife. He looks almost lonely.

Even the most complete family trees, one tracing the Medici family from Giovanni "di Bicci" (1360-1428) and his wife Piccarda Bueri through Giovanni Gastone (1671-1737) and his wife Anne of Saxe-Lauenburg, for example, work patrilineally, tracing descent through the male line.[10] Men's names are set in capital letters or boldfaced or highlighted; their wives' names, when included, are smaller, underneath the names, dates, and titles of the men to whom they are connected or off to the side, after "m" or "=" to indicate their status as wives. When women marry into a family, their names suddenly appear—but where did they come from? Who were *their* grandmothers, *their* mothers, *their* sisters? When women marry out of the family, where do they go? Their names are left dangling on the trees of their families, dead ends on the lines of descent. Are they and their descendants the "irrelevant branches" that have to be pruned?

Out of frustration, trying to identify the women whose names I had stumbled across and trying to sort out the connections between them, I set out to draw my own family trees, linking women, generations of mothers and daughters, aunts and nieces. I searched—not always successfully, as you can see from the family trees included here—for the dates of their birth, the dates of their death, the children who succeeded them. As I drew and then redrew my new genealogical tables, I came to see not a series of individual, isolated women who came from nowhere to be swallowed up in the Tudor, Valois, Habsburg, or Medici families, but networks of related women and patterns of connections between them.

I also began to see significant connections and relationships I couldn't always indicate on my redrawn family trees: There were "genealogical" links that went beyond blood ties. Margaret of Austria, who functioned as regent of the Netherlands from 1519 until her death in 1530, had been betrothed at age three to Charles, the dauphin of France; in 1483 she had been sent to the French court where, for ten years, her care and education were directed by the extraordinary Anne, who acted as regent of France for her brother. The betrothal didn't result in marriage; instead, in 1497, Margaret was sent to the court of Queen Isabella of Castile to marry Juan, heir to his mother's Castile and his father Ferdinand's Aragon. What was the influence of two such politically adept women on Margaret, who would function so successfully as regent for so many years?

If all this seems confusing, you can see why I needed to redraw family trees. Instead of genealogies that focused on kings and their sons, making clear their relationships and connections, I wanted to draw links that moved backward and forward, tracing queens and their grandmothers, mothers, aunts, sisters, daughters, nieces, granddaughters, and grandnieces. I have to admit I enjoyed the process of constructing these new family trees. I made the names of the four women I identified as models big—very big. Isabella of Castile overpowers her husband, Ferdinand of Aragon. She also overshadows him. Wherever I could, I put my women on top.[11] I also eliminated every son I could, including Henry VIII's long-desired Edward, as "issue" with which I was not concerned, an "irrelevant branch" I could prune. I kept only those men through whom lines of power descended to a woman. The names of the men who remain on my redrawn genealogies are so tiny I can hardly read them without my glasses. It's somehow very satisfying to see Henry VIII looking so small. Instead of Francis I and Charles V looming so large on the scene, I could see women—generations of remarkable women.

I could also see the shifting political alliances of early modern Europe from a very different (and revealing) perspective. As I drew my new family trees, I realized that the narrative of early modern European political history looked very different if I focused on women instead of men.

I began my research, as I said, afraid that I might not find enough female rulers to make the project worthwhile. Instead, as I worked, I found more and more women whose stories should be included in my project—too many women, in fact, to make the project, as originally conceived, practicable. But my redrawn family trees had also suggested a way of redefining the "biographical" essays I had originally planned. Instead of perpetuating the tendency to identify a single, extraordinary woman and to focus on her individual life and "unique" accomplishments, the chapters in this volume explore the relationships among women whose lives occupy a place in and perpetuate a continuing, though largely unrecognized, tradition of political rule. Their careers, like their lives, are intertwined, and I have used these pages to explore their personal and political connections.[12]

In choosing my title, I've identified my work here as my own contribution to the debate about female rule. I begin by focusing on the lives of the four powerful women whose careers seemed to me to suggest a range of political models for the queens whose "monstrous regiment" so horrified John Knox: Isabella of Castile, Lady Margaret Beaufort, Caterina Sforza, and Anne of France. Four extended "biographical" chapters then follow, each one focusing on the relationships, connections, and influences that shaped the lives of their female descendants.

The women who assumed political power in succeeding generations in England, Scotland, France, Spain, Portugal, the Holy Roman Empire, the Netherlands, and city-states of Italy were far more numerous—and more successful—than I had imagined, but even more surprising than their numbers and their successes is how completely their names and stories have disappeared from the history of early modern Europe. Aside from Queen Isabella's support of Columbus, "Bloody Mary" and good Queen Bess in England, and the romantic Mary, Queen of Scots, I had learned almost nothing about any of these "monstrous" women in a classroom, through a textbook, or from the pages of the histories and biographies I had read on my own throughout the years.[13]

And so, in addition to analyzing the arguments against female rule and to surveying the lives and connections among the women who constituted this "monstrous regiment," this book has come to reflect as well on the ways that the subject of politics has been shaped and controlled by notions of gender. The "story" of history has been defined by the lists of famous men we have constructed. I have tried to read the past in a different way and to narrate the story from an alternative perspective. I hope, in fact, to have presented a *counter-narrative* here, by focusing on the lives and relationships of women who—like their fathers, husbands, and sons—played important roles in the story of early modern Europe.

I can't claim that my efforts here are either definitive or comprehensive. I have crossed too many chronological, geographical, institutional, and theoretical boundaries to speak authoritatively. Instead, I hope my work will be regarded as exploratory and suggestive. I have tried to summarize, contextualize, and draw together information about female rule and rulers in early modern Europe; perhaps this book is best read as an outline for or a rough draft of a counter-narrative that remains to be written.

By the way, after thinking about it for some time, I decided as I redrew my family trees to let Henry VIII keep two of his six wives—Catherine of Aragon and Anne Boleyn, strong and determined mothers whose daughters became queens.

CHAPTER ONE

FIFTEENTH-CENTURY
FOREMOTHERS

*This subject, Lord, need never to have been discussed because where
there is such union as by the grace of God exists between you and me,
there can be no difference. Already, as my husband, you are king of
Castile, and your orders have to be obeyed here. . . . But since it has
pleased these knights to open this discussion, perhaps it is just as well
that any doubt they have be clarified, as the law of our kingdoms provide[s].*

—Isabella of Castile to Ferdinand of Aragon,
on succession rights, 1475

*My own sweet and most dear King and all my worldly joy, in as hum-
ble a manner as I can think, I recommend me to your Grace and most
heartily beseech Our Lord to bless you. . . . I wis [truly] my very joy,
as I often have showed, . . . there shall never be . . . any good I have
but it shall be yours, and at your commandment.*

—Margaret Beaufort to her son, Henry VII,
king of England, 1499

*. . . and if I have to lose, although I am a woman, I want to lose in a
manly way.*

—Caterina Sforza to her uncle, Ludovico Sforza,
duke of Milan, 1498

*As well, my daughter, with respect to the court, it is not fitting for a
young woman to meddle with or to interfere in many things, and wise*

*men say that one ought to have eyes to look at all things and to see
nothing, ears to hear all and to know nothing, a tongue to answer everyone without speaking a prejudicial word to anyone.*

—Anne of France to her daughter,
Suzanne of Bourbon, c. 1505[1]

Despite John Knox's bitter denunciation, Mary Tudor and Mary Stuart
were not "monsters in nature," nor did their rule represent the sudden
emergence of an unprecedented "monstrous regiment." While the theoretical debate about women's right to govern burned hot, the reality was
that women had and could and did rule—and rule well—even as they were
being told they could not and should not. How, then, did women come
to power in the sixteenth century? In what ways did they represent
themselves as queens and rulers? Where did they turn to find models,
precedents, or guidance?

In compiling our counter-narrative, we will begin with four powerful
women who died early in the sixteenth century: Isabella of Castile (d. 1504),
Margaret Beaufort (d. 1509), Caterina Sforza (d. 1509), and Anne of France
(d. 1522). Each answered questions about female sovereignty in her own
way. Together their lives and careers suggest a range of political models for
the women who were to follow them.

Isabella of Castile (1451-1504), Queen of Castile

Isabella's succession as queen of Castile in 1474 was not unexpected. She
had first been named "princess, legitimate heir and successor to the
kingdoms of Castile and León" some six years earlier, in 1468. Even so, her
succession was not uncomplicated, nor was it uncontested. It was not
complicated because of her sex, however, nor was it contested because she
was a woman: Her rival for the throne of Castile was not a prince but
another princess. Thus the question was not *whether* a woman would rule
in Castile but, rather, *which* woman would rule.

Isabella was the daughter of King Juan II of Castile and his second wife,
Isabel of Portugal. When Isabella was born in 1451, Juan's son by his first
marriage, Enrique, was the Castilian heir apparent, twenty-six years old and
married, expected to produce heirs of his own. Even so, her father signalled
Isabella's place in the succession by announcing the birth of an *infante*, a
title ordinarily reserved for a son of the king. But when a second son,
Alfonso, was born in 1453, Isabella the *infante* became Isabella the *infanta*,
a princess.

When her father died in 1454, Isabella became second in line to the

Castilian throne again, this time behind her younger brother Alfonso, for the newly crowned Enrique still had no children. The year before he had become king, his thirteen-year marriage to Blanche of Navarre had been annulled; the unfortunate Blanche had "failed" to produce an heir for Castile, and despite rumors of Enrique's impotence, she was returned to Navarre in disgrace.[2] A year after he became king, Enrique married once more; like his father, Enrique chose as his second wife a Portuguese princess, Juana.

It took Enrique and his second wife nearly seven years to produce an heir; in late February of 1462 a daughter, also named Juana, was born. In letters dispatched to major cities, Enrique announced the birth of the "most high Princess Doña Juana, my very dear and most beloved daughter and heir."[3] In May the *Cortes*, the parliament of Castile's cities, was convened to confirm Juana as the king's successor. Although rebellion, civil war, and succession crises followed quickly, the "confusions of Castile" were not the result of the birth of a female heir.[4] Juana was never denounced as a "monster in nature," for the succession of a woman to the throne of Castile, although unusual, was not without precedent.

Among those precedents was Sancha of León, the wife of Ferdinand I of Castile. As queen consort, Sancha was praised by contemporary chroniclers for her prudence and justice. When her father Alfonso V died in 1037, Sancha became queen of León in her own right. In a period of transition, when the Christian monarchies of Spain were in the process of shifting from elective to hereditary, her succession is significant for reasons other than her sex: "it affords, it is believed, the first instance of veritable succession to the throne."[5]

When Sancha's husband died in 1065, he left the kingdom of Castile to his older son, Sancho II, and Sancha's kingdom of León to their younger son, Alfonso, but he also left their daughter Urraca absolute sovereignty over the city of Zamora and the title of "queen," which she used all her life. Urraca ruled Zamora peacefully until war broke out between her brothers. After Sancho turned on Alfonso, defeating and exiling him, Urraca went to war against Sancho, who died while besieging her.[6] As a result, Alfonso not only regained León but gained Castile, becoming Alfonso VI, king of a once-more united Castile and León. While Urraca of Zamora remains an intriguing but somewhat elusive figure, her niece and namesake is quite another story. When Alfonso VI's son and heir died, the king turned to his daughter, also named Urraca. As the widow of Count Raymond of Burgundy, she had already succeeded her husband as ruler of his territories. In order to secure his daughter's succession in Castile and León as well, Alfonso VI arranged a second marriage for her, to Alfonso I of Aragon. Instead of a peaceful and profitable union, however, husband and wife went to war. After the death of her father in 1109, Urraca returned to Castile, where she ruled in her own right until 1116, when she recognized her eleven-year-old son by her first marriage as her co-ruler and heir. Throughout the rest of her life, Urraca fought to maintain control of her kingdom. Only after her death in 1126, when her son became Alfonso VII, did Alfonso of Aragon end his fight for Castile and León. In assessing both Urraca and her reign, Bernard Kelley notes the "prevailing tendency" by the queen's contemporaries as well as by modern historians to overlook the years of her rule "as a kind of interregnum to be discussed and dismissed as quickly as possible." But Kelly notes the singular achievement of the woman he calls an "indomitable queen": "she was both a woman and the crowned head of a major western kingdom who ruled in her own right."[7]

The kingdom that Urraca had fought so hard to maintain was divided by her son; when Alfonso VII died in 1157, his older son became Sancho III, king of Castile, and his younger son became Ferdinand II of León.[8] It was left to another queen regnant, Berenguela, to reunite Castile and León.

Berenguela was the daughter of Urraca of Castile's great-grandson Alfonso VIII and his wife, Eleanor of England. When her father died in 1214, Berenguela, separated from her husband Alfonso IX of León, became guardian and regent for the the young Enrique I, her brother. Although she was quickly replaced by disaffected Castilian nobles, when Enrique died in 1217 Berenguela herself became ruler of Castile. Her succession as queen regnant was problematic, however, in part because there was some question about whether she or her sister Blanca was the next legitimate heir to the throne.[9] After receiving the crown, therefore, Berenguela abdicated in favor of her son, who was recognized as King Ferdinand III.

Berenguela's husband invaded Castile. Although he did not succeed in efforts to unseat the young king, Alfonso of León's opposition to Berenguela persisted; when he died in 1230, instead of naming Ferdinand to succeed him in León, his two daughters by his first wife were named as his heirs. Berenguela advised her son "with great prudence," indicating how to gain León without shedding more blood. Negotiating with his half-sisters, Ferdinand exchanged rich dowries for the crown of León, thereby reuniting the kingdoms of Castile and León. Berenguela continued to play a significant role in the kingdom; she advised her son about military and political affairs until her death in 1246.[10]

These examples may seem to offer somewhat problematic precedents for the succession of a queen. Sancha was queen regnant of León but queen-consort of Castile. She had succeeded to the throne of León in her own right, but had she ruled? When her husband died in 1065, he left Sancha's kingdom of León to their son Alfonso, even though Sancha herself did not die until 1067, at the earliest, and perhaps not until 1071. At least

Sancha's inheritance had been undisputed; the successions of both Urraca and Berenguela were accompanied by civil conflict, and both queens "solved" the conflicts by ceding their thrones to their sons. None of these precedents offered an example of female sovereignty more recent than the early thirteenth century. But beyond precedent, Juana's position as her father's heir was assured by law. In the legal code compiled for Alfonso X, Berenguela's grandson, the possibility of a woman's succession to the throne was specifically addressed. *The Seven Divisions (Las Siete Partidas)* both defines the "kingly office" and discusses the qualifications for kingship. A king must possess knowledge of God, love of God, and fear of God, as well as a range of qualifications in thought (vice is condemned), in word (circumspection is enjoined, evil speech condemned), and in deed (appropriate dress is prescribed, anger and hatred proscribed). The king's role as husband and father is detailed, as are his relationships to his court, his people, and his country. Among all of these qualifications of kingship is the law of succession, "The Eldest Son Has Precedence and Superiority over His Other Brothers":

> Superiority, by reason of primogeniture, is a great mark of affection which God bestows upon the sons of kings by distinguishing them from their other brothers who are born after them, for He makes it plain that He gives precedence to, and places above the others, him upon whom He desires to confer this honor, in order that they may obey him and protect him, as they do their father and their lord.

It is "just that no one should have the sovereignty of the kingdom but the eldest son, after the death of his father," but "to avoid many evils which have happened, and which may occur again," primogeniture has been defined by "wise men" to include women:

> Wherefore they ordained that if there were no sons, the eldest daughter should inherit the kingdom. They also decreed that if the eldest son should die before he came into his inheritance, and should leave a son or a daughter born of his lawful wife, he or she, and no other, should have the kingdom.[11]

The "confusions of Castile" did not result, then, from the birth of a princess instead of a prince in 1462. It was Enrique himself who was the focus of dissatisfaction. He was accused of impotence and incompetence, of not being Juan II's legitimate son and of not being Princess Juana's legitimate father, of sympathizing with Jews and Moors and of ignoring his "own" people, particularly the powerful Castilian *grandees*. By 1465, Princess Juana was widely rumored to be the daughter not of Enrique but of Beltrán de la Cueva, Queen Juana's supposed lover. Dissatisfaction, dissension, and disaffection coalesced into defiance. Enrique's opponents "deposed" their king and crowned his half-brother, the eleven-year-old Alfonso, king.

Alfonso "XII," as he was called by his supporters, never became more than "the ghost of a sovereign," as he was known by his opponents. Three years later he fell suddenly ill. On 4 July 1468, Isabella wrote a letter reminding the people that "the succession of the reign and the dominions of Castile and León [belong] to me as legitimate heir and successor." The next day, on 5 July, Alfonso died.

The seventeen-year-old Isabella was urged to press ahead with her claim to be her brother Alfonso's successor, but she chose not to do so. Chroniclers later supplied several motivations for her decision. According to one, Isabella resisted the urging of her advisors because "the death of Alfonso might perhaps be interpreted as an indication from Heaven of its disapproval of their cause." According to another, she rejected these advisors because she wished to avoid "the hardships of war." Yet another attributed her decision to her recognition that "destruction and tyranny" would continue to "increase in the kingdom."[12] Whatever her reasons, Isabella signalled her decision in a letter written some two weeks after Alfonso's death, signing herself "Isabel, by Grace of God princess and legitimate hereditary successor to these kingdoms of Castile and León."[13] Rather than claiming to be Alfonso's heir, she positioned herself as Enrique's.

Although he had assured Queen Juana he had no intention of disinheriting Princess Juana, Enrique met with Isabella and the opposition in September and signed a treaty that named his half-sister as his legitimate successor. The treaty made no specific reference to his daughter or to her claim to the throne. But by his act, Juana of Castile became Juana *la Beltraneja*: illegitimate daughter of a disgraced Queen Juana and her lover Beltrán de la Cueva, instead of legitimate heir of Enrique IV, king of Castile.

Throughout the period of rebellion and civil war that lasted throughout the second half of Enrique's reign—from 1464, through the 1468 succession agreement, until Enrique's death in 1474—various marriage proposals were suggested as a way out of the political crisis. In 1464, before "deposing" Enrique and proclaiming Alfonso king, rebellious nobles had negotiated with the king to name his half-brother as his heir and to arrange for the boy's marriage to Princess Juana, who for the purpose of this agreement was regarded as legitimate. This plan fell apart a few months later.

Isabella was also the focus of various marital projects intended to settle the crisis. In an effort to gain an ally in his struggle with rebellious *grandees*, Enrique had proposed Isabella as a match for Edward IV of England, an offer that Edward declined. In another effort, the king turned to Afonso V of Portugal, his wife's brother and a recent widower. To prevent this

Portuguese alliance and to neutralize Isabella's marriage as a political tool in Enrique's hands, the opposition met with the king in 1466 and proposed instead her marriage to Pedro Giron, one of the rebel leaders. In spite of Isabella's objections, Enrique accepted the compromise, but the bridegroom died on his way to celebrate the union.

By 1468 the political situation changed dramatically. Following Enrique's "decision" to name Isabella as his heir, a double marriage was considered: Afonso V of Portugal, Queen Juana's brother, was again proposed as a match for Isabella, while Juana, princess or *la Beltraneja*, would be married to the Portuguese king's son and heir, Joaõ. Enrique considered this proposal carefully, even asking his queen to travel to Portugal to discuss arrangements with her brother, but Queen Juana refused.[14] Louis XI of France then suggested Isabella's marriage to his brother and heir Charles, duke of Berry and Guyenne. From England came the possibility for an alliance with one of the brothers of King Edward IV, possibly Richard. All of these marriages—with the widowed Portuguese king, with the heir of the king of France, with a brother of the king of England—would have removed Isabella from Castile and almost certainly have jeopardized her claim to the crown.

By the terms of their 1468 agreement, Enrique could arrange a match for Isabella, but he could not force her to accept it; Isabella, for her part, had promised not to marry without Enrique's permission. In 1469, taking the question of her marriage in her own hands, she chose an alliance with Ferdinand of Aragon. She wrote to Enrique announcing her intention and seeking his permission. She began by reminding him of their agreement: "I agreed to submit to your wishes . . . in which it was agreed that the true succession of these said your kingdoms would belong to me as your legitimate heir and successor." Then she sought his permission for her proposal, asking that "Your Highness would . . . consent to the marriage with the . . . prince of Aragon."[15]

Although Enrique's permission was not forthcoming, Isabella and Ferdinand were married on 18 October 1469. The terms of the marriage contract ensured Isabella's rights and her independence: Ferdinand would be prince-consort of Castile, not its king. Ferdinand had to promise "virtual obedience" to Isabella; among other "capitulations," he agreed to live in Castile, to seek permission before leaving the kingdom and before taking any children they might have out of the kingdom, to renew none of his father's claims to Castilian possessions, and to make no government appointments without Isabella's consent. Further, he agreed to provide Isabella a sizeable marriage gift and to serve as her military defender.

By February 1970, Isabella was pregnant. At last, on 26 October, more than a year after his half-sister's marriage, Enrique replied. Declaring Isabella could no longer be considered his heir, he declared Juana once more his legitimate daughter and, therefore, his heir. Despite Enrique's assertions of her legitimacy, the succession question had not been settled when the king died in December of 1474. Conflicting accounts of his dying wishes reflect the confused state of affairs. One report claimed that Enrique had told his confessor, "I declare my daughter to be the heir to the kingdom." Another claimed that, when pressed about his wishes for the succession, the dying king would say nothing. Still another said that Enrique had appointed counselors "who knew his conscience" to settle the succession question, four of them favoring Isabella. In other accounts, Enrique had left a will designating Juana as his heir—a will that was spirited to Portugal for safekeeping, a will that never was found.[16]

Enrique died on 11 December; two days later, on 13 December 1474, Isabella was proclaimed "Queen Proprietess" of Castile. Ferdinand, "as her legitimate husband," was recognized as king. At the church of San Miguel in Segovia, the royal standard raised above her, Isabella took up an unsheathed lance, a symbol of sovereign authority; in the procession that followed, she was proceeded by a rider carrying an upraised naked sword, a symbol of royal justice. Neither ceremony had ever been performed by and for a queen. Ferdinand, meanwhile, was in Aragon. On 16 December he received a letter from Isabella telling him of Enrique's death but not of her coronation. The chronicler Alonso Palencia was with Ferdinand when he received a letter three days later, on 19 December, describing his wife's coronation and the ceremonies. According to Palencia, Ferdinand was surprised—"I have never heard of a queen who usurped this male privilege." His secretary Gonzalez registered more than surprise, shocked not only by Isabella's "insolent action" but by her appropriation of male symbols. He wondered aloud if there were "in antiquity" any "precedent for a queen to be proceeded by this symbol." "Everyone knows that these are conceded to kings," he continued, "but never was known a queen who had usurped this masculine attribute."[17]

Ferdinand was nevertheless confident that he could assert his rights as king. Palencia wrote that Ferdinand felt he would conquer Isabella "with patience"; he "felt certain he would triumph through satisfying assiduously the demands of conjugal love, with which he could easily soften the intransigence that bad advisors had planted in his wife's mind."[18] Speaking for himself, Palencia judged that Isabella was "after all, a woman." His reading of Castilian law led him to conclude that "in the marriage of a crown heiress, even though the husband be of inferior lineage, he must enjoy the scepter and the title of him together with her as well as all the other priorities accorded to males all over the world."[19]

Despite Ferdinand's hopes and Palencia's reading of the laws of succession, Isabella and the Castilian nobility persisted in asserting her role as queen regnant and Ferdinand's as king-consort. Isabella herself announced her position in a letter of 16 December to the towns of Castile, "inviting" them to recognize her as "natural queen" and Ferdinand as "the very illustrious and most powerful Prince . . . , [her] lord, . . . [her] legitimate husband."[20] Fernando del Pulgar, the queen's secretary and chronicler, assembled historical support for Isabella's succession, citing the precedents of the queens whose stories we have briefly mentioned here.

Ferdinand and his allies in Aragon and in Castile, on the other hand, argued that natural and divine law gave precedence to a man over a woman; while law and custom might not exclude women from a throne, in practice, when a woman succeeded, it was her husband who ruled.[21] They also argued that Ferdinand's independent claims to the throne of Castile gave him precedence over Isabella: Ferdinand was the nearest *male* descendant in the Trastamara line.

There matters stood, unresolved even when Ferdinand joined Isabella in Segovia on 2 January. The king-consort was further provoked by learning that, should the queen predecease him, the Castilian throne would pass not to him but to their daughter Isabel, who had been born in 1470. Despite Isabella's efforts at conciliation, Ferdinand threatened to return to Aragon. At last the matter was placed before a council in Segovia on 15 January. About this confrontation Nancy Rubin writes: "That meeting proved to be one of the most extraordinary examinations of female inheritance rights in prefeminist Europe, one whose highly emotional tone would finally be resolved by Isabella's cool logic."[22]

It is at this meeting that Isabella delivered to Ferdinand the words quoted at this outset of this chapter. "This subject"—the subject of succession—did not have to arise, she began. As her husband, Ferdinand was king of Castile. But, the subject having been raised, Isabella appealed to law; the "law of our kingdoms" provided for succession, she reminded him. And Castilian law preferred the inheritance of legitimate daughter in the direct line to a male in a collateral line. Beyond law, Isabella also reminded Ferdinand of the vagaries of male inheritance. If Ferdinand were to die, another, more distant, male relative might claim Castile if women were excluded from succession.[23]

In the end, Ferdinand accepted Isabella's arguments, their agreement reflected in the motto, now famous, which they adopted: "*Tanto monta, monta tanto, Isabel como Fernando*—To stand as high, as high to stand, Isabella as Ferdinand."[24] That he agreed is clear. Why he agreed is another matter.

Motivated by self-interest, fear, or, perhaps, love, Ferdinand accepted the terms Isabella offered, and the two thus established what historian Rafael Altamira calls a "diarchy," a "joint government by two monarchs." There is a qualification to their shared arrangement, however. As Altamira notes, this equality "existed between husband and wife with regard to the Crown's government of Castile. That co-participation was in no wise reflected in the government of Aragon, which was exclusively Ferdinand's prerogative." But, while no similar shared rule was negotiated in Ferdinand's kingdom, he ultimately named Isabella his co-regent in Aragon.[25]

Having settled their own differences, Isabella and Ferdinand were still to face five years of civil war, at least in part motivated by those who defended the twelve-year-old Princess Juana's rights to the throne. Although by February of 1475 most of Castile had recognized Isabella, not all the rebellious *grandees* had. The marquis of Villena, for one, had not. He refused to surrender Juana until a marriage was negotiated for her, a condition Isabella and Ferdinand would not accept. Meanwhile, "Juanista sentiment" was revived in Portugal, where Afonso V, Juana's uncle, decided to intervene. He would marry Princess Juana and invade Castile.

By the end of May the Portuguese king was in Castile. He reached the city of Plasencia, which opened its gates to him. There the forty-three-year-old Afonso, who had once negotiated for Juana as a match for his son, was himself betrothed to the princess. They were jointly proclaimed king and queen of Castile and issued a statement in defense of Juana's claims to the throne. Juana herself claimed that Isabella and Ferdinand had poisoned Enrique and illegally seized the throne. As Ferdinand readied for war against the Portuguese, he prepared a will, one reflecting a changed view of female succession:

> I appoint universal heir . . . our very dear and beloved daughter, princess Isabel. Especially I institute her heir of my kingdoms of Aragon and Sicily, in spite of any laws . . . and customs of the said kingdoms, which may forbid a female to succeed in them.

In his will Ferdinand specifically discounts ambition or love as motivations for his change of heart; "this is not because of ambition, greed, or the inordinate affection I may have for the said princess." Rather, he claims, "I . . . order it in this way due to the great benefit resulting for these kingdoms."[26]

Ferdinand's initial encounter with Afonso was a disaster, his retreating army pillaging the Castilian countryside. At Tordesillas, Isabella's response to her husband's defeat was recorded by an anonymous chronicler. She began conventionally enough, excusing her speech by saying "it may be that women lack discretion to know and strength to dare, and even a tongue to speak." But, as she continued, her words "were more like those of a forceful man than a timid woman." "You may say now that women should not speak of dangers because they are not the ones who suffer them," she began. But, she continued, "nobody was risking more than I"; not only had she "wagered" her husband and king, she had "bet" her knights, her people, and her money. She had suffered their defeat "with an angry heart," she added, "gritting my teeth and clenching my fists." "Revenge itself" seemed to be fighting within her. Her passionate rebuke of Ferdinand and her army is full of references to her sex:

> Of my fury, being a woman, and of your patience, being men, I marvel. And excellent king, my lord, and virtuous knights, if more than I reasonably ought I have extended my words, your virtue pardon such an error, for with daring to complain I have quieted the passion that naturally grows in the heart of women.[27]

The Castilian army recovered, and Afonso and Ferdinand fought on until 1477, when at last Ferdinand declared victory. For his part, Afonso returned to Portugal, taking Juana with him. In 1478 two events signalled an end to the conflict between Portugal and Castile. In June, Isabella gave birth to a son, Juan, and in December the pope revoked the dispensation he had issued to Afonso so that the Portuguese king could marry his own niece. Afonso attempted one more invasion of Castile, but when this failed, Juana's fate was sealed.

To negotiate a peace settlement with Isabella, Afonso sent Beatriz, duchess of Viseu. The two women met in March of 1479. Beatriz was Afonso's sister-in-law, the wife of his brother. But Beatriz was also Isabella's aunt, her mother Isabel of Portugal's sister. The two women were thus joined by family ties even as they were separated by opposing political interests. By the terms of the treaty they eventually negotiated, Princess Isabel was to marry Afonso of Portugal, King Afonso's grandson and heir of Prince João. She would be sent to live under the guardianship of Beatriz of Viseu, who would also be Princess Juana's guardian. Juana could either marry Prince Juan, waiting thirteen or fourteen years until the prince was old enough to be married (by which time Juana would be at least thirty), or she could enter a convent. In either case, she was to give up her claim to the throne of Castile.

In light of these prospects, Princess Juana announced her intention of becoming a nun. Her decision was hardly a happy one, despite the reports of Isabella's chroniclers who attributed to her a variety of pious sentiments. She entered a convent in Portugal in 1479, then left it. She was forced into another convent in 1480, Isabella's own confessor witnessing Juana's profession of her vows. This was not the end of her usefulness as a political tool, however. When Afonso V died in 1481, his son, João II, renewed the promise that Juana should remain in Portugal "unmarried and a nun," then turned around and supported her claim to the Castilian throne in a dispute with Isabella. Juana's attitude to her "choice" of a religious life can best be assessed, as Nancy Rubin argues, by her subsequent behavior:

> During her long life La Beltraneja was to leave the convent repeatedly and live in ducal homes and palaces under the protection of Portuguese kings. Each time she made a lengthy excursion into the Portuguese court, Isabella and Ferdinand protested and enlisted the help of the pope to force her back into the convent. Neither monastic walls nor stark chapels would, however, change La Beltraneja's conviction. To the last days of her life in 1530 La Beltraneja continued to sign her letters *Yo la Reina*, or "I the Queen."[28]

But all that was in the future. For the moment, Isabella's succession was secure.

When her half-brother Enrique IV had died, Isabella was twenty-three years old, a wife and a mother, while Princess Juana was twelve, with all the attendant difficulties of a minority. In the resulting conflict over the succession, Isabella's age and her circumstances favored her, but even so it took five years and her own determination and ability to secure the throne. She had to defeat Juana, but she also had to negotiate with Ferdinand. In her struggle to become queen regnant, she had historical precedents and *The Seven Divisions,* but she had something else as well: Throughout her life she had been surrounded by models of female power and female rule.

From her birth in 1451 until at least 1457 and perhaps 1460, Isabella had remained with her mother. The picture of Isabel of Portugal that is most often drawn is of a young widow who, following the death of her husband Juan II, retired from court to Arevalo, sinking gradually into despair and madness. Her influence over the young Isabella is variously interpreted. A royal widow with a household befitting a queen dowager, Isabel nevertheless "cared for her children personally," "first taught the young children their letters," and "infused her children Isabella and Alfonso with . . . devotional piety," according to one recent, perhaps sentimental, view. Another, darker picture is equally dramatic:

> Isabel grew up with a deeply disturbed mother who locked herself away from the light of day. The child may well have dreaded becoming like her, and suffered tension between that dread and affection for her mother. . . . It is tempting to conjecture that qualities she displayed as an adult . . . were honed in reaction to her mother's condition.[29]

Both views of Queen Isabel may be true, yet neither is complete. As a seventeen-year-old princess, Isabel of Portugal became the second wife of

Juan of Castile. Though young, she was judged "a much more powerful personality than her husband" the king; she was credited, for example, with having engineered the defeat of Juan's favorite, Alvaro de Luna. For this, as the historian J. N. Hillgarth reports, she was celebrated by the marquis of Santillana "as the 'fourth liberator' of mankind, after Judith, Esther, and the Virgin Mary."[30] Devoted *and* disturbed, devoted *or* disturbed, Isabel of Portugal was an influential politician who survived her husband's death by more than forty years and remained a continuing presence in her daughter's life.

Equally important was Isabel of Portugal's mother, Isabel de Barcelos. Daughter of a powerful Portuguese noble, she had married a Portuguese prince; widowed, she arrived in Castile when her granddaughter was two. Chroniclers note that her son-in-law King Juan asked her to attend his privy council; she was, by their account, a "notable woman of great counsel." Following the king's death, Isabel de Barcelos accompanied her daughter to Arevalo, where she, too, exerted her influence in the royal household. One indication of her continuing significance in Castilian affairs is her role in 1454 and 1455 when she and her daughter were instrumental in negotiating with the Portuguese king for Enrique's marriage to Juana of Portugal.[31] When Isabel de Barcelos finally died in 1465, Castile was in the midst of civil war, her granddaughter Isabella busy negotiating the perilous course that would lead to her declaration in 1468 as Enrique's heir.

Yet another strong presence at Arevalo was Maria of Castile, Juan II's sister and Isabella's aunt. Maria married Alfonso V of Aragon, and for nearly twenty years she was "Governor of Aragon," effectively ruling the kingdom for her husband, who spent most of this time in his kingdom of Naples. "Weak in body and constantly attacked by illness," she was nevertheless a woman remarkable for "the energy and constancy with which she pursued her goals."[32] In 1454 she arrived in Castile just after her brother's death to negotiate with the new king, her nephew, on behalf of her husband. She stayed in Arevalo until the year before her death in 1458.[33]

Isabella's biographers stress the relative obscurity of her earliest years, her isolation from court. Accounts of these years also emphasize her lack of the kind of formal, humanistic education her brothers received and her training, instead, in "womanly virtues" and "domestic arts." From another perspective, however, these "isolated" years provided her invaluable lessons in the active role possible for a woman. She spent these formative years surrounded by models of female strength and influence. This royal household of three generations of women represents the sort of "female cluster" described by historian Gerda Lerner as crucial for women's authorization. In such an "inter-generational" group, strong older women "served as models of the *femme forte*, as paragons of female learning and as women of power" for their daughters and granddaughters. Such a "clustering" becomes a means by which "transmittal of knowledge to women becomes a family tradition."[34]

Equally important for Isabella the queen, I would argue, is the presence of politically active women in Ferdinand's life. Although Aragonese succession laws might favor a man, a woman like Maria of Castile, Ferdinand's aunt, might effectively rule the country on behalf of a man.[35] Indeed, Ferdinand's own mother, Juana Enriquez, was just such a woman. As Juan II of Aragon's second wife, she was successful in having her son recognized as his father's heir.[36] The Aragonese king named Juana as "Governor" when Catalonia rebelled, his diplomatic and military activities matched by the "indefatigable" Juana's own maneuverings. The nine-year-old Ferdinand accompanied his mother to Catalonia, where she was successful in her efforts to regain support for her husband.

Juana's influence on her son was significant in ways beyond assuring his succession, however. In assessing the character of Ferdinand, his biographer Jaime Vicens Vives suggests that he resembled his mother more than his father.[37] Vives focuses his discussion of Juana's influence on Ferdinand's personal tastes and preferences, his love for history, music, and personal adornment, but I would argue that she influenced her son in more profound ways, most significantly in his ultimate willingness to negotiate shared rule with Isabella and in his ability to work with her under the terms of their agreement throughout their married life.

Juana Enriquez died in 1468, when Ferdinand was sixteen. He married Isabella the next year, and for the next thirty years, from Isabella's succession in 1474 until her death in 1504, los Reyes Catolicos, "the Catholic kings," managed their dual roles in Castile. How did Isabella reconcile her assertion of political supremacy with her evident acceptance of her traditional subservience as Ferdinand's wife? How, in other words, did she balance her public role as sovereign with her private role as a woman?

Isabella's contemporaries struggled to explain her role as queen. The chronicles of her reign were partisan and propagandistic, representing the contrasting views of her supporters and detractors. Even today historians are no more unified in their views of the queen; biographies of Isabella often share little besides the rough chronology of her life as they interpret and reinterpret her motives, goals, and character. Perhaps the most insightful comment about Isabella remains the judgment of one of her most constant critics, Alfonso de Palencia, Ferdinand's counselor: Isabella was, in his judgment, "mistress of dissimulation and simulation."[38]

Beyond her appropriations of the masculine symbols of authority and justice in her coronation, the queen could, and did, present herself in ways beyond the traditional role of a woman. During the civil war following Enrique's death, "with total disregard for the usual customs of her sex," she rode from city to town to plead for support for her cause. One such foray, before Ferdinand's defeat at Toro in 1475, resulted in a miscarriage. In 1477, denied entrance to a fortress in Trujillo, she summoned an army and, at its head, forced the city to surrender to her. During the ten-year Reconquest, Isabella's military role expanded: "Not only was she a provisioner and quarter master, but she had become a behind-the-scenes administrator and morale booster."[39] An "accomplished strategist," she ultimately moved out from behind the scenes to center stage, taking the field with the Castilian army in Cordoba, Malaga, Baeza, and, at last, in Granada, where she appeared wearing armor and mounted on a warhorse.

Isabella's authority and independence were apparent to those who observed her. The chronicler Palencia collected reports of and complaints about Ferdinand's subordinate role. A foreign traveller in Spain reported that the king didn't seal his letters until Isabella had read them and observed that, while the king's orders were often neglected, "everyone trembled at the name of the queen." Andres de Bernaldéz, a chronicler and curate, judged that the queen was "the most feared and respected queen that ever was in the world," while another contemporary, in Ferdinand's service, concluded that, compared to the king, "in the judgment of many, the queen was of more majestic aspect, of livelier intelligence, of greater soul and more serious conduct."[40] In less flattering terms, she was more intransigent, less willing to compromise, more rigorous, less tolerant.

Yet Isabella's success as queen did not derive ultimately from such appropriations of masculine symbols, roles, and assertions of superiority. Although she deployed such images when they served her advantage, ultimately it was in her role as wife that she succeeded as queen. Isabella had not been trained to rule, had not received the "formal" education her brothers had received; instead, she had been schooled to be a dutiful and virtuous woman, and it is this image, of herself as wife, that she deployed most successfully throughout her reign.

Instruction in the proper role of women had come from a variety of sources. Her father's favorite, Alvaro de Luna, had translated and adapted Boccaccio's *Concerning Famous Women*, publishing his *Book of Famous and Virtuous Women* in 1446; Boccaccio's stories praising the docility and duty of women contrasted sharply to the role assumed by Isabella's mother, Isabel of Portugal, who engineered Luna's fall from power. In this small detail we might see how, by positioning herself as a virtuous wife and presenting her actions as service to her husband, a strong woman could pursue political ends.

A traditional picture of virtuous women is also drawn in *The Book of Good Love,* which formed part of Isabella's curriculum after she left Arevalo. The "womanly virtues" necessary for her life as a dutiful woman were also the focus of a *Garden of Noble Maidens,* a guidebook presented to her in 1468 by Martin de Cordoba. In its emphasis on "chastity, modesty, a sense of shame, and a guarded tongue," it had, as Isabella's biographer Peggy Liss remarks, "little to do with the lives and qualities of the remarkably strong women who had recently been Spain's queens." It also seems to have little to do with the real circumstances of Isabella's life, since it was presented to her just as she had been named Enrique's heir and successor to the throne. The *Garden* contains some "commonplaces about good monarchy," the passages, in Liss's judgment, "obviously a manful attempt to put the best face possible on expectation of a woman ruler."[41]

Yet the lessons of works like these were not lost on Isabella, for it is by using the image of the dutiful and obedient woman—representing in herself the virtues of piety, chastity, silence, self-sacrifice, and modesty—that Isabella succeeded. From the beginning, as she negotiated her role as queen with an angry Ferdinand who threatened to leave Castile, Isabella emphasized her role as his wife: "she would never for any reason have wanted to cause the least humiliation to her most beloved consort, for whose happiness and honor she would sacrifice willingly not only the crown but her own health." She urged Ferdinand "not to leave his beloved wife, for she would not or could not live separated from him."[42] Even as he noted she was feared as queen, Bernaldéz praised Isabella as "a fine example of a good wife." Although Isabella as queen might appear on the battlefield in armor or castigate her army for failures in battle or read Ferdinand's letters before he sealed them, she took care to emphasize her duty as a woman, sleeping surrounded by her ladies during Ferdinand's absences to ensure her reputation for chastity, sewing Ferdinand's shirts with her own hands, instructing her daughters in prayers and needlework. Even as she drew a distinction between her public role as queen and her private life as wife, such acts as these, which she performed as wife, became part of her public image; contemporary chronicles are full of references to her dutiful undertaking of such wifely tasks, and these images reappear in biographies of Isabella even today. As she pushed ahead as queen in her commitment to the Reconquest and the expulsion of the Jews, her image took on mythic tinges as she became identified with the archetypes of Christian womanhood; her contemporaries came to see in her "a second Virgin Mary," her actions "repairing the sin of Eve."[43]

By such means she avoided a challenge to conventional notions of gender and power. She asserted her equality with Ferdinand in their roles as "Catholic Kings," even her political supremacy in Castile, at the same time she asserted her pre-eminent role as dutiful wife to her husband.[44] By her manipulation of this image throughout her reign, by her "dissimulation and simulation," Isabella offered a model of successful queenship that powerful women in the next generation might appropriate for themselves.

Margaret Beaufort (1443-1509), "the King's Mother"

In 1485 Henry Tudor, earl of Richmond, defeated Richard III at Bosworth Field, ending thirty-three years of civil war. He was immediately proclaimed king: His victorious supporters shouted "God save King Henry" after the battle, while Thomas, lord Stanley placed Richard's crown on the head of the new "king." Yet in some way Henry's title also derived from his claim to the crown through his mother, Margaret Beaufort—whose own place in the succession was overlooked when her son became king. Nor was she the only woman passed over in the aftermath of Bosworth; Elizabeth of York had also survived the internecine strife that killed her father, her brothers, and her uncles. Her claim to the throne was also ignored when Henry Tudor, earl of Richmond, became King Henry VII of England.[45]

Just as the late fifteenth century in Castile was a period of political dissension, civil war, and succession crises, the corresponding period in England brought similar social and political conflict. The so-called War of the Roses began in 1455 with a rebellion against Henry VI by Richard of York. The chief opponents in this civil strife were cousins, all descendants of Edward III. As they and their supporters struggled, first one branch of the family and then the other controlled the throne of England.[46] While Henry Tudor's victory at Bosworth seemed to put an end to the bloody contest between Lancaster and York, the new king still faced something of a dilemma.

The fifteenth-century political crisis that resulted in thirty years of civil war had pitted cousin against cousin in a struggle for the crown, but it had also raised questions of a woman's place in the royal succession. The Lancastrians had argued their superior claim to the English throne by *excluding* inheritance through the female line, while the Yorkists had made their claims to the throne *through* the female line. If Henry wanted to justify his right to the throne, he would have to do so through one woman, his mother, even while denying another woman, Elizabeth, the right to make the same claim. Although England had never had a queen regnant, there was no law barring the succession of a woman—but there was no precedent either.

The only example history offered was Matilda, the daughter of Henry I of England and Matilda of Scotland. Born probably in 1102, she was betrothed at age eight to Henry V, king of Germany, and sent to his court to be educated in the language, customs, and duties that would be required of her as queen. The German king had been proclaimed Holy Roman Emperor by the time he married Matilda in 1114, shortly before her twelfth birthday. From 1117, when she acted as Henry's regent in Italy, until her husband's death in 1125, Matilda served an apprenticeship in his government, formally charged with numerous duties by her husband and at the same time gaining political experience from him.[47]

Although she performed her administrative and political duties satisfactorily, Matilda failed in one of her most important duties: She did not provide her husband an heir. When he died in 1125, there was no obvious successor to follow him, and the result was a succession crisis in the empire. As for Matilda, the dowager empress seemed to have only two available options: her husband's family might arrange another marriage for her, perhaps to one of the contenders for the imperial throne, or she might retire to a convent. Although dowager empresses before Matilda had followed one of these two courses, Matilda returned to England instead, where her father faced a succession crisis of his own.

Henry I's son and heir William had died in 1120. While still hoping his second wife, Adela of Louvain, would provide him a son, Henry I arranged in 1127 for the great barons of his kingdom to swear to uphold the rights of his daughter Matilda as his legitimate heir; by the terms of this oath, each man agreed to defend her and her claims if the king died with no son to succeed him. To ensure her position, Henry arranged for Matilda to marry Geoffrey of Anjou in 1128, but what exactly Henry intended is not at all clear now, nor was it any more so to his contemporaries.[48] Was Matilda herself to succeed her father on the throne? Or did Henry intend for Matilda and her husband to rule jointly, as some claimed? Or had Henry planned for Geoffrey to rule in Matilda's name, as still other believed?

Matilda quickly gave birth to two sons, Henry in 1133 and Geoffrey in 1134. These boys offered the English king two potential direct male heirs, but he had not clarified the issue of the succession any further by the time of his death in 1135. The question was, in fact, only more complicated than it had been in 1128: Was Matilda supposed to succeed her father, were Matilda and Geoffrey together to succeed him, was Geoffrey alone to rule, or was the old king's grandson Henry to succeed him, with a regent to rule until the boy reached maturity? But whatever Henry I of England hoped and despite his attempts to secure the throne in some way as his daughter's inheritance, Matilda did not become queen of the English when her father died. Instead, her cousin Stephen of Blois had himself anointed king.[49]

From 1135 until 1141, Matilda pursued her claims to the English throne. With her husband she first invaded Normandy to secure her rights there. Then, in 1139 she appealed her case to the papal court, basing her claim to the crown on her hereditary right and on the oaths that had been sworn to her father. When the hearing was suspended before a judgment was reached, Matilda and her army invaded England. In 1141 Stephen was captured and taken prisoner. He released his supporters from their oaths of allegiance to him, and a compromise seemed to have been reached when Matilda was recognized as "Lady of the English."

But reversal came quickly to Matilda. Stephen's wife, Matilda of Boulogne, led a vigorous offensive on her husband's behalf, and by the end of 1141 Stephen had been restored as king. Civil war in England and Normandy continued, the contenders eventually fighting to a stalemate. Stephen lost Normandy completely, and he failed in his effort to have his son Eustace recognized as his successor. But Matilda, the "Lady of the English," never made good her claim to the English crown, retiring finally to Normandy in 1148. She did not renew her claim even in 1154, when "King" Stephen died. It was her son, Henry, who succeeded Stephen as King Henry II of England.

The new king's mother lived on until 1167, providing her son with "steady help and counsel that has too often been overlooked," in the words of her recent biographer.[50] Beyond "help and counsel," Matilda acted jointly with Henry II in issuing charters, functioned as his viceregent in Normandy, heard cases for and with him and, at times, exerted a restraining influence on him. Henry, for his part, seems to have both authorized and recognized his mother's service on his behalf and to have solicited and respected her advice, relying on not only her administrative experience but also her wider familiarity with European politics. One view of her methods and of the extent of her influence on her son comes from the courtier and chronicler William Map:

> I have heard that his mother's teaching was to this effect, that he should spin out the affairs of everyone, hold long in his own hand all posts that fell in, take the revenues of them, and keep the aspirants to them hanging on in hope; and she supported this advice by an unkind analogy: an unruly hawk, if meat is often offered to it and then snatched away or hid, becomes keener and more inclinably obedient and attentive. He [Henry II] ought also to be much in his own chamber and little in public: he should never confer anything on anyone at the recommendation of any person, unless he had seen and learnt about it.[51]

Map's contemporaries were even more harsh in their judgments. Matilda was criticized for having "compelled" the barons to support her by means of her "loud utterance that nobody could resist." She received supporters who had foresworn their allegiance "ungraciously" and "drove them from her presence in fury after insulting and threatening them." In short, she did not behave as a woman ought; she "put on an extremely arrogant demeanour instead of the modest gait and bearing proper to the gentle sex."[52]

Modern historians are often no more kind, the recently published *Who's Who in Early Medieval England* typical in its reading of Matilda. While noting that her contemporaries judged that the "energy, arrogance, bravery" she displayed were "commendable in a man" but "condemned in a woman," the same gendered views are duplicated in the evaluation of Matilda that follows:

> [S]he successfully retained the loyalty of important English magnates and displayed considerable tenacity in adversity. It was her failure to match this with charm and magnanimity that sealed her fate. Constitutionally, it is hard to see that Matilda represented anything except herself and her family interest.[53]

As a precedent for the succession of a woman to the throne of England—and for her success as queen—the example of Matilda thus did not make for a strong or a clear case in the fifteenth century. Matilda's claim, based both on right of inheritance and on the oaths sworn to her father, had failed, and the result had been civil war. Even so, while many of her contemporaries disliked *her* claim to the throne, they did not dispute *a woman's* right to claim it; although she might be criticized for her behavior *as* a woman, Matilda was not excluded from the succession *because* she was a woman.[54] Rather than objecting to Matilda's sex, Stephen and his supporters argued that their oaths to support her succession had been extorted from them by her father. They also claimed that, on his deathbed, Henry I had changed his mind about his successor and had designated Stephen as his heir in Matilda's place. In any case, they concluded, Stephen had been proclaimed king by "unanimous consent and approval of the bishops and nobles" after Henry's death, his recognition and annointing thus superseding any claim Matilda might make.

The arguments Stephen's supporters used to justify his actions and position are included in John of Salisbury's lengthy report of events to Pope Eugenius III, but John nevertheless defended Matilda's claim to the throne. In his later *Policraticus,* he accepted in principle the rule of a woman. While this work contains what one recent commentator has called "a critical roster" of courtly frivolities, including a "particularly virulent" assault on women, the *Policraticus* does not argue that women should be excluded from sovereignty. Because of the inherent weakness of her sex, a female ruler must struggle to maintain her virtue; even so, her weak nature does not preclude her from exercising sovereignty.[55]

In the kingdom of Castile, as we have seen, the order of succession, including the right of a woman to the throne, was made explicit in *The Seven Divisions,* but when Henry Tudor defeated Richard III at Bosworth, there was no established law defining the English succession.[56] Even if the new king had wanted to justify his claim by citing his Lancastrian descent, his Beaufort credentials were problematic. The first Lancastrian king, Henry IV, was John of Gaunt's son by his first wife, Blanche. Henry V and Henry VI represented this "royal" Lancastrian line. But the Beaufort claim originated with John Beaufort, son of Gaunt and his third wife, Katherine Swynford. This child had been born to Katherine in 1372 while Gaunt was still married to his second wife, Constance of Castile. After Constance's death, Gaunt married his long-time mistress, and in 1396 the pope gave his approval to this marriage and declared that all children born to Gaunt and his third wife—even those who had been born while Gaunt was still married to Constance of Castile—were legitimate. The declaration of legitimacy was confirmed by an act of Parliament in 1397.

But in 1485 some uncertainty about Henry's status as a Lancastrian heir remained. If his Beaufort claim were in fact legitimate, the succession would seem to belong not to Henry but to his mother.[57] Henry's answer to all the questions about his "succession" was brilliant. Instead of claiming the throne by the right of inheritance, Henry Tudor, now Henry VII of England, simply had his succession recognized by Parliament:

> This declaration, a special petition of the Commons assented to by the king and the Lords, was not, strictly speaking, an act of Parliament. Nor did it attempt to justify the Tudor title. It simply stated that the inheritance of the crown resided in "our now sovereign lord King Harry VII and in the heirs of his body lawfully come . . . and in none other."[58]

Henry's title was "good of itself"—it derived not from his Lancastrian origins, not through his Beaufort mother and in her place, but on the field of Bosworth. His victory there was, in his own words, "the true judgment of God in granting him victory over his enemy in the field."[59]

Moreover, although it had been arranged that Henry would marry Elizabeth of York, thus uniting Lancastrian and Yorkist claims, he did not do so immediately.[60] The battle of Bosworth had been fought in August of 1485. Henry was crowned king on 30 October, his title confirmed by Parliament the following November. On 10 December, before adjourning, Parliament asked Henry to marry Elizabeth, but the king did not do so until January of 1486, some five months after Bosworth. She was not crowned queen until 25 November 1487, well after the September 1486 birth of a prince whose own claim to the throne as heir would nullify any potential threat his mother offered as Yorkist heir.

The situation in England in 1485 after Richard III's death was in many ways remarkably similar to the situation in Castile in 1474 at the death of

Enrique IV: for Isabella and Juana, substitute Margaret Beaufort and Elizabeth of York. Yet there is one significant difference. Enrique did not die in a decisive military defeat. If he had, the claims of Isabella and Juana might well have been ignored or superseded, just as those of Margaret Beaufort and Elizabeth of York were following the battle of Bosworth.

The long years of the Lancastrian-Yorkist succession wars might well have made it very difficult for any woman in England to forward a claim to the throne in 1485. But, although she did not gain political authority as queen regnant after the defeat of the Yorkist king, Margaret Beaufort nevertheless wielded considerable political power in the role she assumed thereafter as "the king's mother."[61] Indeed, an alternative history of the Wars of the Roses might be written; for the more familiar and obvious battles of fathers and sons we might well substitute the equally bloody battles fought by mothers on behalf of those same sons.

Margaret's "War of the Roses" was fought initially on a matrimonial battlefield. She was married four times, each alliance a politically expedient skirmish in her war of succession. The first of these unions was in late January or early February of 1450, when William de la Pole, earl of Suffolk, married his seven-year-old son John to the six-year-old Margaret. Suffolk, a Lancastrian supporter of Henry VI, had been awarded Margaret's wardship by the king as acknowledgment of the "notable services" he had performed. As Margaret's recent biographer Linda Simon notes, this marriage was not without implications for the succession:

> As a staunch Lancastrian, unwilling to consider the claims of the family of York, [Suffolk] believed that there was only one real heiress. Margaret Beaufort was a potential queen, and if his ward did not claim the crown for herself, she must pass that glorious inheritance to her son.

Suffolk suffered almost immediately for his presumption; he was indicted for treason, chief among the accusations against him that he had attempted to secure the English throne for his son by marrying the boy to Margaret, "presuming and pretending her to be next inheritable to the crown."[62]

Henry VI dissolved Margaret's marriage to Suffolk's son in 1453. He then granted the wardship and marriage of the nine-year-old girl to his half-brothers, Jasper and Edmund Tudor, this move once again with dynastic significance: "Henry's initial intention in dissolving Lady Margaret's marriage with John de la Pole may have been to nominate Edmund Tudor, earl of Richmond as his heir, in the right of Margaret Beaufort."[63] A twelve-year-old Margaret was married to Edmund Tudor in 1455; by November of 1456 Edmund Tudor was dead, his adolescent widow six months pregnant.

Margaret gave birth to her only son, Henry Tudor, on 28 January 1457. In their study of Margaret Beaufort, Michael Jones and Malcolm Underwood note that her "chief concern" throughout her life was to protect Henry's interests. To this end, the thirteen-year-old widow participated actively in arrangements for her next marriage, her third, to Henry Stafford, a staunch Lancastrian. Discussions for the match began in March 1457, the ceremony taking place on 3 January 1458. Margaret's decision about the alliance was to prove a good one. After Edward IV came to power in 1461, Stafford was reconciled to the Yorkist king, securing a pardon for both himself and for his wife. Wounded fighting for Edward IV and the Yorkists at the battle of Barnet, Stafford never recovered; he died in 1471. Within the year, in fact before the arrangements for Stafford's burial were complete, Margaret married for the fourth time. Her strategy at this point is clear; she married a Yorkist supporter, Thomas Lord Stanley. Once more her marriage reflected her carefully calculated decision.[64]

In the meantime, after his mother's marriage to Stafford, Henry Tudor had become the ward of the Yorkist William Lord Herbert, who intended to marry the young Henry to his own daughter, obviously recognizing what Jones and Underwood call Henry's "long-term political future." In 1469, Henry Tudor's fortunes changed dramatically after Herbert's defeat by Lancastrian forces and with the brief restoration of Henry VI. Margaret's interest was, "first and foremost," the safety of her son, with whom she was reunited in London.

After the Lancastrians were defeated at Barnet, Jasper Tudor and his nephew fled first to Wales, then to France. Edward IV was returned to the throne, but as Stanley's wife, the Lancastrian Margaret Beaufort was intimately involved with the Yorkist court. In 1479, for example, she carried the king's youngest daughter to her christening, while in 1483, during Richard III's coronation, she carried Queen Anne's train, "taking precedence over all other peeresses, even over King Richard's sister."[65] But within the year, Margaret took the "calculated but highly dangerous step" of supporting, perhaps even initiating, the rebellion of Henry Stafford, duke of Buckingham, against King Richard. The Tudor historian Polydore Vergil was later to conclude that she "was commonly called the head of that conspiracy." Head of the plot or not, her "astonishing role in the conspiracy of 1483" is discussed at some length in both of the recent biographies written about her; in their discussion of Margaret's role in events, Jones and Underwood conclude that her participation demonstrated her "ruthless practice of realpolitik."[66] After the insurrection failed, Richard initiated efforts to pass an act of attainder in Parliament against Margaret Beaufort, "mother to the king's great rebel and traitor, Henry, earl of Richmond." Richard charged that she had "conspired and committed high treason, especially by sending messages, writings, and tokens" to her son, and that she had "conspired and imagined the destruction of the king" by supporting Buckingham's treasonous rebellion. But, because of the "good and faithful service" of her husband and "for his sake," she was spared the act of attainder. Her person and her considerable property were to be controlled by her husband, however; Stanley was to keep his wife "so straight with himself" that she could neither communicate with her son "nor practice anything at all" against the king.[67]

Margaret's effort to defeat Richard did not end with Buckingham's defeat. Later in the same year, her efforts to bring Richard III down led to a coup d'etat of a different sort. Margaret's new strategy continued the war she had waged on the matrimonial battlefield, but this time her her effort was to arrange a marriage between her son and Edward IV's daughter Elizabeth. Plans for such a marriage had first been considered while Edward IV was still alive, but at that point Margaret had warned her son not to return to England from the safety of France even if Edward offered such a marriage. Richard III, too, had suggested a marriage between Henry Tudor and one of Edward's daughters. But after the failure of Buckingham's rebellion, Margaret herself pursued the alliance, sending her personal physician to Edward IV's widow, Elizabeth Woodville, then in sanctuary at Westminster with her daughters. Between them, the two women arranged for the marriage of the "Lancastrian" heir Henry Tudor and Elizabeth of York, the oldest surviving heir of Edward IV; in Brittany, Henry Tudor pledged himself to the match on 25 December 1483.

Once her son became king of England, Margaret Beaufort could abandon her matrimonial strategy for a new tactic. She had waged her battle on Henry's behalf by successful marriages, her own and then his. Now she could continue to act on her son's behalf—and her own—as "my lady the King's mother."[68]

At the beginning of her son's reign, Margaret was accorded an honor that was "semi-regal," and she easily dominated both her son's royal household and his queen. One Spanish observer noted that Elizabeth of York "was kept in subjection" by "the king's mother"; another, commenting on the influence of "the king's mother," wrote that "the queen, as is generally the case, does not like it."[69] Margaret's arrangements for the royal household extended even to the birth of a child, her plans compiled in her "Ordinances as to what preparation is to be made against the deliverance of a queen as also for the christening of the child of which she shall be delivered." She directed the arrangement of the "lying-in chamber," the procedure for the queen's retirement to await the birth, the composition of the queen's attendants, and the baptismal ceremony. She established rules for the management and staffing of the royal nursery. Following the birth of her grandson Arthur in 1486, she took over his care. Her role in the lives of her grandchildren extended to her arrangements for their education.[70] After Elizabeth of York's death in 1503, Margaret developed a particularly strong relationship with Henry, heir to the throne after Arthur's death, and she was instrumental in the marriage alliances of her granddaughters Margaret and Mary.

Meanwhile, within the royal households, she lived in close physical proximity to her son. At the residence of Woodstock, for instance, her rooms were linked to his by a shared "withdrawing" room "that belongs to the king's chamber and my lady, his mother's." In the Tower, her rooms were next to her son's bedchamber and council chamber. This physical closeness continued to the end of Henry's life; in 1508, when he was seriously ill, his mother "was in almost constant attendance": Jones and Underwood indicate that "makeshift lodgings were hurriedly erected at Richmond to house her servants as she watched over her son." A year later, as he lay dying, Margaret, "now based in her London house of Coldharbour, made regular journeys by barge along the Thames to the palace of Richmond."[71]

The "king's mother" had a dominant place not only in her son's household but in his kingdom, where her political advice and experience were critical. Henry appointed many of his mother's trusted household officials to positions in his service. The two also shared legal advisors; Jones and Underwood note that "an overlap often existed between the councils of Margaret and her son," with these advisors and even decisions "sometimes passed from one to the other." In 1498 the Spanish ambassador to the court observed that Henry was "much influenced by his mother" and, indeed, that her authority exceeded that of many of his own advisors. Margaret's interest in and influence on Henry's foreign affairs were also considerable; she maintained "friendly" contact with the Yorkist Margaret, duchess of Burgundy, who posed a constant threat to the new Tudor king, for example, and she negotiated at length with the French king on her son's behalf.[72] Most significantly, in the last years of his reign, Henry VII delegated power to his mother's council as a way of relieving the "enormous burden of work" on his own counsellors. From 1499 to 1507 Margaret presided over this court, "her powers" and her authority judged to be "considerable," her role unprecedented: in this position, Jones and Underwood conclude, she "broke new ground."[73]

While she spent a great deal of time in the royal court, the "king's mother" also maintained her own household, which "represented a separate court establishment in its own right, particularly for the numerous aristocrat and gentry women who boarded there."[74] Among those women were the queen's sister, as well as several other "ladies, wards, suitors and scholars."

The "king's mother" negotiated marriages for many of the young women whose rearing she supervised, such political marriages benefitting her son while at the same time demonstrating her own influence and authority.

As he lay dying in 1409, Henry designated his mother as the chief executor of his will. The "culmination of her ceremonial role" within her son's court is indicated by her part in the organization of the burial of her son Henry VII and of the coronation of her grandson Henry VIII; one contemporary account notes that the council arranging these ceremonies was headed by "the mother of the said late king." In both the funeral and the coronation, she was given precedence in the ceremonies. Her "political status" was also "enhanced," if that was possible, by her role in the interim council that governed until Henry VIII's coronation.[75] "My lady the king's grandam," as she then became, "gave instructions for [her grandson's] marriage to Catherine of Aragon and for his coronation."[76]

In their assessment of Margaret Beaufort's role during her son's reign, Jones and Underwood note that Margaret enjoyed a "degree of influence" that gave her "a dominating position within the realm." Throughout the twenty-four years of Henry VII's reign, from his victory at Bosworth in 1485 until his death in 1509, the "king's mother" participated "in every aspect of Tudor ceremony, government and administration and fought for the safeguarding of the dynasty." Hers was, they conclude, "a formidable achievement," even a "partnership."[77]

Margaret Beaufort was able to function successfully and significantly after 1485 not by asserting any claim to rule as queen but by positioning herself instead as "the king's mother." In part this role was, of course, a natural one. Contemporary chroniclers and modern historians alike have remarked on the intensity of the bond between Margaret Beaufort and her son. Jones and Underwood note that the "lack of further offspring was to strengthen the bond between Margaret and her only child," an intense bond no doubt strengthened by the "war of the roses" they had fought together.[78] Part of this notable closeness seems also to have derived from the somewhat unusual circumstances of Henry's early childhood. Following Owen Tudor's death and contrary to the usual practice, the king had not granted Henry's wardship to a nobleman, not even to an obvious candidate like his uncle Jasper Tudor. Instead, Henry was allowed to remain with his mother from his birth in 1457 until 1462, the same critical years that, in an interesting parallel, Isabella of Castile spent in relative isolation with her own mother. Something of the relationship between mother and son can be seen in their letters. Although she addressed her son as "my good king" and "my sweet king," Margaret's expressions of feeling for her son go beyond such conventions. She referred to him as "my dear heart," "my own sweet and most dear king and all my worldly joy," "my dearest and only desired joy in this world." In a letter of 28 January 1501 she closes by referring to the date; on "this day of St. Anne's," she writes, "I did bring into this world my good and gracious prince, king, and only beloved son." Henry's response is equally affectionate. While he apologizes in a letter dated July 1503 for not having written often enough, he addresses himself to "Madam, my most entirely well beloved lady and mother," noting the "great and singular motherly love and affection that it hath pleased you at all times to bear me." In granting a request to her he wrote,

> all of which things according to your desire and pleasure I have, with all my heart and goodwill, given and granted unto you; and, my dame, not only in this but in all other things that I know should be to your honour and pleasure and weal of your soul, I shall be glad to please you as your heart can desire it, and I know well that I am as much bounden so to do, as any creature living, for the great and singular motherly love and affection that it hath pleased you at all times to bear me.[79]

But beyond her "natural" role as Henry Tudor's mother, Margaret Beaufort carefully constructed a public role as "the king's mother." She both cultivated and conveyed her position in a number of ways. In a remarkable move, Parliament declared her a *femme sole*, a "sole person not covered of any husband," an act that allowed her lawful title to her own property without reference to her husband. Such a move, for which she seems to have been responsible, was unprecedented.[80] A vow of chastity, which she took in 1499, further enhanced her autonomous status. She established her own household at Collyweston, where her husband was welcome as a visitor, but where she lived not as his wife but as an independent woman. This too was "novel solution" to a "situation without precedent in England."[81]

During Elizabeth of York's coronation the "king's mother" not only accompanied the king's wife throughout the ceremony, she participated with her, sitting at the queen's right hand. Contemporary chroniclers noted that, throughout her son's reign, she travelled with the king and queen on progresses, royal tours designed "to display the majesty of kingship" as well as "to cement political allegiance."[82] She also used her dress to signal her status; at Christmas of 1487, for example, she wore a mantle and coat "like the queen" and a coronal, a golden circlet; at a ceremony in 1488 she and Elizabeth were dressed identically; in a window commissioned in 1503 for the church of Greyfriars, she was depicted in "robes like a princess, coronal on head and rod of gold in her hand."[83]

Perhaps most significantly, she began to use a new signature. Before about 1499 she used "M. Richmond," for Margaret, countess of Richmond, an aristocratic style emphasizing her title. But after 1499 she began to use the royal style, "Margaret R," in her correspondence, her new signature paralleling her son's "HR" and the queen's "Elizabeth R." The signature was at times combined with an opening announcement, "By the king's mother."[84] Given the identity of the initials in "Richmond" and "*reine*" the signature remains ambiguous, a perfect example of how "the king's mother" could both assert her power and position and at the same time negate any appearance of doing so.

Margaret Beaufort's conception of her role as "the king's mother" had clearly been carefully crafted. As she waged her war of succession on her son's behalf, she was only one of the powerful and determined women who waged their own desperate war over the English succession. She could succeed by taking note of how her contemporaries had succeeded—or how they had failed.

Like Isabella of Castile, Margaret Beaufort's first example had come from her mother. Margaret Beauchamp, daughter of Sir John Beauchamp of Bletsoe, had been an heiress in her own right; following the death of her husband, John Beaufort, duke of Somerset, the dowager duchess had control not only of her own possessions but of those of her husband as well, thus insuring her independence. More important, Somerset had arranged that, in the event of his death, the rights to his daughter's wardship and marriage were to be left in the hands of her mother. Although Henry VI had revoked this agreement after Somerset's death in 1444, Margaret continued to live with her mother, even during the period of her brief "marriage" to John de la Pole in 1449; she remained under her mother's care and guidance, in fact, until 1453, when her wardship was transferred to Jasper and Edmund Tudor. She sustained a strong identification with her mother and her maternal lineage throughout her life.[85]

Beyond the influence of her mother, women of her own generation could provide her with two examples of the possibilities and limits of royal motherhood. The first of these was Cecily Neville, duchess of York. The two women were, in fact, cousins, both descendants of John of Gaunt: Margaret Beaufort was the duke's great-granddaughter through his son John Beaufort, while Cecily Neville was his granddaughter through his daughter Joan. But the two women shared more than blood; the circumstances of their lives are remarkably similar. When her husband Richard of York was attainted, Cecily Neville had acted to protect herself and her children by submitting herself to the king; Henry VI provided for "the relief and sustentation of her and her young children what have not offended against us."[86] When York was killed at Wakefield in 1461, she had acted to preserve her family's claims to the throne by sending her two youngest sons, Richard and George, to safety in Burgundy. After her oldest son Edward became king, Cecily enjoyed considerable influence at his court; a papal legate was told to write to the duchess, who could "rule the king as she pleases." When Edward IV had his father posthumously recognized as "rightful king of England," Cecily thus became a kind of dowager queen.

After the first year of Edward's reign, Cecily's influence waned, in part as a result of her opposition to his marriage to Elizabeth Woodville, in part as Edward came to assert himself as king.[87] This "king's mother" could neither prevent the fratricidal murder of her son George nor keep Richard from attempting to justify his usurpation of the throne by claiming his mother had "conceived [Edward] in adultery" while his father was in exile. As a Yorkist she had struggled so that her family could rule; as a mother she outlived both of her sons who did rule, but who ultimately lost control of the throne.

Cecily Neville was not alone in regarding her son's marriage as "a political blunder of the first magnitude."[88] Elizabeth Woodville was, as Charles T. Wood describes her, "a queen who was prepared to use the allure of her sexual favours and her capacity to withhold them to gain her ends."[89] Those "ends" were the very ends that Cecily Neville had sought and that Margaret Beaufort would seek: safety and political advancement for her children and for herself. From this second Yorkist mother Margaret Beaufort could also learn by example.

When she married Edward IV, Elizabeth Woodville was already a widow and mother. As queen, she sought the advancement of the Woodvilles, her birth family, and of the Greys, the family of her first husband and of her older sons. She used her position as the king's wife to arrange advantageous marriages for her female relatives and to acquire titles, lands, and honors for her male relatives. But the power she wielded as Edward's queen on behalf of the Woodvilles and Greys was viewed "with patriarchal outrage."[90] Most serious, she had attempted to keep her husband's brother Richard from power following Edward IV's death, with disastrous consequences for the boy who should have become Edward V. Something of the very real danger posed by the Greys and the Woodvilles is indicated in Richard's own words; he regarded "the queen, her blood, adherents and affinity" as a threat, claiming they "have intended and daily doth intend to murder and utterly destroy us."[91] As "an object lesson in how not to behave as queen consort," the example of Elizabeth Woodville "could hardly be bettered."[92]

But opinion about her shifted dramatically when the king's wife became a future king's mother:

> As long as she was perceived as a woman who exercised a quasi-sovereignty only for the benefit of self and non-royal kindred, she was hated, but when, after the event, she was seen entirely as a mother, one who had bent every

effort to save her royal sons, almost instantly she took on grandeur, not to say nobility.[93]

This lesson was not lost on Margaret Beaufort. To act for herself or on her own behalf was threatening and would be resisted; to act for her son or on his behalf was acceptable and would be supported.

If she could learn how to cultivate her role from the limited successes of these Yorkist mothers, Margaret Beaufort could also learn from the failures of a Lancastrian queen and mother. Margaret of Anjou offered her perhaps the most potent example of how *not* to craft her role as "the king's mother."

Henry VI's queen has been endlessly vilified, most famously by Shakespeare in his memorable descriptions of her as a "she-wolf of France," a "tiger's heart wrapp'd in a woman's hide." Married to the English king in 1445, when she was fifteen, Margaret had initially failed in her most important duty as queen, the production of a male heir. When her husband was incapacitated in July of 1453, contemporary opinion justified the opposition of Richard of York, who was credited with having perceived that "the king was no ruler." The void left by Henry VI's failure had been filled by the king's wife: "the whole burden of the realm," according to York, had come "to rest in the direction of the queen."[94] When she finally did produce an heir, after eight childless years of marriage, her success became her failure; as one historian has recently commented, the birth of her son "served to . . . bring the queen into politics as a ruthless, even fanatical, supporter of Prince Edward of Lancaster's right to succeed his father."[95]

In an effort to protect her son's rights during her husband's illness, Margaret attempted to secure the regency for herself, a newsletter circulated in January of 1454 reporting that she had "made a bill of five articles," which, if granted by Parliament, would have had the effect of giving her "the whole rule of this land."[96] Although Henry recovered in January of 1455, when he fell ill again in October York was made protector, and the result was civil war. Margaret of Anjou's subsequent efforts to preserve the English crown for her son—her establishment of what amounted to her own court, her leadership of this court party, her negotiations with Scotland and France for support, her ultimate role on the battlefields of the War of the Roses—resulted in the deterioration of her own reputation.

She became, in contemporary opinion "a great and strong labored woman" who "spareth no pain to sue her things to an intent and conclusion to her power." She was judged to be "inexorable" and arrogant: "All marveled at such boldness in a woman, at a man's courage in a woman's breast." For Edward Hall, writing during Henry VIII's reign, Margaret was a "manly woman using to rule and not to be ruled"; deciding "to take upon her the rule and regiment," she fought not for her son but for herself, "desirous of glory and covetous of honor." By the time the Elizabethan chronicler Ralph Holinshed was to describe her, she had become the archetypal virago:

> a woman of great wit, and yet of no greater wit than of haute [high] stomach . . . desirous of glory and covetous of honor, and of reason, policy, counsel, and other gifts and talents of nature belonging to a man; full and flowing of wit and wiliness she lacked nothing, nor of diligence, study, and business she was not unexpert; but yet she had one point of a very woman, for oftentime, when she was vehement and fully bent in a matter, she was suddenly like a weathercock, mutable and turning.[97]

She was widely reported to be sexually promiscuous, her enemies claiming that Edward was not Henry's son at all but the child of Margaret and one of her lovers, most likely Edmund Beaufort, duke of Somerset. Such hostile reprentations of Margaret of Anjou depict her as unnatural and her actions as a violation of woman's nature. And yet, in an interesting way, Margaret of Anjou's role in England was not only a response to the political crisis in that country; the role she assumed as queen and mother had been shaped by the political circumstances of her own childhood and by her own experience of women's abilities and capacities. As Margaret's biographer J. J. Bagley notes, "Politics, war, and administration seemed to be the natural vocations of women in her family."[98]

Margaret of Anjou was the daughter of Isabelle of Lorraine, who both fought for her husband René of Anjou in Sicily and served as his regent there.[99] While her mother was engaged in pursuing and defending René's interests, Margaret spent eight years with her grandmother, Yolande of Aragon, who was regent of Anjou for her oldest son, Louis III. After Louis' death, Yolande remained active in politics and in her family's fortunes, marrying her daughter Marie to the French dauphin and encouraging him in his efforts to recover his throne.[100] Like Isabella of Castile, then, Margaret of Anjou had been shaped by the example of her active and powerful foremothers.[101]

England neither offered such powerful, independent exemplars for women nor accepted them. Indeed, it was Margaret of Anjou herself who became a powerful exemplar for women—an example of the dangers of the independent woman who, ignoring "proper and permissable feminine activity," behaved, or tried to behave, like "ruling princes." I would argue that she became a powerful exemplar for Margaret Beaufort as well, who conducted herself in every way as the mirror image of her contemporary.

Margaret Beaufort seems to have shaped her role as "the king's mother" by learning from the successes and failures of every one of these women who fought for their sons and who outlived them. In constructing her role she seems also to have considered the historical example of Matilda, who attempted to claim and wield authority as England's queen and who failed in this attempt. Matilda was able to negotiate and maintain some degree of power for herself in England only in her role as Henry II's mother.[102]

In her recent analysis of the "personalities and politics" of the Wars of the Roses, Rosemary Horrox has offered a provocative interpretation of Margaret Beaufort, comparing her not to Matilda or to the other women of her generation, as I have done here, but to another contemporary, Richard Neville, the so-called "Kingmaker": "If the earl of Warwick deserves the title of Kingmaker it is less a tribute to his military might than to his skills as a negotiator," she writes. "On this basis," she continues,

> the other Kingmaker of the Wars of the Roses was Margaret Beaufort, who probably deserves the credit for persuading Richard III's opponents to adopt her son, Henry Tudor, as their claimant to the throne.[103]

Such a comparison, so astonishing at first, is, on further reflection, extraordinarily insightful. In pursuit of influence and power, Warwick had married one daughter to the Yorkist George, duke of Clarence, whom he supported in an abortive effort to gain the crown, and the other to the Lancastrian prince Edward, son of Margaret of Anjou, to whom he was reconciled and for whom he also fought. The comparison is also instructive, for the "Kingmaker" was never successful in his efforts to make a king, nor, if he had been, does it seem likely that he could have conducted himself successfully as "the king's father." Margaret Beaufort, by contrast, succeeded in both roles. As "kingmaker," she saw her son become King Henry VII, and as "the king's mother" she was able to understand the potential offered to her by such a role and to use it to her advantage.

Caterina Sforza (1462-1509), Regent of Imola and Forlì

On 30 April 1488, two weeks after the assassination of her husband Girolamo Riario, Caterina Sforza left the fortress of Ravaldino, where she had taken refuge, and was reunited with her children, who had been held hostage by the conspirators who had murdered their father. She made a triumphal tour of the city of Forlì with her eight-year-old son Ottaviano, Girolamo's heir. Within days her husband's assassins had been hunted down and punished, and Caterina had received a delegation from the citizens of Imola, another Riario possession, reaffirming their loyalty to her and her children. Although she had become the effective ruler of both Imola and Forlì, she herself had no legal right to govern these strategically located

Italian cities. In an effort to remedy that situation, Caterina compelled the men of Forlì to swear an oath of allegiance to their "new lord," Ottaviano—and to her as his temporary regent.[104]

To offer his counsel to Caterina, and perhaps to supervise a woman who was not entirely trusted, Cardinal Raffaello Riario, Girolamo's nephew, travelled to Forlì. Also arriving in the city from Milan was an advisor sent by Caterina's uncle, Ludovico Sforza, who had his own reasons for offering to "protect" Ottaviano's interests: He expected to control the city himself. In a letter to Lorenzo de' Medici, one of Ludovico's advisors wrote that "because the Contessa is . . . the sister of the duke [of Milan] and [because] the boy [Ottaviano] is small, it shall fall to us, in the end, to govern that state until he is grown."[105] By August a bull from Rome had also arrived in Forlì, vesting control of Girolamo's possessions in the young Riario heir. The bull named Caterina as Ottaviano's *tutrice et curatrice*, that is, as his guardian and trustee.

Caterina Sforza's birth gave no hint of the role she would come to play for a brief time in the tumultuous world of Italian politics. Her name first appeared in a letter from her father, Galeazzo Maria Sforza, to *his* mother, Bianca Maria Visconti. Galeazzo did not refer to the baby's mother; she was Galeazzo's mistress, Lucrezia Landriani, wife of Giampietro Landriani. Caterina was the second child Lucrezia bore Galeazzo Maria; she would later have two more. In 1466, when Caterina was three years old, her father became duke of Milan, and she became part of the ducal household. Two years later, her father married Bona of Savoy; he legitimized Caterina, and his duchess "adopted" her husband's daughter. According to Pier Desiderio Pasolini, Caterina's biographer, Bona "loved her as a true daughter, bringing her up with maternal love."[106]

Caterina's fortunes began to take shape early in 1473 when the ten-year-old girl was betrothed to Girolamo Riario, nephew of Pope Sixtus IV. Between the time of his betrothal and marriage, Girolamo gained possession of the city of Imola, inherited his older brother's wealth, and, more important, became the *padrone della barca vaticana* ("the captain of the Vatican ship of state")—more prosaically, he became the "designer and executor of papal policies."[107] When Galeazzo Maria Sforza was assassinated in 1476, the pope and his nephew, eager to protect their relationship with the city of Milan, moved quickly to press forward their alliance with the Sforza family. The fourteen-year-old Caterina was married by proxy to Girolamo in January 1477 and left the ducal palace of Milan to join her new husband in late April; she stopped briefly in the Riario city of Imola, leaving on 13 May. By the end of May, she had arrived in Rome.

Ernst Breisach regards Caterina's years in Rome as her "apprenticeship in *quattrocento* politics."[108] While in the papal city the young Caterina observed Girolamo's "partial authorship" of the Pazzi conspiracy against the Medici of Florence, witnessed the resulting war that engulfed the Italian states, and benefited from her ambitious husband's acquisition of the strategically located city of Forlì. During this "apprenticeship" period, Caterina provided Girolamo with an heir, managed the Riario estates, and cultivated personal relationships in pursuit of Riario interests, both political and economic.

Marriage, motherhood, maintaining and manipulating important family relationships and personal contacts: these were the obligations and responsibilities expected of women in her social position. But Caterina's role developed in an unexpected way as a result of her political "apprenticeship." In Pasolini's words, she soon realized that her husband "lacked courage"; in her "bitterness of humiliation," Caterina, as a true "woman of the house of Sforza," was forced to become "ruthless" and "formidable" in her desire to protect her son's future. To this end, in 1483, Caterina found a new occupation. While helping Girolamo gather arms and men in preparation for a threatened war, Breisach reports that Caterina "soon commanded enormous respect"; she also commanded fear, learning what she could accomplish by her "iron discipline cruelly enforced."[109] Her martial activity seems not only to have stimulated her but to have defined her in some essential way. Within months, the effect of her transformation was evident.

On 12 August 1484 Sixtus IV died. On hearing the news of the death of his uncle and patron, Girolamo immediately lifted his siege of the city of Paliano, moving quickly toward Rome. Caterina, who had been living near Girolamo and his troops, also headed for Rome; seven months pregnant, she travelled on horseback. While Girolamo was halted outside the city, denied entry, Caterina rode directly to the Castle Sant'Angelo. She entered the fortress, "standing on her reputation," and had the gates closed behind her. There, "very brave," she announced her intention; she would hold the fortress until the election of a new pope.[110]

Although a woman—and a pregnant woman, at that—she nonetheless compelled admiration and, more important, obedience. A contemporary observer described her:

> Wise, brave, tall, fine-complected, well-made, speaking little, she wore a dress of satin a with train of two-arms' length, a black velvet hat in the French fashion, a man's belt and a purse full of gold ducats, a curved falchion at her side; and among the footsoldiers and the horsemen she was much feared because, when she had a weapon in her hand, she was fierce and cruel.[111]

When urged to compromise, to leave the fortress to resolve the situation or to allow an advisor entrance to talk with her, she responded that they should know that she had "the brains of Duke Galeazzo," her father—and that she possessed a spirit like his as well. She would not surrender.[112]

Ultimately, of course, she did surrender the castle, but not until 25 August, after her husband had been assured that he would retain his possession of Imola and Forlì. Eleven days after seizing the castle, Caterina left it. About the conclusion of the affair, Breisach remarks, "A virago emerged from the Castel Sant'Angelo where a young gentlewoman had entered only days before."[113] At least in part this assessment of her action seems to reflect the attitudes of Caterina's contemporaries: She challenged notions of appropriate female behavior.

Girolamo's rights to Riario possessions in Romagna were confirmed as promised, but he was plagued by financial difficulties and ill health. As her husband's strength failed, Caterina's seemed to grow. By 1487, when the fortress of Ravaldino was captured by conspirators, the governor of Forlì sent word not to Girolamo but to Caterina. She did not hesitate. Pregnant once again, she nevertheless mounted a horse and rode from Imola to Forlì. She was refused entrance to Ravaldino at first, but she effected the surrender of the fortress after three days of negotiations. With Ravaldino once more in her possession, she appointed a new castellan, Tommaso Feo. She returned to Imola immediately, once again by horseback. The day after her return, she gave birth to her seventh child.[114]

There was trouble again in Forlì several months later when enemies of the Riario briefly took control of one of the towers of the city. The governor had regained control of the tower before Caterina arrived. This time she came to judge, not to negotiate; Girolamo had delegated his wife to act for him in Forlì. The conspirators were interrogated in her presence, and she had the authority to condemn them or to pardon them. They were condemned, executed in public, their heads displayed as a warning to others who might contemplate rebellion. According to one contemporary chronicler, "This lady left the fortress as true ambassador of the count her husband, and as a lady of great justice," one who had acted "not by force but by reason."[115]

Several months later Caterina and her family were in residence in Forlì when, on 14 April 1484, Girolamo's enemies stabbed him to death in his own hall after dinner. A horrified witness to the murder ran at once to warn Caterina, who quickly dispatched messengers to her uncle in Milan and to allies in Bologna and sent orders to Tommaso Feo not to surrender the fortress of Ravaldino for any reason. She barricaded herself and her children into her apartments, but the doors eventually gave way, and Caterina was taken prisoner by the conspirators who had assassinated her husband.

Control of the city was eventually placed in the hands of Giovanni Battista Savelli, papal governor of the nearby city of Cesena. In a meeting he arranged with Caterina, Savelli counseled her to return to Imola and to renounce any claims she might make to Forlì on her son's behalf. Caterina refused Savelli's advice. Twice she was taken by Riario enemies to the walls of Ravaldino where she "ordered" Feo to surrender the castle: "Surrender the fortress to them so that I will not be killed with all my children," she pleaded. "They will assassinate me." But Feo remembered her original message and stood firm. "I will surrender to no one," he replied. Frustrated, one of the men holding Caterina threatened her, pressing the point of his weapon to her chest. She responded "quietly": "Do not try to frighten me—do what you will, but do not try to frighten me, because I am the daughter of one who had no fear."[116]

On 16 April Caterina was taken to the fortress for the third time. This time the castellan indicated that he would surrender—if he could first have a private interview with Caterina inside Ravaldino. Although suspicious, Savelli and the council of the city agreed to the meeting because they still held her children as hostages. Caterina entered the fortress.

Once inside Ravaldino, Caterina did not return—not at the end of the three hours she had been granted for her meeting with Tommaso Feo, not at the protests of the citizens who had accompanied her, not after her children were dragged crying to the moat surrounding the fortress. What is clear is that Caterina had no intention of surrendering Ravaldino to her enemies. What is less clear is exactly was she said and did once inside.

Contemporary accounts indicate that Caterina refused to submit to her husband's assassins. When they threatened to kill her children, held as hostages, she responded that she was pregnant once more, another child already growing inside her body.[117] Within a relatively short time, however, accounts of Caterina's reply to her enemies were transformed, the incident metamorphosing into what Pasolini describes as "the legend of the fortress." Among the earliest of these "legendary" accounts is recorded by Niccolò Machiavelli:

> Some Forlì conspirators killed Count Girolamo, their lord, and took his wife and his children, who were small. Since it appeared to them that they could not live secure if they did not become masters of the fortress, and the castellan was not willing to give it to them, Madonna Caterina (so the countess was called) promised the conspirators that if they let her enter it, she would deliver it to them and they might keep her children with them as hostages. Under this faith they let her enter it. As soon as she was inside, she reproved them from the walls for the death of her husband and threatened them with every kind of revenge. And to show that she did not care for her children, she showed them her genital parts, saying that she still had the mode for making more of them.[118]

Ultimately, the "legend of the fortress" came to include the very words Caterina was supposed to have said as she challenged her enemies. In his account of the incident, for example, the Florentine diplomat and historian Guicciardini reported that, when one of the conspirators threatened her children with a knife, Caterina lifted her skirts and cried out, "And isn't it obvious to you, fools, that I have the body with which to make others?"[119]

Whatever Caterina said and did at that moment on the ramparts of the fortress of Ravaldino, her enemies did not convince her to surrender to them by threatening her children. The stalemate lasted for two weeks. Contemporary chroniclers note the uneasiness of the people of Forlì on 29 April: "And on that day the people started to murmur and to fear and to wonder that the envoys sent to the pope had returned no word and no succor." Sensing the mood of the people, Caterina had messages shot into the city:

> My people, people of Forlì! I tell you to punish and kill all enemies. For it I will consider you my good brothers for evermore. Do not hesitate to act, and fear nothing, because the deed will benefit you and your children. And if you fail to act you will regret it in a few days.[120]

When the conspirators realized that they had lost popular support, they decided to kill the Riario children, perhaps to enrage Caterina, who might be tempted into revenging herself on the people of Forlì, turning them against her. But the guards into whose care the children had been placed refused to turn them over to the conspirators. In desperation, the assassins rode out of the city. The people of Forlì filled the streets, raising cries of "*Duca! Duca! Ottaviano! Ottaviano!*" But, the chroniclers reported, many of the men and women began to "behave badly," threatening yet another sack of a city that had been in turmoil for two weeks. A voice was heard rising above the crowd, warning them against more violence because "Madonna would not wish it." And, for the "honor of the merciful and kind lady," it was reported, the people did no "evil." To the cries of "*Duca! Duca! Ottaviano! Ottaviano!*" were added cries of "*Duca! Duca! Contessa! Contessa!*"[121]

The next morning, as we have seen, Caterina left the fortress of Ravaldino in triumph. With her "merciful heart" she gave her thanks to all "as soon as it was possible"—all, that is, but her enemies. Those who had supported the conspirators were hunted down and punished.[122]

Her triumph was relatively short-lived; within months opinion of *Madonna* had begun to shift. As the courageous daughter of Galeazzo Maria Sforza, as the loyal wife of Girolamo Riario, and as the strong mother of Ottaviano, Caterina was "very brave," even "merciful and kind." Though she could be "fierce and cruel," her fierceness and cruelty were understood, even approved. As her father's daughter, she represented Sforza interests; as Girolamo's wife, she defended Riario interests; as Ottaviano's mother, she preserved her son's interests. But once she came to power as regent in Imola and Forlì, she seemed to act in her own interests. Accounts of her rule—and of her nature—shift, sometimes subtly, sometimes dramatically.

The chronicler Leone Cobelli, briefly imprisoned by Caterina, turned against her in his chronicle account; Ludovico Sforza, her uncle, disparaged her "disorderly" way of life; the pope ultimately condemned her as a "daughter of iniquity." Contemporary views like these are paralleled, more subtly, by modern accounts of her life. Even a biography as sympathetic as the one by Ernst Breisach reflects such shifts. About her "merciless" punishment of her husband's assassins, Breisach notes she "ignored her courtly manners and brushed aside all the proper restraints so patiently acquired in the Sforza castle and at the Roman court"; it is, he says, a "bloody vengeance," one that goes beyond "a wounded woman's fury."[123]

The events that resulted in such changed attitudes can be narrated fairly briefly. Having established her position in Imola and Forlì, Caterina heeded the advice of both Rafaello Riario and the advisor sent by Ludovico Sforza, pursuing a policy of moderation. She reduced taxes, skillfully avoided being drawn into hostilities between Florence and Milan, and conducted business with the Bentivogli of Bologna, the Este of Ferrara, the Gonzaga of Mantua, and the Orsini of Rome.[124] But these political decisions are not what affected Caterina's reputation. Attitudes toward the regent of Imola and Forlì changed as the result of her sexual behavior, rather than her political abilities.

Caterina's relationship with Antonio Maria Ordelaffi developed in the summer of 1489, more than a year after her husband's death. The Ordelaffi family had ruled Forlì before the city was handed over to Girolamo Riario, and an alliance with the Ordelaffi might thus seem an acceptable solution for ongoing tensions in Forlì: Caterina was a twenty-six-year-old widow, Antonio Maria the twenty-nine-year-old heir of the Ordelaffi. The prospect of a marriage between the two was celebrated by the people of Forlì. But, in condemning his niece's "disorderly" manner of living, Ludovico Sforza seemed to fear a loss of interest in the strategic city. His letter notes papal interest in the affair; he warns that Innocent VIII (Giovanni Battista Cibo) might remove the city from the Riario and put it in the control of his own son, Franceschetto Cibo. Ultimately, the affair was broken up. In an effort to preserve Riario interests, Cardinal Raffaelo Riario arranged for Ordelaffi's removal from "danger" to safety in Venice.[125]

In 1490 Caterina confounded her critics by consolidating her power—and asserting what Antonia Frasier has called her "sexual freedom of choice." Her first move was against her once-loyal castellan Tommaso Feo, who had helped to effect Ordelaffi's removal. On 30 August she entered Ravaldino with Tommaso's younger brother, Giacomo, and her son Ottaviano. Offended by what she called Tommaso's "indecent behavior," she had her castellan arrested. Caterina described what had happened in a letter to the duke of Ferrara:

> Today at the fourteenth hour it was necessary to proceed with all firmness at my disposal against Tommaso Feo who had been my castellan in said fortress and who during all of today has shown an indecent behavior toward me; thus I had to take him prisoner.[126]

The chronicle accounts, including that of the now antagonistic Cobelli, describe the series of events in Ravaldino as entrapment: Caterina entered the fortress dressed provocatively and deliberately lured Feo into her apartment. But in a confidential letter about the incident, the governor of Caterina's city of Imola notes only that Caterina had acted against Tommaso Feo in concert with her new lover, Tommaso's brother Giacomo.[127]

Caterina appointed Giacomo Feo as the new castellan of Ravaldino. In the months that followed, Caterina restored the governing councils of Forlì and relieved the people of the city of an annual tax that supported soldiers who had occupied the city since the assassination of Girolamo in 1488. But Caterina's relationship with Giacomo scandalized her contemporaries. He was despised for his arrogance and hated for his influence over Caterina. Diplomatic reports to Florence indicate that the two shared "one sentiment": "without [his] presence [she] does not speak; in fact, that which Madonnna says Giacomo confirms, and [vice versa]." Indeed, "they will bear any fate, and Madonna will sacrifice her friends and children and property; they will give their souls to the devil and the state to the Turk before abandoning one another or being separated from one another."[128] In spite of her involvement with Feo and despite the disapproval of her contemporaries, Caterina maintained her control of Imola and Forlì and the neutrality of her cities during the tumultuous events of this same period: a conspiracy against Ottaviano in September 1491, Ludovico's usurpation of power in Milan, and the French invasion of Italy in 1494. Giacomo Feo was brutally assassinated in August of 1495, however, and Caterina's own sons, Ottaviano and Cesare, were among the conspirators. Caterina then revealed that Giacomo had been more than her lover; she had been secretly married to him. Her vengeance against those responsible for Giacomo's death was swift and brutal.[129] Through all the conflict and its aftermath, Caterina survived in power.

A year after Giacomo's assassination, Caterina's "appetite" once more shocked her contemporaries. In October of 1496 a Milanese diplomat reported to Ludovico Sforza that Caterina planned to marry Giovanni de' Medici. While her proposed alliance with the Medici of Florence might disrupt the delicate balance of power in Italy, the relationship was not discussed in terms of its political implications. Instead, it was reported in terms of Caterina's nature as a woman. The Milanese diplomat reporting Caterina's plan to her uncle Ludovico Sforza wrote that the match was intended "to satisfy her appetite."[130] Venetian officials, too, professed shock at her behavior. While noting that "the nature of the female sex excuses her," the Doge nevertheless condemned her conduct, concluding that her failures and mistakes could not be allowed to continue.[131]

Ludovico Sforza received a series of letters about his niece and her relationship. Francesco Tranchedini was able to tell the new duke of Milan about the "many caresses" and "great honors" Caterina bestowed on Giovanni, but he failed to sort out the exact nature of their connection. In January 1497, months after he began reporting to Milan, Franchedini sent a third- or fourth-hand account to Ludovico Sforza; a Florentine who was "very familiar" with Giovanni de' Medici had told Giovanni Bentivoglio of Bologna that Giovanni de' Medici had told him he had married Caterina and that they were keeping their marriage secret. Tranchedi closed his letter on a note of frustration: "cursed is the man who trusts in men," he noted, but even more unfortunate, is the man who trusts "in women."[132]

Caterina's political position was a difficult one. It was acceptable for the duke of Milan to take a mistress; it was not acceptable for the lady of Forlì to take a lover. Just as she had kept her marriage with Giacomo Feo secret, she kept the nature of her relationship with Giovanni de' Medici secret: To admit her marriage would be to place her position as regent for Ottaviano in jeopardy. Complicating her effort to maintain secrecy was another pregnancy. Caterina and Giovanni de' Medici were probably married before the birth of their son in April 1498.[133]

Throughout the period of her marriage to Giovanni de' Medici, Caterina fortified her possessions in Imola and Forlì; work on the fortress of Bubano was completed in 1497. She skillfully negotiated her way out of a proposal from the Gonzaga of Mantua for a marital alliance with her son Ottaviano. More difficult to refuse was a proposal for an alliance between Ottaviano and Lucrezia Borgia, daughter of Pope Alexander VI. Imola and Forlì were papal territories, the pope Caterina's overlord. But Ottaviano's marriage would have necessitated a loss of her position as regent of Imola and Forlì; she would have to relinquish her position in favor of Ottaviano. Caterina avoided the Borgia proposal by claiming that the subject of Ottaviano's marriage would have to be delayed so that the young man could dedicate himself to his preparation as a soldier.

War also threatened Caterina's position. Florence's effort to regain control of the city of Pisa endangered the strategically located cities of Imola and Forlì; at the outset of the conflict, Venice and Milan cooperated, sending help to the Pisans as they fought against Florence. Eventually, however, their cooperation ended; if Venice attacked Florence directly, Caterina's position in Romagna put her in the middle of the conflict. Although she pleaded her neutrality, Venetian mercenaries raided her territories. She received support—of a kind—from Florence, which granted her citizenship and employed her son Ottaviano as a mercenary. Lodovico Sforza sent an advisor and troops. Caterina wrote to him that "war is not for ladies and children like mine." "If I might be more fearful than [is] desirable," she apologized, "your excellency must ascribe that to my being a lady . . . and thus by nature fearful."[134] Given her own past, it is hard to accept her Caterina's characterization of herself as "fearful" by nature. Certainly she was not fearful when she learned that her husband Giovanni's illness, which had kept him from any prominent role in the conflict, had grown more serious. On 15 September she once again undertook an arduous journey on horseback, but she did not reach her husband before he died. Since she had never formally acknowledged her marriage to Giovanni de' Medici, she neither announced the death nor received condolences. Although Venice continued to threaten, soldiers even approaching the city, Forlì ultimately escaped without a direct assault. By spring of 1499 a peace treaty ended the hostilities between Venice and Florence, and Caterina's cities were left in peace. But peace would not remain for long: The French king, Louis XII, invaded Italy.

Some years earlier, in 1494, Charles VIII of France had invaded Italy, claiming to be the rightful king of Naples. He was encouraged, at least initially, by Ludovico Sforza. In response to the French king's successes, Venice had joined with Ferdinand of Aragon and the Emperor Maximilian to form the League of Venice and to expel the French invaders. After the 1495 battle of Fornovo, Charles had left Italy, but France had not abandoned its ambitions. Charles died in April of 1498, and Louis, his nephew and successor, had his own reasons for invading Italy. On his succession, he claimed title not only to France but to Sicily and to Milan.

In return for territory in the Po Valley, Venice aligned itself with France; the treaty of Blois was signed in February 1499. To secure papal support, the new French king arranged an advantageous match for the pope's son, Cesare Borgia, with Charlotte d'Albret, a Navarrese princess. Louis also promised to return control of papal possessions—including Imola and Forlì—to Alexander VI. In a papal bull issued on 9 March 1499, Cesare Borgia was invested with the cities of Imola and Forlì along with other papal territories that had been granted to the Riario. The same bull condemned Caterina Sforza as a "daughter of iniquity."[135]

In 1499, then, as the Italian cities prepared for a renewed French invasion, Caterina moved to solidify her alliances. Her support for her uncle in Milan was firm. Her overtures to Lorenzo de' Medici in Florence resulted in a visit from a Florentine envoy on his first diplomatic mission, Niccolò Machiavelli, who met with Caterina three times between 16 July and 24 July. He sent a favorable report back to Florence, recommending payments to her for past services and a new contract for Ottaviano—but Machiavelli was not authorized to grant her what she wanted, assurances of a Florentine alliance.[136] Even so, Caterina maintained contact with Lorenzo de' Medici, negotiating with him over the return of her late husband Giovanni's possessions, over money Lorenzo had borrowed from Caterina and Ottaviano, and over the guardianship of the son she had born Giovanni.[137]

Although she did not get the alliance with Florence that she had wanted, Caterina still had the support of her uncle in Milan. But by the end of August, Ludovico Sforza had fled from the city, taking refuge with the Emperor Maximilian. In October Louis XII was in Milan. Caterina had not been entirely abandoned; although unable or unwilling to support her openly, Florence did attempt to offer her aid, trying to arrange a treaty for mutual defense for her with, among others, Bologna and Ferrara. The city also offered her refuge; perhaps, at some point in the future, she might be reinstated in her possessions. But Caterina made a different choice. A year earlier, in the letter quoted at the beginning of this chapter, Caterina had written to her uncle in Milan about her intentions: "If I have to lose," she had said, "I want to lose in a manly way." In the event, Caterina did not react in "a manly way": her uncle Lodovico Sforza had already fled, and her kinsman Giovanni Sforza, lord of Pesaro, would soon abandon his possessions as well. Unlike these men, Caterina would not flee. Nor would she surrender.

Instead she prepared the city of Forlì to withstand a siege. She also sent a delegation to Alexander VI requesting a compromise. She may have sent more than letters; it was widely reported that her letters had been treated with a poison intended to kill the pope. The Florentines, who had offered her a refuge, were accused of having aided Caterina; in a papal brief sent to Florence on 21 November 1499, she was again condemned, this time as a "daughter of perdition," for her supposed attempt on Alexander VI's life.[138]

Despite her preparations and despite her son Ottaviano's efforts to ensure Imola's loyalty, that city surrendered to Cesare Borgia on 25 November without offering any resistance. The fortress of Imola held out for some time, however; the castellan finally surrendered on 11 December.[139]

Undaunted, Caterina determined to "show the Borgia that a woman, too, can handle artillery."[140] She sent her son Ottaviano to join her other children in Tuscany and set about final preparations in Forlì, attempting to solidify the citizens' support for her, destroying bridges around the city, and provisioning Ravaldino. She finally withdrew into the fortress with some nine hundred soldiers, advisors, and relatives.[141]

While Caterina was prepared to resist, the citizens of Forlì were not. Despite Caterina's efforts to ensure their loyalty, the citizens decided to surrender to Cesare even before he reached the city. On 18 December a document was sent from Forlì to Cesare offering the city's capitulation; it was signed at once. Cesare Borgia entered the city the next day, 19 December. Although the citizens of Forlì had hoped to avoid the destruction of a siege, their surrender did not, in the end, spare them. Instead, Cesare's troops looted the city.

Then the siege began. When Christmas came and Caterina had not surrendered, Cesare decided to negotiate with her. On 26 December he stood outside Ravaldino. Caterina appeared on the battlements. Cesare began by reminding her that the fortunes of states were mutable—a safe surrender was better than the risk of battle. If she surrendered, she could be assured of a safe haven in Rome, perhaps even a new state. "Surrender! Surrender then, Madonna!" he implored.

"Signor duke," Caterina is reported to have replied, "Fortune helps the intrepid and abandons cowards. I am the daughter of a man who did not know fear. Whatever may come, I am resolved to follow the course until death."[142]

A second attempt to negotiate was made the next day. Again Cesare approached the fortress. Again Caterina rejected his offers. A suit from the the Borgia pope, Alexander VI, followed; the pope's envoy assured Caterina of her safety and that of her children, promised to safeguard and return to her her possessions, and offered a yearly pension. These attempts at negotiation, too, were rejected. The siege of Ravaldino began in earnest on 28 December 1499; the fortress finally fell on 11 January 1500.[143] Cesare's revenge was bloody. Before detailing the horrors, Breisach writes, "For thirty-six hours to be one of Caterina's soldiers or subjects caught in the fortress meant to be a victim of the cruelest torture."[144]

Nor was Caterina spared. A French chronicler commented that, despite her "female body" Caterina "showed a masculine courage."[145] But Cesare's revenge for her "masculine" courage was directed toward her female body; she was taken prisoner and raped by her conqueror. Cesare was said to have boasted that Caterina had "defended her fortress better than her virtue."[146]

Although he possessed both the city and its regent, he had not gained possession of Ottaviano Riario, the heir of Imola and Forlì. Nor could he be assured of his control over the papal territories without Caterina's formal surrender of her son's rights. Cesare maintained possession of Caterina until he completed his Italian conquests and made a triumphal entry into Rome with her late in February. After an attempt at escape, Caterina was imprisoned in the dungeon of the Castel Sant'Angelo; it is grimly ironic that she was defeated and imprisoned in the fortress she herself had once held and from which she had emerged in her first martial and political triumph. Caterina was to be held until she surrendered. Her Riario sons, meanwhile, were less intransigent; Caterina's resistance was an obstacle to their attempts to negotiate new positions and new possessions for themselves. Meanwhile, the Medici threatened to take custody of her son by Giovanni de' Medici. On 30 June 1501, after eighteen months of imprisonment, she finally agreed to renounce her rights as regent of Imola and Forlì and promised to remain in Rome under papal supervision. But on 13 July, after reaching an agreement with Florence, Alexander VI agreed to "graciously set free" Caterina Sforza, that "most noble lady . . . whom we had to detain for certain reasons and for some time."[147]

She spent the rest of her life in Florence, at first trying to regain control of her lost position and possessions. When Alexander VI, the Borgia pope, died in August of 1503, Caterina attempted to regain the cities of Imola and Forlì. She urged Ottaviano to return to Romagna to renewal Riario rule, but her son preferred to remain in Rome, looking instead for a cardinal's hat or a wealthy bride. Despite her ambitions, Imola and Forlì were returned to direct papal rule in 1504.[148]

Caterina spent nearly twelve years in power, from her husband's assassination in April 1488 until the fall of Ravaldino in January of 1500. She lived the last nine years of her life in imprisonment or retirement. She died in Florence on 28 May 1509.

Among her contemporaries Caterina Sforza was not unique in her desire for a public role or in her exercise of power. The kingdoms, duchies, republics, cities, and territories of the Italian states, in fact, offered many precedents for Caterina as she sought to define and forge a political role for herself.[149] Rather than simply listing those women, I will focus instead on two more immediate examples, her grandmother and her stepmother, both of whom had governed in Milan.

Bianca Maria Visconti was the illegitimate daughter—but the only child—of Filippo Maria Visconti, duke of Milan, and Agnese del Maino. In 1433, not yet eight years old, Bianca Maria was betrothed to Francesco Sforza, the illegitimate son of a mercenary soldier who had entered Visconti's service. Despite the proposed alliance, Sforza sided with Venice and Florence against Visconti in 1434. In 1438 he again fought against Milan, but during a period of reconciliation with Filippo Maria he married

Bianca Maria in 1441. Two years later, however, he was once more at war with the Visconti duke, now his father-in-law. For her part, Bianca Maria supported her husband; like her granddaughter after her, "the valorous lady" joined her husband's army on horseback, encouraging the soldiers with her "manly words, full of spirit."[150]

In 1447, threatened once more by Venice, Visconti reconciled with his son-in-law and appealed to him for support; the duke died suddenly, however, and Francesco Sforza found that Filippo Maria had named Alfonso of Aragon, the king of Naples, as his successor in Milan, rather than his daughter Bianca Maria or his son-in-law. From that date until 1454, Francesco Sforza fought, first to gain control of Milan and then to have his position there accepted. In 1448, while Francesco fought against Venice, Bianca Maria rode to the city of Cremona on horseback, encouraged the citizens of the city, and helped in their successful resistance to the Venetians. Bianca Maria's mother, Agnese del Maino, helped her son-in-law as well by gaining control of the city of Pavia for him. The Peace of Lodi (1454) ended the wars with Venice, Naples, and Savoy, among others, and Francesco became the first Sforza duke of Milan.

Bianca Maria Visconti not only provided her husband with a claim to Milan, she presented him with eight children. Equally important, she served him as an advisor. Pasolini describes her political role as pivotal and indicates that she governed with justice. When Francesco died in 1466, their oldest son, the twenty-two-year-old Galeazzo Maria, was at the French court. Bianca Maria ensured the loyalty of the principal citizens of Milan to her son and maintained control of the city until the new duke returned in 1468.

Described by a contemporary as a woman "of pious soul but virile," Bianca Maria had thus been a powerful influence in the ducal household throughout her husband's lifetime and immediately following his death, but she had no official role once her son returned to Milan. While he was in France, Galeazzo Maria had negotiated an alliance with Bona of Savoy, the daughter of Amadeus of Savoy and the sister-in-law of Louis XI of France. Within months of Bona's arrival, Bianca Maria found her position in the court had become "untenable"; she retired to Cremona, a city that had been part of her dowry. She died within a week of her arrival in October 1468, "more from sorrow of heart than sickness of body," according to her doctor.[151]

Meanwhile, Caterina Sforza had been brought to the court of Milan in 1466 by her father, her care and education overseen by her grandmother, Bianca Maria. When Bona of Savoy arrived in Milan, she "adopted" the four children Lucrezia Landriani had borne Galeazzo Maria and undertook their guidance and education. At the ducal palace Caterina was, like her brothers, carefully trained in the humanist tradition; as Pasolini notes, a classical education was more than an "ornament of life" for women, who might be—and often were—called upon to govern.[152]

In 1476, when Galeazzo Maria was assassinated, Bona was worried about his soul and his state. Saving her husband's soul was the easier task of the two; she could negotiate a posthumous absolution for him from Sixtus IV. Ruling Milan provided more difficult. Defeating Ludovico Sforza, her husband's brother, she succeeded in becoming regent for her son Giangaleazzo. Ignoring the political advice and experience of Cecco Simonetta, who had been her husband's chief minister, she relied, instead, on a new lover, Antonio Tassino. She ultimately reconciled with Ludovico Sforza, who then helped her rid herself of Cecco, executed in 1479. But in 1480, Ludovico succeeded in having Bona herself removed as regent, and he assumed power in Milan, first as regent for Giangaleazzo and then by claiming the title of duke for himself. Bona rereated to the French court, where her sister Charlotte was queen, but quickly returned to Milan, where she attempted to bring about the usurper's downfall and restore her son as duke of Milan. She was reconciled to Ludovico after her son's death in 1494 and after Ludovico arranged for her daughter Bianca Maria's marriage to the emperor Maximilian I.

Thus Caterina had seen her grandmother and her stepmother attempting to function as regents after the deaths of their husbands, and she had seen how each of them had failed. Bianca Maria Visconti, capable and just, had been resented by her son and replaced by a daughter-in-law. After her husband's assassination, Bona of Savoy, ill-prepared and incapable, was outmaneuvered and replaced by a powerful man, her son losing his legitimate inheritance. Caterina learned from their example, succeeding where each of these women had failed. Certainly capable and certainly as just as her male contemporaries, she secured her position as regent for Ottaviano by making sure her appointment was official. She kept her position as regent by remaining independent. Despite her contemporaries' reports that she was overwhelmed by love and carried away by her passions, Caterina never allowed her lovers to gain control of her cities; she kept her marriages secret so that she did not have to cede her position as regent. Even when Ottaviano was old enough to govern for himself, she maintained her control over him, at least in part by refusing to allow him to be married. She cultivated good relationships with powerful relatives and neighbors, men like her uncle Ludovico Sforza, who thought to control the strategic cities of Imola and Forlì himself. But she did not allow her relatives or allies to gain power over her or her territories. Despite the unstable political situation in Italy, she was able to preserve her position as regent of Imola and Forlì until Cesare Borgia's conquest.

There is no body of law in the varied Italian kingdoms, republics, duchies, and cities that corresponds to the Spanish *Siete Partidas*, with its provision for female rule; but Niccolò Machiavelli's *The Prince*, arguably the most well-known and influential work of Renaissance political theory, offers by implication acceptance of, if not support for, women rulers. Among all of the questions Machiavelli raises—should a ruler be generous? should a ruler always keep his word? is it better for a ruler to be loved or feared?—he never asks the question, "can a woman govern?" Instead, Machiavelli seems to accept the idea of a female ruler. In his discussion of mercenary soldiers, he notes that they failed Joanna II of Naples. In listing the rulers who met the invading Louis XII of France and "sought his friendship," he includes, without comment, "the Countess of Forlì." In his assessment of the value of fortresses, he notes that there is no evidence of their usefulness to rulers, with the exception of Caterina Sforza, who used the refuge offered by the fortress after her husband was assassinated until she could gain control of her state. In commenting on Caterina's ultimate defeat by Cesare Borgia, he attributes her loss not to her sex—or even to some weakness in her fortress—but to a ruler's failure to avoid the hatred of the people. Stronger than any legal precedent in support of the principle of rule by women, I would argue, is the acceptance, without comment, of the fact of rule by women. Machiavelli seems not to regard sex as an issue for "the prince."[153]

While Caterina could find precedents among her contemporaries and within her own family for her role as a woman ruler, she chose, instead, quite another model. Throughout her life, she patterned herself not on women but on powerful men, especially her father. She could invoke the weakness of her sex when she chose to do so, but more often she vaunted her masculine strength. She held the Castle Sant'Angelo, defying those who wanted her surrender by reminding them that she had the brains and spirit of her father. She refused to surrender Ravaldino, defying her husband's assassins by telling them they couldn't frighten her because she was the daughter of a man who did not know fear. She faced the prospect of defeat in a similar fashion: "although I am a woman, I want to lose in a manly way." And at the last, facing Cesare Borgia, she said she would show him that "a woman too can handle artillery."

Caterina's contemporaries struggled with the ambivalent image she presented: a beautiful and defiant woman wearing a satin dress with a man's purse and knife around her waist, a pregnant wife riding horseback all night and giving birth the next day, a lady displaying the sexual appetites of a man, a mother daring her enemies to kill her children. Her challenge to accepted notions of sexual behavior, as much as her political ambition, seems to have been why and how the "merciful and kind lady" of Forlì was transformed into the "daughter of perdition."

Anne of France (1461-1522), Regent of France

In 1482, exhausted by years of domestic conflict and foreign war and incapacitated by debilitating illness, King Louis XI of France retired to the royal castle of Plessis-les-Tours in Tourraine.[154] To govern in his stead, he gave Pierre de Beaujeu, his son-in-law, the title of lieutenant general, but he seems to have given his daughter Anne the authority to rule. "She is the least foolish of women," he said. "As for wise women, there are none." When he died on 31 August 1483, his son and heir Charles was legally of age to succeed his father, but still young—not quite fourteen—and in poor health. Anne's husband might have presided over the Council convened the day after Louis' death, but the twenty-two-year-old Anne, who "took as much care to disguise her power as others take to parade theirs," became, in the words of one biographer, *roi*—that is, "king"—of France.[155]

Her assumption of power as her brother's regent did not go unchallenged.[156] Immediately following the old king's death, the princes and the nobles whom he had subdued thought to regain power for themselves. Chief among them was Louis, duke of Orléans, who had been forced to marry Jeanne of France, Anne's sister, in 1476; once his father-in-law died, the duke prepared to annul his marriage, hoping both to find a wealthy bride in Brittany and to gain the throne of France for himself. In the meantime, he gathered his allies and travelled quickly to the chateau of Amboise, prepared to take over the regency of the new king, Charles VIII.

Anne, however, had seized control of the young king and had retreated into the castle's keep, accompanied by her husband and her sister Jeanne, wife of the rebellious duke. In the words of Jehanne d'Orliac, Anne's biographer, Anne acted "in guardianship" of her brother, "in obedience" to her husband, and "in alliance" with her sister—to her opponents she presented herself in her role as regent, appointed as guardian of the young king by her father.

Unlike her contemporary Caterina Sforza, Anne chose not to challenge Louis directly from her position in the keep of Amboise; d'Orliac indicates that, before deciding to "reduce" him, she attempted first to "seduce" him. Having halted the advance of her enemies and interrupted their momentum, she organized a series of banquets and processions to welcome the nobles who came to Amboise. More important, she orchestrated concessions, conciliations, and rewards, naming Louis himself lieutenant general of Paris. Still resentful, Louis and his allies accepted all that Anne offered, but they were determined to seize the king. He won the dowager queen, Charlotte of Savoy, to his position—Anne of France had frustrated her mother's desire for authority. Messages were dispatched to his ally in

Brittany, a favorite of Duke Francis II, who reportedly counseled the duke that "it would be better to kill her [Anne] than to let her govern."[157]

Nevertheless, Anne continued to act, asserting her role by signing a series of acts and decrees in her own name, "Anne of France." The stalemate inside Amboise seems to have ended when, after the sudden death of the queen mother, Anne disappeared—taking with her the young king. Not for her the grand gesture of a Caterina Sforza. She was simply gone.

Outmaneuvered for the moment, the duke of Orléans demanded a convocation of the Estates General, the representative assembly of the realm, an appeal that Anne could not ignore.[158] But she prepared for the meeting: She reduced taxes, reformed judicial abuses, and, to secure the support of "the first man of war of his time," married her niece to Louis de la Tremoille. When the Estates convened in Tours on 15 January 1484, the fifteen-year-old Charles appeared, seated on the throne. Anne did not claim a place by his side—she remained behind the scenes.

The first issue to be addressed by the assembly was the formation of a new counsel for the young king. The nobles objected, contending that "the Estates do not have the right to interfere with government."[159] Speaking on behalf of the Estates, Philippe Pot, sire de la Roche and seneschal of Burgundy, replied that it was the people of France—the "sovereign people"—who created the monarchy "by their suffrage." "It is evident," he continued, "that our king is not able to govern public affairs by himself, but [those matters] do not revert to the princes, they belong to all." The ultimate decision of the Estates was in Anne's favor.[160] A council of twelve, all Anne's supporters, was constituted to advise her in her role as regent.

Furious at being outmaneuvered, Louis d'Orléans attempted next a civil rising, demanding that the parliament of Paris support his claims. On 17 January 1484, his representative delivered a speech against Anne, proposing that the guardianship of the king and the administration of the government be turned over to the duke of Orléans.[161] But Charles VIII sent an "official" reply to the parliament, rejecting Louis' proposals:

> If we desire to have continually at our side our very dear and much loved sister, the Dame de Beaujeu, and if we repose entire trust in her, there is no occasion for surprise, seeing that we have no nearer relative or dearer friend.

Like the Estates, the parliament of Paris declared themselves for the regent as the "established and legitimate" authority.[162]

Anne could claim a victory for the moment, but her enemies were not defeated. Louis retreated to Nantes, where, in anticipation of a divorce from his wife Jeanne, he renewed his negotiations with Francis II for an alliance with the heiress Anne of Brittany, and he signed an accord with the English, guaranteeing their support of his cause. He also sought the support of Maximilian of Austria, whose daughter, Margaret, had been in France under Anne's guardianship since the girl's betrothal in 1483 to Charles.[163] Anne responded in kind, fashioning her own alliances for her own ends.[164] The result was the so-called Mad War, which began in 1485. It eventually became a European conflict, pitting Louis and his allies—Brittany, Austria, England, and Spain—against Anne, who occupied Orléans, incited the Flemish against Maximilian, and eventually turned Alain d'Albret against Louis (he was interested in marrying Anne of Brittany himself). After a French victory on 28 July 1488, Louis of Orléans was taken captive, but his allies fought on until 1489, when Francis II, duke of Brittany, died.[165]

The duke's death resulted in a crisis in Brittany. His heir, his only daughter Anne, had been sought in marriage by three powerful men who coveted her inheritance: Louis, duke of Orléans; Alain d'Albret, duke of Guyenne; and Maximilian of Austria, newly elected king of the Romans. Now Charles VIII of France was added to that list. Because an alliance with Maximilian seemed to offer continued independence for Brittany, the young duchess married him by proxy in 1490, strengthening the alliance of Austria, England, and Spain with Brittany.

But that was not the end of the affair. Anne of France pursued her own "alliance" with Brittany; her army captured Nantes, and Charles established his court there while the French army laid seige to Rennes, where Anne of Brittany had retreated. Although she could have joined her husband Maximilian, she decided, instead, to marry Charles VIII of France. By the terms of the marriage contract, the duchy of Brittany would belong to both sovereigns; if Anne died before Charles, the province would revert to France, but if Charles died first, Brittany would be returned to her to rule. A clause inserted in the marriage contract seems to have been designed to ensure that, no matter what, Brittany would remain under French control: "If Charles VIII dies without a male child, Anne of Brittany will marry his successor and remit to him her duchy."[166]

Having defeated her enemies, Anne of France had her own interests to pursue. The duke of Bourbon, her husband's oldest brother, had died in 1488, and despite three marriages, he left no children to succeed him. Charles II of Bourbon, bishop of Lyon, was the second brother; he was ailing and focused on spiritual rather than secular goods. The third brother, Louis, had died in 1482, leaving a son, Pierre. Anne acted ruthlessly to secure the Bourbon title and lands for her husband Pierre—and for herself. She had Louis' marriage, which her father had never recognized, posthumously annulled, and awarded his son, her nephew, the title "Bastard of Liège," depriving him of all his rights. In d'Orliac's words, "she gave herself alone the duchy of the Bourbons":

The primary consequence of this audacious spoliation was that in the center of France was reconstituted a sovereignty analogous to that which the duke of Burgundy had had and which Louis XI had destroyed with so much effort.[167]

Perhaps Anne saw in the new queen a rival for power whom she could not defeat, as d'Orliac suggests. Or perhaps she saw that her brother, by then twenty years old, would not tolerate her role as regent much longer. In either case, Anne of France seems to have learned one clear lesson from her experiences as "ruler" of France: "it is necessary to be rich and independent if one wishes to live."[168] In securing the Bourbon inheritance for her husband, she had gained both riches and independence for herself and for her daughter Suzanne, born on 10 May 1491.

On 28 June, the duke of Orléans was released from prison and reconciled to the new king. On 6 December 1491 Charles VIII married the much-sought-after Anne of Brittany. On 5 July 1492, King Charles VIII and his new queen, his sister Anne and her husband Pierre, and Louis of Orléans took an oath to love and defend one another. Anne relinquished her role as regent and left France, having functioned as its virtual "king" for eight years. She was thirty years old.

Her influence and authority had been disputed, but Anne could find precedent for her role as regent in a long line of women extending back to Capetian times. Although marriage for royal women most often resulted in what André Poulet calls "liberticide," confining them to "a genealogical vocation," the perpetuation of a hereditary kingship in France assumed an unbroken line of succession. To provide for those cases of "natural, accidental or inherent inability to rule," an "efficient substitute was provided for the minor king or the ailing or absent monarch": a regent. Thus we see "the genesis of a vocation" for a royal woman: the "emergence" of her role as a king's "legal replacement."[169]

In Castile, as we have seen, *The Seven Divisions* specifically addressed the issue of female succession and, in the absence of a direct male heir, allowed for the throne to be claimed by a woman. While it was "just" that "no one should have the sovereignty of the kingdom but the eldest son, after the death of his father," it was also clear that the male line could fail; therefore, to "avoid many evils which have happened, and which may occur again," the "eldest daughter should inherit the kingdom" when there was no son to succeed. In France, by contrast, the development of the so-called Salic law in the fourteenth and fifteenth centuries specifically excluded women from inheriting the throne of France. Rather than offering a way to "avoid many evils," the succession of a woman was perceived as a particularly dangerous threat. In the words of the sixteenth-century political theorist Claude de Seyssel,

The first special trait that I find good is that this realm [France] passes by masculine succession and, by virtue of the law which the French call Salic, cannot fall into the hands of a woman. This is excellent, for by falling into the feminine line it can come into the power of a foreigner, a pernicious and dangerous thing, since a ruler from a foreign nation is of a different rearing and condition, of different customs, different language, and a different way of life from the men of the lands he comes to rule. He ordinarily, therefore, wishes to advance those of his nation, to grant them the most important authority in the handling of affairs, and to prefer them to honors and profits.[170]

But, while they were denied the possibility of inheriting the throne themselves, women were not denied access to power. Rather, they were assured a place in the government of France for, as the law of succession developed, a corresponding body of law on regency was also formulated. The law might preclude women from sovereignty, but that same law recognized that women could best be relied on to act as regent. Their very "nature" as women assured their "inviolable right" as guardians of their children. Their "nature" also decreed that they could be relied on to defend the throne for their husbands or sons rather than to take it for themselves. Women were thus preferred to men in the role of regent for a young or an incapacitated king.[171]

As Anne of France assumed her role as guardian and defender of her brother's crown, she could look to the examples of the powerful women who had preceded her over the course of three centuries.[172] Although queens had shared in government from the time of Hugh Capet, the first woman to serve officially as a regent seems to have been Adele of Champagne, the third of Louis VII's wives. During the twenty years of her marriage to Louis she was a "capable and energetic" queen, and after his death in 1180, she attempted, unsuccessfully, to take control of the government for her fifteen-year-old son; despite his relative youth, Philip II resisted his mother's efforts. Nevertheless he continued to rely on her, and in 1190, preparing to leave on crusade, he entrusted her and her brother Archbishop William of Rheims with the regency of his own son, the future Louis VIII. The co-regents were to be supervised by a governing council but, as André Poulet notes, "the dowager was nonetheless officially recognized as the king's replacement."[173]

During his reign Philip refused to share power with either of his two queens, Isabel of Hainault and Ingeborg of Denmark, perhaps perceiving in them a threat to the interests of his son. But after he succeeded to the throne, Philip's son Louis VIII named his wife Blanche of Castile as regent for his son. Poulet indicates something the breadth of the queen-regent's "absolute power": she "legislated, dealt with foreign powers, waged war, arranged marriages." "In short," he concludes, she "imposed herself as sovereign of the realm." Although Louis IX was "under [his mother's] sway far longer than was stipulated by law," he nevertheless "respected her command of statecraft and recalled her to affairs of state when he went on crusade in 1248."[174] He did not, however, appoint his wife Margaret of Provence to function as regent in the event a regency were needed, nor did Blanche's grandson Philip III arrange for a female regent. But her great-grandson Philip IV did, naming his wife Jeanne of Navarre as regent in the eventuality he died before their son Louis X was old enough to succeed him.

Jeanne was never called upon to function as regent, however; she died in 1304. After Philip IV's death in 1314, his three sons succeeded one another and, over the course of the century, women were formally barred from inheriting the French throne: "excluded from inheritance," a royal woman "from then on offered all the legal guarantees to allow her triumph in the regency."[175] Thus in 1338, as he prepared for war against Edward III, the English claimant to his throne, Philip VI looked to his wife Jeanne of Burgundy to function as regent "for existing needs and those which may arise." His grandson Charles V, perhaps fearing that his wife Jeanne of Bourbon might be too powerful, split the regency in 1365, investing her with guardianship of her son Charles and the child's two uncles with the government of the realm.[176]

In 1393 Charles VI followed his father's example in arranging for a regency, naming his wife Isabel of Bavaria as guardian of their son Charles. She was to govern in cooperation with an advisory council. As Charles began to suffer period bouts of insanity, Isabel's role was expanded in a series of ordinances; by 1403, she was "acknowledged as the leader of a new regency council" empowered to mediate and to deal with matters of finance in addition to acting as principal guardian of the dauphin.[177] But like Margaret of Anjou in England and Caterina Sforza in Italy, Isabel was villified and condemned for her political ambitions, for her undisguised pursuit of personal wealth and power. As Rachel Gibbons notes, she was accused of "adultery, incest, moral corruption, treason, avarice and profligacy," her "reputed beauty" used as "'proof' of her evil," her sexual activity necessarily resulting in her "neglect" of her children. "As is often the case today," Gibbon concludes, "the most accessible weapons . . . to use against a woman were criticisms of her looks and her sexual conduct," an "adulterous woman who also neglects her children . . . being totally beyond redemption."[178]

When Isabel's grandson Louis XI named his daughter Anne of France to serve as regent for his son, he was following a long and well-established tradition. Yet in selecting his daughter, rather than his wife, Charlotte of

Savoy, the dauphin's mother, he broke that tradition in some ways. Anne was the first sister of a king to function as regent. For her part, this "least foolish" of women—whose contemporaries referred to her by such titles as "Madam the Regent," "Madam the Governor of the King," or "Madam the Grand"—seems to have been well suited for her role. In his biographical portrait of her, the sixteenth-century chronicler Pierre de Brantôme judges her "the true image of King Louis, her father."[179]

Although his judgment of her is sometimes harsh—she is "a shrewd woman and a cunning if ever there was one," "vindictive in temper like her father," "a sly dissembler, corrupt, full of deceit, and a great hypocrite"—Brantôme nevertheless recognizes that her father's choice for a "guardian and administrator" for Charles VIII was a good one. Anne "governed him so wisely and virtuously that he came to be one of the greatest of the kings of France." With some regret, however, Brantôme notes her husband's lack of control over her: Anne "made him do what she had in her head, for she ruled him and knew how to guide him." Even so, this may have been "all the better," since "he was rather foolish,—indeed very much so."

Brantôme has firsthand evidence for his assessment of the character of the regent, for, as he tells us, he has many letters written from her to his family.[180] In his own judgment, he has never known any French king "talk and write so bravely and imperiously as she did, as much to the great as to the small": "splendid and magnificent by nature and unwilling to diminish by ever so little her early grandeur, she also did many great kindnesses to those whom she liked and took in hand."

This *maitresse femme*, as Brantôme calls her, retired to Bourbon in 1492, after her brother's marriage to Anne of Brittany. Her court at Chantelle, four leagues from Moulins, the governing capital, perhaps recreated the atmosphere of her childhood home: Following his coronation in 1461, her father had established his mother, Marie of Anjou, his wife, Charlotte of Savoy, and his five-month-old daughter Anne in residence at the chateau of Amboise. There, in a household of women living apart from the court, Anne's intelligence had been, in d'Orliac's phrasing, "ripened" by her surroundings and her reading. Now at Chantelle, accompanied by "great numbers of ladies and maids of honour," Anne in her turn formed a generation of women, training and educating them "very wisely and virtuously." Brantôme writes that there were "no ladies or daughters of great houses in her time who did not receive lessons from her, the house of Bourbon being one of the greatest and most splendid in Christendom." Yet Anne did not remain isolated. Perhaps the best indication of her abilities as regent is evidenced by Charles VIII's reliance on her experience. Before undertaking his invasion of Italy, the king arranged for his sister, not his wife, to manage his affairs in his absence: Anne of France would once again have power in her hands, even over the queen and his son, born late in 1492. Under the "express order of the king," Queen Anne was placed under the guardianship of Anne of France during Charles's absence, from 23 August 1494 until October 1495. The government of France was "transported" to Moulins.[181]

In her role Anne could preserve France, but she could not preserve the life of her young nephew, heir to the throne of France. The child died shortly after his third birthday. Meanwhile, Charles had begun his march back to France. The French king returned from his Italian escapades late in 1495; three children were born after his return, two more sons and a daughter, all of whom died. By early 1498, Charles too was dead, leaving no son to succeed him.

In Spain, when her half-brother Enrique had died, Isabella of Castile had been able to claim the throne for herself. But in France, despite her demonstrated ability, Anne could not claim the throne for herself or for her daughter, Suzanne of Bourbon. Instead, the crown passed out of the direct line of descent from father to son—from Charles V to Charles VIII—and to Louis of Orléans. A great-grandson of Charles V, he was descended through a collateral line, the Valois-Orléans. By the terms of the 1491 marriage contract signed by Anne of France, the widowed Anne of Brittany was to marry her husband's successor.

The aim of the 1491 contract had been the union of Brittany with France; the contract drawn in 1498, by contrast, offered independence to Brittany. The duchy would retain its rights and privileges; rather than being joined to the crown of France, it was to be inherited by the second son or oldest daughter born to Anne of Brittany. If her marriage to Louis failed to produce an heir for Brittany, the duchy was to pass to her Breton heirs. But before his long-desired marriage to the heiress of Brittany could take place, Louis had to have his first marriage, to Jeanne of France, annulled. To secure the support of Anne of France, Jeanne's sister, he was willing to grant her concessions. In order to "gain" Brittany, he was willing to lose Bourbon; on the death of Pierre de Bourbon and Anne of France, their daughter would have complete and independent control of Bourbon.[182]

The marriage of Louis XII and Jeanne of France was declared void on 17 December 1498, and Louis was married to Anne of Brittany on 8 January 1499. After the annullment of their marriage Louis "rewarded" Jeanne with the gift of the title "duchess of Berry." She earned a more enduring title for herself, however; after the annullment she retired to a convent. She died in 1505 and was eventually canonized as a saint.

Louis, meanwhile, prepared to resume the French wars in Italy, pressing a claim to the title of duke of Milan.[183] Louis had become king of France only because of the Salic law denying a woman the right to claim the crown of France for herself or to transmit a claim to her children; ironically, then, he laid claim to Milan in right of his grandmother, Valentina Visconti, daughter of Giangaleazzo Visconti, duke of Milan.[184]

But if he were to pursue his interests in Italy, he needed to provide for the administration of France and the protection of his daughter Claude, who had been born in 1499. Anne of France was, once again, the choice. In the words of biographer Marc Chombart de Lauwe, he decided "to call his old adversary to his aid." Anne, for her part, was willing to support the man who had discarded her sister. Louis granted her a number of additional revenues and, in accordance with her wishes, he arranged for the marriage of her daughter Suzanne with her cousin Charles de Montpensier.[185]

Louis made a triumphal entry into the city of Milan on 6 October 1499. But while he gained Italian possessions, he found himself in conflict with the Emperor, with Spain, and with England—a renewal of the enmities that his predecessor Charles had faced. Back in France in 1502, Louis opened negotiations to settle these conflicts, but in 1503 he fell seriously ill. It appeared as if Anne of France would become regent of France once more, the governor of Amboise refusing entry to anyone but Anne or her husband during the king's illness. But at this moment, the queen seized the initiative. At Blois she signed a treaty with the Emperor Maximilian; her daughter Claude would be married to Charles, grandson of both Ferdinand of Aragon and of Maximilian. When he recovered from what had seemed to be a fatal illness, Louis XII did not disavow his wife or the extremely unpopular treaty she had signed; it was, however, rejected by the Estates General in 1506. His daughter Claude would instead be married to the French heir presumptive, Francis of Angoulême, "who is all French," in the words of the deputies of the assembly.[186]

While these events played out in France, Anne of France's life had also undergone significant change. In 1503, her husband died. To prepare her daughter Suzanne for her new role as duchess, Anne of France undertook a task unparalleled in our examination of female rulers: She composed a book for her daughter, a collection of *enseignements*, or teachings, designed to instruct and to guide her. Anne worked rapidly. The book was begun after Pierre de Beaujeu's death in 1503 and presented to Suzanne before her marriage in May 1505. Written on the opening leaf of the manuscript are these words: "This book is mine, Suzanne de Bourbon."[187]

Anne begins her book of instruction to her daughter by justifying its composition: it originates out of the "perfect *natural* love" of a mother for her daughter. In thus committing such an "unnatural" act—a woman writing to another woman on the exercise of power and authority—she justifies her task as, from the outset, natural. Considering the "innumerable and great" dangers of life, the transience of the world, and the suddenness of death, Anne—as a mother—has both the "courage and the desire," despite "the state of our poor fragility," to present a few "little teachings" to her daughter, hoping that in her "ignorance and youth" she will find in them something useful. What follows is a portrait of an ideal princess, a guidebook on governance for Suzanne, not altogether unlike Machiavelli's more famous conduct book for a would-be prince, written some ten years later. In addressing *The Prince* to Lorenzo de' Medici, Machiavelli hoped that his "understanding of the deeds of great men, acquired through a lengthy experience of contemporary politics and through an uninterrupted study of the classics" would prove useful to the new ruler; the book represented "everything I have learned over the course of so many years, and have undergone so many discomforts and dangers to discover," and, as such, he says he could offer "no greater gift."[188] So the *enseignements* from Anne of France to her daughter.

Like her Florentine contemporary, Anne brings to her task her own "lengthy experience of contemporary politics" and wide reading; she also brings an awareness of what is expected of women, whose traditional virtues must be cultivated even as their "poor fragility" must be overcome. To this end, she counsels Suzanne: the "first and principal point above all others," is that she keep herself from "saying, doing, or thinking" anything for which God might "correct" her: "live in great fear and be always on your guard," she warns Suzanne, "lest you be deceived." To "live chastely" and to "better guard her soul from sin," she should always bear in mind that not even one hour of life is sure. Contemplating the uncertainties of life, then, she should avoid those who waste their time in "sweet vanities and foolish pleasure."[189]

But beyond the conventional instructions that occupy much of the book, Anne of France offers her daughter advice intended to help her negotiate the difficult passage of a "fragile" woman in the world of politics, including the words quoted at the outset of this chapter:

> it is not fitting for a young woman to meddle with or to interfere in many things, and wise men say that one ought to have eyes to look at all things and to see nothing, ears to hear all and to know nothing, a tongue to answer everyone without speaking a prejudicial word to anyone.

She must, in sum, conduct herself carefully: "Above all, I counsel you . . . take care of yourself, without asking about anything or seeking to know what others are doing." And she must be discreet: "if by chance it happens that you know something, take care that you do not make it public; whatever is asked of you, do not seem as if you know it."[190]

Anne of France's daughter became duchess of Bourbon upon her father's death in 1503, when she was about twelve years old. In May of 1505, Suzanne married Charles de Montpensier, Anne of France's nephew, whom Anne had "adopted" in his infancy and whom she had raised at Chantelle. In the romantic words of D'Orliac, "Anne . . . realized her dream": the two young people "unified their hearts, formed by her, and the immense domains conquered by her." Bourbon had become "a kingdom within a kingdom."[191]

For the remainder of her life, Anne of France would administer Bourbon, defending its independence, just as her contemporary and rival, Anne of Brittany, fought throughout her life for the continued autonomy of her own province of Brittany. Anne, twice queen of France, died on 9 January 1514. Anne, the "king" of France, died at the age of sixty-one, on 14 November 1522.

Fifteenth-Century Foremothers: Four Models

Among Anne of France's *enseignements* is one that is particularly important for us. It is a reminder for her daughter not to forget the "glory and honor" of her "lineage" as a woman. Foolish women, she advises, think nothing of their foremothers—of their mothers and grandmothers, of their aunts and sisters. But a noble woman remembers the lines of blood and intimacy that bind women together. In remembering the women to whom she is related, she does them honor.[192]

We have examined in detail here the lives of four women. Contemporaries, their lives are intertwined, one with the other. They are inextricably bound together, just as each one of them, in her turn, is bound to her grandmothers, mothers, aunts, sisters, and nieces. In Isabella of Castile, Margaret Beaufort, Caterina Sforza, and Anne of France, we can see models of how women came to power and, having gained it, how they attempted to sustain it.

Isabella of Castile is the model of the queen regnant—of the woman who has inherited power and authority in her own right. While her position is unusual, it is not unprecedented. Castile offered predecessors in her role as queen, as did Naples, Navarre, Scotland, Sicily, Hungary, Poland, and Scandinavia, while many other women inherited titles and provinces as "queens" to govern in their own right.[193]

In Caterina Sforza and Anne of France we see the model of the regent—the woman who has a legally recognized authority to act on behalf of a husband, son, or brother. I have included both of them, for as regents they represent contradictory models, Caterina the "virago," whose desire for power challenged accepted norms of behavior for women, and Anne the *roi*, who crafted a role and persona that allowed her to work within accepted norms. The virago might find herself demonized, like Isabel of Bavaria, or forced from the scene, like Margaret of Anjou, but if she were willing to assume her "natural" role as guardian, she might, like Blanche of Castile and Anne of France, not only find power but considerable respect, and even honor.

In Margaret Beaufort we see the model of what for lack of a better term I will call the "queen *manquant*," that is, a queen who "might have been," a "missing" queen whose claims to rule were overlooked or ignored. Like Matilda of England, Juana *la Beltraneja*, Elizabeth of York, or even Anne of France, Margaret Beaufort is a woman who might have been queen but who, for a variety of reasons, did not become one.[194] Under certain circumstances—and if she were willing to accept those circumstances— such a woman might have considerable power and influence, as Margaret Beaufort did in her carefully constructed role as "the king's mother." But in other cases—if she were either unwilling or unable to conduct herself "appropriately" and accept a role as a wife or a mother instead of the title of queen—such a woman was simply removed from the scene, like Princess Juana in Castile or the younger Blanche of Navarre. In accepting an "appropriate" role, however, she might also effectively be "removed" from the scene, relegated completely to her "natural" role as wife; Elizabeth of York is the obvious example.

These four women also represent the shifting geographical and political boundaries of western Europe in the early modern period. In her connec- tions—by blood, by marriage, by political alliance—Isabella of Castile's "lineage" extends throughout the Iberian peninsula to the Holy Roman Empire and beyond. Margaret Beaufort's extends throughout the British Isles, Caterina Sforza's the Italian peninsula, Anne of France's the kingdom of France. But, as we shall see, their descendants cross geographical and political boundaries as well. One of Isabella's daughters was queen of England, for example; among her granddaughters were queens of England, of France, of Denmark, and of Poland. The "daughters" of England and France travelled less widely, but among Caterina Sforza's "lineage" can be numbered two queens of France, a Holy Roman empress, and a queen of Poland.

In the chapters that follow, then, we will examine the "lineage" of Isabella of Castile, Margaret Beaufort, Caterina Sforza, and Anne of France. We will trace their descendants, the women to whom they were bound, in ties of blood, intimacy, and even enmity, the women who would attempt, with varying degrees of success, to follow the models of female power fashioned by these fifteenth-century foremothers.

CHAPTER 2

THE DAUGHTERS OF
ISABELLA OF CASTILE

Queens and Regents in Spain
andtheHabsburgEmpire

A woman is never feared or respected as a man is, whatever her rank.

—Mary of Austria, Regent of the Netherlands[1]

The daughters of Isabella of Castile—the women to whom she was related by ties of blood, marriage, and alliance—are to be found in royal houses throughout Europe, from the nearby kingdoms of Portugal and Navarre to the more distant lands of Denmark and Hungary. Before examining their roles in the political history of early modern Europe, we will look briefly at the vast and complex empire where they would assume positions as queens and regents in succeeding generations.

Through her marriage to Ferdinand of Aragon, Isabella had united the crowns of Castile and Aragon, but this union was a personal one, threatened after the queen's death in 1504 when her daughter Juana succeeded her as queen, separating Castile from Aragon once more. With its greater wealth and population and with its New World empire, Isabella's kingdom had been the dominant power in the union of *los Reyes Catolicos*, its interests quite different from those of Aragon, a Mediterranean kingdom that laid claim to territory in Italy, Sicily, Sardinia, and Naples. Ultimately, Castile and Aragon would be permanently joined, not *by* Isabella of Castile but *through* her nonetheless, in the person of her daughter Juana's son.

In the western part of the Iberian peninsula, meanwhile, was the independent kingdom of Portugal; by negotiating a series of dynastic marriages between Castilian princesses and Portuguese princes, Isabella aimed at reuniting Portugal with Castile, a "reconquest" that would rival her defeat of the kingdom of Granada and unify the entire peninsula.[2] Despite her efforts, she did not achieve her goal, at least not during her lifetime. But the reunion she sought was temporarily accomplished, once more through her daughter, when Juana's grandson was recognized as king of both Spain and Portugal.

To the east of Castile, in the Pyrenees, lay the kingdom of Navarre, strategically located between Spain and France. Isabella's brother had attempted to unite Castile with the kingdom of Navarre when he married the daughter of Blanche, the queen regnant, but the princess had been returned to her native land, having failed to produce an heir for the Castilian king. Isabella's husband had close ties to Navarre as well, for Eleanor, who succeeded her mother as queen regnant of the kingdom, was Ferdinand's half-sister.[3] When the succession of Eleanor's granddaughter Catherine was disputed by her uncle Jean of Foix, on the ground that a woman should not inherit such a politically important crown, Ferdinand intervened to assure that Catherine would become the queen of Navarre—and that the kingdom would not fall under French control. Still later, after Isabella's death and in pursuit of his own dynastic interests, Ferdinand married Germaine, Jean of Foix's daughter and the niece of Louis XII. Hoping to resist further Spanish encroachment in her independent kingdom, Catherine of Navarre sought the support of the French king. In response, Ferdinand invaded, conquering much of Navarre and incorporating it into Aragon.[4]

The kingdoms of Aragon and Castile were eventually united by Charles, Juana's son, and Spain became a part of his vast inheritance, which included Burgundy, the independent states of the Netherlands, Austria, and, eventually, the imperial crown of the Holy Roman Empire.[5]

The geographical diversity of Spain and of the Habsburg empire to which it was joined offered varied opportunities for the daughters of Isabella of Castile. We will examine their successes—and their failures—as they assumed roles as queens and regents in the generations following Isabella's death.

In pursuit of their geographical and political imperatives, Isabella and Ferdinand arranged a series of dynastic marriages for their children, four daughters and one son. Their first child, Isabel, was born in 1470. It was eight years before a son would be born, and for those years Isabel was recognized as her parents' heir. When Isabella became queen of Castile in 1474, her daughter—not her husband—was recognized as the heir presumptive to her throne. After first objecting, Ferdinand came to accept the Castilian law of succession, as we have seen, eventually naming Isabel as his own heir in Aragon.[6]

The queen made sure that Isabel and the three daughters who followed—Juana, Maria, and Catalina—were carefully educated. They bene-

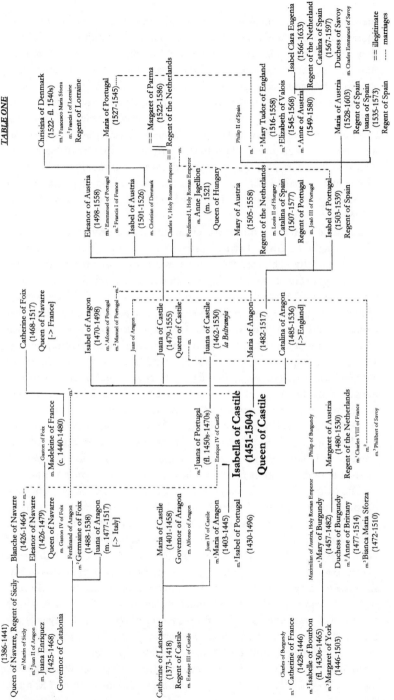

TABLE ONE

fited from an exceptional humanist curriculum, appearing to scholars like Erasmus and Juan Luis Vives as marvels of "feminine learning." In addition, they were instructed in the "feminine accomplishments appropriate to their station," including music and needlework as well as the administration of a royal household. But none of Isabella's daughters was educated in governing, not even the Princess Isabel, who was her mother's heir presumptive. In his analysis of the educational program Isabella devised for her children, Garrett Mattingly concludes that she educated her daughters, like her son, "seriously." Perhaps so. But while they may have been educated "seriously," they were not educated comparably. By contrast, Prince Juan, born in 1478, was trained as a future sovereign, presiding over a kind of "practice" court and instructed in the art of politics as well as the art of war.[7]

It is difficult to account for Isabella's critical omission in the education of her daughters. Given her own background and position, it is hard to understand why she would not have taken care to prepare them for whatever the future might hold. She herself had learned, through hard experience, the "lessons . . . of a warrior and a statesman." First in pursuit of the throne and then as Castile's queen, she had led armies, presided over councils, and dealt with her own rebellious nobility as well as with competing foreign powers. Equally important, she had successfully negotiated her role as queen regnant with Ferdinand as king-consort. Perhaps, as Marvin Lunenfeld speculates, her failure to educate her daughters to rule derived from her sense of her own uniqueness: "Isabella was *sui generis*, hardly believing it likely that any other female, even one of her own brood, would be able to follow in her stern path."[8] For whatever reasons, Isabella's daughters were not prepared to expect, to obtain, or to wield political power; while her "daughters" would come to include a line of effective rulers, her own daughters failed to follow the example of their mother.

The Princess Isabel, for eight years her parents' heir, did not, after all, become queen regnant of Castile. Instead she was consigned to the more conventional role of royal women. As part of the agreement to consolidate her position on the throne of Castile—and to complete the disinheriting of her rival Juana *la Beltraneja*—Queen Isabella agreed to her oldest daughter's marriage to the Portuguese king's grandson, Afonso. By the terms of this agreement, the princess was sent to live under the guardianship of Beatriz of Viseu, who was the Castilian queen's aunt and the Portuguese king's sister-in-law. Isabel remained in Portugal with the duchess for two years, from 1481 to 1483, after which she returned to her mother in Castile. The princess's marriage to Prince Afonso, by then heir apparent in Portugal, was celebrated in 1490, but it was to be a brief one. The prince died in 1491, the twenty-year-old widow returning once more to Castile. Although

Isabella recognized her daughter's grief and her determination not to marry again ("my lord the king promised a year ago not to force her," the queen wrote), the princess was used for a second time as a political tool.[9] In spite of Isabel's determination to become a nun, the Castilian princess was married to the new Portuguese king, Manuel, in 1497.

For a brief period it looked as if she might, after all, become queen of Castile. Within a few weeks of her marriage, her brother Juan died, and the new Portuguese queen and her husband were summoned to Castile. On 29 April 1498 the *Cortes* recognized Manuel and a pregnant Isabel as heirs to the Castilian throne. The *Cortes* in Aragon resisted Ferdinand's efforts to have Isabel proclaimed his heir, however, reserving their decision about the Aragonese succession until the birth of her child. Although Ferdinand argued that the law did of Aragon did not forbid female succession, the *Cortes* would only agree that, if Isabel's baby were a boy, he would be recognized as heir to Aragon. The child was indeed a boy, named Miguel, but his mother, Isabel of Castile, queen of Portugal, died within an hour of his birth.[10]

This was not the end of Isabella of Castile's determined pursuit of a Portuguese *reconquista*. When Prince Miguel died on 20 July 1500, just before his second birthday, the queen decided that her third daughter, Maria, would become the wife of the Portuguese king. Manuel and Maria were married in October. Before her death in 1517, Maria gave birth to eight children. Her oldest son became the king of Portugal as Joaõ III.[11]

While Isabella thus pursued her alliance with the kingdom of Portugal, she also arranged dynastic marriages for her two remaining daughters, the princesses Juana and Catalina. In 1495, the Catholic monarchs signed a treaty with Henry VII of England and with the Emperor Maximilian. The marriage of Isabella's daughter would guarantee this alliance: "the best security that the treaty between Henry and Maximilian will be fulfilled," she and Ferdinand agreed, is "to marry one of their daughters to a son of Maximilian and another to a son of Henry."[12] Thus, Juana of Castile was married to Philip of Austria, and Catalina of Aragon to Prince Arthur of England. Catalina was transformed into Catherine, and her life was to be spent in England where, after Arthur's death, she married his brother, becoming the first of King Henry VIII's six wives. Since her future lay in England, we will postpone her story until the next chapter. Juana would return to Castile after her mother's death, following Isabella to the throne.

Juana's reputation in history is as notorious as her name—she is *Juana la Loca*, or "Juana the Mad." As queen of Castile she was as spectacularly unsuccessful as her mother was successful. References to Juana, named after Ferdinand's mother Juana Enriquez, are frequent in standard histories and biographies—they emphasize her extraordinary beauty and her obsessive love for her husband, Philip of Austria, or Philip "the Handsome." They generally assume, as well, the story of her madness.

As it is generally told, the narrative of Juana's life is fairly simple, a kind of fairy-tale turned horror story. Married to a handsome prince who is as unfaithful as he is charming, the beautiful princess is tormented by her uncontrollable jealousy. Inheriting a strain of madness from her grand-mother, she descends into madness herself. When her mother dies, she becomes queen, but she is unable even to care for herself, much less for her country and her people. Her husband, then her father, and finally her son undertake to act for her as regents. The madwoman is locked away, kept company by her youngest daughter and visited faithfully by her oldest son. In her death, she triumphs—her sons become emperors and her daughters all become queens.

Juana may well have been mad, or she may have become mad, but her story is at once more complicated and more tragic. Certain elements of her tragedy are clear. Her marriage to Philip of Austria, duke of Burgundy, was arranged in 1496, and she left Spain in August of that year. When she finally met the waiting Philip on 18 October, he was so struck by her beauty that he demanded they be married that very day so they could consummate their union without delay. The birth of their first child, Eleanor, in 1498 was followed quickly by the birth of Charles, a son and heir, born in the city of Ghent on 25 February 1500.

Despite the initial attraction between the two, their relationship deteri-orated quickly. In some accounts, Philip is depicted as a kind of sexual psychopath, a ruthless sadist who "held Juana in a vicious cycle of affection, abuse, and intimidation from which she was constitutionally unable to escape," while Juana is portrayed as a woman so "madly in love" that "she allowed herself to be psychologically abused," unable to free herself from her husband's "domination and sexual magnetism." In others Juana is a beautiful but fragile hysteric: "a mercurial temperament subject to soaring changes of disposition, scaling the heights of joy one moment and groveling in a bottomless well of self-pity the next." Modern historians thus differ in their views, but their contradictory assessments of the couple are no more incompatible than the views of Philip and Juana's contemporaries. As Jocelyn Hillgarth makes clear, those who actually met the pair recorded equally inconsistent views: In 1499, for example, a Spanish priest observed that Juana was "so frightened that she could not hold up her head," while in 1500 the Spanish ambassador judged that "in a person so young I do not think one has seen such prudence."[13]

After the deaths, in rapid succession, of Prince Juan of Castile in 1497, of Isabel in 1498, and of Prince Miguel in 1500, the crowns of Aragon and Castile fell to Juana as her parents' heir. Isabella and Ferdinand summoned their daughter and her husband to Spain.[14] Philip ignored their urgent request and put off the journey at first, preferring to send a representative to Spain to act on his behalf, but Juana refused to sign the document appointing Philip's choice of an ambassador. By 1501 Juana was pregnant for a third time, delaying the trip still longer. The archduchess gave birth to another daughter in July, naming the baby Isabel after her Castilian grandmother. When Juana was finally able to travel, she and Philip began their trip to Spain, not by ship, as Ferdinand and Isabella planned, but through France, as Philip preferred. In France, Philip swore fealty as Louis XII's "good neighbor, humble servant, and obedient vassal," but Juana was determined to assert herself as the *Infanta* of Castile rather than as Philip's archduchess and a vassal of France. She refused to kneel to the French king, but she was maneuvered onto her knees forcibly in a gesture of submission by two formidable women we have met before: as Juana approached Anne of Brittany, queen of France, she was either shoved or tripped by Anne of France. Later, when she found herself in yet another "compromising position," Juana responded proudly by refusing to accept an offering of gold coins from the French queen. Her refusal earned the hostility of Anne of Brittany and the anger of her husband.

By the end of January 1502, Juana and Philip arrived in Castile. On 22 May the couple were formally designated Isabella's heirs in Castile, and in September they travelled to Aragon to be recognized as Ferdinand's. The Aragonese *Cortes* recognized Juana as *primogenita succesora*, heir presumptive to the crown, declaring her the "true and lawful heir to the crown, to whom, in default of male heirs, the usage and law of the land require the oath of allegiance." Philip was recognized as her king-consort. But, if Isabella were to predecease Ferdinand, the Aragonese parliament declared that any male child Ferdinand might have in a subsequent marriage would take precedence over Juana. On 27 October Juana became the first woman to whom the Aragonese *Cortes* swore an oath of fealty.

By 19 December Philip was gone, leaving Juana—pregnant again—behind with her parents.[15] His departure was followed almost immediately by his betrayal of Juana and *los Reyes Catolicos*. On 5 April 1503 Philip concluded the treaty of Lyon with France; it provided for the marriage of his son and heir to Louis' daughter and agreed to Ferdinand's renunciation of the kingdom of Naples, which he had just conquered. In 1504 Philip joined his father Maximilian and the French king in yet another treaty against Aragonese interests.

Before Juana rejoined her husband, she gave birth to her fourth child, another son, named Ferdinand after her father, on 10 March 1503. When she finally left Spain in May of 1504, she left this child behind, to be raised by his grandparents. In the meantime, Juana's increasingly erratic behavior,

Philip's perfidy, and Queen Isabella's failing health led to a reeevaluation of the Castilian succession. When she drew her will in October, Isabella named Juana as her successor: the crown of Castile would be inherited by her "dearly beloved daughter" as "universal heiress of all . . . said kingdoms and lands and lordships . . . , proprietress . . . conformable with what I owe and am obliged by law." Juana and Philip—"as her husband"—were to receive "obedience from her subjects." But to exclude Philip from power, Isabella stipulated that Juana appoint no foreigners to office and that she consult the *Cortes* on all decisions. She further ordered, in the event that Juana as queen "does not desire or is not able to engage in government," the regency of Castile fall not to Philip but to Ferdinand. If Juana were incapacitated by absence or illness, her father was to function as her regent until Juana's son and heir, Charles, "shall be at least twenty."

Isabella died on 26 November 1504, and Juana was immediately proclaimed her successor: "Castile, Castile for our sovereign lady, Queen Juana."[16] But in Brussels, Philip had himself proclaimed "King of Castile, Léon, Granada, archduke of Austria, prince of Aragon and Sicily, duke of Burgundy, [and] count of Flanders." What followed was not a smooth succession but a succession crisis. In the new queen's absence, Ferdinand assumed the role of regent of Castile, but his position was vigorously opposed by Juana's husband. Ferdinand convened the *Cortes* in January 1505, and Juana was recognized as "legitimate and proprietary ruler" of Castile and Philip as her husband and consort. But Ferdinand claimed that, by the terms of Isabella's will, Juana had to return to Castile and prove herself capable of rule. In a letter he declared Juana had shown "illness and emotional upheaval" and "disorder" during her previous trip to Castile and that, out of "prudence" and because of "great sorrow," Isabella "did not wish to declare what the impediment was." "Because of the gravity of the situation," he wrote, "it is better that you comprehend the reasons that moved the queen, her mother, to word her will as she did." Since the matter "touches the royal person of Queen Juana, you must all swear a solemn oath to keep this matter secret."[17] The *Cortes* ultimately decided to acknowledge Ferdinand as regent "owing to the incapacity" of Juana. A letter announcing the decision was sent to Philip in Flanders.

In pursuit of his wife's interests, Philip insisted that Juana was capable of ruling and that, as her husband, he had the right to the regency. He was supported by a significant number of the Castilian *grandees*, who were suspicious of the Aragonese king. For his part, Ferdinand solicited a letter from Juana approving of her father's assumption of the regency. But Juana was betrayed by one of her Castilian servants, who turned the document over to Philip. The new Castilian "queen" was forced to substitute a letter in support of Philip:

Since they want in Castile to make out that I am not in my right mind, it is only meet that I should come to my senses again, somewhat, though I ought not to wonder that they raise false testimony against me, since they did so against our Lord. But since the thing has been done so maliciously and at such a time, I bid you . . . speak to my father the king on my behalf, for those who say this of me are acting not only against me but against him, and people say that he is glad of it, so as to have the government of Castile, though I do not believe it, as the king is so great and catholic a sovereign and I his dutiful daughter. I know well that the king my lord [Philip] wrote thither complaining of me in some respect, but such a thing should not go beyond father and children especially as, if I did fly into passions and failed to keep up my proper dignity, it is well known that the only cause of my doing so was jealousy. I am not alone in feeling this passion, for my mother, great and excellent person as she was, was also jealous, but she got over it in time, and so, please God, shall I. Tell everybody [in Castile] . . . that, even if I was in the state that my enemies would wish me to be, I would not deprive the king, my husband, of the government of the realms, and of all the world if it were mine to give.[18]

Ferdinand received the letter, along with reports that indicated Juana's signature on it was either forged or coerced.

It may well be that, at this point, Ferdinand decided on another tack to maintain power in Castile; some reports indicate that he sent an emissary to Portugal to negotiate a marriage with Isabella's old rival, Juana *la Beltraneja*. Through her he could oppose Philip and Juana and claim the crown of Castile for himself. If he did make such an overture, nothing came of it. He did, however, sign a treaty with France; instead of a marriage with Isabella's niece and rival for the throne of Castile, he married the French king's niece, Germaine of Foix. In response, Philip attempted to force Juana to sign a denunciation of her father, but once again she refused. Ferdinand's ambassadors at Philip's court objected to the conditions under which Juana was forced to live; they were finally allowed to see her but not to speak with her.

After Juana gave birth on 13 September 1505 to another daughter, named Mary, Philip decided to travel to Castile to claim the throne. Ferdinand, meanwhile, declared that Juana was sane but a prisoner, publishing a proposal to rescue her. He also prepared for a compromise with Philip that would exclude Juana but benefit both of them. This "iniquitous plot" is described by Martin Hume:

Philip and [Juana] were to be acknowledged by Castile as sovereigns, and their son Charles as heir; but, at the same time, Ferdinand was to be accepted as perpetual governor in his daughter's absence: and in the case of the Queen [Juana] being unwilling or unable to undertake the government, the two Kings, Ferdinand and Philip, were to issue all decrees and grants in their joint names. The revenues of Castile and of the Grand Masterships were to be equally divided between Philip and Ferdinand.[19]

Philip and Juana arrived in Castile on 26 April 1506; as they travelled toward a meeting with Ferdinand, Philip kept his wife in the background. As Hume reports, "Everywhere Philip took the lead, and [Juana] was treated as a consort." Juana resented her husband's efforts, however, and refused to sign documents that Philip prepared for her. The Castilian *grandees* who supported Philip against Ferdinand were increasingly unhappy with Juana's husband and her position as well, noting her isolation and his disregard for their interests.

Philip and Ferdinand finally met in June. Philip was deeply suspicious of his wife and of his father-in-law; he refused to allow Ferdinand to meet with, or even to see, Juana. But on 27 June the two men finally agreed to a treaty of peace, a "hellish compact" that "sealed the fate" of Juana, "whatever might happen."[20] The agreement stated that the queen "on no account wishes to have anything to do with any affair of government or other things." After this categorical statement, it continued: "and, even if she did wish it, it would cause the total loss and destruction of these realms, having regard to her infirmities and passions which are not described here for decency's sake." Juana, therefore, was excluded from governing, and if she should "of her own accord or at the instance of others . . . attempt to interfere in the government or disturbed the arrangement made between the two kings, they will join forces to prevent it." Ferdinand was willing to declare Juana's unfitness, even though it had been over two years since he had seen her. As Hume explains, during that period "both he and Philip had alternately declared she was quite sane and otherwise, as suited their plans." But now, when it suited them both, they agreed "not only that she did not *wish* to govern her country . . . but that if ever she *did* wish, or Castilians wished for her to do so, then her 'passions and infirmities,' so vaguely referred to, would make her rule disastrous."

After signing the document, Ferdinand turned around immediately and denounced it, swearing that he had been coerced and that Juana was, after all, quite fit to rule. He swore to "liberate" Juana from her imprisonment and to return to her the government of Castile. Juana managed to assert herself again in July, when she and Philip were in Valladolid. She refused to enter the city following two banners, insisting that she alone was queen and that one of the banners should be removed. A report to the Spanish ambassador in Rome described one witness's view of Juana's situation:

> It was always the King's [Philip's] intention to do what he has done. The
> *grandees* of the kingdom have united against the Queen and . . . her father,

not only so that she may not reign but also so that she should be made a prisoner. She is under guard in a fortress so that no one may see her or talk with her. She is the most unfortunate woman ever born and would be far better off as the wife of a laborer. It is unbelievable that her own subjects have imprisoned her in her own kingdoms and that there is not one person in the realms who has the courage to lift his voice or his hand to help her.

The Admiral of Castile finally forced Philip to grant him an interview with Juana, and after a two-day meeting with her he reported that "she never gave a random answer."[21] He saw no sign of the insanity that both her father and her husband had, at various times, asserted. On 11 July, under the influence of the Admiral of Castile, the *Cortes* swore allegiance to her as queen of Castile and to Philip only as her consort. Juana appeared in person on 12 July to receive their oath of allegiance.

In the meantime Ferdinand was forced to withdraw from the struggle with Philip. Facing increased opposition in Castile and having his own interests in Naples to pursue, he retreated to Aragon. But Philip's ascendancy in Castile did not last long. By September he was dead. Although Juana declined any role in the government after her husband's death, Ferdinand, on his way to Naples, would not have her declared incompetent, instead issuing orders that she was to be recognized as obeyed as queen regnant.

Juana refused to assume her role as queen, indicating that her father should act in her stead. In this situation, reports about her mental state vary. According to Ferdinand's secretary, "there is no one, big or little, who any longer denies that she is out of her mind, except Juan Lopez, who says that she is as sane as her mother was." Another account attributes her withdrawal from the world not as madness but as an almost stoic resignation; she is "a woman to suffer and behold all the things of this world . . . without change of heart or courage."[22] Sane or insane, competent or incompetent, she was watched carefully by her father's supporters; Ferdinand was now as interested in having her confined as Philip had been.

On 17 January 1507, Queen Juana gave birth to her last child, another daughter, who was named Catalina. When Ferdinand finally arrived in Castile at the end of the year, he assumed the regency for Juana. For nearly fifty years, from 1507 until her death in 1555, Queen Juana of Castile was confined—as prisoner, as recluse, or as madwoman—in the fortress of Tordesillas. Her father continued as regent of Castile until his death in 1516. He was followed as regent by Juana's son Charles.

It is impossible now to determine with certainty whether Juana was, indeed, mad, but there is no question that she was *la Loca*. Most scholars assume without question her incapacity and the necessity of husband, father, and son to rule Castile in her stead. But there is some reason, if not to dismiss, at least to question these assumptions.

The tactic of discrediting and thereby disinheriting a claimant to the Castilian throne is a familiar and successful one; Isabella herself employed it against her niece and rival Juana *la Beltraneja*. It was not enough to declare her rival illegitimate; Isabella forced *that* Juana to renounce her claims and then "imprisoned" her; *la Beltraneja* was consigned to holy orders and "condemned" to life in a convent. There is little doubt now that she was not illegitimate but was in fact her father's legitimate daughter and thus rightful queen of Castile. As Marvin Lunenfeld makes clear,

> It is no longer tenable to maintain that Juana could not possibly have been [Enrique] IV's daughter or that he did not intend she succeed him. A massive campaign of propaganda and the falsification of documents has been uncovered. Isabella was able to create an official history of the advent of her regime to discredit her half-brother and niece but the most authoritative historians deny she had primacy.[23]

Citing recent evidence, Jocelyn Hillgarth also concludes that Juana was "almost certainly" Enrique's daughter. Yet these same scholars, and most others, fail to recognize that the treatment of Juana *la Loca* parallels in an uncanny way that of her namesake and cousin Juana *la Beltraneja*: both were discredited, disinherited, and imprisoned.

But not all scholars assume Juana *la Loca*'s madness. The historian S. B. Chrimes, for example, has considered the claims of Juana's discreditors carefully. He notes that in 1507, Henry VII, the widowed king of England, had entered into serious negotiations with Ferdinand for a marriage with Juana. A treaty for the match was signed in 1508, though the marriage never took place. About the failure of the alliance, Chrimes writes, "the project faded away, not surprisingly because in fact [Juana] was being kept in close confinement, first by Ferdinand and then by [her son Charles], in harsh and sometimes brutal conditions." He continues, "the story of her 'madness' was never, until perhaps towards the end of her long life, more than very successful propaganda put out by her ruthless and unscrupulous father and son." Chrimes indicates that Henry VII, who had met Juana as recently as 1506, "knew or suspected the truth, which oddly enough appears largely to have evaded the serious consideration of modern historians." That Juana was not mad, Chrimes notes, is clear from the "overwhelming weight" of contemporary evidence, which "compels such conclusions."[24] I will add that the fortress of Tordesillas had been used before to imprison "inconvenient" queens, including Maria of Portugal, queen of Castile; Eleanor Teles, queen of Portugal; Blanche of Bourbon, queen of Castile; and Beatrice, princess of Castile.[25]

One of the most curious aspects of Juana's life, at least from our perspective here, is her persistent refusal to associate with, or to be attended by, other women. The reason for her refusal is unclear, though some of her contemporaries attributed it to her unreasonable jealousy—she wanted no rivals for her husband's attentions. Others seemed to blame her isolation from other women on Philip's cruelty. As she travelled through Spain with her husband, a Flemish eyewitness wrote:

> she lived alone away from all women of the world, except for a laundress who . . . washed her clothes in her presence. And in such a state she existed and curbed her passions before her husband, attending to her own needs and waiting on herself like a poor slave. And in such a fashion she followed her husband across the country, one lone woman amid ten or twenty thousand men. It was verily a preposterous sight to behold, a lady of her royal birth and a queen of so many great realms without a single female companion.

At the July 1506 meeting of the *Cortes* Juana was urged to allow herself to be surrounded with ladies at court, as was customary. She agreed to wear Spanish dress, as the *Cortes* also requested, but refused to have women around her. Even after Philip's death she refused the companionship of women; during her last confinement she refused even her aunt's attendance.[26] Given the importance of connections among women we have noticed thus far in our study, it is interesting to speculate about how Juana's isolation may have affected her ability to function independently and successfully in her role as queen.

While we may not be able to conclude with certainty why Juana refused to associate with other women or whether her madness was pure propaganda, we can certainly conclude that she was, like Juana *la Beltraneja*, something of a queen *manquant*, a queen who might or ought to have been, but who was not. Unable, unprepared, unwilling, or unfortunate, she could not forge her own destiny as her mother had been able to do.

If we were to end our story of Isabella's daughters here, we would conclude that, however successful she had been in her own role as queen regnant, she was unsuccessful as a model for her daughters, who were consigned to dynastic marriages and destined for early deaths—Isabel and Maria in Portugal—or for long lives of powerlessness and imprisonment—Juana in Castile and Catalina in England. But, although her own children did not follow her model, Isabella of Castile was nevertheless succeeded by a line of politically capable and powerful "daughters."

As the "founding mother" of succeeding generations of queens and regents, Isabella of Castile must be joined by two contemporaries, Margaret of York and her daughter-in-law, Margaret of Austria. From these three women, together, descended the line of women who are Isabella's true political "daughters." The Habsburg family into which Juana of Castile married had as its motto *Bella gerant alii: tu, felix Austria, nube,* or, "Let others make war: you, happy Austria, marry." While marriage alliances were part of the strategies of all royal and noble families, the Habsburgs were particularly successful.

Margaret of York was the daughter of Cecily Neville and her husband Richard of York, the sister of both Edward IV and Richard III of England. In what her recent biographer has called "the marriage of the century," she became the third wife of Charles the Bold, whose lands included, besides the duchy of Burgundy, a "vast agglomeration" of French fiefs, imperial territories, and independent cities known as the Netherlands.[27] The extent and complexity of Burgundy are indicated by Margaret's new titles: She was duchess of Burgundy, of Lotharingia, of Brabant, of Limbourg, of Luxembourg, and of Guelders; countess of Flanders, of Artois, of Hainault, of Holland, of Zeeland, of Namur, of Zutphen, and of Burgundy (Franche Comté); and the lady of Friesland, of Salins, and of Malines [Mechelen], among others. Although she failed to provide a male heir for Charles, Margaret of York, duchess of Burgundy functioned superlatively as a political advisor and diplomat for the duke and as a mother for his daughter and heir Mary.[28]

After her marriage to the duke, which took place in 1468, Margaret of York also developed a strong relationship with her husband's mother. The dowager duchess, Isabel of Portugal, was a Lancastrian, the granddaughter John of Gaunt, but she was also a relative of the Yorkist Margaret—like Margaret herself, Isabel of Portugal was descended from Edward III of England. Although she was nearly seventy years old when Margaret arrived in Burgundy, the dowager duchess was still politically active, "well able," as Margaret Weightman notes, "to take charge of the marriage negotiations and to receive important diplomatic embassies on behalf of her son."[29]

In Burgundy, Margaret of York played an active role not only in court life but in politics and government, "not merely as the focus of the ducal household," in Weightman's judgment, "but also as an administrator and as the duke's representative": "Traditionally Burgundian duchesses had complemented and assisted the work of their husbands." Charles's mother, for example, had acted as regent of Burgundy, had functioned in the administration of the duchy, had negotiated treaties, and had helped to formulate policy. By 1472 Margaret herself was "actively concerned with affairs of state."[30]

Among Margaret's responsibilities as duchess were regular progresses around the Low Countries; while her husband visited his possessions and campaigned to extend his territory, Margaret also travelled, her progresses an important means of "upholding ducal authority." During the first seven years of her marriage, she spent, by Weightman's calculations, only about a year with her husband; between 1475 and Charles's death in 1477, they did not meet at all. Although the duke was evidently determined to keep his own court "free from silly female influences," his wife and daughter always travelled and lived together. Mary of Burgundy's early education had been supervised by her father's half-sister Anne, but after 1468 it became Margaret of York's task "to give guidance and support to the heiress Mary." For the next nine years, until Mary's marriage, the two were together "almost continually."[31]

Charles of Burgundy died in battle in 1477, and Margaret of York was forced to move quickly and forcefully to protect his heir. In the crisis that followed the duke's death, the thirty-one-year-old Margaret, experienced in government, advised her twenty-year-old stepdaughter and negotiated on her behalf. To guard against further French encroachment—Louis XI claimed a woman could not inherit the duchy—Margaret of York and Mary of Burgundy determined that "only an imperial marriage could save Burgundy from France." Margaret wrote to Maximilian, then archduke of Austria and eventually Holy Roman Emperor, offering him, as she said, "the word of a princess" in support of a marital alliance with Mary of Burgundy. The original marriage contract, as Weightman reports, "cut Maximilian out of the succession, leaving all the Burgundian lands to the children of the marriage and specifying that all Burgundian possessions must be under Burgundian rule." Later, in an act signed by Margaret, her stepdaughter Mary, and Maximilian—and only one Burgundian official—this provision was eliminated, and Mary's inheritance was left to Maximilian in the event of her death.[32] This decision proved to be critical. After five short years—and the births of two children—the young duchess of Burgundy, pregnant with her third child, died in a hunting accident.

When Mary died in 1482, Margaret of York was to have assumed the role of guardian of her stepdaughter's heirs, Philip, then four years old and Margaret, age two. But the Estates General of Flanders refused to turn the children over to Maximilian and the dowager duchess. While Margaret prepared troops to gain possession of them, the Estates signed a treaty with Louis XI, sending the infant Margaret to the French court, while still refusing to relinquish the heir to the dowager duchess or to his father. Maximilian eventually regained control of Philip in 1484; he then entrusted Margaret with the boy's guardianship and education. Margaret established her court in the city of Mechelen, in Brabant, one of her dower possessions; during her stepgrandson's minority, her court there became the de facto ducal palace:

The years 1477-94 were one of the most troubled periods in the whole history of the Burgundian Netherlands. . . . Throughout these difficult years Margaret remained a prominent centre of loyalty to Mary and Maximilian and their heirs. Indeed there were times when her court at Malines [Mechelen] was one of the few places where ducal power and authority was entirely secure.[33]

The relationship between Maximilian and the dowager duchess, who, like Anne of France, came to be known as *Madame la Grande*, was one of "close interdependence": "Margaret needed Maximilian to safeguard her dower but the archduke also needed Margaret." Throughout his son's minority, Margaret remained her son-in-law's "most loyal subject": "her support and advice were an invaluable asset to Maximilian in his government of the Low Countries."[34]

Margaret was forty-eight years old when her stepgrandson Philip of Austria came of age in 1494, inheriting his mother's titles and possessions. Upon his accession, he confirmed the dowager duchess's possessions, in recognition, as he proclaimed,

[of her] good and honest conduct towards our late lord and grandfather, and the great love that she clearly bore towards our late sovereign lady mother and to all her lands and lordships both before and after her marriage, and equally towards our lord and father, and towards us in our minority, how after the death of our late lady mother, she behaved towards us as if she was our real mother . . . and moreover because she has suffered inestimable damange rather than abandon us . . . and because of many other great reasons and considerations.[35]

Although Margaret of York never gave birth to a child of her own, she successfully negotiated a place for herself as a kind of "king's mother," staunchly and faithfully defending the inheritance of her stepdaughter and her stepdaughter's children. Like her contemporary Margaret Beaufort in England, in her role as "mother" she was to serve the next generation as well, for "Madam the Grand" retained her considerable influence during her stepgrandson's rule, welcoming foreign visitors to his court (including his bride, Juana of Castile), selecting administrators and counselors for him, and presiding over many ceremonies, including the christening of Philip and Juana's first two children, Eleanor and Charles.

Margaret of York played an important role in the life of her stepgranddaughter as well, though Margaret of Austria spent relatively little of her childhood with the older Margaret. Nevertheless, as Weightman notes, the younger Margaret "inherited much from her step-grandmother, acquiring both her personal treasures and her public servants"; but "the young woman seems to have inherited much more than material goods and servants from her namesake." Under the influence of three notable "mothers"—Margaret of York among them—Margaret of Austria was one of the most accomplished rulers of the early modern period. She was to serve as regent of the Netherlands for twenty years, at the same time shaping another generation of women whom she trained at her court and for whom she herself was to provide an influential model of female sovereignty.[36]

Named after her stepgrandmother, Margaret of Austria was born on 10 January 1480. When Mary of Burgundy died on 27 March 1482, at the age of twenty-seven, her daughter was just two years old. The Estates General of Flanders refused to accept Maximilian as his children's regent, however, pursuing instead a course of reconciliation with France. Louis XI, in an effort to settle his ongoing war with Burgundy, offered the Estates a treaty of peace, which included a proposed marriage between Margaret and his son and heir, Charles. Despite the vigorous opposition of both Maximilian and Margaret of York, the Estates agreed to the offer. Maximilian was forced to sign the treaty of Arras on 23 December, and Margaret was sent from Ghent "under guard"; on 24 April, just three years old, she was delivered to the French. The dauphin's sister met her at the border. Taking possession of the little girl, Anne of France and her husband needed to make sure of her health and fitness. Margaret was undressed so that she could be examined, "at which they were well content, being greatly pleased in every way."[37] On 2 June, at Amboise, she was betrothed to the dauphin Charles, then aged thirteen; they were "married" the following day.

Margaret of Austria spent the next ten years, until 1493, in France, in the care of a woman whom we have discussed before. After Louis XI died on 31 August 1483, his son Charles became king of France and, as his wife, Margaret, just three years old, became *la petite reine*, "the little queen." Throughout her childhood and adolescence, her education and training were supervised by her sister-in-law Anne, the regent of France. The regent established Margaret's court at Amboise, "organized according to the strictest royal norms." She appointed a governess and directed Margaret's education. The "little queen" became the "pet and plaything" not only of her husband but of Louis of Orléans, who would eventually succeed Charles VIII as king of France. There, too, was Louise of Savoy, Anne of France's niece, three years older than the young Margaret.[38]

Despite the treaty intended to end hostilities, Anne of France, as regent, was forced to pursue her father's war against Burgundy. After Margaret was sent to France, Maximilian of Austria had gone to war, first with the rebellious Flemish states. By 1485 he had regained control of much of his late wife's Burgundian territory and of his son and heir. In 1486 he was elected king of the Romans; with the help of Spain, England, and Brittany, he renewed his war with France. In 1490, as we have seen, he negotiated a marriage with Anne of Brittany. But Anne of France invaded Brittany, and by 1491 *la petite reine* had been replaced. The eleven-year-old Margaret had heard that her "husband" was going "to marry another wife," and although Charles VIII had assured her that he would "have no other," he married Anne of Brittany on 6 December 1491.[39]

Maximilian's loss of Anne of Brittany has received far more attention than Margaret's loss of her husband and of her position as queen of France. Her biographer Jane de Iongh, however, indicates something of the effect of her radical change of circumstance:

> The child experienced her degradation as a whiplash, as a shame and a humiliation, against which her self-respect, cultivated in the surroundings of royalty, rose in bitterest revolt. For the first time the power of treachery and deceit invaded her consciousness, and it engraved upon her nature a motif of cynicism which, softened by the influence of time and of a beneficent humor, was to become one of her most attractive characteristics.[40]

While de Iongh's description of Margaret's situation is fictionalized, it is important to note the very real extent of Margaret's personal loss and change in status. She herself responded to Charles's rejection by saying that "by reason of her youth, those who had counted on her fortune could never say or suspect that this had come upon her through any fault of her own."[41] For more than eight years she had been Charles's wife, raised to be and treated as the queen of France; suddenly, at age eleven, she was no longer a French queen, but neither was she sent home. She could no longer remain in the royal residence of Amboise, but she was not returned to Burgundy either. Instead, she was sent to the castle of Melun, where she remained a hostage in France for two years.

When Charles VIII decided to pursue his conquests in Italy, he needed peace with Maximilian. By the terms of the treaty of Senlis, signed in May 1493, Margaret of Austria, no longer *la petite reine* of France, was returned to her father along with the disputed provinces of Artois, Charolais, and Franche Comté, which Louis had demanded as her dowry.

Margaret of York awaited her stepdaughter and greeted her upon her arrival in the Flemish city of Cambrai. The two returned to the dowager duchess's court at Mechelen, where the younger Margaret would remain for the next four years. While his daughter had been in France, Maximilian had regained control of all of his Austrian possessions and of his wife's duchy of Burgundy and possessions in the Netherlands; as Margaret returned from France, he had been elected Holy Roman Emperor following his own father's death. In 1494, as Charles VIII invaded Italy, the new emperor allied himself with the pope, Spain, Venice, and Milan in the "Holy League" against the French. In 1494, in support of his alliance, "happy Austria" was married again, to Bianca Maria Sforza.[42] In 1496 Maximilian himself campaigned in Italy, and, to strengthen his Spanish alliance, arranged for two Habsburg marriages. His son, Philip of Burgundy, would be married to Juana of Castile, while his daughter Margaret of Austria, one-time "queen" of France, would marry the son and heir of Ferdinand and Isabella.

Philip's marriage to Juana took place first, as we have seen, in 1496. The ships that brought the Spanish princess to Flanders would, on their return voyage, take Margaret of Austria to Spain. But before she left Mechelen, a ceremonial marriage by proxy was celebrated. On 5 November 1496, Margaret of Austria was married to the Spanish *infante*, Prince Juan. She was sixteen years old.

Her voyage to Castile was a difficult one. After weeks of bad weather, she finally set sail on 22 January 1497, ten days after her seventeenth birthday. In the midst of a terrible storm, she wrote a two-line epitaph, which, as the incident is sometimes narrated, she tied into her hand, along with money for her burial: *Cy-gist Margot, la gentil' damoiselle / Qu'ha deux marys et encore est pucelle* ("Here lies Margot, the gentle maiden / Who had two husbands and is virgin still.") About this incident, de Iongh comments,

> Among the primitively egocentric utterances of her fellow-rulers, "Margot" in the storms . . . reveals an ironical self-criticism, a humorous sense of proportion, that are the more surprising in a seventeen-year-old girl who could have known only the norms of princely pride. She was already more than the Archduchess of Austria, Princess [by her second marriage] of the Asturias, Queen of Granada and Léon; she was a woman who in the face of death dared to express with a smile her belief in the relativity of all values.[43]

Margaret survived her trip, finally arriving in Spain on 8 March. She was greeted by Ferdinand and her new husband, Prince Juan. "If you could see her," the Spanish chronicler Peter Martyr wrote, "you would believe that you were contemplating Venus herself."[44] Together they travelled to the city of Burgos, where Margaret of Austria met her new mother-in-law, Isabella of Castile. Having conquered fear on her trip to Spain, she conquered her new husband and his parents. Her formal wedding with Juan took place on 3 April 1497. Just as Maximilian had arranged the marriage to secure his allies and to further his dynastic pursuit, Isabella and Ferdinand hoped, by this marriage, to expand their own power: for *los Reyes Catolicos*, "the twin crowns of Castile and Aragon would now be linked to the Holy Roman Empire, thus surrounding France and making Spain the most powerful kingdom in Europe."[45]

But Margaret was much stronger than her prince, as Peter Martyr noted on 13 June 1497:

> our young Prince is becoming pallid, consumed with passion. The doctors

and the King himself beg the Queen to intervene and separate the newlyweds. They ask her to seek a respite in the incessant acts of love and they warn of the dangers that these will incur. Again and again they call her attention to the paleness of her son's face and his fatigued manner, adding that the sickness is attacking his marrow and weakening his very being. They urge that a remedy be applied before it is too late.

Isabella, while not ignoring the warning, did not separate the newlyweds. "Man does not have the power to tear asunder those whom God has joined together," she is reported to have said.[46] By 9 October, just six months after his marriage, Prince Juan was dead, and Margaret of Austria was a widow. She was also pregnant for what turned out to be the first and only time in her life. Late in 1497 or early in 1498, she gave birth to a daughter, stillborn. The child was premature, an "unformed mass of flesh worthy of grief."[47]

Margaret of Austria had remained in France after her husband dissolved their marriage, a discarded "wife" but a valuable hostage. She also remained in Spain after Prince Juan's death, perhaps, as Rubin contends, "as a daughter," or perhaps for a second time as a political hostage, as de Iongh suggests:

> Ferdinand was glad to have in his hands a weapon against his ally Emperor Maximilian, and particularly against his son-in-law Duke Philip the Handsome, who . . . had appropriated the title of Prince of Castile and whose influence on his daughter Juana Ferdinand not unjustly feared.[48]

Whatever the circumstances of her life in Castile after Juan's death, Margaret did spend her time profitably, both teaching and learning. She tutored her sister-in-law Catalina of Aragon, betrothed to Prince Arthur of England, in English, while she herself learned practical lessons in politics and government from her "mother," the queen of Castile.

Eventually, though, Margaret was returned to Burgundy. She arrived in the Netherlands in September 1499, spending much of the next two years once more with Margaret of York at Mechelen. Already her father was planning to use her again to further his political ambitions. Many candidates for her remarriage were proposed: Ludovico Sforza, duke of Milan; the king of Scotland; Arthur, Prince of Wales (who had already been betrothed to her sister-in-law Catalina of Aragon); and the king of Hungary, among others.

While Maximilian deliberated, his son Philip of Burgundy decided the matter. With the death of Prince Juan of Castile, Philip's wife Juana had become the heir to the crowns of Castile and Aragon, and Philip was interested in having himself recognized as the future ruler of Spain. To this end, he wanted peace with France. He suggested yet another double marriage: his son and heir Charles would be married to Claude, infant daughter of Louis XII and Anne of Brittany, while his sister Margaret would be married to Philibert of Savoy, the French king's nephew. The duchy of Savoy, bordering France and Milan, was strategically located. And Louise of Savoy, Margaret's childhood companion during her days as "queen" of France, was Philibert's sister.

Like Philip of Austria, Philibert was nicknamed "the Handsome." Having arranged the marriage, Philip expected his sister to sign a document indicating that she had not been pressured or coerced into the match, a document that she refused to sign.[49] This was, perhaps, an early indication of the understandable antipathy to France that Margaret would demonstrate throughout the rest of her life. The marriage contract was validated nevertheless, on 26 September 1501, and once again Margaret left Flanders. She set off for a proxy marriage, accompanied by Margaret of York. The ceremony took place late on 28 November, the marriage with Philibert taking place shortly thereafter, on 4 December.

After her arrival in Savoy, Margaret recognized that her husband had no interest in government and no political influence. He had placed the government of Savoy in the hands of his illegitimate brother René, the so-called Grand Bastard of Savoy, to whom he had given the title "Lieu-tenant-General of the States of Savoy." Having had the best of models in Margaret of York, Anne of France, and Isabella of Castile, Margaret of Austria for the first time became more than a wife and political pawn:

> She dealt with the Grand Bastard swiftly and effectively. Charged with having conspired with the dangerous Swiss, he saw himself condemned as a traitor to his country, robbed of his dignity and his possessions and even of the letter of legitimacy granted him a few years earlier. . . . From this first political struggle . . . Margaret emerged as conqueror and absolute monarch of Savoy.

Although she joined her husband in courtly amusements, she found herself "wielding the actual power" in Savoy; her husband "basked in the sun of his popularity and, amused at the masculine interests of his so very feminine consort, gladly left the worry of governing to her."[50]

As she began her political career, interested not only in domestic affairs but in foreign policy, Margaret of Austria had a distinct advantage over the rulers who were her "colleagues." Although young and as yet unpracticed, she was neither sheltered nor inexperienced; her marriages and her travel had brought her into contact with all the European powers. Her father was archduke of Austria and the Holy Roman Emperor. Her brother was duke of Burgundy. She had spent eight years in France and knew Louis XII, Anne of Brittany, and Anne of France. Louise of Savoy, by then the mother of the heir presumptive to Louis' French throne, was her childhood companion and sister-in-law. She had spent three years in Spain with Isabella of Castile and Ferdinand of Aragon. Jane de Iongh's now dated and clearly gendered description of Margaret of Austria serves nonetheless as a balance to historical accounts that do no more than mention her name in passing, if they refer to her at all:

> In addition to all this rich experience she possessed one privilege that was more powerful the less it was known and recognized: she was a woman. . . . Tact, insight, flexibility that is stronger than the strongest fortress, intuition and charm, womanly levelheadedness and common sense made up the arsenal upon which she was to base her power. Margaret, with velvet gloves and a smile on her lips, was often to appear more powerful than the plumed and armored figures of her masculine opponents.[51]

Although Margaret's tenure in Savoy was to be brief, it was to be important for her future career. She would never again be a wife, but she would be a ruler. In Savoy, having identified and appointed trustworthy advisors and assistants, many of whom would serve her throughout her life, she began to apply the lessons of politics and government she had learned in France and Spain. But by September of 1504 Philibert was dead.

Margaret's first reaction to the loss of her husband was to try to throw herself out a window. Her attempt at suicide thwarted, she threw herself into passionate grieving instead, refusing to be separated from Philibert's body. According to a contemporary account, "immediately after her husband's death" the grief-stricken young woman also "cut off her beautiful golden hair, and had the same done to her own ladies."[52] Although she was eventually convinced to bury her husband, she had his heart embalmed so she could keep it with her. She withdrew from society and, six months later, began the construction of a mausoleum for Philibert's interment. While such behavior would label her sister-in-law Juana as *la Loca* and result in her being stripped of power and confined, that was not to be Margaret's fate.

In her retirement Margaret adopted the motto which she would keep for the remainder of her life: *Fortune. Infortune. Fort. Une.* This "enigmatical inscription," which she had inscribed throughout the church where Philibert's body was interred, has been variously interpreted. It is most often simply translated into a three-word English equivalent, "fortune, infortune [misfortune], fortune," a kind of "resume of her life" as "a plaything of fortune." But the devise is clearly four words, not three, and perhaps can best be interpreted as "Fortune tries a woman very strongly."[53]

Margaret remained in Savoy for two years after Philibert's death, conducting affairs for Philibert's brother and successor, still a minor, and struggling to obtain her dower income. For a time it looked as if she might once again be a marital pawn; her father was proposing a match with the recently widowed Henvy VII of England, but this time Margaret's refusal was determined. Maximilian's agent reported to the Emperor on 20 July 1506 that "the Archduchess Margaret decidedly refuses to marry Henry VII, although he [the agent], at first by himself, and afterwards conjointly with the Imperial ambassador . . . daily pressed her during a whole month to consent." On 8 August another report was sent to Maximilian; Margaret said that "although an obedient daughter, she will never agree to so unreasonable a marriage." On 24 September Maximilian wrote to the English king indicating that, while "he had not been able to persuade his daughter . . . to marry him," he intended to travel to Savoy himself "in order to persuade her."[54]

But before Maximilian could try to persuade his daughter into a fourth marriage, fortune—or "infortune"—intervened. On 25 September, just a day after Maximilian wrote to Henry VII, Margaret's brother Philip of Burgundy died. His death meant that Margaret was once more on her way back to the Netherlands

In 1506 Margaret of Austria was twenty-six years old; she had been married three times, repudiated once, and widowed twice. Although Philip's wife Juana would survive her husband by nearly fifty years, she was not to act as guardian for the four children she had left behind in the Netherlands—Eleanor, Charles, Isabel, and Mary—nor was she to serve as regent for her son. Instead Maximilian looked to his daughter to act as regent for Charles, Philip's heir in Burgundy (and Juana's heir in Spain). Margaret left Savoy on 29 October 1506, and on 18 March 1507, her father signed a document naming her regent of the Netherlands. About the new regent a contemporary chronicler noted "She has tested . . . the loyalty, the service, the kindness and the constancy of some; the falsity, the unkindness, the meanness and the frivolity of others, the perseverance and the mutability of diverse human affections."[55] She was the first of three strong women who would rule the Netherlands for most of the sixteenth century.

Margaret of Austria would serve as regent for nearly twenty years. Her first appointment extended from 1507 to 1515, her second from 1519 to 1530. Before examining her accomplishments in detail, we will pause here to examine the role of the regent in Habsburg possessions. In his recent examination of the Habsburg empire, Andrew Wheatcroft notes that "The policy of using the Habsburg kin, both male and female, as regents has attracted little attention." He continues,

A viceroy, such as the viceroy of the Indies, or of Naples, could be anyone who "acted in the name and with the authority of the supreme ruler." A regent was of a higher order, and endowed with the quality of sovereignty, personally and not vicariously. . . . A regent could . . . take the place of the Universal Emperor better than any viceroy. . . . It is hard to think of any other royal or noble house that made such a practice of distributing power amongst members, secure in the knowledge that, like a paid official, they would relinquish office and estates upon command.

In this "mobilization of the lineage," Margaret of Austria, as regent, would act as guardian for Philip's children and would arrange for their education. She would also manage the government of the Netherlands for the six-year-old Charles until he came of age.[57]

She set up her court at Mechelen, where Margaret of York, who had died in 1505, had established her own ducal establishment. One of Margaret's first decisions as regent was to travel with her nephew Charles throughout the provinces of the Low Countries. Another was, like Anne of France, to obtain for herself some property she could call her own—"in our old age," she wrote to her father, "we [do not have] any foot of land or house where we can retire without danger from others."[58] She asked particularly for the county of Burgundy (Franche Comté), which adjoined her dower lands in Savoy. By 1509, Margaret had a range of titles: "Governess-General" of the Netherlands, archduchess of Austria, duchess of Burgundy, dowager duchess of Savoy, and countess of Burgundy among them.

And although she had rejected Henry VII's offer of marriage, she negotiated new trade relations with him quite successfully. Less successfully, she was forced into the "Gelderland war," which she managed to settle in October of 1508 with the assistance of Louis XII, once her youthful companion and now the French king. The next month, in November, she travelled to Cambrai, where she represented both her father Maximilian and her former father-in-law, Ferdinand of Aragon, in a series of international negotiations. Maximilian did not seem to have complete faith in his daughter, warning her that she could be duped, after which she would have learned to "take better care."[59] Despite her father's hesitancy, Margaret proved herself an able negotiator; "Madam Margaret," one chronicler reported, "has seen and experienced more at her youthful age . . . than any lady on record, however long her life." Another noted,

This princess had a man's talent for managing business; in fact she was more capable than most men, for she added to her talents the fascination of her sex, brought up as she had been to hide her own feelings, conciliate her opponents, and persuade all parties that she was acting blindly in their interests.

Still another, noting how well she dealt with one powerful representative, commented that she was "so successful in charming him that he could refuse her nothing."[60]

The treaty was concluded on 10 December 1508. Publicly, peace was declared between Maximilian and Louis XII, and Louis was invested with the duchy of Milan. But a secret treaty was also negotiated, one that united Maximilian, Louis XII, Ferdinand of Aragon, and Pope Julius II against Venice; the kings of England and Hungary were also invited to join the League of Cambrai. While each of the men who were parties to the agreement had territorial and personal ambitions, Margaret had her own as well, for she aimed to secure peace in the Netherlands. In thanks for her success in guaranteeing peace for them, the states of the Netherlands voted her a substantial monetary gift.[61]

Throughout the years of war that resulted, Margaret maintained peace in the Low Countries. Working with a council that included advisors who had accompanied her to Mechelen from Savoy, she assured the continued success of trade. She supervised the education of the children in her care. She also pursued her "womanly" responsibilities, spinning, weaving, and sewing, modelling herself, it seems, upon Isabella of Castile. She sent her father "good linen shirts"; "I have received by this bearer some beautiful shirts . . . which you have helped to make with your own hand," Maximilian wrote, adding, "I am delighted." She sent him recipes and prescriptions for his health, for which he was also thankful. She sent some political advice as well, carefully constructing her role as a woman and his "one and only daughter" rather than as his equal and an experienced politician in her own right. Maximilian was less pleased by her political "prescriptions" than her advice about his health. Chastised for a "rude and ungracious" letter she sent, Margaret replied as a "good daughter":

> I know that it is not my business to interfere in your said affairs, as I am an inexperienced woman in such matters; nevertheless the great duty I have towards you emboldens me to . . . beg of you . . . to take care whilst there is yet time.[62]

She also prepared for the future by arranging political marriages for her nieces. This "trade in princesses" began when a Portuguese match was suggested for Eleanor, Isabel, or Mary. Nothing was settled with Portugal, but a match was arranged for Isabel with Christian II, king of Denmark, Norway, and Sweden, who had a rather frightening reputation as the "Nero of the North." A double alliance would be made with Bohemia and Hungary as well; Mary of Austria would marry Louis, the crown prince of Bohemia and Hungary, while Ferdinand of Austria would marry Louis' sister Anne.[63] Eleanor was to be reserved for a match with France or England.

In 1513, long after the principles of the Cambrai treaty had been abandoned, Maximilian and a new ally, the young Henry VIII of England, defeated the French, recapturing Tournai, a Burgundian possession. Margaret travelled with her nephew Charles to Lille to meet the victors. There she met the English king's favorite, Charles Brandon, duke of Suffolk, and rumors quickly spread that she would marry him. Both Henry and Maximilian objected. Margaret responded to the English king through a letter she addressed to his ambassador. She acknowledged Brandon's "virtue" and the "grace of his person," but she denied any interest in yet another marriage. Although Brandon had pursued her, she told him she had been "too much unhappy in husbands." She had refused both his gifts and his proposal. But the rumors continued, and Margaret wrote again to the ambassador noting that she was "abashed" that the "unhappy bruit" of a forthcoming marriage "hath run not only here but on all parts, as well in Germany as in all countries." She was "constrained by honor" to object to the "fantasies of people" and urged further efforts to end the matter.[64]

Early in 1514, Margaret's old rival Anne of Brittany died in France. She had given birth to two daughters, but not to a son and heir. Louis XII seems briefly to have considered an offer of marriage to Margaret, but instead a match was arranged with her oldest niece, Eleanor. As soon as the marriage was arranged, however, Louis betrayed his agreement and married Mary Tudor, Henry VIII's younger sister instead, renewing Margaret of Austria's suspicion of the French.

By 1515, Charles of Ghent, son and heir of Philip of Austria and Juana of Castile, was fifteen years old. He was declared of age by Maximilian, who apparently did not consult with Margaret before he made his decision. In a letter to the estates of Flanders the young man announced his "emancipation." He also received a letter from Maximilian, who reminded the newly "emancipated" young man "to remember the way [your aunt and regent] laboured during your minority in the administration of your country" and advised him to "communicate your chief and most arduous business to her, and . . . take and use her good advice and council," noting that from her the young Charles could count on "more comfort, help, and support than from any other." He concluded his letter with a touching reminder to Charles: "you are her whole heart, hope, and heir."[65]

But Charles's new counselors were eager to raise the young man's suspicions about his aunt. There is little doubt that during her tenure as regent Margaret had angered many—like her male contemporaries, she had not hesitated to use her power and authority, sometimes arbitrarily. She had at times insulted members of the Estates, on one notable occasion angering the nobles of the powerful Order of the Golden Fleece: "Ah, Messeigneurs! if I were such a man as I am a woman, I would make you bring your statutes to me and make you sing out passages from them!"[66] On 20 August, before her nephew's council, Margaret presented a letter to Charles:

> Monseigneur, as I evidently perceive, after having had such long patience, that by diverse means they [Charles's counselors] try to give you suspicions of me, your humble aunt, to withdraw me from your goodwill and confidence, which would indeed be a poor recompense for the services which I have rendered you until now, I am constrained to excuse myself. . . . I am . . . your only aunt, and have no other son nor heir but you, and I know of no one to whom your honour is dearer than to me. You can rest assured, Monseigneur, that when it pleases you to make use of my services . . . I will serve you well and loyally, not sparing my person or my goods, as I have done heretofore. But if you are pleased to give ear to what they tell you against me and allow me to be treated as I see they have begun to do, I would much rather look after my own small affairs and gracefully retire, as I have already begged the emperor to allow me to do.[67]

Her nephew wisely reconsidered, dismissing the suspicions that had been raised about Margaret's regency. When his grandfather Ferdinand of Aragon died on 23 January 1516, Charles became king of Aragon, Naples, and Sicily and regent of Castile for his "mad" mother, Juana. Before he left for Spain to claim his inheritance and his titles, he needed to appoint a regent, and Maximilian advised him to turn to Margaret of Austria once more. In a letter to Charles, Maximilian reminded his grandson that he, his daughter, and Charles were "one and the same thing corresponding to one and the same desire." In February 1517 he travelled to the Netherlands to make sure that his daughter and his grandson were reconciled. It was agreed among them that Margaret of Austria would once more become regent of the Netherlands.

Charles confirmed Margaret in her regency, and on 8 September, accompanied by his sister Eleanor, he departed for Spain. On his arrival, one of his first duties was to visit his mother in Tordesillas; once there, he attempted to remove his youngest sister, Catalina, but witnessing his mother's grief, he left her there. On 24 July 1519, from Saragossa, he issued an edict giving Margaret the authority to act in the Netherlands in his name:

> we have ordained that our very dear lady and aunt, the Lady Margaret, archduchess of Austria, dowager of Savoy, etc., shall sign from henceforth all letters, acts, and documents with her own hand, which are issued for us, and for our business over there, . . . that she shall have the care of . . . our finances, and that she *alone* shall provide and dispose of the appointments of

our country, for we have given and left the disposal of them to her, assisted by the chief and other members of our privy council.[68]

Eleanor of Austria's marriage took place during this trip to Spain; she became the third wife of Manuel of Portugal—who had previously been married to two of her aunts, Isabel and Maria of Castile, Queen Isabella's daughters.[69]

While Charles was in Spain, the Emperor Maximilian's health began to fail. In August 1518 he called together the electors of Rome to secure the imperial title for his grandson. But on 12 January 1519, before he could complete his task, he died, and it was left to Margaret to ensure her nephew's election. His competition for the imperial throne included men with whom she was intimately familiar: Henry VIII of England and Louis XII of France. Margaret's campaign on behalf of her nephew was vigorous, even brutal—and ultimately successful. On 28 June 1519, the seven electors named Charles of Austria and Burgundy, King of Spain, Naples, and Sicily, as Holy Roman Emperor.[70]

On 1 July 1519, in Barcelona, Charles praised the "great, inestimable, and praiseworthy" service of the "very dear lady and aunt, Lady Margaret." For the last ten years of her life, until her death on 1 December 1530, Margaret of Austria would continue to serve her nephew as regent of the Netherlands. During her second tenure, under constant threats of war with the French and in spite of economic pressures, she extended Habsburg territories in the Low Countries: by 1524, Friesland had been brought under control and Gelders had been subdued; by 1528, she had annexed the bishop of Utrecht's lands.

But if she is known at all, the achievement for which Margaret of Austria is most remembered is the so-called Ladies' Peace of 1529, which settled years of strife. On 24 February 1525, while he campaigned against the Emperor Charles in Italy, Francis I, who had succeeded Louis XII as king of France, was captured at the battle of Pavia. He was sent to Spain. During his imprisonment, his mother Louise of Savoy became regent of France. In August she wrote to her childhood companion and former sister-in-law, Margaret of Austria, for a truce so that she could negotiate for her son's release, a request to which Margaret agreed, though she earned an angry reaction from Charles, whom she had not consulted. Francis's release was finally negotiated by the treaty of Madrid; among its other provisions, the agreement aimed at securing the peace between Charles and the French king by a double marriage. Charles's sister, the recently widowed Eleanor, would marry Francis, whose first wife, Claude, had also just died. Eleanor's infant daughter Maria of Portugal would marry Francis's son and heir, the

French dauphin, another Francis. The French king was released from captivity on 17 March 1526.

But Francis had no intention of keeping to the terms of his treaty, which had committed him, besides his marriage to Eleanor, to serious territorial loss and had sent his two sons to Spain as hostages. Once back in France, he renewed his war with Charles; on 22 May 1526 Francis allied himself with Venice, Milan, England, and the pope. The League of Cognac aimed at Charles, targeting his Italian possessions. War broke out once more. It dragged on for two more years, until May of 1528, when Margaret of Austria, in what would be one of her last acts as regent of the Netherlands, conceived of a plan to end it. In a letter to her chief steward, Margaret of Austria explained the reasons for her proposed "Ladies' Peace":

> First, that the bitterness of the reproaches written and spoken on either side were such that ill will and hatred were the inevitable consequences. The hostilities also which ensued were so fierce that neither of the two sovereigns could compromise his dignity by being the first to talk of reconciliation, a challenge having been given and accepted for settling the differences and disputes by single combat. On the other hand, how easy for ladies . . . to make the first advances in such an undertaking! Secondly, that it is only by a mutual forgiveness of all offences, and the total oblivion of the causes of war . . . that the idea of peace could be entertained. This could not be thought of or proposed by the princes without a sacrifice of what they held most precious, their honour; but ladies might well come forward in a measure for submitting the gratification of private hatred and revenge to the far nobler principle of the welfare of nations.

Continuing with a third point, that as women they could "relieve" the men they represented of the responsibilities for the concessions that would be made, Margaret concluded that she and Louise of Savoy, "as the mother of the king and the aunt of the emperor" would have as their goal "one sole object, which they had mutually at heart": "the general good of Europe in the reconciliation of these two great princes."[71]

Charles invested his aunt with the power to negotiate for him, and three women—Margaret of Austria, Louise of Savoy, and Louise's daughter Marguerite of Angoulême—planned to meet at the neutral city of Cambrai. Before she left, Margaret was warned not to go because the French king would take her hostage, as her nephew had taken him hostage. But Margaret rejected such an idea, saying "she had no mistrust or fear of any sort as regarded Madame Louise or the king, and that if any of her councillors or courtiers were afraid, they might go home."[72]

The regent arrived in Cambrai on 5 July 1529 at three o'clock in the afternoon; Louise and her daughter arrived two hours later. The two older women, although they had been sisters-in-law, had not met since Margaret had begun her journey to Savoy for her wedding with Philibert. On a personal level, the terms of the agreement they reached arranged for the ransom of Louise's grandsons from their captivity in France, and Francis agreed to celebrate his marriage to Margaret's niece, the widowed queen of Portugal. Further, the agreement they reached confirmed most of the territorial advantages the treaty of Madrid had awarded to the empire. Margaret of Austria once again proved her skills as a negotiator—and her willingness to use whatever means necessary, including bribery, to get the terms she wanted. The "Ladies' Peace" was formally concluded on 5 August. But the two "ladies" had agreed that they would continue their negotiations, securing their peace still more firmly by arranging double marriages between Louise's grandchildren and Charles's children. They never completed their plans, however.

Back in the Netherlands, Margaret grew increasingly ill. She knew she was dying, and she wrote to her nephew Charles on 30 November 1530:

> I have no regrets whatever, save for the privation of your presence, and that I can neither see nor speak with you once more before my death. . . . I turn back to you the government of [your lands], in which I believe I have loyally acquitted myself. . . . I particularly commend to you peace.[73]

She died the next day, 1 December 1530. She was buried in Savoy, next to her third husband Philibert.

Although she did not have any children, this "daughter" of Isabella of Castile nevertheless proved herself, like her mother-in-law, a formative influence on long and successful line of political daughters. But before we examine the accomplishments of these women in the Habsburg empire in the generations that followed, we will pause and return to Spain to look briefly at the life of Margaret's contemporary, Germaine of Foix.

In March of 1506, little more than a year after Isabella of Castile's death, Ferdinand of Aragon married the eighteen-year-old Germaine. If her name is mentioned in histories at all, it is either in passing or with contempt. She is dismissed as a kind of sixteenth-century bimbo, a trophy wife for an aging king. Yet, as we have seen over and over again, such marriages were the rule rather than the exception, and in any case the young Germaine was a pawn in the game of political chess played between the Aragonese king and Louis of France, Germaine's uncle, and hardly a scheming young woman intent on snagging a wealthy and powerful older man.

Certainly the Castilian reaction to Ferdinand's second marriage was strongly negative; he was generally regarded as having dishonored Isabella. But Ferdinand had good reasons for this alliance. He needed to secure the

French king's support as he maneuvered with Philip of Burgundy, Juana's husband and his rival for control of Castile, and he needed an heir—a male heir.[74] Germaine herself, born in 1488, was the daughter of Jean of Foix and of Marie of Orléans, Louis XII's sister. By the terms of the treaty of Blois, dated 12 October 1505, Germaine was betrothed to Ferdinand. The French king agreed to cede his claims to the kingdom of Naples to her, and Ferdinand agreed to recognize Germaine's title as queen of Aragon (an agreement he failed to keep). Louis, for his part, hoped that Ferdinand would support the claims of Germaine's brother, Gaston of Foix, to the throne of Navarre.[75]

The wedding of Ferdinand of Aragon and Germaine of Foix was celebrated in Valencia. After their marriage on 22 March 1506, they were crowned in Naples, and in 1507 the new Aragonese queen travelled to meet her stepdaughter Juana, who reportedly greeted her warmly and showed her every mark of respect. Germaine gave birth to a son named Juan in 1509, although the baby died almost immediately. That was the last child Ferdinand would have. After Germaine's brother died in 1512, his claims to the crown of Navarre passed to his sister, lending justification to Ferdinand's invasion of the kingdom. In 1515 Ferdinand was on his way to Seville when he fell ill; Germaine, presiding over the *Cortes* of Aragon in his absence, reached him two days before he died, on 23 January 1516.

When he died Ferdinand left the kingdom of Naples to his daughter Juana—not, as he had promised, to Germaine. But his widow stayed in Spain, serving as vice-regent of Valencia. We catch a glimpse of her again, when she attended her stepgrandson's coronation as Holy Roman Emperor in 1519. She went first to Mechelen to join Margaret of Austria, and the two then travelled together to Aix-la-Chapelle. At the ceremony she sat next to the regent of the Netherlands. She married again in the same year; her second husband was John of Brandenburg, who became governor of Valencia. In 1524 she resumed her role as vice-regent. When her second husband died she married another Ferdinand of Aragon, this one the duke of Calabria. She died in Valencia on 18 October 1538, having spent more than twenty years in Aragon. Thus Germaine served twice as Charles's representative in Valencia. She proved herself a woman to be reckoned with; while, as Isabella's successor, she cannot comfortably be considered as a "daughter" of the Castilian queen, she deserves more than a footnote in the story of Ferdinand's life.

Among Isabella of Castile's "daughters" in the generation of Habsburg women who followed Margaret of Austria, several served as regents, governing various parts of the empire for Charles and, later, for *his* son and heir Philip II. We will briefly look at how each of these women participated in government and politics during the sixteenth century.

As we have seen, Margaret of Austria was not only regent of the Netherlands but the guardian of her nephew and nieces, who addressed her for the rest of her life as their aunt and *bonne mere*. She oversaw the education of her nieces Eleanor, Isabel, and Mary. They were tutored along with their brother Charles, receiving additional instruction in the "feminine accomplishments" that women needed to learn, including, of course, needlework. But they also learned more from Margaret of Austria.

Born in 1505, Mary of Austria was the third daughter born to Philip of Austria and Juana of Castile.[76] When she was just six months old, on 17 March 1506, her grandfather Maximilian concluded an agreement for her marriage to an as-yet-unborn heir to the throne of Hungary and Bohemia. The marriage was confirmed in 1507 after the birth of Louis of Hungary, and in 1514, when she was eight years old, she left her aunt's court at Mechelen and travelled to Maximilian's court in Vienna in preparation for the conclusion of his proposed alliance. To that end, in the summer of 1515, she was betrothed to Louis. Maximilian, who had proposed a double alliance, originally planned that one of his grandsons—either Charles or Ferdinand—would marry Louis' sister Anne of Bohemia, but instead he decided to marry the twelve-year-old princess himself. After the formal betrothal ceremonies, the two "little queens" remained together in Vienna. In 1516 Maximilian changed his mind about Anne and secured a papal dispensation that would allow his grandson Ferdinand to marry her instead. On 24 July 1516 the fourteen-year-old Anne knelt next to Maximilian, renounced her title as "empress," and was married by proxy to Maximilian's grandson. Following this ceremony, the "little queens," now sisters-in-law, were sent to Innsbruck.[77]

Mary of Austria's marriage to Louis of Hungary and Bohemia was celebrated on 11 December 1520, and the following May, not yet sixteen years old, she left for Hungary along with her sister-in-law Anne. By 1524, the strong wife of a weak man, she had negotiated considerable influence and authority for herself; by 1525, in a "spectacular coup," she gained even more when she assumed control of one powerful political faction and put down the threat, for the moment, of another.[78] A friend wrote to the humanist scholar Erasmus expressing the hope and regret of many: "If she could only be changed into a king, our affairs would be in better shape." The Venetian ambassador at the Hungary court recorded a description of Mary:

> The most serene queen is about twenty-two years old, of diminutive stature, long and narrow face, rather comely, very spare, with a slight color, black eyes, her under lip rather thick, lively, never quiet either at home or abroad. Rides admirably, and manages a horse with as much address as the best

horseman. She is a good shot with the crossbow, is intellectual, and has the heart to do anything.

But her active and intellectual nature seemed to endanger her "natural" role as a woman, however: "It is generally supposed that by reason of her natural volatility and from too much exercise and motion she will have no posterity."[79] And despite a "heart" that promised she could "do anything," Mary could not unite the country, and when the Turks invaded, Louis of Hungary was killed.

On 30 August 1526, the day after her husband's death, Mary wrote to her brother Ferdinand, notifying him of the Hungarian defeat and sending him a warning: "I fear the Turk will not stop at my lord brother's borders."[80] Shortly thereafter, an urgent message was sent to the archduke, urging him to come immediately to Hungary's aid; until he could arrive, troops were requested to support Mary "so that the kingdom does not fall away from us entirely and Your Serene Highness can the better come into Hungary with her help."[81] But Ferdinand was concerned with what was going on in Bohemia, where he had been elected king, and instead of coming himself he named Mary as his regent. Throughout 1526 she worked to secure her brother Ferdinand's election to the crown of Hungary. On 14 February 1527 she asked him to allow her to resign from her regency, but he preferred her to remain. She continued until the summer of 1527, when Ferdinand finally arrived in Hungary. On 29 October he was crowned king.

Relieved of the responsibility of her position, what followed were years "of aimless wandering, of financial worries, ill health, and loneliness."[82] In 1528 she rejected her aunt's proposal for a marriage to James V of Scotland, writing to the regent and to her brother Ferdinand that, having loved her husband, she did not wish another marriage; in 1530 she rejected another proposed husband, Frederick of Bavaria.

In 1528 she also rejected Ferdinand's request that she resume her regency in Hungary: "such affairs need a person wiser and older than I am," she wrote. Drawn into Ferdinand's affairs in 1529, she still demurred, noting that she did not wish to act "like those women who interfere in many things which are not demanded of them." But in 1530, after her aunt Margaret of Austria's death, she received yet another letter from her brother: "I advise you that it has pleased God to take to himself madam, our aunt, the first day of this month, God rest her soul." He concluded on a rather ominous note of warning: "And I think this might perchance cause your affairs to take a different course."[83]

Ferdinand's letter was quickly followed by a letter dated 3 January 1531 from her brother Charles V; the emperor requested that she assume the regency of the Netherlands. As her biographer Jane de Iongh states Mary's dilemma, on the one hand she could remain a queen "without a country, without a crown, without money," but with some measure of independence. On the other she could assume the regency of the Netherlands, which offered action, responsibilities, and power—but no independence. In her response of 29 January, Mary agreed to take over the regency for Charles. In October she was invested with the power to uphold the law, to receive petitions, to supervise legislation and finances, to command the army, and to head the various governors of the provinces: "In short, she received the right to perform everything that could serve to maintain the sovereign's authority and the welfare of the country."[84]

She was also to help the emperor in arranging the marriages of her nieces, for Charles, like his Habsburg grandfather, decided to follow the course of "happy Austria" in using marriage to effect in arranging political alliances. His sister Isabel's two daughters, Dorotea and Christina, had been at Margaret of Austria's court when the old regent died, and Mary, in turn, became their guardian. In 1532 an envoy from the duke of Milan arrived to arrange a marriage with Dorotea, but Charles tried again to form an alliance with James V of Scotland. Since his sister Mary had refused the king, Charles hoped James could be persuaded to accept his niece instead, but the king refused, preferring an alliance with France.[85] The duke of Milan, meanwhile, changed his mind about Dorotea and proposed a marriage with the younger Christina, then eleven years old. Charles agreed not only to a marriage by proxy but to an immediate consummation once Christina could travel to Milan. At this, Mary of Austria responded, for once, as her biographer notes, abandoning "the humble attitude of modest pupil" that she had adopted with her brother and speaking with "a conviction and a confidence in her own judgment that cannot have escaped Charles despite the careful terms in which her letter was couched":

> I reply to Your Majesty . . . only to unburden my conscience . . . and to warn you of the difficulties I think I discern. . . . I am of the opinion that it contravenes the law of God and all reason to have her marry so young, before she is twelve years old. . . . I hold it not only contrary to God's command, but I am moreover convinced that you may endanger her life, should she become pregnant before she is altogether a woman. It has often happened that in such cases neither the mother nor the child has survived the birth.
>
> Monseigneur, I am aware that I have said more about this matter, and that I express myself more clumsily, than is desirable. I beg you to forgive me, for my conscience and the love I bear the child compel me to it.[86]

Charles refused to consider his sister's objections to the marriage, but Mary managed to delay. She put off the marriage by proxy first by telling the Milanese envoy that Christina was ill and then by leaving for "serious affairs" in another part of the Netherlands. The ceremony was finally celebrated on 28 September 1532, but Mary postponed the girl's departure. In early 1533, after Christina's twelfth birthday, the regent could delay no longer, and she was forced to send her niece to Milan on 11 March. The regent immediately fell ill and requested that she be relieved of her position, but Charles refused. A little more than a year later, Dorotea was married to Elector Palatine Frederick and left her aunt, but Mary was not to remain alone for long. Within a few months, Christina, a widow at the age of fourteen, returned to her aunt. Henry VIII immediately sought her hand in marriage, but once again Mary objected to the proposed alliance. This time her delaying tactics were more effective; although her brother urged her to negotiate with the English king, by 1539 Henry had been excommunicated, ending any chance that Christina of Denmark would become Henry VIII's fourth wife.[87]

Until 1555 Mary of Austria served her brother Charles as regent, determined "to centralize the government of the provinces," and she succeeded in achieving among them a greater internal unity and for them some measure of independence from France and the empire. Throughout her tenure she also struggled "with the military threats and financial burdens laid on the Netherlands by the European politics of Charles V."[88] In 1535 she and her sister Eleanor, who had been married to Francis I of France, attempted another "ladies' peace" of the sort negotiated by their aunt and Francis's mother in 1529. To end the ongoing war between their brother and Eleanor's husband, they met at Cambrai, but unlike their predecessors, they could find no solutions.

Like her aunt, Mary of Austria sought peace for the Netherlands, but, in de Iongh's words, as "representative of the Emperor, who paid scarcely any attention to her problems," as "Regent versus her subjects, who refused to keep the treasury filled and instead threatened revolt," and as "a woman versus her generals, who did not wish to take notice of her commands," she struggled, forced into war in 1537 against the French and from 1538 to 1540 facing a revolt in Ghent.[89] On 14 October 1540, after he subdued the rebellion, Charles renewed Mary's appointment as his regent.

In 1543, war with France began again, with further recurrences in 1551, 1552, and 1553. Mary was also forced to mediate between her brothers, when Ferdinand objected to Charles's intention to resign as emperor and place the government of the Netherlands in the hands of his son Philip II. When she learned of her brother's intentions, Mary let him know that she, too, would resign her role, sending him a thoughtful analysis of her reasons for her decision and, more generally, of the difficulties faced by women in power. In late August 1555 she sent the emperor the letter quoted at the outset of this chapter:

> I . . . have sufficient experience (beside the fact that the books, Holy Scripture as well as others, are full of it) to know that it is impossible for a woman in peacetime, and even more in time of war, to do her duty as regent towards God, her sovereign, and her own sense of honor. For in peacetime it is unavoidable, in addition to all the meetings and cares of daily affairs which any government brings with it, that whoever guides the government of these provinces must mix with as many people as possible, in order to win the sympathy of both nobility and middle classes. . . . For a woman, especially if she is a widow, it is not feasible to mix thus freely with people. Of necessity I myself have had to do more in this respect than I really wanted. Moreover, a woman is never so much respected and feared as a man, whatever her position.
>
> If one is conducting the government of these countries in time of war, and one cannot in person enter the battle, one is faced with an insoluble problem. One receives all the blows and is blamed for all mistakes made by others, and is reproached if one does not carry out what everyone thinks he can demand. All the complainants can be heard throughout the entire country. But the accused stands alone and cannot answer for herself everywhere at once. And if things then do not go as expected, it is not difficult to make the people believe that the woman who heads the government is to blame for everything, and for this reason she is hated and held in contempt by the people.[90]

But the emperor and his son both urged her to continue as regent despite her determined and well-considered decision. Once more she wrote about her role as a woman in power. "I regard my release . . . as an unalterable fact," she began, continuing:

> My conscience is troubled by carrying on this function without satisfying all its demands. The more experience I have of it, the more I have realized that I am unable to accomplish my task properly
>
> I am of the opinion that whoever acts as regent for a ruler must have more understanding of affairs than the person who governs on his own account and is therefore only responsible to God. If he does whatever lies within his power, he has done his duty. But a regent has to account not only to God, but also to his sovereign and his sovereign's subjects.
>
> And even if I possessed all the aptitudes necessary to govern well, and I am far from doing so, experience has taught me that a woman is not suited to the purpose, neither in peacetime nor in time of war. . . . I have often done more than was fitting for my position and vocation as a woman, out of eagerness to serve you and accomplish my task as well as possible. Your Majesty also knows what insurmountable difficulties we would have met with if you had not been in the country yourself during the last war.

Difficulties which I could not have removed, because as a woman I was compelled to leave the conduct of war to others.[91]

Beyond the difficulties and uncertainties, Mary also appealed to her age. She loved her nephew Philip, she wrote, but would hate to start over by trying to serve a new "master"; "it is difficult for someone like me, who has served you till the end, to have to think in my old age of learning my ABC all over again." She continued, "It is suitable that a woman of fifty who has served for at least twenty-four years" should be "content" with having served "one God and one master." She couldn't face the prospect of "a young generation" to whose "ways I cannot and would not wish to accommodate myself."[92]

Continuing, she appealed to her brother for permission "to arrange my life as a private person." Her sister Eleanor, the queen of France, had again been widowed, and Mary wanted to retire with her to Spain, near her brother, where she would be able to "withdraw from all affairs of government"—if she stayed in the Netherlands, she feared she would be once more "drawn into" politics "more than I wish." She expressed fear about leaving the Low Countries, however; although she was the daughter of Juana of Castile, who had just died at Tordesillas, Mary had never lived in Spain. If her Eleanor were to die, she wrote, "I would be all alone in a country where I know nobody, where the way of life is different from what I am used to, and where I might feel a stranger." Nevertheless, "the advantages are greater than the drawbacks," and in the event that she could not adjust to the country "and its ways," she would still "have the time . . . to be able to go back to the Netherlands."[93]

Charles V finally agreed to his sister's resignation of the post she had held so long. She announced her decision on 24 September 1555, dismissing her household on 1 October. On 25 October, authority was transferred to her nephew Philip. Her departure for Spain finally took place a nearly a year later; with Charles and her sister Eleanor, she sailed from Ghent on 15 September 1556.

Her happy retirement did not last long. Her sister Eleanor died early in 1558. Mary was "so much affected," wrote one observer, "that it is a heart-rending sight." In her grief she travelled to her brother Charles, apparently to ask his advice about how she should arrange her life after her sister's death. Charles had one answer: He wanted her to return to the Netherlands to resume her role as regent. He promised her a home and a sizable income, but she refused. From the Netherlands, her nephew Philip sent a memorandum to an advisor urging him to convince his aunt to return: "Explain to her how great the necessity is. Remind her of the love and devotion she has always shown. . . . Explain to her what a support her presence will mean." And the bottom line: "Finally offer her a large income and great authority and give her hope that there will be peace and that this will last a long time, as the rulers are all exhausted." Her brother added his urging to his son's request and, when he became ill in August, she finally relented. She would assume the regency once more.[94]

But Charles died on 21 September. His death affected Mary profoundly. She died within a few weeks, on 18 October 1558.

While she had followed her aunt Margaret of Austria in the regency and had governed successfully, Mary had never enjoyed her role. In Jane de Iongh's comparison of the two women we may find the reasons for Margaret's relish of her role and Mary's struggle: "That Mary of Hungary suffered more from her lack of power as a woman than her predecessor, the truly feminine Margaret of Austria, was undoubtedly the consequence of her own qualities." De Iongh continues:

> In the continual struggle for power in which her position as the Emperor's representative involved her . . . , Mary would have preferred to use the weapons she possessed by nature and which her masculine adversaries were accustomed to use against her. Mary of Hungary was hard, authoritarian, hot-tempered, and unyielding. She possessed unlimited physical and mental courage, and never doubted her own right. . . . She lacked completely all the feminine characteristics by which Margaret of Austria had so often triumphed: tact, flexibility, the power to adapt herself, humor, and charm. . . . What Margaret had been able to put right by a smile, a word of praise or a joke, Mary aggravated by a cynical remark, a biting comment. Margaret had been able to laugh and forgive; Mary neither forgave nor forgot.[95]

However personally unhappy, Mary of Austria had served so well as regent for her brother that he forced her to continue long after she wished to quit and urged her to take up the position again even after she had resigned.

Just as he relied on his sister Mary in the Netherlands, Charles V, ruler of Spain, Burgundy, and the Holy Roman Empire, needed reliable regents to function as his representative in other parts of his vast empire. He inherited possessions that extended across Europe, from the Iberian peninsula east to the Netherlands and Austria, south to Italy, and west, across the Atlantic, to the New World. He succeeded to the crown of Aragon after the death of his grandfather, Ferdinand, and functioned as well as "king" of Castile although his mother Juana was nominally the queen until her death in 1555. While his aunt Margaret of Austria governed for him in the Netherlands, he had ceded his Austrian lands to his brother Ferdinand in 1522. To govern in Spain while he secured the imperial election, he had appointed his spiritual guide, Adrian of Utrecht, who proved unable to suppress the revolt against Charles in 1519, forcing his return, although by then he was at war with the French in Italy. He remained in Spain until 1529; in 1526, he married Isabel of Portugal, as he said to his brother, "as the only sure way of securing stability in the Spanish kingdoms in his absence."[96]

The daughter of Maria of Aragon and Manuel of Portugal, Isabel of Portugal was Charles's cousin. She was also a true "daughter" of Isabella of Castile. When Charles was forced to leave Spain for the empire, he appointed his wife as his regent, a role she fulfilled admirably. The *Cortes* recognized her position on 27 July 1527. She took her duties as regent seriously and was personally involved, as well, in the education of her two children, Philip, born in May 1527, and Maria, born in 1528.[97] Charles returned to Spain in April 1533, and when he left again in April 1535, Isabel was regent once more. But after Isabel's early death in 1539, at the age of thirty-six, Andrew Wheatcroft indicates Charles was "hamstrung" because he "could find no one to replace her effectively." He would not "countenance the appointment of any of his male kin whom he judged inadequate to the role," nor any female "unless she was married, widowed, or old enough to be widowed."[98] Ultimately his son, Philip II, was old enough to act on his behalf; Charles appointed him to act as his representative in Spain in 1543. The same year Philip married Maria of Portugal. By 1545, Maria had given birth to a son and heir, Carlos, and had died.

In 1554, when Philip left Spain for his second marriage, this one to Mary Tudor, queen of England, he turned to his sister Juana to act as regent of Spain in his place. Juana, born in 1535, had been married to Prince Joaõ of Portugal, her cousin, in 1552, but he had died on 2 January 1554, just three weeks after she had given birth to a son, Sebastian. The widowed Juana, "discreet" and "religious," left behind her infant son to be raised by his grandmother Catalina, regent of Portugal.[99]

As Philip prepared to leave Spain, his father advised him about negotiations for his second marriage and about a regency. In a letter of 1 April 1554, he agreed with his son about his proposals for the government of Spain in his absence, calling them "very prudent." He continued, expressing something of the worry about male advisors that underlay the choice of a woman for a regent:

> I also agree with your choice of the Princess [of Portugal], my daughter, so I am sending you the powers signed and suppose you will already have sent for her to come from Portugal. Above all, let me urge you to see to it that the counsellors who are to surround her be dispassionate men of character and authority. Lay down rules for their guidance in case of conflicts, and try to limit the sphere of each one as far as it is possible without hindering them in the exercise of their offices.

"The instructions and restrictions may be drawn up on the model of those issued for [Mary of Austria]," he wrote,

> but as the princess is of a more active disposition (and even under [Mary of Austria] there was a great deal of disorder) be sure to insist upon it that she and her advisors be moderate in all things, and forbear from those new interpretations of their instructions of which they have sometimes been known to be lavish.

As regent, the widowed Juana would need "some woman of position and exemplary character to be near her," Charles advised, but he cautioned that his son should "specify the number of ladies she may have, so that they [presumably courtiers or advisors] may not always be importuning her to accept more." Juana had evidently lived lavishly in Portugal, and the emperor wrote that Philip should make sure her household was "of reasonable size," for the money needed to keep her in the state she enjoyed in Portugal would be "altogether too much."[100]

As Philip II's recent biographer notes, Juana of Spain "chose to spend the rest of her life in the service of the crown." A few details of her regency can be gleaned from Philip's biography, indicating the issues that occupied her attention. In 1558, her father Charles V, retired in Spain, advised her to "take a hard line against the Lutheran cells" in Castile, while in 1559, "in letter after letter," her brother pleaded with her for money: "The lack of money is so great that I don't know what to say," he wrote, continuing, "I am in worse straits tha[n] you could possibly imagine." "You need to find money from there," she replied to him at one point, "because here all is consumed and spent." Later in that year Juana and her council "sanctioned an ill-fated military expedition into North Africa."[101] In the same year she was again faced with "alarming" news about Lutherans in Valladolid. Philip urged her to monitor the situation with "all care and diligence," while her father urged her to take measures against the "heretics." She issued a strict censorship order, had a new Index prepared, increased the activity of the Inquisition, and, at a series of *autos de fe*, several heretics were executed.[102]

In December of 1559 Philip was again in Spain, preparing for his third marriage, this one to Elizabeth of Valois. Juana was called upon to arrange for the new queen's reception. She was also entrusted with the guardianship of Don Juan, her father Charles V's illegitimate son, who had been born in 1547.[103] After Philip's return to Spain, Juana's regency ended. About her, Philip's biographer Henry Kamen writes:

> The princess Juana, always relegated to the background by historians because she abstained from any political role after her short regency in 1554-9, was the effective centre of Philip's family circle. When Philip returned to Spain

in 1559 she bought a group of houses in the middle of Madrid . . . [which] became her home and retreat. All her energies were dedicated to helping her brother. Philip in his turn lavished affection on her. She was the inseparable companion of queens Elizabeth [of Valois] and Anne [of Austria, Philip's fourth wife]. In 1572 she fell seriously ill, and never recovered. Her early death, in September 1573 at the age of thirty-eight, was a severe blow to the king, who had leaned on her for advice and affection. Philip was at her bedside when she died.[104]

Philip II did not rely only on his sister Juana as he governed. His sister Maria of Austria, with whom he also had a close relationship, married her cousin Maximilian II in 1548, and he had served as regent of Spain for his brother-in-law and cousin. But Maximilian succeeded to the imperial throne, taking him away from Spain and the regency. In his place, Philip relied on his sister Juana, as we have seen. After Maximilian's death in 1576, the empress Maria returned to Spain, where she, like her sister before her, "played a crucial role" for her brother. She took up residence in Madrid after her return in 1581. Philip had considered making her regent of the Netherlands in 1578, and now he wanted her to assume the role of regent of Portugal, but she declined the job.[105] In 1585, however, she agreed to act as his representative in Spain while he travelled to Savoy for the marriage of his daughter.[106]

Meanwhile, after the resignation of Mary of Austria, the Netherlands also needed a new regent. In 1559 Philip appointed his half-sister, Margaret, who was Charles V's illegitimate daughter, born in 1522 to Charles's mistress, "a Flemish girl." In the 1530s she had been sent to Italy to marry a Medici prince; after his death she had married Ottavio Farnese, duke of Parma, and she is traditionally known as Margaret of Parma. At the time she assumed the regency of the Netherlands for her half-brother, she was thirty-seven years old, "thoroughly Italianised," and "almost masculine" in appearance: "She walked like a man and her enemies made unkind remarks about the thick growth of hair on her upper lip."[107] More important than her physical appearance, however, she had been born in the Netherlands and proved a successful regent: "Duchess Margaret of Parma was . . . an excellent choice to govern the provinces which traditionally had thrived under princesses of the ruling house."[108] She left Italy to serve her half-brother in that capacity until 1567, during an extraordinary period of political and religious turmoil. When her son, Alessandro Farnese, was appointed in 1579 to serve as Philip's representative in the Netherlands, Margaret of Parma once more returned to her political role, in aid of her son. She functioned as head of civil administration while he assumed command of the military. She retired to Italy in 1583 and died in 1586.

As Philip grew older, he had come increasingly to rely on his daughter,

Isabel—Isabel Clara Eugenia—to help him in Spain. In March of 1588, the ministers of Henry III of France, his contemporary, announced that King Philip was "mad": "The grand chancellor assured his awed dinner guests in Paris that while Philip's councillors debated state affairs, his eldest daughter, Isabel, was signing documents and in control of government." This "scandalous" announcement derived from reports made by Philip's ambassador in Paris, who had told the king's mother, Catherine de' Medici, about the significance of Isabel's role in her father's government. Rumors were also spreading in Spain that, if Philip were "incapacitated," it would be Isabel who would "take control of the government" of her father's kingdom, and not her half-brother Philip III.[109]

Her potential to function for her father as a "regent" had been noted as early as 1574, when an eight-year-old Isabel was suggested as regent of the Netherlands. She obviously would have been a figurehead then, but from an early age she had been extremely close to her father, who had played a "direct role" in raising her and her sister Catalina. Isabel, in particular, had emulated her father, and he had allowed her "to take part in his office work." By 1586, she was able to be a significant help and advisor to her father; she "read him the letters and despatches he had to deal with, adding her suggestions on how they should be answered." He "even gave her access to the most important papers of state."[110]

In 1592, Philip proposed Isabel for the throne of France, not as a bride for a ruling king but as queen regnant—the last Valois king of France had died, and Isabel, through her mother Elizabeth, Philip's second wife, had a claim to the throne. As a Catholic, she was preferable to the closest male claimant, Henry of Navarre, a Protestant, but as a woman she had a distinct disadvantage. A challenge to French Salic law never had to be made, however, since Henry converted to Catholicism and assumed the French throne as Henry IV.[111]

As his death neared, Philip might have been well advised to name his daughter Isabel as his successor in Spain, for his son Philip III had no experience for the responsibilities he assumed in 1595. The king "had made no previous attempt to bring him into the process of government, an attitude which contrasts with the confidence he had place in . . . Isabel when she was even younger." Despite the fact that Philip III was, by all reports, "very childish," in poor health, knew nothing "of matters of state," and "appeared to have little intellectual capacity," his sex seemed to determine his father's choice of Philip III as his successor. But, while she would not take her father's place in Spain, Isabel would have a role in government nonetheless; Philip arranged for her marriage to her cousin Albert of Austria, and "the two would become joint rulers" of the Netherlands.[112] On 11 September 1598, as Philip lay dying, he told his daughter that he was sorry he would not live to see her marriage, but he asked that she "govern the Netherlands well" with her husband's help. Philip II died two days later. In April 1599 Isabel married the archduke of Austria, as her father had arranged, and after the ceremony in April 1599, the two took up their positions in the Netherlands. By then, the seven northern provinces (the United Provinces) of the Low Countries had become independent; from April 1599 until Albert's death in 1621, the two governed the ten southern provinces of the Netherlands as regents for Isabel's brother Philip III.

Philip III of Spain has generally been dismissed as "a weak, dimwitted monarch who preferred hunting and traveling to governing"; most historians have focused their interest on Philip's favorite, the duke of Lerma, to whom he "turned over the reigns of power," rather than on the king himself. But in her recent work, Magdalena Sánchez has examined the roles of three women in Philip's court: his wife, Margaret of Austria, who was also his cousin; the empress Maria, his aunt; and Maria's daughter, Margaret of the Cross. Together, "the empress, the queen, and the nun" exercised considerable power in Philip III's court. Unlike the other women whom we have examined here, theirs was an informal role, but, as Sánchez notes, they had considerable influence, nonetheless:

> The continued political impact of Empress Maria, Margaret of the Cross, and Margaret of Austria exemplifies the manner in which female relatives of kings, emperors, and other rulers influenced policy despite male attempts to eliminate or at least circumscribe women's involvement in politics.

Although the informal power negotiated by royal women is beyond our scope here, it is important to note that recent works, like that of Sánchez, are now beginning, in her words, to "tackle" the "constant, one-dimensional, simplified portrayal" of such women, which has kept them out of discussions and analyses of early modern politics.[113]

Philip III of Spain died in 1621, the same year Albert of Austria died. He was succeeded by his son Philip IV, who appointed his aunt Isabel to rule the Netherlands as sole regent. She served him in that capacity until her death in 1633, when she was sixty-seven years old.

With the death of Isabel Clara Eugenia, we have come to the end of our look at the line of daughters descended from Isabella of Castile. Throughout the early modern period, from Isabella's death at the beginning of the sixteenth century through Isabel's death in the middle of the seventeenth— for five generations—the Castilian queen's descendants had assumed roles as queens and regents throughout the Habsburg empire that was to their inheritance. Yet in our examination of her daughters, we have omitted one line of descent—her daughter Catalina of Aragon had travelled to England to be the wife of Henry VIII. In England, Catalina became Catherine, and I have chosen to delay our discussion of this daughter of Isabella until our next chapter.

CHAPTER THREE

THE DAUGHTERS OF MARGARET BEAUFORT

Queens and Regents in England and Scotland

And wit you . . . that this realm stood never as it doth now, nor never like to be so evil rule in it, for every lord prideth who may be greatest party and most friends, and they think to get the king my son in their hands, and then they will rule all as they will.

—Margaret Tudor, Queen and Regent of Scotland[1]

When Isabella of Castile's youngest daughter left Spain to become the wife of Margaret Beaufort's grandson, she left behind not only her home but her name. In England, Catalina was transformed into Catherine; on 14 November 1501, as Catherine of Aragon, she was married to Arthur, eldest son and heir of Henry VII. Within five months of this marriage, she underwent yet another transformation: Her fifteen-year-old husband died, and from the status as Princess of Wales, wife of the heir to the throne, Catherine was reduced to the role of Princess Dowager, a widow and a political nonentity.

Just as her sister-in-law Margaret of Austria had remained in Spain after the sudden death of her young husband, Prince Juan, Catherine of Aragon stayed in England after Arthur's death, a hostage, or a pawn, in the political game being played by her father, Ferdinand of Aragon, and her father-in-law, Henry VII. After considerable maneuvering and manipulation—theirs—and shame and despair—hers—she was eventually married to Arthur's younger brother, King Henry VIII, in 1509.

Catherine of Aragon thus provides a bridge to the line of women we will examine in this chapter, for her daughter became the first queen regnant of England; in Mary Tudor's veins ran the blood not only of her grandmother Isabella of Castile but also of her great-grandmother Margaret Beaufort. Three descendants of Margaret Beaufort, "the king's mother," eventually ruled as queens in their own right: In addition to Mary, whose reign so outraged John Knox, were Elizabeth Tudor, who succeeded her half-sister as queen of England, and their cousin Mary Stuart, queen of Scotland. We could add a fourth to this list, the unfortunate Lady Jane Grey, who was "queen" for nine days. But these women—their lives fictionalized and popularized through numerous biographies, historical novels, television series, and feature films—were preceded by a generation of women, also "daughters" of Margaret Beaufort, whose struggles for power and position are today much less familiar.

As a king notorious for his marital misadventures, Henry VIII looms large in the popular imagination, and the six women he married are equally familiar, at least for the roles they played as one of the much-married king's six wives: Catherine of Aragon, the abandoned wife; Anne Boleyn, "of the thousand days"; Jane Seymour, the "entirely beloved" mother of Henry's long-desired son; Anne of Cleves, the "Flemish mare"; Catherine Howard, the "rose without a thorn"; and Catherine Parr, the "obedient" and "agreeable" woman who nursed the king through his final years. There is even a rhyme that serves as a mneumonic device for remembering them: "divorced, beheaded, died; divorced, beheaded, survived." Despite their titles, Alison Weir's *The Six Wives of Henry VIII*, Antonia Fraser's *The Wives of Henry VIII*, and David Loades's *Henry VIII and His Queens* are as much about the king himself as about the women who were his queens. Henry's queens are of interest not for themselves or for the political role they played (or failed to play), but for their ordinal position in a series of marriages. Even an avowedly "feminist" work like Karen Lindsey's *Divorced, Beheaded, Survived: A Feminist Reinterpretation of the Wives of Henry VIII* focuses more on Henry the husband than on his six queens.[2] Loades is at least clear about his intentions: "This is a book about a king. It is not about six women, although they are very important to the story."[3] Aside from these multiple biographies, there is a large literature on most of Henry's queens, and at least a few of the more recent biographies have begun to shift their focus from examining these women as wives to exploring their role as queens.

Although Catherine of Aragon's biography has been written and rewritten, Garrett Mattingly's 1941 *Catherine of Aragon*, recently reprinted, remains the basis of all more recent accounts of her life.[4] I will not summarize her story here, the details of which are well known from both scholarly and popular sources. Instead, I will briefly examine her actions as queen—the ways she attempted to construct a role like her mother Isabella's and the ways she failed where her mother had succeeded.

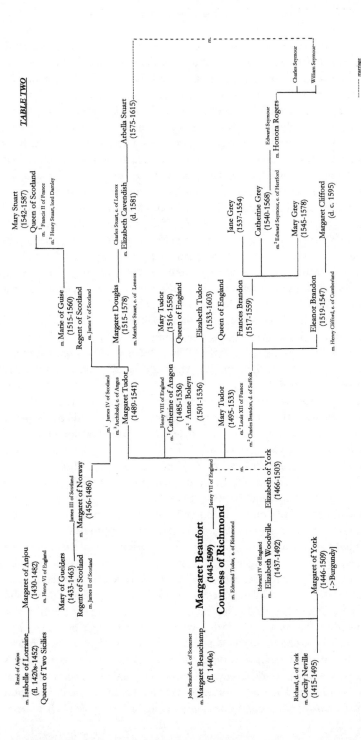

TABLE TWO

------ marriage

The young widow waited nearly seven years after Arthur's death to know her future, living in a sort of royal limbo; in this, if nowhere else, we can see that Catherine is most unlike her mother. Isabella did not wait for her fate to be decided by others. Rather than accept a match of her brother's making, one that would forward his political ends, Isabella of Castile chose for herself, gambling on a marriage to Ferdinand of Aragon to forward her own political goals. But Isabella's daughter was different. Between Arthur's death on 2 April 1502 and her eventual marriage to his brother Henry VIII on 11 June 1509, Catherine of Aragon remained in England, isolated and powerless in the Tudor court, waiting for the decisions of others.

After Elizabeth of York's death in 1503, Henry VII briefly considered making his son's widow his own wife; the possibility that Catherine of Aragon would become her former father-in-law's second queen was discussed between the English king and the Spanish monarchs, but Isabella objected strongly; such a marriage would be an "evil thing," she wrote, "the mere mention of which offends our ears."[5] Instead, a contract that would unite Catherine and her dead husband's brother was signed on 23 June; while the sixteen-year-old widow waited for the twelve-year-old Henry to reach the marriageable age of fifteen, her father and her once-and-future father-in-law "negotiated" over the payment of the rest of her dowry and her dower rights in what Mattingly has called an "extraordinary contest of meanness."

By the terms of this second marriage treaty, Catherine was to be provided for by Henry VII, but neither the English king nor Catherine's father supplied her with the money she needed to maintain her household, and when Isabella of Castile died in November of 1504, the English king rejected the Spanish alliance; on 27 June 1505 Prince Henry formally "renounced" his betrothal to Catherine, indicating that the agreement had been negotiated in his minority without his consent. While the English abandonment of the marriage contract is generally explained in political terms, we might speculate what, if any, part the disapproval of "the king's mother" might have played in Henry VII's decision to repudiate the match he had so recently arranged for his heir. Mattingly asserts, without explanation, that Margaret Beaufort "had never approved of [Catherine] as a bride for the Prince of Wales and treated her with open hostility."[6] It would be interesting to know why, if Mattingly is correct, Margaret Beaufort was opposed to the match. Given her strict piety, we might be tempted to explain her disapproval in religious terms: Pope Julius II had hesitated before granting the dispensation needed for the English prince to marry his brother's widow, issuing it only after some delay and under some pressure, and even Henry VII was reported to have doubts about the dispensation "much on his conscience."[7] The course of English history would have been radically different if Margaret Beaufort's opposition to the match, whatever its source, had prevailed.

For the moment, at any rate, and for whatever reasons, the proposed marriage between Prince Henry and Catherine of Aragon had been rejected, and Henry VII began negotiations for another royal match for his surviving son and heir. An alliance with the empire or with France seemed more advantageous than an alliance with Ferdinand; among the brides considered for the English prince were Eleanor of Austria, Catherine's niece, whose mother Juana was nominally the new queen regnant of Castile, and Claude of France, the only child of Louis XII and Anne of Brittany. But even under these circumstances, the Spanish princess did not return to Spain. Instead, the bride/widow/bride-to-be/rejected bride remained in England, ignored alike by Henry VII and by Ferdinand.

Her letters to her father repeat endlessly her need for money.[8] In 1505 she prefaced her request by apologizing; "Hitherto I have not wished to let Your Highness know the affairs here," she began, "that I might not give you annoyance." But, she continued, "Your Highness shall know, as I have often written to you, that since I came into England I have not had a single *maravedi*, except a certain sum which was given me for food." Her condition "does not weigh upon her," she explains, "except that it concerns the service of Your Highness, doing the contrary of that which ought to be done": "I entreat Your Highness that you will consider that I am your daughter." A year later she was still appealing to her father: "I have written many times to Your Highness, supplicating you to order a remedy for my extreme necessity, of which . . . I have never had answer." "I am in the greatest trouble and anguish in the world," she remonstrated: "On this account I supplicate Your Highness to command to remedy this, and that as quickly as may be; for certainly I shall not be able to live in this manner." "Now I supplicate Your Highness," she wrote, "for the love of our Lord, that you consider how I am your daughter, and that after Him . . . I have no other good nor remedy, except in Your Highness." Still later she reminded Ferdinand once more that it was his duty as her father "to succour a young princess who is living in a foreign land without protection."

Neither Henry nor Ferdinand was inclined to relieve the unfortunate princess, but in 1506 her position as a nonentity at the Tudor court was ended by an unexpected set of circumstances. Blown off course on their long-delayed voyage to Spain after Isabella's death, Philip of Austria and Juana of Castile, Catherine's sister, landed in England in January.[9] As Philip solicited Henry's support against his wife's father, Ferdinand, in a canny move of his own, sent his daughter Catherine formal credentials to serve as his ambassador in England. Thereafter Catherine's letters to her father contain political reports, rumors, and reflections in addition to her repeated requests for money.[10] Her advice to him, however, was deferential; "Let not Your Highness think that I say this by way of advising you," she wrote, on one occasion, "since I do not say of myself anything in the world that can warn Your Highness which you will not have well before prepared for." As she was "personally interested" in the continued good relations between England and Spain, she thanked her father for his consideration:

> And, since I see with how much affection Your Highness desire this may come to effect, there will be no need to supplicate you [or] that I labour at it, except to kiss your hands for the favour that, for my part, in this affair I receive, who may find such new obligation to love Your Highness more, and give myself to serve you in every respect, since I esteem the affairs of the king of England, my lord, more mine than my own.

In another letter she noted that Henry had "acknowledged" her "diligence" in performing her duties as ambassador; to "content" him she wrote that she was "glad to let him know" that she was only carrying out her father's orders:

> I . . . act as hitherto Your Highness has rightly commanded me, according to that which falls in most with the service of Your Highness. And that nothing may be hindered by me, I do as I have always done, since I cannot improve upon it.

This letter concludes with her promise that she would continue to act according to her father's desires "until Your Highness sends to give remedy in my life, which is greatly needed": "And thus I conclude, supplicating Your Highness so to act that I may be here favoured by Your Highness, and that you may shew that you hold me in esteem, although I may not merit it."

When Henry VII died on 21 April 1509, his mother Margaret Beaufort functioned unofficially but effectively as regent for her grandson until he reached the age of eighteen. Although it was reported to Ferdinand that the new king had expressed some reservation about marrying his brother's widow, Henry VIII decided, after all, to marry the woman to whom he had been betrothed in 1503 and whom he had rejected in 1505.[11] In a letter to Margaret of Austria announcing his decision, Henry claimed the marriage to Catherine had been his father's deathbed wish. For her part, in the first letter she wrote to her father after her marriage, the new queen alluded to her new role in England, as liaison between her father and her new husband: "I have performed the office of ambassador as Your Highness sent to command, and as was known by the king my lord who is, and places himself entirely, in the hands of Your Highness, as of so entire a father and lord."

She continued, "And Your Highness may believe me, that he is such in keeping obedience to Your Highness as could never have been thought, from which I increase in infinite pleasure as much as reason requires."[12]

As her mother's political daughter, Catherine of Aragon began to follow an interesting course as queen of England. In her relationship with her new—and younger—husband, Catherine adopted the public role as wife favored by her mother. While Henry disguised himself to participate in the masks performed as part of court festivities, for example, Catherine was content to function as her husband's admiring audience, applauding his performance rather than joining in with him. She "never disappointed him" by "failing to be completely surprised when he revealed himself." Similarly, while Henry danced with a variety of ladies of the court, Catherine sat by, watching him and praising his grace and skill. And while Henry competed in the "mimic combats" of the tournaments he enjoyed, she again assumed the "essential" role as audience for his display of prowess. In short, as Mattingly notes, the princess Henry had "rescued" and "set upon his throne" seemed the "chief trophy" of the new king and "the necessary audience for all his triumphs."[13]

Beyond the passive role she was content to play in public, however, Catherine assumed a more active role in private. Before her marriage to Henry, she had come to function as her father's representative at the English court; although she had been replaced as Spanish ambassador early in 1508, she continued in her role as a strong, if unofficial, advocate for Spain and for Ferdinand's policies after her marriage. As David Loades notes, it is "hard to estimate" the extent of her influence in Henry's foreign affairs, but she was the young king's most trusted counselor.[14] To the extent that she influenced her less experienced husband, then, Catherine's political role can be regarded as significant, yet her role is somewhat complicated, for rather than acting on her own or as a result of her own judgment, she remained, as Loades notes, "her father's ambassador": Her advice to her husband followed her father's instructions to her. She wrote daily to Ferdinand about the state of affairs in the English court, her letters reflecting her view (and his) that England was, in Loades' terms, "an appanage of Spain." Shortly after her marriage, for example, she wrote, "I know that in this life I have no other good except that of being your daughter." About her husband, the "most strong" reason she had to love him, she affirmed, was "his being the so true son of Your Highness, with desire of greater obedience and love to serve you than ever son had to his father." She concluded, "His Highness and I are very hearty to the service of Your Highness."[15]

The young English king, eager to exercise his martial skills on the field of battle, was determined to play a role in the conflict between his father-in-law and Louis XII of France, and Catherine the queen made sure her husband entered the dispute as an ally of Spain. In 1510, she helped to negotiate the treaty between England and Spain that ensured Henry's support of Ferdinand. This alliance was reaffirmed in 1511, when Henry joined the Holy League and signed a second treaty with Ferdinand that committed him to an invasion of France to take place before April 1512. Henry kept his part of the agreement, sending an English army to Spain, where it was to be joined by Ferdinand's troops. But the Spanish soldiers never arrived; the presence of an English army had allowed Ferdinand to seize Navarre, but the absence of Spanish support kept the English king from pursuing his own interests in France.

Despite Ferdinand's betrayal, Henry signed yet another treaty with his father-in-law on 18 April 1513 committing him to declaring war on France within four weeks. Once more he had been influenced by the queen. "The King is bent on war," reported a Venetian observer, who continued, "the Council is averse to it; the Queen will have it; and the wisest councillors in England cannot stand against the Queen."[16] But Henry discovered that his father-in-law had betrayed him again, having already signed a year-long truce with Louis XII—on 1 April. Infuriated, he turned his anger against his wife, who was, in Loades' terms, "a hostage to diplomatic fortune"; he accepted her explanations of her father's decisions and Ferdinand's own excuses, then decided to carry on with the planned invasion on his own. As he departed for France in 1513, he named Catherine "Governor of the Realm" during his absence. Her powers extended beyond those given to other royal women who had served previously as regents in England; she was not only to administer the government in Henry's absence but she was to be "captain general" of all of of his forces that remained in England.

Thus Isabella of Castile's daughter assumed the role of queen regent of England. While Henry captured two insignificant French towns, Thérouanne and Tournai, Catherine enjoyed a much more significant military triumph at home. With the king's departure, English troops had been sent north to defend the border with Scotland. After Anne of Brittany appealed to James IV of Scotland to help France, the Scots king obliged, crossing into England in August, just as Henry was celebrating his victory at Thérouanne. Under Catherine's direction, an army was raised and headed north, by some accounts sent on its way after an inspiring oration delivered by the queen herself. Whether she delivered the speech or not, she was, by all accounts, "the center and soul of the army." Once the troops were on their way, she turned her attention to the defense of London, raising an army of 60,000, which "she, herself, meant to lead." By the beginning of September this reserve army was ready, but before she could assume command, the Scots were defeated at the battle of Flodden, James IV dying on the field. Catherine's victory in the north was, in Loades' words, "far more devastating and significant than anything which Henry achieved" in France.[17]

Henry seems to have had "no misgivings" about enjoying the military victory of his wife, who thoughtfully attributed her success to God rather than to her own ability: "The matter is so marvelous . . . that it seemeth to be of God's doing alone," she tactfully wrote.[18] And when Henry returned to England, Catherine was, Mattingly writes, "glad to exchange her regency for her husband."[19] But Catherine's triumph as regent of England was shortlived, overshadowed by her failure as a wife. Shortly after Flodden, Catherine suffered yet another in what was becoming a long series of miscarriages. She had not provided the king of England with an heir. As queen regent, she had won a military battle; as queen consort, she was still losing the war.

The Spanish ambassador complained to Ferdinand that the king had lost his daughter's support—Catherine had, he wrote, been persuaded "to forget Spain, and gain the love of the English."[20] "If so," Loades writes about this report, "it was a lesson which she had been slow to learn."[21] It seems to have been a lesson Catherine learned too late, for if Ferdinand had lost his daughter's support, she had lost her husband's. As early as 1514, Henry may have begun to consider, at least briefly, a divorce and remarriage, possibly to a French princess.[22] Whether or not he seriously considered replacing Catherine as his queen, he replaced her as a sexual partner; Elizabeth Blount was publicly recognized as his mistress. Although Catherine finally gave birth on 18 February 1516 to a child who survived, a daughter named Mary, the royal mistress gave Henry a son, whom the king named Henry Fitzroy, in 1519.

There was no question about Henry's pride in his daughter Mary. A separate court was established for the princess, and great care was taken with her education.[23] Henry also began to negotiate for a politically advantageous alliance for his daughter almost immediately after her birth. The two-year-old Mary was betrothed to the French dauphin in 1518 and then, after Henry's French alliance was broken, to the Holy Roman Emperor Charles V in 1521. Quickly thereafter—"before the ink was dry on the Anglo-Imperial treaty," as Loades writes—Henry attempted to use Mary "as bait to undermine Scotland's traditional relationship with France," suggesting a betrothal with his nephew, the nine-year-old James V. But in 1525, with the defeat and capture of the French king at the battle of Pavia, Charles could afford to abandon his alliance with Henry. Rather than wait for his English cousin to be old enough to marry, he married another cousin, Isabel of Portugal, instead. Thus Mary was again a "disposable asset" her father could use, but, as Loades notes, this was a "limited advantage" for Henry, because "neither the French nor the Scots were eager to seek her hand" and because questions about her status in the succession were being asked.[24] One contemporary observer expressed a widespread conclusion when he wrote that "it does not seem very probable that the daughter of the king of England will bring that kingdom with her as dower."[25]

If Henry had no male heir, would his daughter succeed him on the English throne? If she did inherit the kingdom, what role would her husband have? In 1525, rather than clarifying the situation, Henry further complicated it. In July his six-year-old son Henry Fitzroy was created duke of Richmond and Somerset and proclaimed "Lord Admiral of England, Wales, and Ireland, of Normandy, Gascony and Aquitaine, Knight of the Garter, Keeper of the City and Castle of Carlisle, and first peer of England."[26] After "uncharacteristically" and openly protesting her husband's decision, Catherine's objections were answered with a change that, in Mattingly's words, "redounded to her harm." The nine-year-old princess was sent to Ludlow Castle as nominal head of the council of the Welsh Marches. This ordinarily would have been accompanied by recognition of her status as Princess of Wales, an "unequivocal recognition of her status as heir," but the title was never formally conferred.[27]

Shortly after Princess Mary left for Wales in the autumn of 1525, Henry VIII began the courtly dalliance with Anne Boleyn that eventually changed the course of English history. At some point during the winter of the following year, the king decided to divorce his wife, informing the queen of his intentions in spring of 1527. The six-year saga of the king's "Great Matter" is not our concern here, nor is Catherine's part as an abandoned wife in this drama.[28] Rather than the role she chose to play, I am interested in the role she chose not to play.

Catherine of Aragon decided not to fight to maintain her position as queen or her daughter's claim to the throne of England—or, at least, not to fight actively. Loades, in fact, calls Catherine's "policy" in the protracted struggle with Henry one of "masterly inactivity."[29] "Masterly" or not, her role in the divorce drama was reactive rather than active, paralleling her initial public role as queen, as passive observer of her husband's occupations rather than active participant in them. Unlike Isabella of Castile, Catherine of Aragon did not become a "warrior queen" during the divorce crisis; instead, she continued her role as a dutiful wife, embracing her suffering, even characterizing her persecution as a martyrdom.

The queen resisted all her husband's maneuverings, refusing his attempts to cajole her as well as his efforts to force her to agree to a divorce. She also rejected the solution to the crisis suggested by Lorenzo Campeggio, the papal legate sent to England by Clement VII: If Catherine would retire to a convent, Henry could be allowed to remarry. Indeed, the queen displayed a great deal of personal strength during the six years she fought against the divorce, but in her staunch opposition to the king she was neither pragmatic nor political. As heartless as Henry's decision might have been, the royal divorce he sought was not unprecedented. Among Catherine's own ancestors, for example, Enrique IV had divorced his first wife, Blanche of Navarre, after thirteen years of marriage—"she" had failed to produce an heir for the newly crowned king of Castile, and Enrique replaced her with Juana of Portugal.[30] In the immediately preceding generation, the childless Louis XII of France had divorced his wife of more than twenty years in order to secure Brittany and in the hope that a new queen could provide him an heir; similarly, René of Lorraine, titular king of Naples, Sicily, and Jerusalem, had divorced his first wife Jeanne d'Harcourt, who had failed to provide *him* with an heir, in order to marry Philippa of Guelders, who bore him eleven children.[31] Closer to home and more recently, Charles Brandon, duke of Suffolk had "bigamously married" Henry VIII's sister Mary in 1515, after her brief marriage to Louis XII, and then had applied to Clement VII for a bull to dissolve his earlier marriage; the same pope had also granted Henry's older sister Margaret, the widowed queen of Scotland, a divorce from her second husband in 1527.[32]

Unwilling or unable to accept the political reality of dynastic divorce— and the compromise offered to her by her husband and the pope—Catherine was equally disappointed by her nephew Charles, whom she "badgered ceaselessly to put diplomatic pressure on her errant husband," and by the pope, who failed to "declare unequivocally in her favour."[33] Nor would the queen follow the advice of her supporters in England, who urged her to more active resistance. Unlike her mother, she would not go to war to defend her title or her daughter's position: "I shall not ask His Holiness for war," she wrote, adding "that is a thing I would rather die than provoke." In a letter to Charles V, Eustace Chapuys, the imperial ambassador in England, concluded that "The queen . . . is so overscrupulous that she would consider herself damned eternally were she to consent to anything that might provoke a war." To her nephew, Catherine herself not only reiterated her opposition to war but refused offers of escape: To disobey the king "would be a sin against the law and against my lawful husband of which I shall never be guilty." Although she complained that "political considerations"—her husband's, the emperor's the pope's—denied her justice, in the end she would neither stand aside for her rival not stand up for herself and her daughter. She preferred instead to "bear the cross" of her "tribulation." Her view of her situation is clear: "I am told. . . that the next parliament is to decide whether I am to suffer martyrdom. If it is to be so, I hope it may be a meritorious act. . . . I do not . . . fear for there is no punishment from God except for neglected duty." "I could not endure so much," she wrote still later, "did I not think these things suffered for God's sake."[34]

For his part, Henry can hardly be praised, but neither can he be condemned as ruthless, at least not at this point in his marital career. It took him six years before he finally arranged for himself the divorce he wanted, and while, over the course of those years, he abandoned Catherine, isolated her from her friends and her daughter, and lodged her in a series of remote country homes, his treatment of her was fairly restrained by contemporary standards. We have only to remember Isabella of Castile's unrelenting pursuit of her rival Juana *la Beltraneja* or Philip of Burgundy's unremitting cruelty to Juana *la Loca* to judge Henry's rather cautious treatment of Catherine.

Perhaps the king's reluctance to move against his wife came from his own insight into what she could do if she chose to oppose him more actively. "The lady Catherine is a proud, stubborn woman of very high courage," he told his council in 1535:

> If she took it into her head to take her daughter's part, she could quite easily take the field, muster a great array, and wage against me a war as fierce as any her mother Isabella ever waged in Spain.[35]

But Catherine did not "take the field" as her mother had done on more than one occasion in defense of her title. On the day of her death in 1536, she wrote one last loving and admonitory letter to Henry, addressing him as her "most dear lord, king, and husband":

> The hour of my death now drawing on, the tender love I owe you forceth me, my case being such, to commend myself to you, and to put you in remembrance with a few words of the health and safeguard of your soul which you ought to prefer before all worldly matters, and before the care and pampering of your body, for the which you have cast me into many calamities and yourself into many troubles. For my part, I pardon you everything, and I wish and devoutly pray God that He will pardon you also. . . . I make this vow, that mine eyes desire you above all things.[36]

Whether we regard her as principled and courageous or as proud and intransigent, as foolish and impractical or as noble and dutiful—or as all of these—Catherine of Aragon is the last of Isabella of Castile's ill-fated daughters, whose unfortunate lives differed so notably from their mother's. For whatever reason, Catherine chose not to follow in her mother's footsteps as a warrior queen. But in the end, she managed to succeed where her mother failed. Juana of Castile did inherit Isabella's throne, but she never ruled as her mother had; Catherine of Aragon ensured that her daughter not only inherited the crown of England but that she came to the throne as a queen regnant. It is an irony that when Mary Tudor became queen, she seemed only too anxious to find a husband to rule in her place.

As Henry's second queen, Anne Boleyn was no more successful than Catherine had been in providing Henry with a male heir, and though Henry never gave up his pursuit of sons, when he died in 1546, after marrying six women, he had managed to produce only one frail boy who would not survive to maturity. Our interest here is not in following the details of Henry's marital misadventures any further, but I would like to note two further points about the women Henry VIII married before moving on in our examination of the "daughters" of Margaret Beaufort.

The first is a detail about the connections of the woman whose power intrigued not only the king but generations of historians who seem to be equally under her spell. Anne Boleyn's character and motivations remain as elusive, as incomprehensible even, as Catherine of Aragon's. Villified by her opponents as an English Jezebel, Messalina, or Agrippina, accused of witchcraft and incest, dismissed as the king's concubine, his "goggle-eyed whore," and ultimately executed by the husband who had turned his kingdom upside down to make her his wife, she was praised by her supporters as a saint, the "elect of God" who had done more than anyone else to bring true religion into England. Recent studies of Henry's second queen have begun to focus less on the mystery of her sexual attraction and more on her informed and skillful participation in Tudor politics and religion.[37] What I would like to emphasize here is the contact she had with two of the most powerful women of the early sixteenth century.

In the summer of 1513, while Catherine of Aragon prepared to assume her role as regent of England, Anne Boleyn began the training that would prepare her for the role she would eventually play in Tudor history; when she was twelve years old, the daughter of Thomas Boleyn, a minor courtier, and of Elizabeth Howard, daughter of the powerful earl of Surrey, she was sent to the Habsburg court of Margaret of Austria at Mechelen. The move, according to Anne's biographer Eric Ives, was in recognition not only of her "potential" but also of what the "opportunities which a training at the premier court of Europe" could offer a young woman of such promise. At Margaret of Austria's court, not only was Anne carefully educated, but she was surrounded by the "elite of Europe," where she was able to observe at first hand "the leaders of Europe who would so affect her later career." Chief among these leaders, clearly, was the regent herself, whom Ives identifies as providing an important model for the young woman who would later seize the opportunity to make herself a queen: "Anne Boleyn could have had no better mentor," he concludes.[38]

By the spring of 1515, Anne Boleyn left Mechelen and the court of the

Habsburg regent, but she did not return to England. Instead, she departed for the court of Francis I, where she would become part of the household of his wife, Claude, the eldest daughter of Louis XII and Anne of Brittany. The young Englishwoman spent seven years at the French queen's court, where, again in Ives's words, she could "soak in the sophisticated atmosphere around her."[39] While she was in France, she would have had the opportunity to acquire more than courtly sophistication and refinement. While in France she would also have observed the king's mother, Louise of Savoy, whom we have met before and whom we will meet again.[40] Although little is known about Anne Boleyn's life in France, she arrived there as Louise was acting as regent of France for her son.

With our focus on restoring women to the political history of early modern Europe and on tracing the connections between them, I think it is important to consider the influence that women like Margaret of Austria and Louise of Savoy might have had on an intelligent, ambitious, and capable young woman. Anne could observe in Margaret of Austria a woman who, as regent, was invested with political authority, who functioned successfully in that role, and who was widely recognized and appreciated for her abilities, while in Louise of Savoy she could observe a woman who was not only authorized to rule directly as regent for her son but who also exerted considerable power indirectly, through her personal influence over him.

We can never fully understand the complex variety of forces that motivated Anne Boleyn or the reasons for the choices she made and actions she took. As Ives notes, any attempt to "penetrate" her "inner character or her private personality" will defeat us; as we struggle to understand "what we can," he argues, it is important to "enter the extrovert world in which she lived." As part of that world, I think we need to consider the powerful shaping influence of two noteworthy regents on the woman who—whatever else she may or may not have been—was an "astute and determined politician." Anne Boleyn was neither a pawn nor a plaything; as Loades notes, she "played politics for high stakes, not as an agent but as a principal." "In that sense," he concludes, "her execution was in itself a tribute to her power."[41]

The final point to be made about Henry and his queens is that he ended his life much as he began, by appointing his last wife regent, just as he had appointed his first. Despite his determination to leave his crown to a son rather than to a daughter, he seems not to have regarded women as incapable of or unfit for rule. Catherine of Aragon's regency, though brief, had produced the resounding victory of the English over the Scots, and throughout his reign the English king had many dealings with Margaret of Austria. In 1544, before he left for war in France, he did not hesitate to designate his sixth wife, Catherine Parr, as governor and protector of the realm in his absence. On 7 July the king announced to his council that the queen would serve as regent: "The Queen's Highness shall be regent in his grace's absence; and that His Highness' progress shall pass and bear test in her name, as in like cases heretofore hath been accustomed."[42] Catherine functioned in this capacity from 14 July until Henry's return on 30 September, and while as regent she did not have to raise an army or conduct a war while the king was in France, she was given the guardianship of Henry's son, Prince Edward, and she made use of her regency to reorganize the royal school where the future king was being educated. Long regarded only as a capable nurse for an aging and irritable king and as a surrogate mother for his three children, Catherine Parr is now being recognized for her religious and political role at the end of Henry VIII's reign.[43]

But our interest here is not with the role of queen consort, however, no matter how powerful or influential such queens could be. Even so, it is worth noting that, while the role of queen regnant might be unprecedented in England when John Knox launched his "blast" against the "monstrous regiment" of Mary Tudor in 1558, rule by a woman was not. Even without acknowledging the long history of continental queens, Knox could have found in England several examples of women who had exercised "regiment," either unofficially, like Margaret Beaufort, or officially, like Catherine of Aragon and Catherine Parr.

While savagely attacking Marie of Guise, the regent of Scotland, and her daughter Mary Stuart, the queen regnant, Knox also conveniently overlooked the regency of Margaret Tudor, Mary Stuart's grandmother. Born on 28 November 1489, Margaret was the eldest daughter of Henry VII and Elizabeth of York, four years younger than their son and heir Arthur.[44] Her grandmother Margaret Beaufort was present at her birth and supervised her granddaughter's education; though the English princess was, as her biographer Hester Chapman notes, "more carefully educated than most princesses of her day," Margaret Beaufort could not interest her namesake "in the intellectual projects for which she herself became celebrated."[45] By 1496 the English king was engaged in negotiations to arrange for the marriage of his first-born daughter.

Henry VII had established his Tudor dynasty in 1485, with his defeat of Richard III at the battle of Bosworth. But his position was not unchallenged, and among those who were interested in unseating him was Margaret of York, sister of Edward IV and Richard III. Despite the fact that her niece Elizabeth of York was Henry's wife and queen of England, the dowager duchess of Burgundy continued to intrigue against the king who had defeated and killed her brother. With her support, a young man named Perkin Warbeck had been acknowledged as one of the missing "princes in the Tower," Richard of York.[46] In 1495, as "Richard IV," Warbeck was welcomed to the court of James IV; the Scots king, evidently believing Warbeck's claims, had arranged for the marriage of the young "king" of England to a kinswoman, Lady Katherine Gordon. In response, Henry VII prepared for war—but he also attempted to gain the support of the Scots king in August 1556 by proposing a marriage with his daughter Margaret. The Scots king "replied," in Hester Chapman's words, "by an attempted invasion."[47]

By 1497 James had agreed to withdraw his support from Warbeck, and he negotiated a seventeen-year truce guaranteeing peace with the English king. The marriage of the nine-year-old Margaret and the twenty-five-year-old James was to seal the treaty, but the king's plans were blocked by two formidable opponents: his wife and his mother. "The Queen and my mother are very much against the marriage," Henry indicated to the Spanish ambassador at his court, continuing, "They say if the marriage were concluded we should be obliged to send the princess directly to Scotland, in which case they fear the king of Scotland would not *wait*, but injure her and endanger her health."[48] Margaret Beaufort, whose early pregnancy was widely believed to have permanently injured her, prevailed in this dispute, and her granddaughter's marriage was delayed.

The English king was not without some reservations of his own about the alliance. "Supposing, which God forbid, that all my male progeny were to become extinct and the kingdom devolve by law upon Margaret's heirs," he is reported to have reflected at the time of her betrothal. In such an eventuality, "Will England be damaged thereby or rather benefited?" But with two sons, the likelihood that Margaret would succeed to the throne as queen of England, while theoretically possible, was not great. And, as the king reasoned, if Margaret were to become queen, England would not suffer: "since it ever happens that the less becomes subservient to the greater, the accession will be that of Scotland to England."[49]

The treaty that negotiated the marriage of King James IV and Princess Margaret was signed on 24 January 1502. The Tudor princess left for her new home in July of 1503, eighteen months later. Before she left England, her brother Arthur died, bringing her that much closer to the throne. Since her mother's death quickly followed, preparations for the young queen's departure were made by her grandmother, Margaret Beaufort.[50] The new Scots queen remained with her grandmother at Collyweston for three weeks before setting off on her journey to Edinburgh on 8 July. On 30 July she crossed the border at Berwick. Margaret met her new husband for the first time on 3 August, five days before their marriage was celebrated.[51]

When the new queen of Scotland arrived at Stirling, her dower castle, she found a nursery there already occupied by her husband's seven illegitimate children, including a daughter her own age. Since she did not immediately produce an heir for her husband, eighteen months after their marriage her husband legitimized his eldest son, James Stewart, earl of Moray.[52] But on 21 February 1507, just three months after her seventeenth birthday, Margaret Tudor gave birth to a son. He was baptized two days later and proclaimed "Prince of Scotland and the Isles and Duke of Rothesay," titles that, as Margaret's biographer Maria Perry notes, "clearly distinguished the little Prince of the blood" from that other James, the king's illegitimate son. But the prince died a year later, on 27 February 1508; a daughter, born on the following 15 July, lived only a few hours. Margaret was pregnant again in 1509 when her father Henry VII died.

When Henry VIII succeeded his father as king of England, Henry VII's earlier questions about Margaret's status as heir to the English throne became more than hypothetical. For the moment, the queen of Scotland was the heir presumptive of the king of England; the child she was carrying might inherit the crowns of both Scotland and England. When Margaret gave birth to a son, Arthur, in October 1509, the prince's future thus seemed great. But this child, too, lived only a few brief months; by July of 1510, he was dead. Convinced that the deaths of his first three legitimate children were a judgment by God, James at first planned a pilgrimage to the Holy Land and then considered a crusade. Ultimately he settled on a visit to a shrine in Scotland instead. By 1511 Margaret was pregnant again; on 11 April 1512 the birth of another son, christened James, seemed to signal to the Scots king that God's favor had been restored. By May Margaret was pregnant again, for the fifth time, and in June Henry's English armies were routed in Spain.

Thus when his brother-in-law sent an embassy to Scotland, James felt the time was right to press the English king for a legacy due Margaret. In the midst of preparations for his planned invasion of France, Henry hoped to secure peace in the north; he would send Margaret's inheritance "on condition" that James "keep his oath . . . that none of us shall invade the other."[53] Henry's ambassador indicated to Margaret that it was her responsibility "to preserve a good understanding between the two crowns." Margaret "promised to do her best for peace," but she also pressed for her legacy, which included jewels that had been left to her by her brother Arthur and a small bequest from her grandmother Margaret Beaufort.[54]

Events overtook James IV of Scotland. In November Margaret's fifth pregnancy ended in the premature birth of a daughter who died within hours. James renewed his plan for a pilgrimage to the Holy Land; to secure his safe passage through France, he agreed to send aid to Louis XII; the result was his excommunication. As her husband moved closer to declaring war on her brother, Margaret made one last appeal to Henry, sending him and Queen Catherine gifts and letter in which she addressed the king as "Right excellent, right high and mighty prince, our dearest and best beloved brother." "We cannot think that of your mind, or by your command, we are so fremdly [strangely] dealt with," she wrote, indicating that she was "ashamed" over the dispute about her legacy. She continued, "would God had never word been thereof," indicating that the matter was "not worth such estimation as in your diverse letters of the same." She concluded that, as queen of Scotland, "we lack nothing; our husband is ever the longer the better to us, as knows God."[55]

When Anne of Brittany, queen of France, appealed to James IV of Scotland for his support of her husband against England, her appeal was couched in the terms of medieval romance. She sent the Scots king tokens and a request that he do battle on her behalf: "For my sake . . . march forth, were it only but three feet, on to English ground."[56] And if this failed to persuade him, she sent a more practical second letter enclosing money for his expenses. Margaret attempted to dissuade her husband with tears, accusations of infidelity, and anger: "What a folly, what a blindness . . . to make this war yours! Keep your promise to England, and enjoy peace at home. . . . Should [the French queen's] letters prove more powerful than the cries of your little son?"[57]

Her husband's decision to go to war transformed Margaret from queen consort to queen regent; as he prepared to leave Scotland, James arranged for a regency government to be headed by his wife. The queen, for her part, continued to attempt to dissuade her husband from going to war against her brother, reminding him that the English were "a mighty people" and warning him that her dreams had given her omens of his failure. She also suggested a way out of the confrontation. She believed that Catherine of Aragon would accompany the English army, and Margaret proposed a meeting with the English queen: "I hear the queen my sister will be with the army in her husband's absence; if we shall meet, who knows what God, by our means, may bring to pass?"[58] But there was to be no "ladies' peace" for James IV and Henry VIII. Catherine did not come north with her English army, and Margaret did not travel with her husband and his.

The Scots king crossed into England on 22 August. On 9 September he was dead, defeated at the battle of Flodden by the English troops his sister-in-law, Catherine of Aragon, had sent north. His seventeen-month-old son became James V of Scotland. Pregnant again, Margaret acted decisively upon receiving the news of her husband's death. According to Perry, the regent "moved with speed and resolution," securing her son in the safety of Stirling castle and ensuring his coronation twelve days later, on 21 September. She seized the treasury, then summoned a council that approved her husband's will designating her as regent, thereby becoming de facto ruler of Scotland. The new king and his mother were "styled" as "James, by God's Grace, King of the Scots and Margaret, Queen of Scotland and testamentary *tutrix* of the same."[59]

In an interesting analysis of the situation in Scotland in the aftermath of Flodden, Perry writes that the "manhood of a nation had been wiped out." Margaret had become, in Perry's terms, "queen of a country full of despairing widows and fatherless young men." In the tide of violence that erupted, the queen regent acted to defend the country for which she was now responsible. A proclamation designed to prevent the violation of property and of women (a telling combination) was issued on 26 September, followed quickly by a second in the new king's name. Recognizing that the "wives and widows" of his father's supporters were "desolate," and acknowledging "their daughters . . . being heirs to them," it made rape and robbery of these women treasonable offences. Since many of these "desolate" women had no legal status, Margaret's council took up their cases, and to replace those council members lost at Flodden, Margaret suggested her own candidates for bishop to the pope.[60] She also attempted to repair the break with England. A week after her son's coronation she wrote to her brother Henry asking him not to invade Scotland, and a month later sent a letter to her sister-in-law appealing for her consideration "in the blow" that had "fallen" upon her.[61]

Margaret's position was a difficult one. She had to negotiate between those who desired revenge for Flodden and those who wanted peace. The situation was further complicated by the succession; the heir presumptive to the throne was now John Stuart, duke of Albany, who was in France at the court of Louis XII. Margaret's council wanted Albany recalled, though the French king, who said that he wanted to do "everything befitting an ally," cautiously wrote to know the regent's wishes.[62] Henry VIII, meanwhile, saw himself as his nephew's "natural guardian" and wanted the boy sent to England; his ambassador informed Margaret that her son should be "ordered and ruled by the King's Grace."[63]

It seems inevitable that the widowed and pregnant queen would find the question of her remarriage under discussion by both Louis and Henry. Anne of Brittany was ill, and the French king considered marrying Margaret Tudor himself even before his second queen died. By March, when Margaret was eight months pregnant, the English ambassador was writing to Henry that "by sundry reports that are made unto me, I am informed that if the French king be disposed to marry her upon knowledge thereof had, he shall have her at his pleasure." Henry, on the other hand, suggested a suitable marriage for his widowed sister might be to the Emperor Maximilian, whose heir Charles was Catherine of Aragon's nephew; the idea that Margaret would "make a good match" for the emperor was also noted in Venice.[64] Both prospective husbands made offers for her hand in 1514, after the birth on 12 April of her second son, Alexander.

Margaret's situation seemed more stable immediately afterward, and the Scots nobility signalled its support of her and her regency: "Madame, . . . we are content to stand in one mind and will to concur with all the lords of the realm to the pleasure of our master the King's grace, your grace and for the common weal."[65] But when her brother once again pressed her to send her sons to England—reminding her that, as he still had no children, James V was his heir—dissension was renewed. On 14 August she secretly married Archibald Douglas, earl of Angus. Since the Douglas family was an enormously influential one, her alliance with Angus had serious political implications, suggested by the immediate reaction of the council:

> We have shown heretofore our willingness to honour the Queen contrary to the ancient law and custom of this kingdom. . . . We suffered and obeyed her authority the whiles she herself kept her right by keeping her widow-hood. Now she has quit it by marrying, why should we not choose another to succeed in the place she has voluntarily left?[66]

Margaret's decision to remarry illustrates one of the many dilemmas of women and rule. A mother's desire to protect her minor son's interests could lead her to ally herself with a powerful man, but such alliances brought risks with them. Margaret Beaufort had been notably successful in her series of political marriages to preserve her son's claims to the throne of England. Her husbands, whether Lancastrian or Yorkist, had neither challenged nor spoiled her son's prospects—but, then, Henry had not inherited the crown as a child, either. Margaret of Anjou, by contrast, fought desperately to preserve the crown for *her* son, who as King Henry VI's heir should have succeeded his father on the throne. Her alliances with powerful men like Warwick "the kingmaker" and Edmund Beaufort, duke of Somerset, were failures, although both had fought for her and her son. Complicating Margaret of Anjou's situation was her foreignness. Unlike her contemporary Margaret Beaufort, she was not English, and the suspicion and resentment that had accompanied her marriage to Henry VI grew more virulent as she fought for power. In her defeat, she lost her crown, her son, and her reputation, ending her days in "exile" in the country of her birth.[67]

Like Margaret of Anjou, Margaret Tudor was a foreigner in the country of her regency. Although her marriage to James IV had confirmed the intended "perpetual peace" between the neighboring realms, tensions between the countries had persisted; after James IV's death, fear of English domination was renewed, fed by Henry VIII's influence over his sister and his interest in the guardianship of his nephews. Margaret herself contributed to these fears; she seemed to regard herself, in Chapman's terms, "as her brother's Vicereine."[68]

By marrying Angus, Margaret might have intended to neutralize both foreign influence—French and English—and her own foreignness. But the council insisted she had terminated her regency by marrying without its consent; for her part, Margaret argued that James IV's will had not limited her regency in any way. She then proceeded to name Angus as co-regent, a move that did not help her situation. In response the council insisted that, by law, a widow who remarried forfeited the guardianship of her children; the nobles wanted Albany recalled and named regent in Margaret's place. Margaret again insisted that she had been named regent by the terms of her husband's will, that this will had made no conditions on her regency, and that it had been confirmed by an act of Parliament.

In addition to her legal position, Margaret counted on support of the people, to whom she could appeal "as the widow of their adored King and the mother of his children."[69] She determined on a more conciliatory course and arranged to meet with the council once more, even agreeing to recall Albany. Arriving in Edinburgh on 12 September, she was "wildly cheered" by the people, their evident support convincing several more influential lords to her side. But it was not enough. She would later write that her "adversaries" had continued "in their malice and proceeds in their parliament, usurping the king's authority," as if she and her supporters "were of no reputation, reputing us as rebels."[70] She retreated once more to Stirling with her sons.

By November her situation had become so tenuous that she appealed to Henry VIII for help. "I beseech you that you would make haste with your army, both by sea and land," she wrote in her desperation, noting that she was, as well, "at great expenses . . . and my money is near wasted." Henry's support would "revenge" her enemies, who had already laid siege to the castle of St. Andrews and who threatened a siege against her as well, but Margaret was aware, as well, of the memory of Flodden:

> There is some of the lords that dread that your army shall do them scathe, and that their lands shall be destroyed with the fury of the army: wherefore I would that you wrote to them that their lands nor goods shall not be hurt, and, if so be, that they shall be recompensed double and treble.

Her opponents—her "party adversary"—had recalled Albany, and Margaret wanted her brother to prevent Albany's arrival in Scotland. Meanwhile, she planned to "keep this castle" with her children, who were well. In a subtle way she reminded her brother that his own interests lay in defending her and her sons: "The king, my son, and his brother, prosper well, and are right lifelike children." She appealed to him by claiming that "all the welfare of me and my children lies in your hands." Fearing that her enemies would "counterfeit" her letters, Margaret closed by telling Henry that if she was compelled to write to him "for concord," the letter would be signed merely "Margaret R." and "no more." If she wrote on her own, she would sign herself "Your loving sister."

But Henry did not enter actively into the conflict in Scotland. He had his own political interests to pursue. As his older sister Margaret struggled in Scotland, he had concluded his war with France. A treaty of peace between the two countries was signed on 7 August 1514, and as part of the peace, Henry arranged for the marriage of his younger sister Mary to the just-widowed Louis XII. On 13 August a proxy marriage was celebrated, but the new "queen of France" had only left England in October; thus in November Henry was was not interested in disturbing his relationship with France by invading Scotland. Instead he suggested that Margaret flee with her children and take refuge with him in England.

The Scots queen responded that she would be "gladder" to follow her brother's advice than to be made "the greatest lady of the world," but that it was "impossible to be performed by any manner of fashion" she, her husband, or their supporters could devise.[71] On the one hand she was surrounded by "watch and spies" and feared to "disclose" her counsel to anyone "but God," and on the other she had no money and feared that her "poverty" would force her to "consent to some of their [her enemies'] minds." Her letter shows that she had still not given up on the idea that her brother would come to her aid with an army; she could "defend" herself from her "enemies," she wrote, if she had "sufficient expenses to [until] the coming" of Henry's help.

Her letter contains, as well, a touching—and carefully calculated—picture of her special plight as queen: "If I were such a woman that might go with bairn in mine arm, I trow I should not be long from you, whose presence I desire most of any man." But Margaret was not "such a woman"; she was a queen and, for the moment, regent of Scotland. Relatively quickly, however, her regency came to an end. In January 1515 Louis XII died, and his successor Francis was not so interested in keeping Albany in France. Henry attempted to persuade the new French king to preserve the peace and prevent Albany from leaving; Henry would renew his treaty with France if Francis "would promise not to send the Duke of Albany into Scotland."[72] For his part, Francis wanted the treaty renewed without conditions, and he got what he wanted. On 2 April Albany began his trip back to Scotland; on 5 April the English king and the French king renewed their peace treaty.

Albany arrived in Scotland on 17 May 1515, and at first his relationship with the regent was cordial. But on 12 July parliament declared him regent of Scotland, and he was formally invested with the "sword and sceptre" that symbolized his rule. Since it was obvious even to his supporters that his own claim to the throne precluded him from being the best guardian for the young king and his brother, custody of the princes was to be given over to others, selected by the queen but from a slate of candidates forwarded by parliament. Even in her defeat, Margaret demonstrated her political skill. She retreated into Stirling castle with her children, her husband, and a few servants. An eyewitness described her defiance of the delegation of lords who came to take custody of her children:

> And when she saw the lords within three yards of the gates, she bade them stand, and demanded the cause of their coming. . . . They told her they had come from the duke [Albany] and parliament to demand "deliverance of the king and his brother." Without hesitation, she defied them, and then she caused the portcullis be letten down, and made answer, saying that the castle was her own feoffment, given to her by the king her late husband . . . and that her said late husband had made her *protectrix*, and given her authority to have the keeping and government of her said children, wherefore she could in no wise deliver them to any person.

"It was," as Maria Perry describes it, "a superb *coup de théâtre*, calculated to impress the crowds thronging the castle approach." It was, as well, a superb political statement, for the portcullis itself was "a device forming part of the Beaufort arms," which were in turn part of the "royal arms of England."[73] It would also seem that the king's mother was alluding to her Beaufort grandmother, that other Margaret, "the king's mother." All in all, it was a performance worthy of, and similar to one staged by, Caterina Sforza.

Despite her husband's plea for her to surrender her sons and despite her own physical state—she was pregnant again—Margaret would not compromise. She had taken the only action she could take. While she waited for relief from her brother, who failed to come to her aid, and from her husband, who came to her aid but failed, she planned her strategy. If she was besieged, she would appear on the battlements, where she would "set the young King upon the walls in the sight of all persons crowned, and the sceptre in his hand," aware that such a display would make it "manifestly known to every person that the war shall be made against the King's own person."[74]

On 6 August, Albany arrived outside Stirling with 7,000 men and heavy artillery, and the queen lost her nerve. She abandoned her plan and surrendered. In another deliberately calculated gesture, however, she made her son, the king, hand over the castle to Albany. In a letter to her brother dated 20 August, she seemed to be pleased with the turn of events, writing that her relations with the new regent were peaceful: "Brother, I am determined that I and my said cousin [Albany] shall take one part, for I know it is most for my profit." Through her "diligence" she wrote that she hoped to "keep the peace betwixt the realms" and expressed her desire that her brother would do likewise. She indicated that her children were also well: "I have presence of my children at my pleasure, and enter to them whenever I will."[75] On the same day she consented to Albany's regency, handing over to him "charge and keeping of the King and his brother."[76]

But both her letter and her "consent" had been coerced. She preserved the truth of the situation in a document she entitled "A remembrance of an information by me, Margaret queen of Scots." There she wrote about the disobedience of the lords and their threats to her, indicating that after her husband's death they had tried to force her marriage with Albany. As for Albany himself, he had sent "tokens" to her "for marriage": "Whereupon I was driven by force either to steal away and leave my said children or to marry . . . , seeing the suspicion that the said duke was in, and the pretence that his father made before him to the crown of Scotland." Her "tender children" had been forced from her, and all of her supporters, except Angus, had deserted her. She concluded:

> And for to say that ever I was agreeable, content, or pleased that the said duke of Albany should come into Scotland, or that ever he did justice, or meddled with justice, but only vexed and troubled me and my friends, it appeareth in the said supplication, which I am ready to justify, point by point.[77]

Her brother again offered Margaret asylum in England, indicating that she would be well provided for; she would lack neither "stuff, household, nor money." She arranged for her escape, outlining the plan in a "credence" given to Henry's representative Lord Dacre and forwarded to her brother.[78] She began by describing the conditions of her life:

> First, the said queen sheweth that the duke of Albany hath compelled and constrained her to subscribe and write diverse letters contrary to her own mind, and against all right and conscience; and [he] keepeth her so straitly in Edinburgh that neither she can nor may see nor send to the king and prince her children, nor to other her friends, for her relief and comfort in her causes, and therefore from thence she can make none escape.

Albany had also "withheld" from her "all the profits and revenues of her land," so that she found herself "at extreme poverty." Driven by such circumstances, she wrote, she would attempt to escape Scotland. She would "feign herself to be sick" and leave Edinburgh, retiring to Linlithgow, "with the consent of the said duke," where she would "take her chamber," naturally enough since she was nearing the end of her pregnancy; she was, she wrote, within "six weeks of her lying down." On the "first or second night of her coming thither" she would "depart without any man or woman with her" except her husband and "four or five servants" who would "not be privy to any part of her purpose." If her first attempt failed, she would try again, making sure some diversion—some "ruffling"—distracted Albany and his men.

But her initial plan was successful. After staying in Linlithgow for forty-eight hours, she disappeared on 13 September, spending a night in a stronghold that belonged to the Douglas family. She made an attempt to get her sons from Stirling castle, but abandoned that effort and arrived in England, quickly moving toward the fortress of Harbottle. There, on 7 October, she gave birth to a daughter, whom she named Margaret. She wrote to Albany on 10 October announcing the child's birth, asserting once more her rightful place as her son's regent and demanding her restoration.

Margaret's premature labor and delivery had weakened her, and she remained so seriously ill that she was not informed of the death, on 18 December, of Alexander, the younger of her two sons; the news was kept from her until she recovered somewhat.[79] In March she was composing an eight-page catalogue of the wrongs she had suffered in Scotland, and the story of her plight elicited much sympathy and support not only in England but throughout the courts of Europe, excepting, of course, in France.[80] Finally, in April, Margaret was strong enough to leave the north for London; Angus, however, had decided to come to terms with Albany and left for Scotland. The queen was reunited on 3 May 1516 with her brother, whom she had not seen since he was twelve years old.

She spent the next year in England, alternately pleading with Henry for political and financial support and negotiating with Albany for her return to Scotland. Albany, in the meantime, had had his own troubles with the fractious Scots lords and decided to return to France. The lords agreed to recall their queen; on 18 May 1517, twelve months after her arrival in England, Margaret Tudor left for Scotland once more, believing that she would resume her position as regent. Instead, when she arrived in June she was denied access to her son and learned that the regency had been offered to James Hamilton, earl of Arran. The grandson of James II, Arran was, after Albany, next in line to the throne. She also discovered that her husband had deserted her. In a letter to her "dearest brother" she wrote that she was "sore troubled" by Angus "every day more and more." He had taken control of her property and of her rents so that, she wrote, "I get never a penny." He had also taken a mistress, though she did not tell her brother so directly, alluding instead to another "evil" that she would "cause a servant" to "show Your Grace." She raised the possibility of a divorce, softening the news with something of an apology for the marriage in the first place and suggesting that a remarriage, if it occurred, would come at Henry's advice:

> I am so minded . . . , an [if] I may by law of God and to my honour, to part with him, for I wit well he loves me not, as he sheweth to me daily. Wherefore I beseech Your Grace, when it comes to that point, as I trust it shall, to be a kind prince and brother to me, for I shall never marry but where you will bid me, nor never to part from Your Grace, for I will never with my will abide into Scotland.[81]

Henry had not yet embarked upon his own efforts for a divorce, though by then he had begun his relationship with Elizabeth Blount. Nevertheless, he was offended by Margaret's suggestion that she would seek a divorce and occupied with his own personal and political affairs. Abandoned by her husband and his supporters, her appeals to her brother ignored, Margaret also found that the Scots lords had no intention of honoring the conditions they had agreed upon for her return; "the cause that I came hither most for was for the king my son's sake," she wrote to her brother, "and I am holden from him like a stranger, and not like his mother, which doth me great displeasure in my heart, considering I have no other comfort here but him."[82] Arran, meanwhile, found himself outmaneuvered by Angus and his supporters and in a reversal took up the queen's cause. Together they decided to negotiate with Albany for his return to Scotland.

Margaret's decision to accept Arran's support and to recall Albany provoked warnings and admonitions from England, but no direct aid. For the first time, as Perry notes, Margaret seemed to see that her future lay in Scotland rather than in England: "I must cause me to please *this* realm, when I have my life here."[83] Later, in explaining her decision, she was to describe her new determination: "I would be contented with" what "was for the good of the king my son's person," she wrote. That is, she had decided "that I should be a good Scotswoman."[84] Thus the political game in Scotland continued. Albany returned from France on 18 November 1521. He seized power immediately, and Angus and his supporters were exiled. Albany and Margaret together resumed control of the government, the duke as regent and Margaret as queen mother. In responding to a series of fifteen charges levelled against her in England, Margaret replied in a long letter, written in 1522, to what she characterized as the "right sharp" articles. She began by asserting that, as she had gotten "no remedy" from her brother, she had determined to act for herself; "considering I am mother to the king of this realm," she wrote, she had acted for her son's honor and her own. She justified her break with Angus as well, who, "if he had desired my company or my love" would have acted "more kindly" toward her.

She had sought Henry's assistance again and again, but it had not been forthcoming; although her brother had supported her "in general words," it "must be the deed" that would help. She rejected a series of rumors about her personal behavior, including one that she had begun a sexual relationship with Albany. She ended with a keen insight into the problems she had caused herself:

> I took my lord of Angus against all Scotland's will and did him the honour that I could, where-through I lost the keeping of my sons, my house of Stirling, my rule of the realm which I had by right, that might not have been taken from me, and all this for his sake. . . .
>
> [S]ince I took him at mine own pleasure, I will not be boasted [threatened] to take him now.[85]

But relations between England and Scotland remained strained, and war threatened. Margaret worked ceaselessly to maintain the peace, her efforts earning her Henry's good graces once more. Henry suggested a marriage between his daughter, Princess Mary, and Margaret's son, James V, but the Scots parliament rejected his offer. In 1523 Henry sent additional troops north and in June commenced a series of border raids. Albany, meanwhile, had been back in France for reinforcements and with those French troops entered England. He was forced to withdraw, and on 31 May 1524 he left Scotland for France, never to return.

After Albany's departure, Margaret wrote to her brother that her twelve-year-old son should "have his proper position of authority and throw off the governance usurped by Albany."[86] Fearful of her intentions and of continued French influence in Scotland, Henry responded by advising Margaret to be reconciled with Angus, who had shown up at the English court and convinced the English king that he would support the English cause in Scotland. With Arran's support, she wrote to Henry rejecting his proposal that Angus should return to Scotland and the regency, asking him to "remember well" her many letters to him and "to make not long delay in helping of the king my son to put him to freedom and out of danger of his enemies, for now is the time."[87] She minimized her political power and authority, reminding him, "I am but a woman and may do little." He, by contrast, could affect the situation for better or worse. If he ignored Margaret's advice—"do Your Grace the contrary"—it would affect James V; "the king my son will be the longer from his liberty and his person in danger."

But, as if to contradict her statement that as a woman she could do little, she told Henry that her son "will be ruled by me" and that she had "labored and broken many lords from the ways of the duke of Albany to his [her son's] way that he may be put out of danger and that he and his lords may rule this realm" with, of course, "the help and assistance" of Henry, in whom was "all" her "trust." She rejected any notion that Angus would "help" her brother or the cause for peace, attacking as well the idea that Henry should rely on the advice of others: "methinks, dearest brother the king, methinks that he [Angus] nor no other should be heard in that matter so well as I your sister, nor that you may get so much honor to do for their request as for me."

In August James V opened parliament flanked by his mother and the earl of Arran. The boy moved "to deprive the duke of Albany of his government," and after some opposition from Albany's supporters, the lords agreed.[88] But by November 1526 Angus was in Scotland. As the parliament met, he seized control of Edinburgh. Margaret and the king were in Holyroodhouse, which the queen defended despite protests that she not oppose with force her "lawful husband." Angus retreated, and the parliament confirmed Margaret's regency.

Louise of Savoy, regent of France for her son Francis, responded to the situation immediately by offering the queen a pension and a renewal of an alliance with France. Margaret rejected the offer, however, and agreed at last to accept a reconciliation with Angus. But her agreement to be reconciled *with* her husband did not mean she intended to accept him *as* her husband. She continued in her suit for a divorce, and she took a lover, Henry Stewart. As a result, her uneasy relationship with Angus broke down. He had custody of the king, and when he faced Margaret's army on the field, he had her son by his side so that she could not attack. The lord of Arran and many of Margaret's supporters deserted her and her cause, joining Angus instead.

Angus controlled the king entirely; he dismissed James's tutor and replaced the young king's household officials with Douglas supporters. On 14 June 1526 he had the king declared of age, but that did not mean that James was to rule. Angus defeated all attempts made by Margaret and Stewart to rescue the king. Late in 1527 Margaret finally received her divorce from Angus, and in April 1528 she married Stewart. Her brother was offended by her "foolish and evil" behavior, and in a moment of supreme blindness, since by this time he himself was seeking a divorce from Catherine of Aragon, he judged it "impossible for anyone to lead a more shameful life" than his sister. "Turn to God's word," he wrote to his sister, "and for the weal of your soul, avoid eternal damnation. . . . Relinquish the adulterous company of him that is not, nor may not be, of right, your husband."[89]

Despite some initial objection to his mother's remarriage, the young king joined his mother and her new husband in May when he managed to escape from Angus. At last he entered into his majority and his role as king.

In recognition of Henry Stewart's support and "for the great love I bear my dearest mother," he created Margaret's third husband the earl Methven. Together they besieged Angus and his supporters. Angus eventually surrendered in November 1528, leaving Scotland for England, taking with him his and Margaret Tudor's daughter, the thirteen-year-old Lady Margaret Douglas.

James V set about consolidating his power in Scotland, and for the next eight years, his mother and her husband were his most reliable advisers. Margaret mediated between her son and her brother, for Henry had continued to support Angus, who remained at the English court with Lady Margaret. When the alliance of mother and son was ultimately broken, as it was, the source of their disagreement was, ironically, James's marriage plans. The king, then twenty-five years old, wanted to marry his already-married mistress Lady Margaret Douglas of Lochleven, the mother of his son James Stewart. When he discovered that his mother had been in correspondence with her brother about his intentions, he sent her away from court.[90] English ambassadors in Scotland reported to Henry VIII that Margaret was "weary of Scotland and fully determined to come into England." She had earned her son's "high displeasure" for having "intermeddled" in his affairs; specifically, she had tried to arrange a meeting between her son and her brother. James had accused his mother of receiving bribes "to betray him" from the English king.[91]

Mother and son were reconciled, however, and the king abandoned his plan to marry his mistress. He arranged for a truce with England and even agreed to meet with his uncle; instead, when he left Scotland he went to France, where he planned to marry Marie of Bourbon, daughter of the duke of Vendôme. Once at the French court, however, he changed his mind, preferring the French king's fourteen-year-old daughter, Madeleine. They were married on New Year's Day 1537 and returned Scotland in May. By July Madeleine was dead.

Margaret, meanwhile, had resumed her role as regent of Scotland while her son was in France. She had also decided to divorce her third husband, Henry Stewart, but when her son returned to Scotland, he put an end to her suit. Pleading poverty and ill-treatment, Margaret turned once more to her brother; she would return to England. Then, within months of the death of his first queen, James married another French wife, Marie of Guise.[92] After her arrival in Scotland, the new queen worked to reconcile her husband and his mother. Marie gave birth to her son James in May 1539 and quickly became pregnant again. The second child was also a boy, but disaster struck in April 1541 when the two young princes died within a week of one another. Margaret, who knew only too well the pain of losing her children, comforted her son and his wife. She died as the year ended, on 18 October.

In a number of striking ways the lives of Margaret Tudor and her sister-in-law Catherine of Aragon are parallel, yet in their responses to political and domestic turmoil they are almost mirror images. They were both foreign queens in the lands in which they spent their lives, their marriages intended to seal peace treaties between uneasy allies, Catherine's between Spain and England, Margaret's between England and Scotland. The initial success of these political alliances was affected by each woman's initial "failure" to produce the requisite male heirs, though Margaret eventually "succeeded" where Catherine continued to "fail." Both women were empowered as regents by their husbands at the same moment; Catherine of Aragon, as her husband's regent, defeated James IV at Flodden, while Margaret Tudor, left behind in Scotland, was acting as her husband's regent.

But there the parallels end, and we may come closer to understanding Catherine of Aragon's passive resistance to her husband's divorce project, in fact, if we view her decisions in light of her sister-in-law's. In Scotland the English Margaret Tudor was initially accepted as her son's regent, but she remained nonetheless a foreign queen. Her marriage to Angus may have been an effort to neutralize both her own "foreignness" and the foreign influence of the English king on affairs in Scotland. She gained strong supporters as a result, but she also gained powerful enemies. The endless difficulties of Margaret's regency may well have influenced Catherine of Aragon's decision *not* to follow the advice of her supporters in England to move against Henry and pursue a regency for her own child.

Like Margaret Tudor, Catherine as queen and as mother was well loved by the people of England, but as regent she would inevitably face suspicions about Spanish influences on her decisions. And by the mid 1530s, when her supporters were urging her to take to the field against her husband, Catherine had also been able to assess the reaction throughout the courts of Europe to Margaret Tudor's leading an army into battle against her husband Angus. Catherine's mother, Isabella of Castile, was reknowned for having led armies, but she had fought for and with her husband against mutual enemies. She had never raised an army against Ferdinand. Even if Catherine had chosen to follow her mother's lead as a warrior queen, overthrowing her husband and establishing herself as regent for Mary, she would inevitably have faced the same shocked reactions throughout Europe and the same opposition in England that Margaret had faced in Scotland. Moreover Henry's strong condemnation of Margaret's 1527 divorce may have suggested another course of action to Catherine. She may have been convinced that her husband would, at last, come to his senses and give up his own pursuit of a divorce. But Catherine's husband never gave up his "great matter," and when the queen—who had been reassigned the title of "Princess Dowager"—died in 1536, she was neither reconciled to him nor assured of her daughter's position. A 1532 act of succession had declared Mary illegitimate and named Anne Boleyn's daughter Elizabeth as the king's legitimate successor, failing the birth of a male heir. By contrast, for all the tumult she endured in her life, Margaret Tudor spent her last years in relative peace, and when she died in 1541 she left her son on the throne of Scotland.

Despite the objections of the Scots lords to having a woman rule over them, Margaret Tudor had not been the only woman to have struggled for power as regent of Scotland for a minor son, nor had she been the first to succeed. Indeed, as Antonia Fraser notes, "there had been no adult succession to the Scots throne since the fourteenth century," necessitating a series of royal minorities.[93] In the early fifteenth century one of Margaret Tudor's own Beaufort foremothers had been queen of Scotland, forced to struggle, like Margaret, to control the regency for her son. The daughter of Margaret Holland and John Beaufort, duke of Somerset, Joan Beaufort had been married to James I of Scotland in 1424.[94] When the king was assassinated in 1437, Queen Joan, assuming guardianship of her six-year-old son, had her husband's assassins captured and killed, but the Scots lords refused to accept her as regent. Citing the "ancient law and custom" of Scotland that forbade rule by a woman (the same argument that would be made when Margaret Tudor attempted to assume the regency), they named Archibald Douglas as regent instead. In response—and to acquire a male protector for herself and her son—the widowed queen married James Stewart in 1439. Her bid for power failed. The Douglases, however, also lost the regency, which was turned over to two rivals. The result was civil war, which lasted until James II reached the age of eighteen and assumed power himself. In 1449 King James II married Mary of Guelders, who was more successful in getting and keeping control of her minor son than her predecessor, Joan Beaufort, had been.[95] When James II was killed in a skirmish again English forces in 1460, Mary of Guelders, queen of Scotland, assumed the regency for her son James III, then about eight years old. She governed ably as regent, even sending help to Margaret of Anjou in England. But Mary of Guelders died in 1463, before James III reached his majority.

Thus Margaret Tudor's efforts to rule as regent for her minor son were not unprecedented. Whatever the opposition of the Scots lords to a female ruler, when Margaret's son James V died in 1542, he left only a daughter, Mary, to succeed him. Although the regency had initially been in the hands of James Hamilton, earl of Arran, by April 1554 Marie of Guise had replaced him, her position as queen regent "ratified by the Estates of Scotland."[96]

She served as regent until her death in 1560 and seems to have taken to heart the advice of her brother, the duke of Guise, to "deal in Scotland in a spirit of conciliation, introducing much gentleness and moderation into the administration of justice." She attempted to steer a judicious middle course for herself, acting in Fraser's words, "gently and slowly by the use of Parliament," introducing more equitable administration of the law into a country "where administration was either non-existent or archaic in the extreme," aiming for stability in economic matters, and proceeding with "balance and political acumen" in her dealings with the Scots lords, whom she judged to be "jealous and suspicious." She knew the difficulty of her task: "whenever it is a question of meeting out justice or punishment," she wrote, the lords "find these things insupportable, thinking always that one wants to give them new laws and change theirs, which in fact have much need of amendment."[97]

Her family predicted that her "tender" methods would result in her failure. Her enemies condemned her as full of "craft and subtleties"; she had a "queenly mind," but "the heart of a man of war." John Knox, her most virulent critic, described her regency in an oft-quoted passage: "a crown [was] put upon her head, as seemly a sight . . . as to put a saddle upon the back of an unruly cow." But her supporters described her differently. The Catholic bishop John Lesley judged her to be a "princess most prudent and very well instructed in sweetness, comely and honest manners and integrity of life":

> Through use and experience, she knew much of our affairs and was very expert, in so far that none was of the nobility and of the common people except very few obscure persons whose engine, mind and manners she knew not perfectly and very well. . . . [S]he did justice with all diligence all her days. . . . [S]he likewise in virtues and many offices of humanity far overcame many other women. . . . [T]herefore she won the hearts of all . . . with wit and wisdom.

Lesley's view was surely as partisan Knox's, but, as Rosalind Marshall writes, "it is interesting to note" that the English chronicler Holinshed's estimation of the regent is much closer to Lesley's than to Knox's: In his view Mary of Guise was "wise and very prudent." During her regency "she kept good justice and was well obeyed in all parts of the realm."[98]

In Scotland, then, the daughters of Margaret Beaufort, "the king's mother," included not only a "king's mother," Margaret Tudor, and a "queen's mother," Marie of Guise, both of whom functioned as queen regents for their children, but a queen regnant as well, Mary Stuart. In England, Margaret Beaufort's descendants included two more queens regnant, Mary and Elizabeth Tudor. We might push the total to three if we

include Lady Jane Grey, queen of England for nine days; the granddaughter
of Henry VIII's younger sister, Mary Tudor, she was manipulated onto the
throne for her brief reign after Edward VI's death in 1553 and was executed
in 1554 at the age of sixteen. It is easy to dismiss or to overlook a woman
who was "queen" under such circumstances. As historian Carole Levin
notes, many historians "have continued to accept the conventional notion
of Lady Jane Grey as a weak, powerless victim of political intrigue." While
acknowledging the "clear historical roots" of this assessment, Levin suggests
that she "was actually a far stronger figure than this picture would lead us
to believe":

> Though it is true, as many historians have argued, that Lady Jane Grey was
> a pawn in the political intrigue of 1553, she was also a strongly determined
> and articulate woman not afraid to speak out for what she believed, no matter
> what the consequences. Lady Jane Grey is worth noting not only for her
> political position, but also as an example of a sixteenth-century Protestant
> woman who died steadfast to her faith.[99]

While we may conclude that, whatever her political acumen, a nine-
days' queen should not be counted as a queen regnant, we might instead
consider Lady Jane Grey as one of a striking number of queens *manquant*
among the "daughters" of Margaret Beaufort, who, as we have seen, could
herself be viewed as a queen who should have been or who might have
been.

By the terms of the 1543 act of succession, confirmed by his will, Henry
VIII had determined that, if his three children died without heirs of their
own to succeed them, the crown should pass to the heirs of his younger
sister Mary, who had died in 1533; the English king thus set aside the claims
of his older sister and of her descendants in favor of the claims of Frances
and Eleanor Brandon.[100] In his "device" for the succession, Edward VI
followed his father in passing over the claims of Margaret Tudor's descendants, but he also set aside the claims of Frances Brandon herself in favor of
her three daughters, Jane, Catherine, and Mary Grey. After the brief "reign"
of Jane Grey, Edward VI was followed on the throne by his older half-sister
Mary Tudor. When Elizabeth Tudor, the last of Henry VIII's children,
succeeded her half-sister as queen regnant in 1558, her immediate heirs, by
the terms of her father's and brother's decisions, were her cousins Catherine
and Mary, Frances Brandon's surviving daughters. But she still had to
contend with the claims of Margaret Tudor's granddaughter Mary Stuart
and with the claims of Margaret Tudor's daughter Lady Margaret Douglas
and *her* son, Henry, lord Darnley. In 1575 yet another claimant was born,
Arbella Stuart, Lady Margaret Douglas's granddaughter and, thus, Margaret
Tudor's great-granddaughter.[101]

Lady Margaret Douglas had married Matthew Stewart, earl of Lennox, who was himself a descendant of James II of Scotland; when her son Henry, lord Darnley married Mary Stuart, queen of Scots, uniting and reinforcing these claims, Lady Margaret Douglas was imprisoned. In 1574 she arranged for her younger son, Charles, earl of Lennox, to marry Elizabeth Cavendish, the daughter of Bess of Hardwick, then countess of Shrewsbury; Queen Elizabeth sent Lady Margaret to the Tower once more. She was released by November of the next year, however, when she wrote to her niece Mary Stuart to announce the birth of her granddaughter Arbella.[102]

Little is known about the early period of Arbella Stuart's life. Her father died in April of 1576, when she was about six months old; in 1582, when her mother died, she was sent to live with her grandmother Elizabeth Hardwick, "Bess," as she was known, whose fourth marriage had been to George Talbot, earl of Shrewsbury. Talbot was Mary Stuart's "guardian" while she was imprisoned in England; "Much has been speculated about Stuart's relationship with her aunt, the exiled Scottish queen, during the years that Stuart lived in that politically charged household," writes Sara Jane Steen. But, she adds, "Little . . . is known of their association." Nonetheless, Steen concludes that Arbella's subsequent "letters and actions suggest that she was influenced by Mary of Scots's trial and execution."[103]

Throughout her childhood, Arbella Stuart was "useful" to Queen Elizabeth as a "marrigeable property": "As a claimant who could bring the dowry of a crown, she was a commodity, one of high worth on the matrimonial market," but her status as a claimant "fluctuated with English and European politics and the rise and fall of Elizabeth's favor."[104] Margaret Tudor's descendants had been cut out of the succession by Elizabeth's father and half-brother, but the queen had also acted to bar the descendants of Mary Tudor from the throne. In such a complicated situation, James VI of Scotland, Mary Stuart's son, seemed to have the best claim to the English throne: he was the oldest unquestionably legitimate male descendant of Henry VII and Henry VIII. But he was also unquestionably a foreigner, and foreign birth was generally regarded as a bar to the English succession. After James VI, Margaret Tudor's daughter, Lady Margaret Douglas, might be considered "next in line" for the English crown. She had been born in England and had spent much of her life at the English court, but as Steen notes, she was older than Elizabeth Tudor and "unlikely to outlive" her. Lady Margaret's oldest son, Darnley, had married Mary Stuart, but he died in 1567; her younger son, Charles, was thus next in line for the throne, after James VI. After Charles's death in 1575, his daughter Arbella would inherit his claim.

When Arbella was still a child, her grandmother had promised her to the four-year-old son of Robert Dudley, earl of Leicester, who, perhaps fortunately for Bess of Hardwick, died; the queen had been angered by the proposal and took upon herself the task of arranging Arbella's future. Elizabeth used Arbella as a "bargaining chip in foreign policy, tantalizing continental nobility with the prospect of marriage accompanied by the declaration of succession."[105] At various times those prospective alliances included Esmé Stuart, who had inherited Arbella's Lennox title and lands after her father's death; the king of Scotland himself, James VI; Rainutio Farnese, the son of the duke of Parma; Henry IV of France; the prince of Condé; and the duke of Nevers. Various alliances with members of the English nobility were also proposed, including Robert Cecil.[106]

But none of these marriages ever took place. Arbella came briefly to court in 1587 and again in 1588, but she was sent away in disgrace for some offense. At the time it was rumored, on the one hand, that her presumption had resulted in her dismissal, on the other that a romance with the earl of Essex had precipitated her removal from court. Arbella herself, writing about the incident later, indicated that at first she had enjoyed the queen's approval. Queen Elizabeth had examined the young woman for herself when she arrived at court and "by trial did pronounce me an eaglet of her own kind . . . worthy . . . even yet to carry her thunderbolt."[107]

It wasn't until 1591 that Arbella was recalled to court, during the period when her marriage to the son of the duke of Farnese was being discussed. She remained with the court into the summer of 1592, but when the duke died and marriage negotiations failed, she was once again dismissed. She was with her grandmother later in that year when a plot to abduct her came to light. A Catholic priest revealed a plan to kidnap Arbella and then marry her to a foreign Catholic noble, who would invade England and claim the throne on the young woman's behalf. Arbella was not implicated in the plot, but neither was she recalled to court by the queen.

Despite the dazzling array of marriages proposed for Arbella, the queen was no more interested in finding a husband for Arbella than she was in finding one for herself. Instead, she left the young woman in the care of her grandmother. Arbella was well educated, but she was completely isolated, and she came to regard her seclusion as an imprisonment rather than a retirement. Life at Hardwick Hall grew intolerable. A twenty-seven-year-old woman, she still slept in her grandmother's bedroom and had her nose "tweaked" for punishment.[108] After a decade of being cut off from court and court contacts, in 1602 Arbella sought permission from Bess of Hardwick to "present" herself to the queen, but even that "small and ordinary liberty" was denied to her, at which she "despaired."[109]

At last she took matters into her own hands. Arbella proposed a marriage with Edward Seymour, Lady Catherine Grey's grandson and thus, himself, a claimant to the English throne—despite the fact that Elizabeth I had declared Catherine Grey's marriage invalid and the children of that marriage illegitimate. On Christmas Day Arbella sent a message to Seymour's grandfather, the earl of Hertford, indicating that she would be interested in an alliance with his grandson. If the earl approved, he should send his grandson to her in disguise so that they could meet one another and, after having met, "see how they could like."[110]

But Arbella's plot failed. The earl of Hertford forwarded her message to Sir Robert Cecil, and within days Henry Brounker was sent to Hardwick Hall to investigate. By January he had cleared things up to his own satisfaction and the queen's. Arbella apologized in a letter to the queen, expressing her sorrow for having given "the least cause of offense"; "I humbly prostrate myself at Your Majesty's feet," she wrote, "craving pardon" and hoping that, out of "princely clemency," the queen would "signify" her "gracious remission" to Arbella's grandmother, whose "discomfort" she, Arbella, would be until then.[111]

Arbella was "forgiven," but her restrictions were "redoubled." "Educated for command," as Steen notes, "Stuart seemed powerless, politically and personally enclosed: chaste, with no opportunity to be otherwise; silenced, forbidden unmonitored conversations or letters; and obedient, under the very real threat of the Tower or death."[112] Although she acknowledged herself as a "poor silly infant and wretch," Arbella insisted that she had taken as "great care" to preserve the queen's "royal lineage from any blot as any whosoever"; she would, she wrote, have judged herself "unworthy of life" if she had "degenerated from the most reknowned stock whereof it is my greatest honor to be a branch."[113]

Despite her apologies, Arbella's efforts to escape her confinement continued. She fabricated another marriage plot, used her poor health to effect a move to another residence, and ultimately attempted to escape. The escape failed, however, and early in March Arbella was once more at Hardwick Hall, under investigation. This time her apologies were less abject:

> When it shall please Her Majesty to afford me those ordinary rights which other subjects cannot be debarred of justly, I shall endeavor to receive them as thankfully now as if they had been in due time offered.

She would bear her yoke, she wrote, "as long as I think good to convince them that impose it of hardness of heart," and then "shake it off when I think good to take my Christian liberty." If it were "denied" her, the "whole world" would be "made judge upon what cause, or color, or how justly given or taken and by whom." If she could be left to be her "own woman," then everyone's "trouble" would cease.[114]

Queen Elizabeth died on 24 March 1603, just days after Arbella's letter was written. Arbella acknowledged the authority of the queen's successor, James VI of Scotland, now James I of England, and she was once more welcomed at court. Again rumors about a prospective marriage for her circulated, but in July two plots against the new king were discovered, one of which included a plan to place Arbella on the English throne. She was cleared of suspicion, and while in the years that followed she was able to exert a certain amount of influence and patronage, she remained both unmarried and without adequate financial support. By the end of 1609 she was again under guard; "rumors abounded" about her political plans, her religious preferences, and her marriage prospects. She was investigated once more, cleared of suspicion once more, and restored to favor once more. By 1610 she had taken her destiny into her own hands, secretly arranging to marry.

Arbella Stuart married William Seymour, Edward Seymour's younger brother, on 22 June. By early July, both were imprisoned and under investigation, Seymour in the Tower and Arbella in a private residence in Lambeth. In a letter to her husband written shortly after their arrest, Arbella wrote that she had heard he was not well, suggesting his illness represented the "sympathy" between them since she herself had been sick at the same time. She looked forward to a return of the king's favor, however, and wanted to make sure that Seymour's "grief of mind" did not "work" upon his body. If they were not "able to live to" the return of the king's favor, she wrote, "I for my part shall think myself a pattern of misfortune in enjoying so great a blessing as you so little a while."[115]

Arbella's belief that James would restore the pair to favor derived at least in part from her conviction that the king had given her permission to marry a husband of her own choice. In a letter to the king she wrote that his "neglect" of her and her lack of money "drove" her to her "contract" with Seymour before she informed the king of her intentions; nevertheless, she wrote,

> I humbly beseech Your Majesty to consider how impossible it was for me to imagine it could be offensive unto Your Majesty, having few days before given me your royal consent to bestow myself on any subject of Your Majesty's (which . . . likewise Your Majesty had done long since), besides never having been either prohibited any or spoken to for any in this land by your Majesty these seven years that I have lived in Your Majesty's house I could not conceive that Your Majesty regarded my marriage at all.[116]

Despite Arbella's hopes, in January 1611 William Seymour was condemned to life imprisonment, and she was exiled to the north of England, where she was to live out her life guarded by the bishop of Durham. She attempted to fight the decision, at first by law, but when the courts failed her, she again fell ill. As Steen notes, she "became—whether by policy, from illness, or some combination of the two—too weak to travel."[117] She was sent on her way north on 21 March, but she travelled only six miles before stopping. There she remained until 1 April, when King James had her examined by a physician, who determined that she was, as she claimed, too weak to travel. By the end of April James was insisting that Arbella be forced to leave for Durham, but again she appealed, using her continued illness. She was granted an extension until 5 June, but on 3 June she escaped from custody, "cross-dressed like one of Shakespeare's heroines."[118]

Her husband had escaped from the Tower, and the pair planned to be reunited in France. Arbella reached Calais on 5 June, but she was caught immediately and returned to England, this time to imprisonment in the Tower. She was never charged with a crime, but, despite numerous appeals to James I, she remained there until her death on 25 September 1615. Seymour, meanwhile, remained in France. He returned to England five months after Arbella died, restored to the king's favor.[119]

Arbella's imprisonment in the Tower sounds a note we have heard before, for it is generally claimed that she became insane. "The primary source for the idea that Stuart became deranged," Steen writes, "was court observer and letter-writer John Chamberlain, who in 1613 and 1614 repeatedly commented on Stuart's distraction; in April 1613, for example, he wrote that she was said to be 'cracked in her brain.'" The Lieutenant of the Tower, too, described Arbella's "fits of distemper and convulsions."[120] Most later historians have accepted the diagnosis that Arbella Stuart "lost her sanity," but Steen effectively disputes the notion that she spent the last years of her life "as a lunatic prisoner." The evidence does "suggest that Stuart indeed was distressed, perhaps even intermittently delusional," suffering from illnesses that were "physiological, strategic, or a combination of the two," but also that Arbella "remained active on her own behalf."[121]

Throughout the period of her supposed madness, Arbella Stuart continued to manage her financial affairs. Her relatives and friends continued to work for her release, and various political supporters continued to focus on her as a replacement for King James. At least one rescue attempt was made, and at least one plot to place her on the throne dates from this period, unlikely efforts if she were "irrecoverably deranged":

> The phrase "went insane" conveniently labels Stuart a female hysteric, a woman exhibiting the mental instability and melancholia often attributed to learned women, thus allowing observers such as John Chamberlain to dismiss her transgressions of the code of appropriate female behavior as "madness," without calling the system into question. Those who were acquainted with

and attended Stuart consistently characterized her illnesses either as intentionally deceitful and obstinate or as psychosomatic in origin . . . , as arising from her grief of her unquiet mind.[122]

James and his examiners may well have used "madness" as a way of explaining Arbella's gender "transgressions," as Steen suggests, but such a determination was an effective political tool as well, as we have seen. If Arbella Stuart were "cracked in her brain," her continued "imprisonment" in the Tower could be justified, and she could more effectively be eliminated as a rival or as a threat.

In her assessment of what she calls Arbella Stuart's "oppositional drama," Steen provides a final comment on her significance as a descendant of Margaret Beaufort:

> Raised to rule and always aware of her rank, Lady Arbella Stuart was not silent or obedient, nor was she passive in response to the forces arrayed against her. Articulate in her anger, she struggled to command her destiny through whatever means were available, from ruse to overt defiance. She understood that she was a political commodity and used both her mind and body in her attempts to achieve control of her life. . . . Even though she did not attain her goals, Stuart pushed the social and political system to its limits, delineating for us what those limits were for a royal woman of her era. King James remained so compulsively fearful of Stuart, the unruly female within his own family, that nearly three years after her death he had his Privy Council investigate whether she had given birth to a child that had been secretly conveyed across the sea.[123]

In placing her among the women we have examined thus far, it is possible to see how closely Arbella's story parallels those of other women whose claims to the throne for themselves or their children resulted in their containment as nuns, lunatics, exiles, or prisoners. In Spain, for example, Juana *la Beltraneja* was discredited as illegitimate and compelled to become a nun, while Juana of Castile was declared insane and secluded (or imprisoned) at Tordesillas. In England, Margaret of Anjou had fought to maintain the crown for her son; having lost her son, she was defeated, discredited, and exiled. Lady Jane Grey was imprisoned in the Tower after her brief rule, but no further action was taken against her. It was only after an unsuccessful rebellion against Queen Mary that her imprisonment was not enough, and she was executed. The potential threats offered by such women could be controlled in other ways, however, if they were willing to accept more traditional and subordinate female roles. Elizabeth of York offered no challenge to the new Tudor king because he married her. She became a queen consort rather than a queen regnant, her own claims to the succession united with her husband's in their children. And having worked to secure her son's succession throughout her lifetime, Margaret Beaufort was certainly no challenge to his kingship; she was, as we have seen, able to exert considerable influence in her "natural" role as his mother.

In this discussion of the "daughters" of Lady Margaret Beaufort, I have until this point omitted any discussion of the three most well known queens of the early modern period, at least for English speakers, Mary Stuart, Mary Tudor, and Elizabeth Tudor. Their lives and reigns have attracted so much attention that I have focused on less well known women here. But having examined the lives of these "other" daughters of Margaret Beaufort in detail, we can now see certain patterns that may help us to see the more familiar figures in a new light.

In her discussion of Margaret Tudor, Patricia Buchanan compares her to her granddaughter Mary Stuart, queen of Scots. In the same way, Sara Jayne Steen notes the influence on Arbella Stuart of her aunt, Mary Stuart. Buchanan and Steen point us in the right direction: If we move beyond the examination of individual lives, we can better see how generations of women responded in similar ways and under similar conditions.

Margaret Beaufort's descendants are as remarkable for their marriage patterns as the Habsburgs are for theirs—but we can contrast the political choices made by "happy Austria" to the personal choices made in "un-happy" England and Scotland. The "king's mother" had brilliantly used marriage to her political advantage; as she maneuvered to secure her son's succession, she contracted important alliances among influential English nobles to insure her own safety and her son's future. Her granddaughters and great-granddaughters, including Margaret and Mary Tudor, Lady Margaret Douglas, the Grey sisters, Margaret Clifford, and Arbella Stuart, all attempted to emulate Margaret Beaufort's marital decision-making. But they missed the point. There is nothing to suggest that Margaret Beaufort was ever motivated by personal preference, sexual desire, or emotional pique; her decisions were political calculations.[124]

Like so many of her Tudor forebears, Mary Stuart miscalculated badly. Marie of Guise had arranged a dynastic marriage for her daughter while Mary was still a child; but after Francis II's death, political calculation seems to have played a relatively small part in her choice of Darnley and then Bothwell. The results of her ill-considered choices were disastrous: her loss of her throne, her flight from Scotland, her long imprisonment in England, and her ultimate execution.

Queen Mary Tudor was no more successful than her Stuart cousin in her marital decision-making. None of the dynastic alliances Henry VIII had considered during her childhood had ever taken place. When Mary finally became queen, it was as queen regnant of England. The 1554 act of parliament "concerning regal power" directly addressed the extent of Mary's authority. It confirmed her inheritance of the crown "with all dignities, honors, prerogatives, authorities, jurisdictions, and preeminences thereunto annexed, united, and belonging, by the divine providence of Almighty God"; she was the "very true and undoubted heir and inheritrix thereof." As "sovereign supreme governor and queen," she had "all regal power" in "as full, large, and ample manner as it hath done heretofore to any other her most noble progenitors, kings of this realm." Noting that "malicious and ignorant persons" had committed the "error and folly" of thinking that "the most ancient statues of this realm," in mentioning only "the name of king," had precluded the succession of a queen, the act clarified Mary's rights as queen:

> For the avoiding and clear extinguishment of which said error or doubt, and for a plain declaration of the laws of this realm in that behalf, be it declared and enacted by the authority of this present parliament that the law of this realm is and ever hath been and ought to be understood that the kingly or regal office of the realm, and all dignities, prerogative royal, power, preem-inences, privileges, authorities, and jurisdictions thereunto annexed, united, or belonging, being invested either in male or female, are and be and ought to be as fully, wholly, absolutely, and entirely deemed, judged, accepted, invested, and taken in the one as in the other.[125]

In spite of her advisors and Parliament, Mary insisted on marrying Philip of Spain. The terms of the marriage treaty negotiated on her behalf limited Philip's role to what Constance Jordan has called "cer-emonial space," maintaining for the queen "the arena of substantive political decisions." The subsequent "failure of the legislation intended to limit Philip's power" was due less to the inherent nature of a female sovereign than to Mary herself, who "repeatedly declined to exercise the independence of mind that the law had authorized." One letter from Mary will serve to illustrate her conception of her role as queen regnant. "Consider the miserable plight into which this country has now fallen," she wrote to Charles V in early 1555. Unless her husband Philip "comes to remedy matters . . . great danger will ensue from lack of a firm hand."[126] Perhaps the best analysis of Mary's inability to negotiate the relationship between her sex and her role as queen comes from her biographer Carolly Erickson:

> [Her father] was her benchmark of political power; beside him all other authority faded. Mary drew strength from the fact that she was Henry's daughter . . . and she was aware of having inherited his authority along with his throne and title. Yet everything she had been taught since childhood

robbed her of that strength and contradicted that authority. She had been trained to mistrust her judgment, fear her weakness, and feel shame for her sinfulness. She had never been taught to confront the world; instead her gaze had been turned inward, to focus on guarding her chastity and cultivating the gestures, expressions and tones of voice that symbolized it. . . . In short, Mary was now raised to a political status that conflicted with her sexual status at every turn. The interplay between the two was to form an inescapable backdrop to her troubled reign.[127]

When Elizabeth followed her half-sister on England's throne, she made yet another marital choice. She is as famous as her father for her marital adventures, but rather than his notoriety as a much-married king, she is recognized for her never-married status. A great deal has been written about the political and psychological motivations for her decision, and a great deal more about her use of her *potential* marriage as a political tool and her manipulation of her virginity as a political symbol.[128] Less has been said, however, about the precedents for her decision to remain unmarried.

If we look beyond Elizabeth I in sixteenth-century England, we will see a number of women whose status as unmarried women gave them access to political power. In her essay on women at the court of Charlemagne, for example, Janet Nelson questions whether the Holy Roman Emperor's court did not offer an early "case of monstrous regiment." Needing "their political help within the household and the court," Charlemagne decided that his daughters should have considerable political power—and that, with such power, they should remain unmarried. In Nelson's terms they "kept the keys of the inner doors: the keys of power," but as unmarried women they offered "no rivalry as potential heirs to formal power," nor did they have children "with claims to a share in rulership or patrimony." Even while they had considerable power, however, they had no authority, their positions "ancillary, dependent on their father and on his survival."[129]

Still, as John Carmi Parsons notes, "virginity or chastity in fact extended the power of many [women] from . . . exalted lineages."[130] Among them were Elvira Ramírez, the tenth-century regent of León. As a *devota*, a consecrated virgin, and the abbess of a monastery, she was regent for her nephew Ramiro III, who succeeded to the throne when he was five years old, preferred over the young king's mother, Teresa, a foreign-born queen.[131] Similarly, Pauline Stafford notes that the chronicler Goscelin claimed that English throne was offered to the royal nun Edith, daughter of King Edgar, after her brother Edward's death:

> The great men wanted to make her ruler, preferring a mature woman to an ignorant infant. They even offered their daughters to be consecrated nuns in exchange for her. Like Christ, Edith refuses a kingdom. The question is not

of Goscelin's historical accuracy—his is an unlikely interpretation of the 970s—but of his ability to think female rule was acceptable. He confronts the question squarely, and uses the unusual argument that many nations have been ruled by women. . . . In the Europe of the late tenth century this was indeed the case.[132]

Among those tenth-century female rulers was Matilda, the daughter of Adelheid of Burgundy and Otto I and the abbess of Quedlinburg. When her brother Otto II went to Italy, she acted as regent for him; a contemporary chronicler wrote that she governed "without female levity, using the skills of her talented ancestors and parents to restore the stubborn officials of barbarian kings to peace and obedience." The "skills" she used to "restore" peace and obedience included leading an army against the "barbarians." When the claims of her brother's son Otto III to succeed his father as Holy Roman Emperor were disputed, Matilda successfully fought off the challenge, "holding the empire together" with the aid of her mother, Adelheid, and sister-in-law, Theophano.[133]

Elizabeth Tudor's situation was, of course, quite different, but it is interesting to see that, like these earlier women, her virginity seemed integral to her ability to get and maintain her position. She succeeded where her half-sister and her cousin failed. A queen's foreign marriage offered many potential threats to political stability, as did a marriage to one of her subjects. Like her tenth-century foremothers, Elizabeth I effectively used her position as a "consecrated" virgin, committed to her country rather than to her religion, when she became queen. In Margaret King's words, her "heroic virginity" seemed "more in the pattern of the great saints than of a modern woman" and "set her apart from the other women of her realm."[134]

Elizabeth I's oration before the troops at Tilbury on 9 August 1588 is most often cited as an example of her ability to negotiate her sex and her role as queen. "I know I have the body but of a weak and feeble woman," she said, "but I have the heart and stomach of a king, and of a king of England, too."[135] Believing in her absolute authority, she nevertheless recognized her need as a woman to construct that authority. "One of the significant tasks, and in the end one of the major achievements of her reign," writes Patricia-Ann Lee, "entailed the creation of herself as a living icon of royal authority," a "persona" that "shaped her subjects' perception of her queenship" and that, in turn, was "shaped by her understanding of what they expected her to be."[136]

Among Elizabeth Tudor's earliest speeches to Parliament is one that that indicates, in Allison Heisch's words, her sense of her "identity as a monarch."[137] Only three days after Mary Tudor's death, the new queen addressed parliament, acknowedging at the outset the "weak" nature of woman. "My Lords," she began, "the law of nature moveth me to sorrow for my sister. The burden that is fallen upon me maketh me amazed." But she did not stop there. "And yet," she continued, "considering I am God's creature, ordained to obey his appointment, I will thereto yield, desiring from the bottom of my heart that I may have assistance of His Grace to be the minister of His heavenly will in this office now committed to me." She referred to her sex—"I am but one body naturally considered"—even while overcoming it—"though by His permission a body politic to govern."[138]

Unlike so many of Margaret Beaufort's descendants, Elizabeth Tudor saw that marriage was not an end in itself but a means to an end. It was a tool that could be used in getting and maintaining power, but it wasn't the only tool. Like her foremother, this daughter of Margaret Beaufort recognized that her success lay in fashioning a workable identity for herself. Since it wasn't possible for her to become queen, Margaret Beaufort had become "the king's mother"; since it wasn't safe for her to become a wife, Queen Elizabeth "married" England, becoming the "mother" of her people.

CHAPTER FOUR

THE DAUGHTERS OF
CATERINA SFORZA

Rulers and Regents in Italy

*Let Your Highness, I beg of you, keep a tranquil mind and attend
wholly to military affairs, for I intend to govern the state with the help
of these magnificent gentlemen and officials in such a manner that you
will suffer no wrong, and all that is possible will be done for the good of
your subjects. And if anyone should write or tell you of disorders of
which you have not heard from me, you may be certain that it is a lie,
because, since I not only give audience to officials but allow all your subjects to speak to me whenever they choose, no disturbance can arise without my knowledge.*

—Isabella d'Este, Marchioness and Regent
of Mantua, 30 June 1495[1]

While the various kingdoms, duchies, republics, city- states, and territories
of Italy did not allow women the kind of power and influence exercised
by English regents and queens, they nonetheless offered many opportunities
for women to play a variety of political roles. In the absence of a male heir,
a woman could inherit her father's title and transmit it to her husband or
children. As the only child of Filippo Maria Visconti, Bianca Maria could
therefore transfer her claim to Milan to her husband, who became the first
Sforza duke of Milan.[2] A woman could, of course, assume the role of regent
in the event of her father's or husband's absence or, following his death, for
her minor son. Thus Bona of Savoy claimed the title of regent of Milan for
her son Giangaleazzo, Caterina Sforza's half-brother, and Caterina herself
could claim the regency of Imola and Forlì for her son Ottaviano. We have
already discussed the precedents to whom Caterina could look as she

struggled to maintain power as regent of Imola and Forlì. Before we turn to our examination of the women who were to follow her, we will pause briefly to note several of her contemporaries.

When Giovanni III, king of Cyprus, died in 1458, he was succeeded on the throne by his daughter Carlotta of Lusignan. Carlotta did not rule Cyprus for long, however. By 1460 she had been deposed by her half-brother Giacomo, who had himself crowned in her place.[3] In an effort to gain support for his rule, the new king of Cyprus sought a political alliance through marriage and, turning to the republic of Venice, requested a bride. In response, the signory selected Caterina Cornaro, the daughter of Fiorenza Crispo and Marco Cornaro, who, interestingly, "happened to hold most of the island of Cyprus in mortgage."[4] On 30 July 1468 the betrothal of the fourteen-year-old Caterina to Giacomo was celebrated by proxy in Venice.

But Caterina did not travel immediately to Cyprus to meet her new husband; instead, she remained in Venice for four years more years. In the mean time, Giacomo seems to have considered carefully other possible marital alliances, most notably the suggestion of Ferdinand of Naples that the king of Cyprus marry *his* daughter, but Giacomo hesitated and was eventually persuaded to accept the marriage he had already negotiated. In 1472 Caterina finally left for Cyprus, where her marriage to Giacomo was formalized. Within the year he died, leaving his wife, then pregnant, to succeed him.

Immediately after her husband's death, Caterina acted to preserve Cyprus for her unborn child. A regency council was established, and Caterina, recognizing that "her throne was on a volcano" (*stava apicato a un chavelo*), sent word of Giacomo's death to Venice, which responded by sending troops to Cyprus to protect the young queen.[5] Meanwhile, on learning of the situation in Cyprus, Carlotta of Lusignan, who had taken refuge in Rome after Giacomo's usurpation, prepared to reassert her claim to the throne. Her supporters forced their way into the Lusignan palace, killing several members of Caterina's household, including her uncle and cousin, but the queen herself escaped. When Venetian troops arrived, the conspirators were hunted down and order was restored. On 28 August 1473, the queen of Cyprus gave birth to a son, who was baptized Giacomo III on 26 September 1473.

But the son for whom Caterina struggled to preserve the crown of Cyprus died in 1474, just a year old, and once again Carlotta of Lusignan conspired to effect her rival's overthrow, this time with the aid of Ferdinand of Naples. In response, the republic of Venice sent Caterina's father and mother to Cyprus and ordered that Giacomo's mother, sister, and illegitimate son be sent to Venice. Denied motherhood, Caterina seems to have turned her energies to sovereignty, supported by her subjects: she "recalled

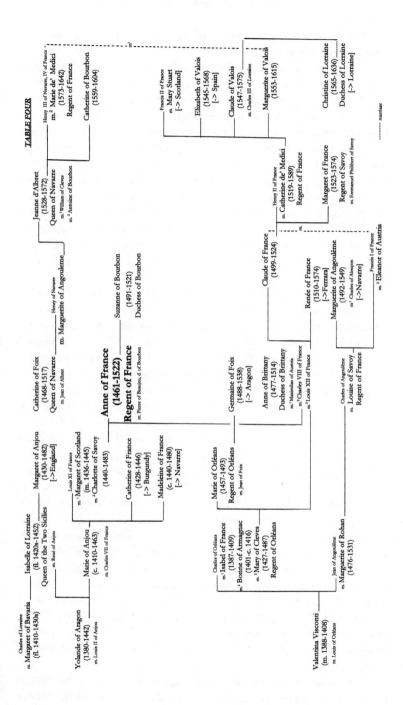

TABLE FOUR

Charles of Lorraine
m. Margaret of Bavaria
(fl. 1410-1430s)

Isabelle of Lorraine
(fl. 1420s-1452)
Queen of the Two Sicilies
m. René of Anjou

Margaret of Anjou
(1430-1482)
[-> England]

Catherine of Foix
(1468-1517)
Queen of Navarre
m. Jean of Albret

Jeanne d'Albret
(1528-1572)
Queen of Navarre
m.¹ William of Cleves
m.² Antoine of Bourbon

Henry III of Navarre, IV of France
m.² Marie de' Medici
(1573-1642)
Regent of France

Yolande of Aragon
(1380-1442)
m. Louis II of Anjou

Marie of Anjou
(c. 1410-1463)
m. Charles VII of France

Louis XI of France
m.¹ Margaret of Scotland (m. 1436-1445)
m.² Charlotte of Savoy
(1440-1483)

Catherine of France
(1428-1446)
[-> Burgundy]

Madeleine of France
(c. 1440-1480)
[-> Navarre]

Henry of Navarre
m. Marguerite of Angoulême

Suzanne of Bourbon
(1491-1521)
Duchess of Bourbon

Catherine of Bourbon
(1559-1604)

**Anne of France
(1461-1522)
Regent of France**
m. Pierre of Beaujeu, d. of Bourbon

Germaine of Foix
(1488-1538)
[-> Aragon]

Anne of Brittany
(1477-1514)
Duchess of Brittany
m.¹ Maximilian of Austria
m.² Charles VIII of France
m.³ Louis XII of France

Marie of Orléans
(1457-1493)
Regent of Orléans
m. Jean of Foix

Claude of France
(1499-1524)

Henry II of France
m. Catherine de' Medici
(1519-1589)
Regent of France

Francis II of France
m. Mary Stuart
[-> Scotland]

Elizabeth of Valois
(1545-1568)
[-> Spain]

Claude of Valois
(1547-1575)
m. Charles III of Lorraine

Marguerite of Valois
(1553-1615)

Margaret of France
(1523-1574)
Regent of Savoy
m. Emmanuel Philibert of Savoy

Christine of Lorraine
(1565-1636)
Duchess of Lorraine
[-> Lorraine]

Renée of France
(1510-1574)
[->Ferrara]

Marguerite of Angoulême
(1492-1549)
m.¹ Charles of Alençon
[->Navarre]

Charles of Angoulême
m. Louise of Savoy
Regent of France

Francis I of France
m.² Eleanor of Austria

Charles of Orléans
m.¹ Isabel of France
(1387-1409)
m.² Bonne of Armagnac
(1401-c. 1416)
m.³ Mary of Cleves
(1427-1487)
Regent of Orléans

Jean of Angoulême
m. Marguerite of Rohan
(1476-1531)

Valentina Visconti
(m. 1388-1408)
m. Louis of Orléans

- - - - - marriage

to [them] those memories of independence which flattered their pride," a contemporary commented.[6]

The counselors and commissioners sent from Venice inexorably assumed more and more power in Cyprus. Caterina protested to the doge, complaining, for example, that one of the Venetian envoys "without respect or reverence would enter her chamber when he would."[7] Even her brother was won over by those who sought to relieve Caterina of her crown; pressure was exerted to convince her that the best course of action for her was to abdicate. Finally, in 1489, "the unhappy lady yielded . . . to persuasion and threats." Her decision to abdicate her throne was described by a Venetian ambassador as having been made as a result of "full and free determination."[8] She returned to Venice and was "freed" from the rule of Cyprus in a formal ceremony; in return, she was awarded the castle and town of Asolo. She took possession of her new "kingdom" on 11 October 1489, just as Caterina Sforza was consolidating her position as regent of Imola and Forlì.

"We cannot tell whether the exiled Queen of Cyprus was really satisfied with her mimic Court, her empty title," muses historian Marian Andrews, "or whether, like a wise woman, she made the best of that which was within her reach, and ceased to sigh for the unattainable."[9] What we do know is that she governed Asolo efficiently for nearly twenty years. Though her "kingdom" was limited, Caterina Cornaro dispensed justice, founded charitable institutions, patronized artists, welcomed intellectuals, and was loved by her "subjects." At last, when the combined forces of the Holy Roman Empire, France, and Spain invaded Italy and threatened Asolo, she was forced to return to Venice. She died there on 10 July 1510 and was buried the next day in the Cornaro chapel.

Among the many visitors to Asolo during Caterina Cornaro's residence there was Isabella d'Este, yet another of Caterina Sforza's contemporaries. Renowned as "the first lady of the world" (*la prima donna del mondo*), Isabella was the daughter of Eleanora of Aragon and Ercole d'Este, duke of Ferrara, the granddaughter of that Ferdinand of Naples who had attempted to lure Giacomo of Cyprus away from his Venetian bride.[10] In 1480 Isabella, not yet six years old, was betrothed to Francesco Gonzaga, son and heir of the marquis of Mantua. Just days after this alliance was negotiated, Bona of Savoy and her brother-in-law Ludovico Sforza travelled from Milan to the court of Ferrara hoping to arrange Ludovico's marriage to Isabella. Disappointed of their original objective, they accepted Isabella's younger sister Beatrice instead. On 28 May the betrothals of both girls were publicly proclaimed.

As the sister-in-law of Ludovico Sforza, Isabella d'Este was thus related to Caterina Sforza by marriage, but she was also related to the *Madonna* of

Imola and Forlì by circumstance and vocation as well. As the wife of Francesco Gonzaga, whom she married in 1490, she came to play an important role in Italian politics. Like Caterina Sforza's cities, Mantua was strategically located; it lay between the rival cities Milan and Venice, and good relations with both were critical. Within a year of her marriage, Isabella found herself entrusted with the government of Mantua during her husband's absence; among the responsibilities she assumed was maintaining good relationships with both of her powerful neighbors. In addition, she faced the usual task of producing an heir; by the end of 1492, in addition to her administration of Mantua, she had given birth to a child, but rather than the desired son, the baby was a girl. "You will have heard that I have a daughter," she wrote to her sister Beatrice in Milan, "and that both she and I are doing well, although I am sorry not to have a son."[11]

Isabella was called upon again in Mantua when her husband, as captain-general of the Venetian army, joined the combined forces of Spain, England, and the Holy Roman Empire determined to drive the invading French out of Naples. According to her biographer Julia Cartwright, "she took up the reigns of government . . . and administered affairs with a prudence and sagacity which excited the wonders of grey-haired councillors."[12]

After Charles VIII retreated from Naples, Francesco returned briefly to Mantua, but by January of 1496 he was once more in command of the Venetian army, leaving Isabella again in control. To improve her understanding of affairs of state, she added architecture, agriculture, and industry to her ongoing humanist studies.[13] During her husband's absence she also gave birth to her second child, another daughter, in July; again, she was disappointed, more disappointed than her husband, who assured her that sons would follow but that, in the meantime, "if ever a father had reason to be satisfied with his daughters, it was he."[14]

Despite his eight years of service to Venice, Francesco Gonzaga was dismissed from his position as captain-general in 1497, ostensibly for his French sympathies. In an effort to regain his position, he offered to surrender his wife and children to Venice as hostages, but his offer was rejected. Aside from the insult to her husband, Isabella suffered another loss as well, with the death of her young sister Beatrice, Ludovico Sforza's wife. Isabella set about reconciling her husband and her brother-in-law, and when Charles VIII died in 1498 and Louis XII announced his intention of pursuing his claim to the duchy of Milan, their reconciliation seemed inevitable.[15] Under this threat, Ludovico Sforza renewed his alliance with the Holy Roman Empire, and Francesco Gonzaga was offered military command of their combined forces, a post he ultimately accepted despite his hope to regain his position of captain-general of Venice, which had allied itself with the French. In 1499 the French invaded, and Lodovico Sforza was forced out of Milan.[16] Francesco Gonzaga immediately offered his services to Louis XII, though Isabella persisted in her allegiance to her sister's husband and offered refuge to Milanese fleeing the French. After Ludovico's capture by the French in 1500 at the battle of Novara, she turned her attention to cultivating the victors.

Within a month of Ludovico's defeat, Isabella gave birth to a son, Federico, and his birth gave the marchioness and her husband an opportunity to make a conciliatory gesture to the French. Accordingly, Cesare Borgia, who had defeated and brutalized the defiant Caterina Sforza in 1499, was solicited by Isabella d'Este to act as one of her son's godfathers.[17] As Cesare continued his conquests in Italy, Isabella grudgingly welcomed his sister Lucrezia as her brother's bride and, once more governing Mantua on her husband's behalf, negotiated with Cesare over the betrothal of her son Federico to Cesare's daughter.[18]

In her letters she also kept her husband advised about political matters. "I cannot conceal my fears for your person and state," she wrote while Francesco was with Louis XII in Milan:

> There is a report here—whether it has come from Milan by letter or word of mouth, I do not know—that Your Excellency has spoken angry words against [Cesare Borgia] before the Most Christian King [Louis] and the Pope's servants, and whether this is true or not, they will doubtless reach the ears of [Cesare], who, having already shown that he does not scruple to conspire against those of his own blood, will, I am certain, not hesitate to plot against your person.

Warning her husband that his "natural goodness" led him to "take no precautions" for his "safety," she urged him to guard against poison—if not for his own sake, then for hers and "that of our little son." She closed her letter with a postscript: "My dearest lord, do not laugh at my fears and say that women are cowards and always afraid, because *their* malignity is far greater than my fears and your own courage."[19]

But the situation in Italy shifted radically after the death of Pope Alexander VI in August of 1503. His son Cesare Borgia lost his Italian conquests almost as quickly as he had gained them.[20] Isabella, meanwhile, remained in Mantua, still acting as regent for Francesco, who fought first for Julius II, leading the papal army against Bologna, and then for Louis XII, helping conduct the siege of Genoa. Isabella herself was invited to France in 1507 by Louis and Anne of Brittany; despite her renowned love of travel, it was a trip she could not take. As Cartwright notes, Isabella's continued presence in Mantua was "urgently required" during Francesco's absences.[21] Her role became even more critical when the pope and the

French king combined forces in 1508 to attack Venice. Francesco was part of the defeat of Venice at the battle of Cannae on 14 May, but on 9 August he was taken prisoner.

When Louis XII and Maximilian asked her to send her son Federico as a hostage, in exchange for her husband's freedom, Isabella replied in a way that makes for a sharp contrast between the regent of Mantua and the regent of Imola and Forlì:

> As to the demand for our dearest first-born son Federico, besides being a cruel and almost inhuman thing for any one who knows the meaning of a mother's love, there are many causes which render it difficult and impossible. Although we are quite sure that his person would be well cared for and protected by His Majesty, how could we wish him to run the risk of this long and difficult journey, putting aside the child's tender and delicate age? And you must know what comfort and solace, in his father's present unhappy condition, we find in the presence of this dear son, the hope and joy of all our people and subjects. To deprive us of him would be to deprive us of life itself, and of all we count good and precious. If you take Federico away you might as well take away our life and state at once; . . . we will suffer any loss rather than part from our son, and this you may take to be our deliberate and unchanging resolution.[22]

Despite his mother's "deliberate and unchanging resolution," Federico became a hostage for his father's good behavior after all. Julius II eventually negotiated Francesco Gonzaga's release on 10 July 1510 on the condition that Federico be sent to Rome, where he would be the hostage of the pope instead of the Republic of Venice. Isabella's son became a papal favorite, accompanying Julius II everywhere; "O Madonna!" one of Isabella's correspondents wrote from Rome, "you have indeed a rare son, and I think you will find more comfort in him than in anything else in the world."[23]

His imprisonment had taken a toll on Francesco Gonzaga's health, and he was forced to give up his military career, retiring to Mantua, where, as Cartwright indicates, "he depended more and more on his wife" who had an increasingly large part "in the management of public affairs." Isabella's Latin teacher, Mario Equicola, wrote to her brother that "everything is referred to Madonna, and not a leaf is allowed to stir without her knowledge and consent."[24] Beyond Mantua, Isabella attempted to effect the reconciliation of her brother, the duke of Ferrara, to Julius II. When that effort failed and the threat of war loomed again, a "congress" met in Mantua in 1512, where Isabella "displayed her usual tact and ability in the conduct of negotiations"; she knew, "above all, how to govern others without ever allowing her influence to appear."[25]

While her husband remained in Mantua over the course of the next few years, Isabella travelled widely throughout Italy, visiting Milan, Rome, and Naples. She returned to Mantua by the end of 1518, however, as Francesco grew increasingly ill. On the morning of 29 March 1519, he drew up a will naming Federico as his successor, with Isabella to act as his "guardian and advisor" until the young man reached the age of twenty-two; he died late the same day. When Pope Leo X considered making the twenty-year-old Federico his captain-general in 1520, he hesitated, wondering how Mantua could be governed in the young man's absence. The answer, of course, was Isabella, who governed Mantua after her son took up his new position. Once Federico returned to Mantua and took up the administration of his state "in his own right," he "rarely referred things to her or asked her advice."[26]

No longer needed in Mantua, Isabella decided to travel; she was in Rome, for instance, when it was sacked by imperial troops in 1527. She had fortified the Palazza Colonna, where she was in residence, offering shelter and protection to ambassadors from Mantua, Ferrara, Urbino, and Venice. It was, one biographer notes, "almost the only building in all of Rome to escape serious damage in the terrible sack."[27] In 1528 she was in Ferrara for the marriage of her nephew Ercole to Renée of France, Louis XII's daughter, and in 1529 she travelled to Bologna for the meeting between Pope Clement and the newly elected Holy Roman Emperor, Charles V. She was there for more than the spectacle of the emperor's coronation, however: she intended "to promote the interests of the Gonzaga family," "to help her brother Alfonso in his effort to keep Ferrara an Este duchy," and to "use her influence to have her nephew Francesco Sforza confirmed in his Milan duchy."[28] Her efforts were successful, and the new emperor travelled to Mantua immediately following the events in Bologna; there, on 8 April, he changed the status of Mantua, creating a new duchy, and Isabella d'Este's son became the first duke of Mantua.

With this success, mother and son were reunited, and when Federico travelled to Montferrat in 1531, where his marriage to Margherita di Montferrat was celebrated, Isabella "once more administered the State in her son's absence." This was the last occasion she took "any active part in public affairs," her biographer Julia Cartwright notes.[29] Isabella continued to travel, as her health permitted, with one last visit to Ferrara in 1538, her birthplace, before her death on 13 February 1539.

Isabella d'Este is more widely known today for the humanist intellectuals she collected at Mantua and for her patronage of artists like Mantegna, da Vinci, and Raphael than for her political role. Her sister-in-law, Lucrezia Borgia, is also rather well known, having earned a notoriety that rivals that of her contemporary Caterina Sforza, to whom Lucrezia was related by her first marriage. Accused of poisoning her husband and of incest with both father and brother, she was probably guilty of neither.[30] Less well known, she too played a notable role in Italian politics.

Lucrezia Borgia was the daughter of Cardinal Rodrigo Borgia, later Pope Alexander VI, and his mistress Vanozza Cattanei. Born in April 1480, she was raised in Rome, but her father looked to his native Spain for her future, arranging her betrothal in 1491 to Don Juan de Centelles, lord of Val D'Agora in Valencia, and then, when the first contract was annulled, to Don Gaspare d'Aversa, who was also living in Valencia. But that betrothal was also broken when, after his election as pope in 1492, her father arranged for her marriage to Giovanni Sforza; their marriage was celebrated on 12 June 1493.[31]

Unsettled by Charles VIII's threatened invasion of Italy and by "Vatican intrigues," the bridegroom left Rome after his marriage and returned, without his bride, to Pesaro for the summer and fall. But Giovanni returned to Rome in November, "seduced by the prospect" of his thirteen-year-old bride's dowry.[32] In 1494 Lucrezia finally left Rome for Pesaro, where she was living when Charles VIII's threatened invasion became a reality. She returned to Rome in the autumn of 1495; having become "expert at court life," she "played hostess" there for her father. But in the changed world of Italian politics, Alexander VI no longer had need of a Sforza alliance, and he decided that Lucrezia's marriage should be annulled on the basis of nonconsummation.

Giovanni angrily rejected the annullment, implying as it did his impotence, and appealed to his uncle Ludovico Sforza for aid. Ludovico was in need of papal support as he fought against Charles VIII, and, fearful that he could lose Milan to the French, proposed a test for Giovanni—he could prove the validity of his marriage if he consummated it, publicly, in the presence of members of both the Borgia and Sforza families. After Giovanni rejected this proposal, Ludovico then suggested that Giovanni prove his virility in front of just one person, but again the proposal was angrily refused. Giovanni, for his part, reminded the pope and his uncle that his first wife, Maddalena Gonzaga, had died in childbirth; under those circumstances, he argued, there could be little question of his ability to consummate a marriage. He charged that Alexander wanted to dissolve the marriage because Alexander wanted his daughter for himself. Giovanni's angry charge of incest was, as Ivan Cloulas notes, "almost certainly untrue," but it has become an indelible part of the Lucrezia's unsavory reputation nonetheless. Even while he indicates that there is no evidence to support such a charge, Cloulas, as only one example, says that Sforza's "outrageous accusation" was not "conjured . . . out of the blue." The "outrageous charge," he believes, arose out of the "shows of affection" between the pope and Lucrezia and between Cesare and his sister.[33]

Failing such "shows of affection" to members of her family, a woman like Caterina Sforza or, as we shall see, Jeanne of Navarre could be constructed as an unwomanly monster, but, as we have seen with Margaret Beaufort, as we see here in the case of Lucrezia Borgia, and as we will see in the next chapter, intimate and loving "shows of affection" could also be used against a woman, raising the suggestion of "neurotic" and "obsessive" attachment or even incest. However "outrageous" such "accusations" and suggestions, they nevertheless remain part of each woman's story. Thus Cloulas, even while dismissing incest, nevertheless incorporates it into his story of Lucrezia Borgia.

Alexander, instead of expressing outrage at his son-in-law's "outrageous accusation," replied to Giovanni in "letters full of consideration" for the young man's "honorable" reputation: "Giovanni would only have to claim a momentary physical deficiency caused by an evil spell." Or, he could agree to the annullment by claiming that his marriage was invalid because of Lucrezia's previous betrothals.[34] Giovanni agreed to have the legality of his marriage examined, but a commission charged with the investigation found no irregularities, despite Alexander VI's obvious desire to have them found. The only remaining argument was nonconsummation, and under pressure from his uncle Ludovico and with financial inducements from the pope, Giovanni Sforza finally agreed. On 18 November 1497 he signed a "confession" of impotence, and on 22 December Lucrezia Borgia's first marriage was formally annulled. She was declared to be *intacta*, that is, a virgin.

Several new alliances were immediately suggested for her, including one with Ottaviano Sforza, Caterina's son. But on 29 June 1498 she was married by proxy to Alfonso of Aragon, the illegitimate son of Alfonso II, king of Naples, who made his son duke of Bisceglie. The formal ceremony took place in Rome in July.[35] When Alexander VI and his son allied themselves with the French, who planned to invade Naples, Alfonso left Rome without his wife. Shortly thereafter, Alexander VI appointed his daughter governor of Spoleto and Foligno, "an important office usually reserved for cardinals and prelates."[36]

Just nineteen years old, Lucrezia was no "figurehead"; as Cloulas notes, she "threw herself into her task," taking "great pains" to "administer the city well." Apparently reassured of his father-in-law's intentions, Alfonso reclaimed his wife, and the two returned to Rome, where Lucrezia gave birth to a son, whom she named Rodrigo after her father. In July of 1500 Alfonso was attacked by assassins in Rome. As he did not die (Lucrezia's ministrations are credited with his recovery), on 18 August he was strangled in his bed, probably under Cesare Borgia's orders. Lucrezia was dismissed from Rome, her letters from this period signed *La Infelicissima*—"the most unhappy of ladies."[37]

By July of 1501 Louis XII of France and Ferdinand of Aragon had defeated Naples. While her father campaigned in Italy, Lucrezia returned to Rome to administer his affairs.[38] But Lucrezia's remarriage could provide her father another political ally, and so a third husband was found for her, Alfonso d'Este, Isabella d'Este's brother, son and heir to the duke of Ferrara. After initially opposing the alliance, the duke was compelled to agree. Lucrezia and Alfonso d'Este were married on 30 December 1501. Contemporary accounts of Lucrezia, just twenty-one years old at the time of her third marriage, counter the more salacious and vicious gossip that still surrounds her name. Her new sister-in-law viewed Lucrezia with suspicion; nevertheless, Isabella d'Este's agent reported to her that Lucrezia was "full of charm and grace," and one of Isabella's ladies-in-waiting, too, grudgingly admitted that if Lucrezia "is not noticeably beautiful, she stands out thanks to the sweetness of her expression." A chronicler in Ferrara reported, "She is full of tact, prudent, intelligent, animated, pleasing, very amiable. . . . Her quick mind makes her eyes sparkle."[39]

Despite d'Este fears and Isabella's suspicions, Lucrezia proved, in Carwright's words, "an excellent wife to Alfonso." She bore her husband four children, including his son and heir Ercole, who succeeded his father as duke of Ferrara in 1534. After Alexander VI's death, Lucrezia no longer played a political role in Italy, but she "edified the people of Ferrara by the charitable institutions which she founded," and, like her sister-in-law's court at Mantua, Ferrara became a center for artists and intellectuals.[40] She died on 24 June 1519, just thirty-nine years old.

Before we move on to discuss the powerful women who were to follow Caterina Sforza, we should note two more of her contemporaries. While neither played the kind of political role in Italy that Caterina Cornaro or Lucrezia Borgia did, each nonetheless contributed in her own way to the story of women and power in Italy.

Bianca Maria Sforza became the wife of the widowed Maximilian of Austria in 1493.[41] Maximilian's first wife, Mary of Burgundy, had died in 1482, and his second "wife," Anne of Brittany, had renounced her proxy marriage to Maximilian and married Charles VIII of France instead.[42] Thus Maximilian was available when Ludovico Sforza, in need of an imperial alliance, offered his niece and an immense dowry; by the time of their marriage, celebrated on 30 November, Bianca Maria's husband had become Holy Roman Emperor.[43]

Bianca Maria arrived in Innsbruck on 23 December, but her husband was in Vienna, and he did not bother to greet his new wife until 9 March. When they did meet, Maximilian decided that Bianca Maria, while "as fair" as Mary of Burgundy, was "inferior in wisdom and good sense," though she "might improve in time." He seems to have decided rather quickly that Bianca Maria wouldn't, after all, improve; he complained of her extravagance, her "foolish tricks," and her passionate friendship for one of her ladies, Violante Caimi. Then he virtually abandoned his empress, leaving her behind in Innsbruck.[44] Bianca Maria nevertheless was to prove a strong ally to her uncle. She gave Ludovico Sforza "hospitable welcome" at her castle in Innsbruck when he was forced to flee Milan in 1499, and after his ultimate defeat and capture, she raised and educated his two sons, Maximilian and Francesco.[45]

A similar role is played by another of Caterina Sforza's contemporaries, Lucrezia de' Medici, a cousin by marriage.[46] The wife of Jacopo Salviati, whom she wed in 1488, Lucrezia was allowed to remain in Florence after her family was exiled in 1494. In working ceaselessly for the restoration of the Medici, she became "one of the leading conspirators on her family's behalf."[47] After her brother Giovanni became Pope Leo X, she moved to Rome, where she exerted considerable influence, promoting a series of protégés and receiving numerous benefits. She had eleven children of her own, in addition to which, by the terms of Caterina Sforza's will, she became the guardian of Caterina's son, Giovanni di Giovanni de' Medici.[48] While Lucrezia's husband "could never control the precociously headstrong" child, the "tougher" Lucrezia "gradually came to acquire an influence over Giovanni that she never lost." The "terrifying youth" became the famed soldier popularly known as Giovanni delle Bande Nere.[49] In 1516 he married Lucrezia's daughter Maria Salviati; we will encounter both mother and daughter again.

Among the "daughters" of Caterina Sforza who exerted their influence in the generations following the death of the *Madonna* of Imola and Forlì was her niece Bona, named after her grandmother Bona of Savoy.[50] Raised at the brilliant Renaissance court of Milan, Bona Sforza was well educated, her studies including the discipline of statecraft as well as languages, literature, and music, more traditional occupations for women. In 1518 the Emperor Maximilian, the long-standing ally of Milan who had married the unfortunate Bianca Maria Sforza, arranged the young woman's marriage to Sigismund, the king of Poland; the formal wedding ceremony and coronation took place in Naples on 18 April 1518.[51]

Bona proved a more successful wife, mother, and politician than her aunt Bianca Maria had been. As a wife and mother, she promptly bore her husband six children. As a politician, Bona proved herself skillful in maintaining good relations with the contending European powers:

Bona desired to keep a hold on Italy, north and south. In the north, we have noted her connection with Milan. In the south she was the duchess of Bari and granddaughter of the duke of Rossano and lord of Naples. To keep a hold on Milan she would have to stand in with France. . . . To retain a hold in the south required the good graces of Spain and the Hapsburgs, for, although Naples was not ruled from Madrid, her rulers were Spaniards. The favor of the papacy was also requisite, for without it no power survived long in that region.

Bona was able to manipulate this "unstable balance" of powers to Poland's advantage by her "adroit and even devious diplomacy."[52]

Nor did she ignore domestic politics, where her aim was to strengthen royal power. Thus "she undertook to make Poland a centralized national state in accord with the pattern emerging in Spain, France and England," working to check and balance "the power of the lords, lay and clerical."[53] She handled the appointment of bishops (with papal permission and her husband's consent), undertook agricultural reform, regained crown lands that had been granted to the nobility, and arranged for her ten-year-old son to be crowned king during his father's lifetime. She began a vast building program, provided for mercenary armies, and arranged a series of politically advantageous marriages for her children.[54] Along the way she enriched herself as well as the royal treasury, which drew criticism, though her efforts "to relieve Poland by bringing in the revenues from her Italian estates" drew no praise.[55]

As her husband's health failed, Bona Sforza "became the real ruler of Poland," and whatever criticism she endured in her own day, her achievements have been recognized by some modern historians:

> Bona exerted a powerful influence on the form of the modern Polish state not only by reason of her intellectual gifts but even more because she possessed a profound feeling for the essential needs of the state. She fused completely the foreign Italian strand with the emerging Polish national movement. In the social and economic sphere she aspired through her excellent reforms to create a strong authority based on just distribution of goods. In many respects Bona was ahead of her times and that was the tragedy of her life.[56]

The "tragedy" of her life occured after her husband's death, when Bona's son Sigismund Augustus, now king of Poland, rejected the political marriage his mother had arranged for him with Anne of Ferrara, daughter of the duke of Ferrara and his wife Renée, the daughter of Louis XII of France. Sigismund preferred Barbara Radziwill, daughter of a Lithuanian noble, whom he married secretly in 1547.[57] Bona was not the only one to object to her son's marriage; the Polish diet insisted that Sigismund repudiate his bride, but at length, in the face of Sigismund's insistence, they accepted her. Barbara died shortly and childless in 1551, and although Bona had reconciled herself to her daughter-in-law, she was suspected of having poisoned her.[58]

Bona was not reconciled to her son, however, and she decided to return to her Italian duchy of Bari for health reasons, as she claimed. Her son opposed her departure from Poland. "She wants to get back to Italy just to get her hands on all the properties of Bari, Rossano and Naples and to cut me off from my rightful inheritance from my grandmother," he objected, adding that as queen dowager she "should not be permitted to leave" Poland, even if it meant she should be imprisoned—"though it would grieve" him "greatly." It would, after all, be a "genteel incarceration."[59] But the Polish diet agreed that Bona should be allowed to go, and she left Poland in November of 1556, nearly forty years after her marriage in 1518. Her return to Italy gave her no peace, however. Philip II of Spain, having defeated the French in Italy, was determined that she should cede to him her claims in Naples and "appropriated" much of the income from her estates. She died in poverty in 1557 and was buried in Bari.

Despite her talents and abilities, Bona Sforza was resented in Poland, viewed with a mixture of dislike and suspicion. Roland Bainton's assessment of her sounds a note that is by now very familiar:

> Bona had several counts against her. She was a woman. Of course a woman could exert a powerful influence. Witness Isabella in Spain and Elizabeth in England. But Bona was resented in Poland, when as the old king grew enfeebled, she usurped authority, not only from him but also from the nobles. . . . A further count was that she was not Polish. Isabella was Castillian and Elizabeth an English Tudor. Italianism, was, to be sure, for a period very much the vogue in Cracow. At the same time many Poles resented the Italians and especially one reared in the atmosphere of the political intrigue characteristic of the despots of the Italian Renaissance. . . . Added to all this was her manner. Tomicki, her most faithful chancellor, confided to a complainer that the queen was imperious, blustering and badgering. Sometimes she was brutal. When a blind archbishop stood in her way she told him she wished he had lost not only his eyes but his tongue. Her yoke chafed.[60]

Before moving on in our discussion of the "daughters" of Caterina Sforza, we will pause to note one of Bona Sforza's contemporaries, Renée of France, whose life parallels Bona's in many ways and intersects with hers in another. We have already noted the moment when the lives of the two women intersected: Bona Sforza had arranged for the marriage of her son, Sigismund Augustus, to Renée's daughter, Anne.

The parallels with Bona Sforza are apparent in this brief outline of Renée's life.

The younger daughter of Louis XII of France and Anne of Brittany, Renée was married to Lucrezia Borgia's son Ercole d'Este in 1528.[61] Renée's "Italian career" as the duchess of Ferrara was a disaster, husband and wife mismatched in the extreme. Renée remained French in her language and sympathy, and her slowness in acquiring "even a rudimentary knowledge" of Italian "remained steadily against her, keeping her, apart from any other consideration, a very isolated person in her own establishment." She "persistently refused to identify herself with her husband's interests," clinging "with stupid pathos" even to the French manner of dress.[62]

Thus isolated, Renée turned to other pursuits, and her court at Ferrara became a safe haven for intellectuals like Olympia Morata, Vittoria Colonna, and the French poet Clément Marot, and a refuge for French Huguenots.[63] John Calvin visited Renée's court in 1536, and under his influence she was converted in 1540. In retaliation, Ercole dismissed and imprisoned members of his wife's household staff. Although she had been granted exemptions by Pope Paul III in 1543, in 1554 she was brought before the Inquisition by Julius II. Ercole separated his wife from her children and imprisoned her. "We kept her shut up for fifteen days, with only people who had no sort of Lutheran tendencies to wait upon her," he wrote, adding, "We also threatened to confiscate all her property."[64] In spite of all the pressures, Renée withstood her examination by the Inquisition, and a formal sentence was passed against her. She was condemned for heresy and again imprisoned by Ercole. A week later, she recanted, however, and those she had formerly befriended did not befriend her. Calvin's response was shocked: "What shall I say, except that constancy is a very rare virtue among the great of this world?" Olympia Morata said she was not surprised by the recantation, since she had always believed Renée's was a weak mind (une tête legère).[65]

Renée lived apart from her husband after her release. In 1559, after her husband's death and estranged from her son Alfonso, she returned to France after thirty years in Ferrara, settling on her estates near Montargis. During the wars of religion that raged after her return, she was besieged by her son-in-law Francis, duke of Guise. When he threatened to destroy the walls of her fortress, Renée proved herself something of a true "daughter" of Caterina Sforza when she replied that "she would herself mount the battlements and see if he dare kill a King's daughter."[66]

Renée and Montargis withstood the siege, and in the religious persecution that followed, she offered a haven to French Huguenots "to her own constant peril." Under the circumstances, John Calvin, who seems to have been as "inconstant" as the woman whose inconstancy he had bewailed, resumed his friendship with Renée, and his correspondence to her indicates his recognition at last of her courage. This courage led her to write "imploring letters" to her son in 1569, protesting his persecution of those suspected of following reformed religion and to providing a haven for Huguenots again in the same year. But her son ignored her pleas, and, under threat, she was forced to send away those who had come to her for protection. She reportedly told the king's envoy that "if she had his sword in her hands, he would deserve to die, as a messenger of death."[67]

Both her son and the French king attempted to take control of Renée's income and possessions. Her daughter Anne, by then wife of the duke of Nemours, recovered a document by which Louis XII, Renée's father, had given her a claim to her mother's independent Brittany, which she was forced to cede; "little by little," as one biographer notes, "all her lands were being taken from her":

> Gisors and Vernon were given to the Duc d'Alençon, Caen and Falaise had been seized by Alfonso [her son] for debts, Chartres and Montargis were to belong to the Duchess of Nemours [her daughter Anna], but Renée was suffered to remain as a pensioner in her own castle. Her son Alfonso was furious and wrote the most bitter letters to his mother, whom he never forgave, for yielding any possible claim to [Brittany].[68]

In 1572 Renée was in Paris for the marriage of Henry of Navarre and Marguerite of Angoulême. Lodging with her daughter Anne, whose Catholic husband was the duke of Nemours, Renée escaped the bloodbath of the St. Bartholomew massacre. She was escorted back to Montargis, all Huguenot services forbidden. There, "broken in health and spirit," she "ruled her great castle . . . in lonely state," "neglected and forgotten by her sons and daughters, on whom she had bestowed all that remained of her possessions." She dictated her last will and testament just before her death on 2 July 1574. In proudly listing her titles, she contrasted the state to which she had fallen with the state she had been born and raised to occupy:

> We, Renée of France, Duchess of Chartres, Countess of Gisors, Lady of Montargis, widow and dowager of the late Monseigneur of good memory Ercole II of Ferrara, Daughter of the lady King Louis XII and the late Queen Anne, Duchess of Brétagne.[69]

Also deeply influenced by the reformed religion was Caterina Cibo, a "daughter" of Caterina Sforza in more ways than one. Her mother was Maddelena de' Medici, the younger sister of that Lucrezia de' Medici who was the guardian of Caterina Sforza's son. But, as "one of the famous 'warrior women' of Italy," Caterina Cibo can also been seen as "a rival of her name-sake Caterina Sforza, the lady of Forli."[70] Born near Florence in 1501, Caterina Cibo was the daughter of Franceschetto Cibo, whose brother was Pope Innocent VIII. Her mother Maddalena also had important papal connections; she was the niece of Clement VII and the sister of Innocent X.[71] As a girl Caterina was well educated in Rome, learning Latin, Greek, and Hebrew. At the age of twelve she was betrothed to Giovanni Maria Varano, heir to Camerino, a tiny principality in the Umbrian marches, not too far from Assisi. By the time she was married in 1520, her husband had become duke of Camerino, though his succession was challenged by his nephew. In 1523 the young wife gave birth to a daughter, but because affairs remained unsettled in Camerino, she preferred Rome, where Clement VII had become pope. By 1527, however, her husband had died, and Caterina, who succeeded him, returned to Camerino.[72]

There she was attacked and imprisoned by her husband's illegitimate son Rodolfo Varano. Another period of turmoil ensued, involving Francesco Maria della Rovere, the duke of Urbino, whom Clement VII solicited in support of his niece. Peace was restored, and Caterina's daughter Giulia was betrothed to Guidobaldo, the duke of Urbino's son. But after Clement's death an attempt was again made to wrest control of Camerino from Caterina, this time by another member of the Varano family, Matteo. On 13 April 1534 he entered the city and made his way into Caterina's fortress, where he insisted that he would settle the succession by marrying her daughter himself. When Caterina refused, Matteo threatened to kill her. But rather than a "rival" of her namesake, I would argue that Caterina Cibo proved herself a worthy "daughter," although her tactics were certainly different:

> She, with a strong soul worthy of immortal fame, not only denied his request, but seeing that he stood over her with a drawn sword, and with his hand raised to strike, she fell upon her knees, and raising her veil, bent her head forwards, recommending her soul to God.[73]

Realizing that the city had been roused in defense of its duchess, Matteo retreated, taking Caterina with him. The rebel and his captive were overtaken, however, and after Caterina returned to the city she had twenty of Matteo's followers executed. In a letter to her brother, the cardinal of Marseilles, she described the events and her reaction to them:

> Having told you the outrage they have here committed, you will understand that they deserved sentence of death, for they are evil livers and assassins. . . . It will certainly appear to your Lordship, as it does to us, a wild dream, that sixty persons should set out to pillage Camerino, should dare to take me

prisoner, then should carry me off without a word, and escape without being killed! . . . For my rescue I do indeed return thanks to God, and that all should have ended so well.[74]

For the moment things had "ended so well," but after her uncle's death, the new pope, Paul III, wanted Caterina's daughter to be married to a Farnese, one of his relatives. Despite being summoned to Rome and threatened with excommunication, Caterina held to the Urbino marriage, and her daughter Giulia was married to Guidobaldo della Rovere later in 1534. Caterina Cibo eventually handed over control of Camerino to her daughter and her new son-in-law, but they were replaced almost immediately by a representative sent by the pope to administer the duchy. Caterina Cibo spent the rest of her life, some twenty years, in Florence, where she died on 17 February 1557.[75]

While Caterina Cibo was about to retire into obscurity in Florence, another daughter of Caterina Sforza was just about to emerge. In 1532 Caterina de' Medici was married to Henry of Orléans, second son of Francis I of France. Her great-aunt Caterina Cibo helped to prepare the young woman's trousseau and, on 1 September, was one of the women who travelled with the younger Caterina from Florence to Villefrance, where she boarded a ship for the rest of the journey to her new home. Once in France, Caterina became Catherine, and, quite unexpectedly, she became *dauphine* and later queen. There, too, she became regent of France, her power and influence in her adoptive country extending for some twenty years. We will reserve our discussion of her regency until the next chapter, when we pick up the career of Catherine de' Medici in France.

For now we will focus on the influences that helped to shape this daughter of Caterina Sforza. Caterina de' Medici was by family ties as well as by circumstance the "daughter" of the *Madonna* of Imola and Forlì. Her father was Lorenzo de' Medici, grandson of the famous Lorenzo "the Magnificent," while her mother, Madeleine de la Tour d'Auvergne, countess of Boulogne, had connections to French royalty.[76] Both parents died within two weeks of their daughter's birth, leaving Caterina's care and education in the hands of the Medici family. In his biography of her, Mark Strage calls it "odd" that "generations of assiduous searching" have revealed "virtually nothing" about Caterina's early life, "those formative years of childhood and young adolescence" which "forever shape character and help determine future behavior."[77] Perhaps so, if by "virtually nothing" Strage means the "documentation," "diplomatic dispatches," "state papers," and "letters" that he indicates are lacking. But something important, surely, can be said about Caterina's "formative years" if we note the series of strong women who raised her and if we are willing to consider the profound influence they must have had on the young woman who became queen and then virtual ruler of France.[78]

Immediately after the death of her parents, Caterina de' Medici's care was entrusted to her grandmother Alfonsina Orsini, who had dominated her son Lorenzo di Piero, "determined to make him a powerful ruler."[79] Alfonsina was, in Theodore Rabb's words, "famous for maintaining the family's backbone amidst male pusillanimity."[80] The baby remained with her grandmother in Florence for a year, until Alfonsina's death, when Caterina was transferred to Rome and the guardianship, first, of her great-aunt Lucrezia de' Medici, whom we have met before as the guardian of Caterina Sforza's son Giovanni, and then, in 1524, to her aunt Clarice de' Medici, about whom Pope Leo X reportedly said "that it would have been well for the family if Clarice had been the man."[81] The young Caterina and her aunt remained in Rome until 1525, when they returned to Florence. In 1527 Clarice and her eight-year-old niece were there when, after Rome was sacked by the troops of the Emperor Charles V, the city rose against the Medici to expel them. Clarice castigated her male relatives for their weakness, daring them to resist by reminding them that "the Medici palace is not a stable for mules." As a contemporary chronicler noted, "The Lady Clarice had great power of tongue."[82]

Despite her courage, Clarice was eventually forced not only to leave Florence but to leave Caterina behind as well. The last legitimate survivor of the senior Medici line, the girl became a "prisoner of the Republic" and was placed in a convent for safekeeping. By 1529 Clement had come to terms with Charles V, and the two united to restore the Medici in Florence. Then, as R. J. Knecht reports, "political hotheads allegedly wanted Catherine killed or exposed on the town walls as a target for enemy gunfire; others suggested that she should be sent to a brothel."[83] Instead it was decided that she should be sent to more secure convent, a move she resisted, fearing she would be killed instead. When three senators arrived to transfer her, she cut off all her hair and put on the dress of a nun, daring them to take her by force. The eleven-year-old Caterina reportedly asked, "Will they dare now to remove me . . . and to appear before the eyes of the people in the streets employed in the crime of forcibly carrying off a nun from her convent?"[84] Faced with the girl's refusal to change her clothes, the senators eventually had to take her as she was.

After the Medici were restored to power in Florence in 1530, Caterina was moved again, this time to Rome, where she was welcomed by her uncle Clement VII and housed in the Vatican. Her marriage became for him an important political tool, and among the alliances considered were unions with Ercole d'Este, Isabella d'Este's nephew; with James V of Scotland, Margaret Tudor's son; with Henry, earl of Richmond, Henry

VIII's illegitimate son who threatened the inheritance of Catherine of Aragon's daughter; with Federico Gonzaga, Isabella d'Este's son; and with Francesco Sforza, who had been raised by Bianca Maria Sforza. Ultimately the alliance with France was the one Clement accepted.

Although Francis wanted his future daughter-in-law to be sent to France as soon as the betrothal was arranged in 1531, Clement refused; instead, Caterina was returned to Florence, where she was place in the care of Lucrezia de' Medici's daughter Maria Salviati, by then the widow of Caterina Sforza's son Giovanni delle Bande Nere. In the spring of 1533 the young Caterina was one of the women who welcomed Margaret of Austria to the city; by September, accompanied by Maria Salviata and Caterina Cibo, her life shaped by a series of powerful models and political turmoil, this daughter of Caterina Sforza left for France. We will resume her story in our next chapter.

Meanwhile, yet another "daughter" of Caterina Sforza had been born in the same year as Caterina de' Medici. Isabella Jagellion was in fact related to *Madonna*: She was the daughter of Caterina Sforza's niece Bona and her husband, the king of Poland. Raised in Cracow, Isabella had the benefit of a humanist education that included the study of Polish, Italian, Latin, and, as is evident from her life, "the art of political patience and compromise."[85] In 1539 she was married to the fifty-two-year-old king of Hungary, John Zápolya, who, like Isabella's father, was resisting the eastward expansion of the Holy Roman Empire.[86] Zápolya had recently concluded a ten-year war with Emperor Ferdinand, the terms of which divided Hungary. Under the treaty of Varda, the western section of Hungary was joined to the empire, Ferdinand recognized as king of Hungary; the eastern portion was granted to Zápolya, recognized as king of Transylvania. If he died without an heir, Transylvania would become part of the empire. But a year after their marriage, Isabella gave birth to a son, John Sigismund. After the child's birth, Zápolya formally rejected the treaty he had made with Ferdinand. Two weeks later he died, naming his wife as queen regent for his newborn son. In Roland Bainton's words, "Isabella took up the campaign for the infant." On hearing the news of the death of the king of Hungary, Isabella's father sent a letter of advice to his daughter:

> Do not allow yourself to be crushed by grief. The course of prudence is that reason should rule the emotions. It becomes a prince to bear with composure that which cannot be altered. To succumb to immoderate weeping is to contest the will of God, whose judgments are a great abyss.

Her mother Bona wrote as well, advising Isabella not "to be mired in grief." "After the sorrow of the night comes the joy of the morning," she reminded her daughter.[87]

Isabella seems to have followed her parents' advice about overcoming her grief; during the course of the next few years she faced a great deal of political turmoil. Immediately after her husband's death, one of the guardians he had named for his son usurped Isabella's authority, but by 1542 the Estates of Transylvania "confirmed Isabella as queen regent and recognized Sigismund as their prince."[88] In a series of events that recall the life of Caterina Sforza, the emperor laid siege to the castle of Olah where Isabella was residing, relief coming to her from the Turkish sultan. After breaking the siege, the sultan asked to see Isabella's son. According to a contemporary chronicle account, "She was frightened and suggested to her advisers that she go alone with presents, or, if this would not do, that she take the boy." But, despite her fears, she took the advice of her advisers and sent her son to the sultan, who returned the boy to her unharmed: "The queen thanked the Sultan for returning her son, begged to be taken under his protection, promised not to remarry and sent a present to his daughter." The sultan, for his part, "promised to do his best" for Isabella.[89]

For the next five years, as David Daniel indicates, there was an "endemic triangular contest for hegemony" between the the Habsburg empire, the Turks, and Isabella. But in 1547 the emperor and the sultan signed a truce, and Isabella was forced to retire with her son to the territory of Opole, assigned to her by the emperor. Isabella refused to give up; instead, she "began to prepare the way for a return to Transylvania," negotiating with the Turks and with opponents of the Habsburgs. By 1555, she had "established a residence on the Polish-Hungary border"; by 1556, the estates had "reaffirmed her sixteen-year-old son as their prince." The Habsburgs, Daniel notes, "did not regain control of Transylvania until the end of the eighteenth century."[90]

From 1556 until her death on 20 September 1559, Isabella ruled as queen regent for her son, "actively" governing Transylvania:

> Fearful that she would again be expelled, she trusted few, fought hard to maintain her extensive authority and independence of action, and proved willing to act decisively. Yet she was also willing to make necessary compromises to secure her own position and that of her son. She kept the office of *voivode* [lieutenant] vacant so that none could challenge her authority. . . .
>
> Isabella likewise extended limited [religious] toleration to her subjects, viewing this as a necessary concession to bring peace to the kingdom and strengthen her political influence and security.[91]

In 1558 she was, as Bainton notes, "the first ruler to issue an edict of universal toleration"; the edict granted that "each" person be permitted to

> observe the faith of his preference with new or ancient ceremonies, permitting freedom of choice to each according to preference, provided no harm

be done to any, that neither the followers of the new religion are to do despite to the old, nor are the old in any way to injure the followers of the new.[92]

While her own religious views can be debated, what is clear is that Isabella used her edict "to fulfill her dynastic and political responsibilities." As Daniel concludes, "She used the Reformation and its advocates as she saw fit, on her own terms, for her own reasons, to secure for her son the rightful inheritance of the father he never knew."[93]

Having ventured into eastern Europe, where Caterina Sforza's niece Bona Sforza and grand-niece Isabella Jagellion struggled to preserve power for their families, we will return once more to the Italian peninsula. There, in the duchy of Savoy, we will find one final worthy "daughter" of Caterina Sforza.

The woman who was to govern Savoy in the late sixteenth century was Margaret of France, the youngest daughter of Francis I and his wife Claude, who herself was the daughter of Anne, duchess of Brittany.[94] Although the poet Ronsard had written that "thousands and thousands of great lords" had sought to marry Margaret, she was twenty-three years old and unmarried when her father died in 1547. Her brother succeeded to the French throne as Henry II, his wife Catherine de' Medici, by then Margaret's dear friend and companion, becoming queen of France. The new king set about finding a husband for his sister, and she is reported to have commented, "If my brother can find me a husband, alliance with whom may honour and advantage his kingdom, . . . then will I marry in order to please the King."[95]

Henry's choice as a husband for his sister was Philip II of Spain, whose first wife had just died, but the two kings were unable to settle their differences over disputed territories in Navarre and Piedmont. The duke of Parma, illegitimate son of Pope Paul III, suggested an alliance with *his* son Alessandro Farnese, but the French king did not seriously consider that as a worthy match for his sister. Instead, an earlier project was revived, a marriage to Emmanuel Philibert of Savoy.

Francis I had considered an alliance with Savoy for his daughter as early as 1526, when Margaret was three years old. It was a particularly attractive proposal. Francis's mother was Louise of Savoy, the sister of Charles III, duke of Savoy, who suggested a marriage between his son and heir, Louis, and the French king's daughter, but the project had been abandoned after the boy's death. In 1538 the duke had revived the possibility, suggesting his younger son, Emmanuel Philibert, prince of Piedmont, but by then the duke of Savoy had lost much of his territory, and Francis had rejected the match.[96]

And so Margaret of France remained unmarried. War between France and Spain resumed in 1552, and Emmanuel Philibert fought for the imperial forces; by 1554 he had won renown on the battlefield and had regained the territories that his father had lost. His potential as a bridegroom had thus improved, and matches for him were suggested with, among others, Elizabeth Tudor and Juana of Castile, but he preferred an alliance with France and a marriage to Margaret of France. In 1556, as part of the truce of Vaucelles, Henry II of France negotiated a marriage between his sister Margaret and Emmanuel Philibert. But the truce did not hold, and by 1556 Spain and France were at war once more, Emmanuel Philibert resuming his command of Spanish troops. They fought on until 1558, when peace negotiations resumed under the direction of Christine, the dowager duchess of Lorraine, niece of the Emperor Charles V. The resulting treaty of Cateau-Cambrésis was to include two marriages. At first it was proposed that Elizabeth of Valois, the oldest daughter of Henry II and Catherine de' Medici, would marry Don Carlos, son of Philip II of Spain, while the French king's second daughter, Claude, would marry Emmanuel Philibert. But Claude was already betrothed to the young duke of Lorraine, Christine of Lorraine's son, and she objected. And so it was agreed that Margaret of France would, after all, become the wife of Emmanuel Philibert, duke of Savoy.[97]

The marriage took place in Paris on 4 July 1559, some twenty years after it had originally been proposed. Despite her age—Margaret was thirty-eight—the new duchess of Savoy became pregnant, though it was at first feared that her pregnancy was the same "delusion" that had "obsessed" Mary Tudor.[98] Margaret seems to have had some doubts herself about her pregnancy, writing to her husband, "I trust that what I have been told is true. I pray to our Lord that it may be, and that you now have hopes of a fine child."[99] A "fine child" it turned out to be, since it was a son, born on 12 January 1562, his birth believed by some to be a miracle, by others to be fraud. Margaret's devotion to Charles Emmanuel is criticized by her biographer Winifred Stephens, who decides that if the duchess "had one weakness," it was "her idolisation of her child." The "coddling" and "cosseting"—Stephens's words—the boy received seem hardly to merit such disdain. Margaret cared for her son until he reached the age of ten, devoting herself to watching over his diet and exercise. Despite the "softness of his nurture," he "quickly took" to the more rigorous training he received when he "passed under his father's control."[100]

Margaret's situation in Savoy might have been difficult, as difficult as her aunt Renée's in Ferrara. Her father and her brother had, for thirty years, occupied much of the duchy of Savoy, and France still occupied territory in Piedmont. Her husband, in return, had repeatedly fought against France. But Margaret, interested in state affairs, devoted herself to Savoy as thoroughly as she devoted herself to the rearing of her child. "French as she was," in Stephens's words, "the Duchess threw herself entirely" into her husband's effort to rid his territory of the French soldiers who remained.[101]

During Emmanuel Philibert's absence from Savoy in 1561, he appointed Margaret to act as his regent. She was not inexperienced in her role as governor. In 1550 her brother had created her duchess of Berry where, Stephens notes, "she was a stateswoman equally interested in the commercial and social as well as in the intellectual development of her subjects." Stephens concludes that, "as governor of this province," Margaret had proved herself the "true descendant" of her grandfather Louis XII, the "inheretrix of those gifts which rendered him one of the best of French kings": "It is no exaggeration . . . to say that in ruling her province Margaret displayed a greater gift for government than any male member of her house."[102]

After Charles IX succeeded to the throne, Catherine de' Medici, regent for her son, refused to negotiate a return of the disputed territory to Savoy, claiming that the matter would have to wait for the king to reach his majority. But after civil war erupted in France, she needed Savoy's support, and she reopened negotiations, agreeing to surrender three of the five cities to him in 1562. The surrender, as Stephens notes, "was universally regarded as due to Margaret's diplomacy," one contemporary writing that "her wisdom" had "taken the fortress."[103]

When Emmanuel Philibert fell seriously ill in August 1563, his ministers despaired of his life and feared a minority, but Margaret again took control of her husband's affairs:

> She presided over the Council. She arranged for the future government of the state in the even of her husband's death. To quiet the fears of his ministers, who trembled lest the heir might be carried off by France of Spain, she parted with her son, sending him to Turin, so that the ministers might keep the infant prince under their observation.[104]

Emmanuel Philibert recovered from his illness, but Margaret acted as his regent again in 1566 and in 1568, on both occasions during his absences.

Even with the 1562 surrender of territory, Savoy was not completely rid of the French, who continued to hold Pinerola, Savigliano, and Perosa. Throughout the rest of her life, Margaret continued to work to regain these cities. In August of 1574, she hosted her nephew Henry, the new French king, as he travelled from Poland back to France, by means of "her festivities" intending "to win from the King of France which the French still held in Piedmont." He agreed to surrender them unconditionally to her; her "last political act" was the treaty of Turin, which returned Perosa, Savigliano, and Pinerolo to Savoy.[105]

Margaret did not enjoy her success for long. She had planned to join her husband and her nephew, travelling to meet the French court at Lyon; her old friend Catherine de' Medici was looking forward to her arrival. But her son Charles Emmanuel suddenly fell ill, and she remained behind to nurse the twelve-year-old. She wrote to her husband on 12 September mentioning that she was also ill: "My sickness would be nothing," she wrote, "did it not keep me from my son."[106] Her son survived, but she did not. She died two days later. In September 1575, a year after her death, the treaty of Turin was ratified.

There remains one further woman to mention here, Maria de' Medici, who was born just the year before Margaret of Savoy's death. She was Caterina Sforza's direct descendant, the great-granddaughter of Caterina's son Giovanni delle Bande Nere and Maria Salviati. In 1600 she was married to Henry IV of France where, after her husband's assassination in 1610, she would become, like her foremother Caterina Sforza, regent for her son. The story of this "daughter" of Caterina Sforza will be told in the next chapter, along with those of other women who came to power as queens and regents in France.

CHAPTER FIVE

THE DAUGHTERS OF ANNE OF FRANCE

Queens and Regents in France and French Navarre

[On] the first day of January I lost my husband, and [on] the first day of January my son became king of France. [On] the day of the Conversion of Saint Paul [25 January] my son was in great danger of dying, and on the same day he was annointed and crowned in the church of Rheims. . . . Anne, queen of France, . . . left to me the administration of her goods, of her fortune, and of her daughters, even of Madame Claude, queen of France and wife of my son, which I have honorably and courteously carried out; everyone knows it, truth acknowledges it, experience demonstrates it, [and it] is openly reported.

—Louise of Savoy, Regent of France[1]

Before her death in 1522, Anne of France, *Madame la grande*, had already lost the daughter for whom she had so carefully composed her series of *enseignements*; Suzanne, duchess of Bourbon died in 1521. Nevertheless, the former regent had already witnessed the rise to power of the first of a series of formidable "daughters" who were to succeed her in sixteenth-century France, women who were to dominate the throne that, as women, they were legally barred from inheriting.[2]

Louise of Savoy was related by blood and by marriage to *Madame*. Through her father, Philip II of Savoy, Louise was related to Anne of France by blood: Her father's sister was Charlotte of Savoy, queen of France and Anne of France's mother. Through her mother, Marguerite of Bourbon, Louise was related to Anne of France by marriage: Her mother's brother was Anne of France's husband.[3] Despite such royal connections, however, there was little in Louise of Savoy's early life to suggest the role she would later come to play in royal government.

Louis XI of France had married Charlotte of Savoy in order to secure his border with Italy; to strengthen his alliance with Savoy, he awarded his new queen's younger brother Philip the title of count of Bresse. Then, in an effort to contain the threat posed to his throne by the Orléans branch of the Valois family, he forced Louis of Orléans to marry his daughter Jeanne in 1476, as we have seen. In 1478, to further both endeavors, he arranged the betrothal of his two-year-old niece Louise to Charles of Angoulême, twenty years her senior, who represented the Angoulême branch of the Valois family tree.[4]

Louise's mother Marguerite of Bourbon died in 1483, when the girl was seven years old. After the death of his wife, Philip of Savoy sent his daughter to Amboise to be raised and educated by Anne of France, Louis XI's daughter. There Louise joined Margaret of Austria, who had been sent to France at about the same time to be raised as its "queen." In a 1972 essay about Louise, John F. Freeman describes the education that she would have received under the "supervision" of her aunt; "one may assume," he writes, "she learned the traditional fare of home management and principles of Christian morality." Certainly "home management" and "Christian morality" would have been part of her training, but she certainly learned much more. Louise's biographer Dorothy Mayer presents a more insightful assessment of the education that the girl received; "Above all," Mayer writes, she was able to observe "the exercise of power by a woman."[5]

When Louis XI died in 1483, his daughter Anne became de facto ruler of France as regent for her brother, Charles VIII. In an effort to "escape the matrimonial fate prescribed for him," Charles of Angoulême took part in the "Mad War" that began in 1485; after he was defeated in 1487, the "price of his submission" was his marriage to Louise, which took place on 16 February 1488, when she was twelve years old.[6] But Louise apparently did not begin living with her husband until 1491, when she was about fifteen.[7] At that point she joined her husband's household at Cognac, which included his mistress Jeanne de Polignac and several illegitimate children.[8]

Rather than antagonism, the two women, wife and mistress, forged durable bonds, and it might be said that in her husband's mistress Louise found another influential tutor. Jeanne became Louise's "permanent ally" and companion; Louise took into her service Jeanne's brothers. Louise accepted Jeanne's children into her household; Jeanne, in turn, raised Louise's children, Marguerite, born in 1492, and Francis, who, according to Louise, had his "first experience of earthly light at Cognac" on the afternoon of 12 September 1494. While Jeanne de Polignac "nursed Francis

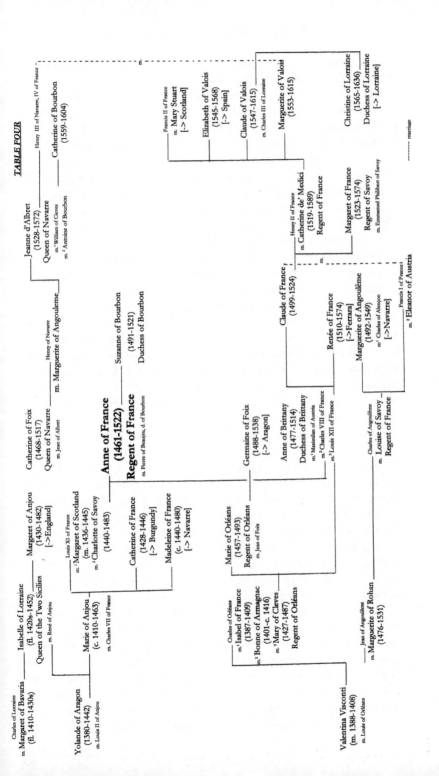

TABLE FOUR

Charles of Lorraine
m. Margaret of Bavaria
(fl. 1410-1430s)

Margaret of Anjou
(1430-1482)
[->England]

Isabelle of Lorraine
(fl. 1420s-1452)
Queen of the Two Sicilies
m. René of Anjou

Catherine of Foix
(1468-1517)
Queen of Navarre
m. Jean of Albret

Jeanne d'Albret
(1528-1572)
Queen of Navarre
m. ¹ William of Cleves
m. ² Antoine of Bourbon

Henry III of Navarre, IV of France

Catherine of Bourbon
(1559-1604)

Henry of Navarre
m. Marguerite of Angoulême

Yolande of Aragon
(1380-1442)
m. Louis II of Anjou

Marie of Anjou
(c. 1410-1463)
m. Charles VII of France

Louis XI of France
m. ¹ Margaret of Scotland
(m. 1436-1445)
m. ² Charlotte of Savoy
(1440-1483)

Anne of France
(1461-1522)
Regent of France
m. Pierre of Beaujeu, d. of Bourbon

Suzanne of Bourbon
(1491-1521)
Duchess of Bourbon

Catherine of France
(1428-1446)
[-> Burgundy]

Madeleine of France
(c. 1440-1480)
[-> Navarre]

Francis II of France
m. Mary Stuart
[-> Scotland]

Elizabeth of Valois
(1545-1568)
[-> Spain]

Claude of Valois
(1547-1615)
m. Charles III of Lorraine

Marguerite of Valois
(1553-1615)

Christine of Lorraine
(1565-1636)
Duchess of Lorraine
[-> Lorraine]

Henry II of France
m. Catherine de' Medici
(1519-1589)
Regent of France

Margaret of France
(1523-1574)
Regent of Savoy
m. Emmanuel Philibert of Savoy

Claude of France
(1499-1524)

Renée of France
(1510-1574)
[->Ferrara]

Marguerite of Angoulême
(1492-1549)
m ¹ Charles of Alençon
[->Navarre]

Charles of Angoulême
m. Louise of Savoy
Regent of France

Francis I of France
m. ² Eleanor of Austria

Germaine of Foix
(1488-1538)
[-> Aragon]

Anne of Brittany
(1477-1514)
Duchess of Brittany
m.¹ Maximilian of Austria
m.² Charles VIII of France
m.¹ Louis XII of France

Marie of Orléans
(1457-1493)
Regent of Orléans
m. Jean of Foix

Charles of Orléans
m.¹ Isabel of France
(1387-1409)
m.² Bonne of Armagnac
(1401-c. 1416)
m.³ Mary of Cleves
(1427-1487)
Regent of Orléans

Jean of Angoulême
m. Marguerite of Rohan
(1476-1531)

Valentina Visconti
(m. 1388-1408)
m. Louis of Orléans

------- marriage

. . . through his first seven years," Louise would later arrange advantageous marriages for her husband's illegitimate children.[9]

But events far away from Cognac were to affect Louise of Savoy's life and her children's future. In 1495, the son of King Charles VIII died, and on his way to the dauphin's funeral, Louise of Savoy's husband became ill. He died a month later, on 1 January 1496. In his will Charles of Angoulême named his wife as "tutoress and guardian" of Marguerite and Francis "with full powers"; but since Louise was still a minor herself and thus precluded from "exercising full tutorship," he had also provided for an eight-man committee, including his cousin Louis of Orléans, to administer his affairs. The king settled the disputed question of the guardianship of Francis—who with the death of the *dauphin* and of his father had become second in line to the throne after Louis of Orléans, now heir presumptive. The widow was to maintain custody of her children, while Louis, an "honorary guardian," would control her business affairs. In the event of her remarriage, she would lose her guardianship and her property.[10]

For the next two years, Louise of Savoy remained at Cognac. But in 1498 Charles VIII died, leaving no child of his own to succeed him, and Louis, duke of Orléans became Louis XII, king of France. He married Anne of Brittany, Charles VIII's widow, but until they had children, Francis of Angoulême became the king's heir presumptive. Louise and her children were moved to Amboise, and the new king appointed a guardian for Francis, Pierre de Rohan, seigneur de Gié. Louise's hatred of Gié was immediate and undying; the first entry in a journal she later compiled provides vivid evidence of her regard for her son's new guardian. "[On] the day of the Conversion of Saint Paul, 25 January, about two o'clock in the afternoon, my king, my lord, my Caesar, and my son was carried across the fields outside Amboise by a hack that had been given to him by Marshal de Gié," she began, "and the danger was so great that those who were present thought it beyond repair." But the seemingly irreparable "danger" was repaired: "However, God—Protector of widows and Defender of orphans—foreseeing all things, did not abandon me, knowing that if this accident had suddenly taken from me my love, I would have been too unfortunate."[11] No harm came to the young Francis.

Despite Gié's authority over her household, Louise seems nevertheless to have maintained custody of her children for some time, sleeping in the same room with them and directing their education. But by 1505 Gié gained "complete authority" over the "person" of the young Francis. The boy was removed from his mother at night so that Gié's representatives might "keep watch over him." Louise herself was offered a number of marriage proposals, including an alliance with Alfonso d'Este and Henry VII of England, but she rejected any inducement to remarry.[12]

The king, meanwhile, had begun to prepare for the succession if he were to die without a son and heir. A daughter, Claude, had been born in 1499; and when Louis had fallen ill in 1503, his wife Anne of Brittany had seized the initiative, arranging a marriage between her daughter and Charles, the future Holy Roman Emperor. Regaining his health, Louis disavowed both the match and Gié, whose actions during the king's illness had appeared treasonable. After another serious illness in April 1505, the king arranged for the betrothal of his daughter to the heir presumptive, Francis of Angoulême, and for the government of France should he die while his successor was still a minor:

> Louis . . . stipulated that if he died before Francis reached fourteen, the recognized legal age for royal majority, a regency would be established whereby Queen Anne and Louise of Savoy would share authority as guardians of the royal children. . . . Louise was thus recognized as the legal guardian of her two children, but the greater signficance lay with her designation as regent. Her duty to oversee Francis' health, welfare, and education assured her a privileged status at the royal court.[13]

The betrothal of the king's daughter and the king's heir was celebrated on 21 May 1506, when Claude was seven and Francis twelve. On 3 August 1508 the young Francis left his mother and Amboise for the king's court at Plessis-les-Tours, and despite his prospects and her assurances of a place in a regency, Louise was not altogether happy: "My son left Amboise to be a man of court, and left me all alone," she later wrote.[14] By 1509, her daughter, too, was gone; Marguerite left her mother to be married to Charles, duke of Alençon.

During her separation from her son, Louise noted his travels and every illness and injury he suffered, dutifully recording them later in her journal. She continued to have personal contact with him as well; in 1514, for example, he travelled with her on a journey from Cognac to Angoulême; "demonstrating the love" that he had for her, his mother, he "chose to go on foot" and provided her "good company."[15] But even though his future looked promising, Francis's destiny was not assured. Anne of Brittany might still provide her husband Louis XII an heir. In late 1509, ten years after Claude's birth, that possibility threatened; the queen was pregnant, but the baby, born in April of 1510, was a girl, Renée. In 1512 the queen was again pregnant. In January 1513 she gave birth to a son who did not survive. Louise of Savoy recorded the birth and death in her journal with some satisfaction; the baby was not able to "delay the elevation" of her "Caesar," she wrote, because the baby "lacked life."[16] After the queen's death in January of 1514, Francis—and his mother—grew more confident; the heir presumptive's marriage with Claude was celebrated in May of that year.

But, despite Francis's doubt that the widowed king would "commit the folly of marrying again," that is exactly what Louis XII did. The wedding of the "extremely old and feeble" king, as Louise of Savoy described him, and Henry VIII's sister, the "young" Mary Tudor, took place in October 1514.[17]

Although Louis may still have hoped to produce a male heir of his own to succeed him, by January 1515 he was dead.[18] Louise of Savoy's son became King Francis I, Louise herself recognized as "the king's mother," *Madame Mère du Roi*. Elizabeth McCartney notes that Louise of Savoy's status as *mater regis* was both acknowledged and appreciated by her contemporaries, among them Pope Leo X:

> Some months after Francis' accession, Leo sent congratulations to the French royal court, praising Louise's piety, devotion and maternal vigilance; he particularly emphasized her diligence in her "labeurs grant [*sic*]," noting that her accomplishments provided further testimony of God's omnipotence.[19]

Charles Brandon, the duke of Suffolk, sent Henry VIII an equally glowing assessment of the king's mother: "Sir, it is she who runs all, and so may she well; for I never saw a woman like to her, both for wit, honour and dignity. She hath a great stroke in all matters with the King her son."[20] The Venetian ambassador, meanwhile, judged that "the Most Christian King's most illustrious mother . . . would prove the greatest and most faithful friend Venice ever had."[21]

Like the young Henry VIII in England, anxious to win glory for himself shortly after his accession to the throne, Francis I was almost immediately attracted to the possibility of armed conflict. In order to renew French claims in Italy, he began to prepare for a military expedition, designating his mother, rather than his wife, to function as regent of France in his absence. "All the princes and nobles of our blood will accompany us," Francis wrote, "And in consideration of this, we have decided to leave the government of our realm to our well beloved and dear Lady and Mother . . . in whom we have entire and perfect confidence." Because of her "virtue and prudence," she would, he proclaimed, "know how to acquit this trust."[22] McCartney assesses the significance of Francis's decision:

> First, he noted that his mother was qualified to act as regent by virtue of her wisdom and prudence, and because of the "great and singular love" that she held for his subjects. Next, he placed in her hands full authority to decide issues of government (including domestic and foreign affairs) as well as security of the realm and judicial matters. And he bestowed on her specific obligations regarding the appointment of royal officers and the right to fill

vacant benefices, to grant remissions for crimes, and to confirm privileges of government usually enacted during ceremonial entries into cities.[23]

It is interesting to note how Louise of Savoy's first regency has been treated by historians. In his 1937 biography of Francis I, for example, Francis Hackett devotes considerable attention to the new king's Italian campaign, but does not mention Louise's regency, while R. J. Knecht, writing in 1982, indicates simply that "Francis informed 'the good towns' of his kingdom that he was about to leave for Italy and that his mother would be regent in his absence." Among those who have focused on the mother rather than on her son, Millicent Fawcett ignores Louise's first regency entirely, while John Freeman writes in general terms of her government as regent, noting that on two occasions the king "secured his reign against ambitious nobles by conferring the regency upon his mother," but "[w]hile Regent Louise did nothing without consulting with the close relatives and great nobles who made up the innermost circle of the unwieldy King's Council."[24] Even Mayer's biography, in its discussion of Louise's "first regency," focuses on Francis's military exploits rather than Louise's activities.[25]

McCartney, by contrast, analyzes with some care Louise's first tenure as regent. Francis specified that, as regent, his mother was to work "in consultation with governmental bureaus, and, particularly, with ranking members of the *Parlement* of Paris." While Knecht concludes that Louise's powers as regent were "limited, since the chancellor took the great seal with him to Italy," McCartney provides an alternative view:

> He [Francis] allowed for the possibility that exceptional issues could arise in his absence, but took care to limit them by taking with him to Italy the royal seal needed to affirm important legislation. As a result, royal power effectively remained with him and any pressing concerns must await his return, particularly those regarding royal policy and important matters of justice.

Louise was still empowered "to exercise privileges symbolic of her son's sovereign authority," however, including the right to fill vacant benefices and to grant pardons. After initial objections by the *Parlement* to Louise's powers as regent "dissipated," regent and parliament were able to work successfully together: "routine affairs of government continued without interference from the regent," while "Louise diligently attended to matters touching her rights to oversee royal policy."[26]

Louise herself commented only briefly on her role as regent. She noted in her journal that she had a dream some months before Francis became king in which the ceiling of her room began to fall in upon her. "I believe that it was a sign that it would be necessary that all this house would depend on me," she wrote, "and that by divine permission I would take the burden."[27] This is her only allusion to her role as regent—she has taken up "the burden," *la charge*. Her other journal entries about this period record her fears for her son and an omen presaging battle. A "celestial forecast" on 14 August—a "terrible" sign in the heavens, "having the figure of a comet"—frightened her; she interpreted it to mean that Francis would face a "great danger against the Swiss," who were defending Milan. A month later, on 13 September, she noted that her son had defeated the Swiss. She "went by foot" to the church of Notre Dame des Fontaines in Amboise to "commend" the one "whom I love more than myself—that is my son, glorious and triumphant second Caesar." Later on the same day, the very day Francis was victorious at the battle of Marignano, she noted that a "flaming torch the length of a lance" was seen "in several places" in the skies of Flanders, and that it seemed as if it would fall on houses. But, although it was as bright as "a hundred torches," it made only a "great light" and no flames. This marvel, too, she seemed to have recorded because she interpreted it as a sign of her son's victory. For the month of December, she noted the conclusion of Francis's Italian adventures, including his reception in Rome by Leo X and his peace agreement with England.[28] Notably absent from her journal is any indication of her own dealings in the king's absence.

Francis returned home early in 1516, and thus Louise's first tenure as regent was only a few months' duration, from July of 1515 until the king's return early the next year. Louise continued to be an extremely influential force in her son's government, however, even after the period of her official role ended. Relations with England remained strained, and in 1521 the English ambassador in France suggested to Cardinal Wolsey that he apply to the king's mother for help:

> I have seen in diverse things since I came hither . . . that when the French king would stick at some points, and speak very great words, yet my Lady [Louise] would qualify the matter; and sometimes when the king is not contented he will say nay, and then my Lady must require him, and at her request he will be contented, for he is so obeissant to her that he will refuse nothing that she requireth him to do.

Even so, the ambassador did not consider her influence on her son to be entirely for the good, since he added, "and if it had not been for her he would have done wonders."[29] Francis "eventually agreed" to a "comprimit," or conference, regarding the ongoing dispute, "very grudgingly, and in deference, he said, to his mother."[30] Cardinal Wolsey, for his part, urged English envoys in France to promote "unity, peace and concord": they were to "exhort, stir and move by all means and ways to them possible." Wolsey particularly recommended that they address themselves to Louise of Savoy, "the mother and nourisher of peace."[31]

In other matters, however, Louise's influence on Francis has been interpreted more negatively. In 1521, Anne of France's daughter Suzanne of Bourbon died, leaving her possessions and title to her husband, Charles of Montpensier, constable of France. In the event of his remarriage, Suzanne's will stipulated that the title and property were to be inherited by the children of that marriage. But Louise of Savoy and Francis I both claimed title to the Bourbon inheritance after Suzanne's death, Louise by inheritance through the right of Margaret of Bourbon, her mother, and Francis by right of escheat, that is, by reversion to the crown after the death, without heir, of the duchess. Their claims were disputed by Anne of France, and the issue was placed before the parliament of Paris. After Anne's death in 1522, the *Parlement* adjourned without a decision. Francis eventually awarded some of the Bourbon property to his mother and confiscated the rest of it himself.

Charles of Montpensier had already complicated the question of the Bourbon inheritance by proposing a marriage to Francis's sister-in-law Renée, younger daughter of Louis XII, even before Suzanne died. After her death, such an alliance might have seemed a reasonable solution to the disputed Bourbon inheritance, but Montpensier may somehow have involved himself with Louise of Savoy as well. For some historians a romantic relationship gone bad is at the root of the conflict about the Bourbon inheritance. Fawcett, for instance, argues that Charles of Montpensier's "rather nauseous flirtation with Louise, who was thirteen years his senior" was the source of the dispute. The two had agreed to marry as soon as Suzanne of Bourbon died, and Louise, "with the infatuation sometimes seen in a middle-aged woman for a young lover," had worked for Montpensier's advancement. Her intrigues on his behalf had dealt him "a blow" that he "never forgave," however. He "added insult" to the "injury" of his rejection of Louise "by saying that his former court to her was but a feint to cover his real love for her daughter Margaret." For her part, "the rage of Louise knew no bounds." Rejected by her faithless lover, she "worked so indefatigably" for Montpensier's ruin that he was forced to commit treason—he "deserted" France and defected to the Emperor Charles V.[32]

In addressing the rumored relationship between Charles of Montpensier and Louise of Savoy, Knecht asks, "Did he reject an offer of marriage from the queen mother, as is often claimed?" The answer: "There is some evidence for this." As evidence Knecht refers a diplomatic report from the imperial ambassador in England indicating that Louise was "much in love with" Montpensier but that he had refused to marry her. A second contemporary chronicle indicates that a marriage project had been broached, though it was a political arrangement by which Louise "hoped to gain possession of Bourbon's lands" rather than a passionate affair.[33] Knecht has here only concurred with Mayer's earlier analysis: "On what evidence does the report of Louise's love for Bourbon rest?" she had asked, citing the same "evidence" and concluding that such "gossip" was not enough "to warrant succeeding generations of historians in attributing the vilest motives to all Louise's actions."[34]

Following Mayer, more recent analyses of Louise of Savoy's role in this conflict do not ascribe Charles of Montpensier's treason to a failed romance with the queen mother. Freeman mentions what he calls the "domestic issue with the most far-reaching consequences" only in terms of Francis's "chance to reclaim Bourbon's estates" and his ultimate decision to award "some of Bourbon's estates . . . to Louise," while McCartney, who also omits discussion of any romance, assumes Louise's role as an agent in the dispute: the queen mother "sought the inheritance for herself" and commissioned her secretary Etienne Le Blanc to "chart her ancestry," his "tracing" of "the fortunes of the house of Bourbon" intended to support her claims. Le Blanc's completed history is an "impressive piece of historiographical research," McCartney concludes, one that uses "an abundance of archival sources" to "support Louise's claims to the Bourbon properties."[35]

There the question of Louise of Savoy's relationship, if any, to Charles of Montpensier must remain for the moment. Complicating the dispute over Bourbon lands and Montpensier's defection are larger events. On 27 April 1522 French troops just outside Milan were defeated by imperial forces at a battle known as "la Bicocca," the name of a nearby country home, and in August English forces invaded Picardy. By October the English were only fifty miles from Paris. Once more Francis went to war. On 12 August 1523 he again appointed Louise of Savoy as his regent. A letter announcing his decision cited Louise's experience and outlined her considerable powers in his absence.[36]

Louise of Savoy's second regency lasted considerably longer than her first, because on 24 February 1525 the French king was defeated and captured at the battle of Pavia. He was taken first to Pavia itself (where he was served dinner by Charles of Montpensier), then on to Genoa. From there he was sent to Naples. By June he was in Barcelona, and in July he was sent on to Madrid, where he would remain until February 1526, when his release was finally arranged.

Just after his capture, Francis wrote to his mother to "inform" her "of the extent" of his "misfortune"; "of everything," he wrote, "nothing is left but my honour and my life." He begged her "not to lose heart," but to "exercise" her "customary prudence." He recommended to her his "little children," who were, he reminded her, also hers. He signed himself her "humble and obedient son." Louise responded: "I cannot better begin this letter than by thanking our Saviour that it has pleased him to preserve your honour, your life, and your health." "On my part," she continued, "I shall support the misfortune in such a manner for the succour of your little children and the affairs of your kingdom that I shall not give you occasion for more pain."[37]

In governing France while her son the king was in captivity, Louise of Savoy "faced" what Knecht describes as a "threefold task": "first, to defend the kingdom against the threat of foreign invasion; secondly, to uphold the crown's authority in respect of bodies like the Parlement; and thirdly, to secure her son's release on terms that were not excessively harsh."[38] In her execution of these tasks, Louise has earned widespread respect. Freeman judges that the regent "was primarily responsible for keeping France intact" during the king's captivity, and even the disapproving Fawcett grudgingly admits that "in such moments even Louise showed herself great and admirable."[39]

To defend France from invasion she mobilized forces for defense, securing the country's borders. She successfully negotiated an alliance with Henry VIII (treaty of the Moore, 1525) and, in Italy, with the pope and the Venetians (League of Cognac, 1526). In upolding the crown's authority, Louise was equally successful. Immediately after the king's capture, McCartney notes that some members of the *Parlement* of Paris were moved to "contest Louise's right to act as regent by promoting an alternate regent," the duke of Vendôme, but that this effort failed.[40] Louise ultimately proved her competency, "more tactful" in her dealings with the parliament "than her son had been": "She flattered it, enlisted its co-operation in organizing the defence of northern France and enlarged her council at its suggestion."[41] And finally, to secure her son's release, she made every effort to raise the money needed to ransom Francis. The chancellor of France assured the captive king that the "said lady has managed so well that the rea[l]m is on its accustomed footing."[42] She then undertook negotiations resulting in the treaty of Madrid, which Francis signed on 14 January 1526. The terms of this agreement were punishing, however: Francis was to renounce all his claims to Italy; he was to pardon Charles of Montpensier and restore to him his confiscated estates; the French king's two sons were to be held as hostages by the emperor to guarantee Francis's fulfillment of the terms of the treaty; and, finally, Francis was to marry Isabel of Portugal, Charles V's widowed sister.[43]

The French king was finally released from his captivity in March—on the 17th of that month Francis was exchanged for his two sons, the *dauphin* Francis and his younger brother Henry. With her son's return, Louise's second regency ended. But, although his sons were hostages to ensure his compliance with the terms of the treaty of Madrid, Francis did not honor his agreement. While negotiating the treaty, Louise had decided that accepting the terms offered was better than the king's continued absence, but once the king had returned to his kingdom, she is said to have advised him "not to observe promises made under duress."[44]

Peace between Francis I and Charles V was not achieved until 3 August 1529 when the treaty of Cambrai, the so-called Ladies' Peace, was negotiated by the king of France's mother, Louise of Savoy, and the Holy Roman Emperor's aunt, Margaret of Austria. The two women were more than representatives of their male relatives, however. They were personally and intimately related. They had spent years together as children, both raised by Anne of France; Louise had been sent to the regent by her father in 1483, the same year Margaret had arrived to be raised and educated as "queen" of France. They were together until 1491, when Margaret was rejected as a wife by Charles VIII. Margaret had ultimately married the son and heir of Isabella and Ferdinand, Juan of Castile and Aragon, but after his early death, she had then married Philibert of Savoy, Louise of Savoy's brother. Thus the two women who met to negotiate an end of hostilities knew each other well; each had much to bargain for, and they bargained hard, but the regent of the Netherlands was in the stronger position. By the terms of the treaty the two women devised, Francis agreed to give up his claims in Italy, to pay a heavy ransom for his sons, and to marry the emperor's sister, whom he had agreed to marry in 1526.[45]

Although the terms were difficult, the treaty of Cambrai was the last political achievement of a determined woman. In a final personal achievement, aging, ill, and increasingly weak, Louise of Savoy travelled to meet the grandchildren whose release she had negotiated, a journey made against the advice of her physicians. Freeman uses Louise's effort to illustrate "the depth of her emotional attachment to her family": they were "more than diplomatic pawns" to her, he notes, as if this were somehow surprising. The children arrived in France on 1 July 1530, and by Christmas the king was writing that his mother, with "her gout and colics added to her pains of the stomach," was nearing death. She died the next year, on 22 September 1531.[46]

Despite her remarkable achievements, Louise of Savoy has not been treated well by most historians—when she has been treated at all. In his 1972 essay, John Freeman surveys historical opinion, which, before the twentieth century, can generally summed up by quoting the nineteenth-century entry in the Larousse encyclopedia: "Spiteful, revengeful, greedy for money and power, she wasted no time to exercise her disastrous influence over the conduct of public affairs."[47] In noting more recent treatment of Louise, which has begun to correct this picture, Freeman indicates that Louise's biographers have ignored "the most obvious factor" in considering her role: "she was a woman." Those who have "ignored" this "obvious factor" have, he observes, ascribed to Louise "the characteristics of a man": that is, that she spent much of her life "in the service of the state." Here Freeman alludes to Mayer, who in her concluding assessments of Louise of Savoy had written that she was a "woman who had passed her life in the service of the State."[48] Freeman discounts such views, concluding instead that Louise's role in sixteenth-century politics is best regarded as a case "maternal opportunism." Her "concern for her son" took precedence over everything else," he claims.

Once again we see the ambivalence with which women of power and authority are viewed. Even while arguing we cannot simply dismiss Louise of Savoy as a "possessive mother," Freeman in essence does just that. He may believe that his attention to her sex rights a wrong done by historians like Mayer who "ignore" the fact that Louise is a woman, but his treatment of her career as a "case of maternal opportunism" does the regent no justice. Mayer overlooks neither Louise's sex nor that her role as "the king's mother" gave her access to power. Rather, Mayer might be said to have preceded Freeman in analyzing Louise's role as "maternal opportunism":

> Louise . . . was completely mistress of herself and her aim was power. Power which she would exercise through a son who adored her, whose every thought she understood, whom she had trained and for whom her approval was paramount. She . . . was convinced he would be King, and when that day came, she intended that it should be his mother to whom he should turn for guidance.

But the "great regent," as the king's mother, did not seek power as a means of self-aggrandizement: "Louise used her power for France, her policy was perspicacious and her alliances farsighted."[49] For our part, we can note here that a king's role in extending his power is not usually dismissed as self-aggrandizement, nor is preserving that power for his son a "case of paternal opportunism." A king devoted to his son's personal and political well-being is not a "possessive father." Such judgments are preserved for women like Margaret Beaufort and Louise of Savoy. Similarly, if a woman like Caterina Sforza is willing to risk the lives of her children, held as hostages, for the preservation of her city, she is regarded as a monster, while a man like Francis, risking the lives of his hostage children when he repudiated the treaty of Madrid, is not a monster—he is a king, doing what he must for the preservation of his state.[50]

And it needs hardly be said that a woman's sexuality is treated vastly different than her male counterpart's. After becoming a widow at age nineteen, Louise of Savoy remained unmarried, devoting herself to her family members and their positions; she rejected for herself all of the marriage proposals that might have taken her away from France, even while they might have been advantageous for her. The mere suggestion that she might have considered a political alliance with Charles of Montpensier—or even that she might have wanted to marry him because she loved him—has earned her both derision and scandal. While her son, to name only one example, could amuse himself with a string of mistresses, and while her contemporary Henry VIII could have six wives, the idea that Louise, a woman in her mid-forties, might marry a man some thirteen years her junior has offended and incensed generations of historians: In the eighteenth century she was a "miserable prostitute, avaricious, false, cruel and pleasure seeking," for example. She had a "big nose," a nineteenth-century historian wrote, "sensual and coarse, a sanguine nose, like those of all strong base natures, passionate temperaments, often unhealthy."[51] Modern historians are more judicious in their views of this episode in Louise's life, even while they continue to regard her devotion to her son and her expressions of love for him as obsessive.[52]

Suspect, too, is Louise of Savoy's daughter Marguerite of Angoulême, who in 1509, at the age of seventeen, was married to the duke of Alençon.[53] Marguerite was devoted to her brother—her mother, in fact, referred to the three of them as "our trinity"—*nôtre trinité*—and after her brother's accession she spent much of her time with him at court, where, along with her mother, "she was a sort of viceroy."[54] Her intense devotion to her brother led historians, beginning in the eighteenth century, to conclude that their relationship was an incestuous one—a view that is now thoroughly discredited, but one which nonetheless finds its way into modern histories.[55]

Marguerite of Angoulême's most important political effort was made on her brother's behalf when, after his defeat at Pavia, he was held hostage by Charles V. Marguerite undertook a four-month trip to Spain to secure his release from the emperor. She arrived in time to nurse a critically ill Francis back to health, but she failed in her efforts to negotiate an end to his captivity. Nevertheless, she returned to France "a heroine"; in later years Francis is reported to have "often said" that "without her he would have died, and that forever would he recognize his obligation and love her for it." Meanwhile, Marguerite's husband, who had escaped capture at Pavia, had died, and in January of 1527, the woman who has been called the "virtual queen of France" married Henry d'Albret, king of Navarre.[56]

We should pause here for a moment to consider Claude, who was the "real," as opposed to virtual, queen of France. Despite Louis XII's divorce from the childless Jeanne, his subsequent marriage to Anne of Brittany (his predecessor's widow), and his final six-month union with the seventeen-year-old Mary Tudor, the French king never produced the requisite male heir. When he died, he was survived only by Claude and Renée, the daughters of his queen Anne of Brittany.[57] As a woman, Claude could not succeed her father, denied the throne by the so-called Salic law. But Louis secured at least some future for his oldest daughter, negotiating with Louise of Savoy for Claude's marriage to Francis of Angoulême, afterward Francis I.

But as queen consort Claude had no political role; she is conspicuously absent from the "trinity" of Francis, his mother, and his sister, mostly absent from court, often replaced on ceremonial occasions by Louise of Savoy. Indeed, Claude reminds us of no one so much as Elizabeth of York, who married the man who defeated her Yorkist uncle on the battlefield and then claimed the English throne for himself.[58] Both women, daughters of kings, were precluded from claiming the crowns of their respective kingdoms, Elizabeth by circumstance and Claude by law. Like Elizabeth of York, then, Claude might best be viewed as a queen *manquant*, denied both authority and power, dominated by her husband's mother, and relegated to the role of child-bearing. Over the course of nine years Claude dutifully provided her husband with children—Louise, Charlotte, Francis, Henry, Madeleine, Charles, and Margaret—then died in July of 1524, twenty-five years old.[59]

Marguerite of Angoulême, however, was a different kind of woman than her sister-in-law Claude. Politically astute, she made as much of her role as queen consort as she had her role as "virtual" queen. Her husband, the king of Navarre, was the son of Catherine of Foix. In 1512 he had been forced to flee with his mother to the French court after Ferdinand of Aragon conquered Haute Navarre. As queen regnant, Catherine of Navarre retained control over Basse Navarre and the counties of Soule and Béarn, as well as her French possessions. After her death in 1517, her son assumed his title as "ruler-in-exile" of the kingdom.[60] In marrying Henry d'Albret, Marguerite ironically became a "virtual" queen of another sort, acquiring the title of queen if not the actual kingdom.

Marguerite's daughter Jeanne d'Albret, future queen of Navarre, was born at Fountainebleu in November of 1528, but the birth of a child did not keep Marguerite from continuing her political service to her brother; in 1529, she accompanied *her* mother Louise of Savoy to negotiate the treaty of Cambrai with Margaret of Austria. On her return to France, Marguerite supervised her brother's children at Blois. Little is known of Jeanne's life at this point, though she seems to have spent at least part of it in the royal nursery with her cousins; she is not regularly mentioned in her mother's letters, or at least not in those that survive, and only in 1532 is a *gouvernante* provided for her. This seeming lack of interest in her own child, as well as her documented concern for her brother's children, has led to Marguerite's condemnation by many historians; whatever her accomplishments as a politician, writer, or thinker, they are undercut by her failure as a mother.[61] But in detailing the political and religious occupations of Marguerite of Angoulême after her daughter's birth, Nancy Roelker puts the picture into a different perspective: "Jeanne's absentee mother was the most prominent 'career-woman' in Europe."[62]

From about 1530, Jeanne seems to have been established in Alençon, which Marguerite had inherited from her first husband. By 1532 Jeanne was in the care of Aymée de Lafayette, who had accompanied Marguerite on her diplomatic mission to Spain to negotiate Francis's release. After 1532 we can catch glimpses of Marguerite's visits to Alençon and Jeanne's visits to her mother at various places where the court was in residence.[63] Little is certain about the formal education the future queen of Navarre received, but as the granddaughter of a woman whose motto was *libris et liberis*, "for books and for children," and as the daughter of a woman who both patronized humanist scholars and who was herself a writer, Jeanne seems likely to have received the best of educations. Her nominal tutor was the humanist Nicolas Bourbon, whose attacks on the Catholic church had landed him in considerable difficulties. In some danger, he left France for two years, travelling to England where he received the support of Anne Boleyn. Despite the lack of specific detail about Jeanne's curriculum and instruction, Roelker concludes, "There is no doubt that Marguerite's daughter was given an education designed to implement the humanist ideal, that is, the development of both character and intellect through absorption of the classic writings which were the models of the Renaissance."[64]

In 1537 the young princess of Navarre became the source of conflict between her father and her uncle. Despite his earlier promises to help Henry d'Albret recover Haute Navarre from Spain, Francis I had not done so, and Henry had come to regard his daughter as his "principal asset" in his attempt to regain his kingdom. He began secretly negotiating with Charles V for a marriage between Jeanne and the emperor's son, Philip.[65] Francis retaliated, and as Roelker notes, Jeanne "became an instrument of her uncle's policy" as well as of her father's, the "object of rival intrigues": "To become a pawn in the power-struggle of two such men as Henri d'Albret and François I was to acquire an uncomfortable kind of importance—as instrument rather than a human being."[66]

Marguerite seemed at first to support her husband in his efforts to arrange an imperial marriage for their daughter, but when Francis objected, he appealed to Marguerite. Her political decision was relayed in personal terms. Roelker quotes one of Marguerite's letters to Francis from this period: "All my life I have wanted to serve you not as a sister but as a brother." Forced to delay a visit to court because of Jeanne's illness, she continued, "You do me great wrong, Monseigneur, if you think that, compared to the desire I have to see you, either husband or child would count at all."[67]

By the summer of 1538, the ten-year-old Jeanne of Navarre had been ordered to the royal castle of Plessis-les-Tours, where she would spend the next ten years. Despite Marguerite's protestations that her service to her brother is paramount, there is contemporary testimony of her concern for her daughter as well. In January of 1540, learning that Jeanne was "at death's door," her "virtuous mother . . . declared that she would go at once to her daughter." Travelling in haste and at night, she arrived to discover that Jeanne "was still in this world." Marguerite's reaction was not the common one, however. This uncommon woman did not "express wild and uncontrolled joy (as many would have)," but, rather, "lifted her hands to Heaven and loudly praised God's goodness."[68]

During the year between 1540 and 1541, Jeanne's father continuing his efforts to marry her to Philip of Spain, while Francis negotiated for her marriage to William de la Marck, duke of Cleves.[69] Francis signed a contract for the marriage of Jeanne of Navarre and Duke William on 16 July 1540, announcing his plans to the girl and her mother at Fountainebleu, at which time the young princess seems to have signified that she was "content" with her uncle's arrangement. However agreeable mother and daughter may have been, Jeanne's father was not, and he continued to bargain for an alliance with Charles V, apparently to the extent of plotting to kidnap his daughter.

But Jeanne and Marguerite did not remain "content" with the Cleves alliance either. The reasons for Marguerite's opposition to her brother's plan are not clear, but that she opposed it is. To delay the marriage, she pleaded both her daughter's age and health and her own illness. And whether through her parents' efforts or due to her own objections, Jeanne, too, protested the alliance.[70] Nevertheless, on 9 May 1541 the twelve-year-old princess was brought to court to meet with the duke of Cleves, and on 13 June their formal betrothal was celebrated. Jeanne's participation in the ceremony is variously reported. While the duke's chancellor noted that, when "asked each in turn if they were willing to marry each other," each "replied in the affirmative," Jeanne's own historian was later to write that "she never replied either yes or no, but said, 'Don't press me.'" The princess herself secretly prepared a written "explicit protest" to her marriage: "I, Jehanne de Navarre," she wrote, "say and declare and protest again . . . that the marriage proposed between me and the Duke of Cleves is against my will, that I have never consented to it, and that I never will." Anything that she might say or do that seemed to signify her approval was only done "because of force, against my will, out of fear of the King, of my father the

King, and of my mother the Queen, who had me threatened and beaten."
The declaration concluded with an appeal to God and to her witnesses to
show "the force, violence, and constraint which has been used against me
to make me enter . . . the said marriage."[71]

The ceremony went forward, despite the fact that Jeanne did not walk
to the altar; she had to be carried. This, too, has been variously interpreted.
Either she refused as an act of protest, or, as was later reported, she couldn't
walk because she was immobilized by her clothing and jewels: "The bride
was so weighted with jewels and with her gown of gold and silver stuff that
her body was too weak to walk to church."[72] Whatever the reason, she
was carried to the altar, and afterward the duke and the new duchess
performed a ritual consummation of their match: "The bridegroom was led
to the bride's bed, into which he put only one foot, in the presence of the
uncle, the father, and the mother of the bride."[73] The bridegroom left
shortly after for Cleves, which was then being threatened by Charles V.

Jeanne, meanwhile, remained behind in France. Letters from Marguerite
and her daughter to the duke contain no hint of their former objections.
By 1543 Jeanne was deemed old enough to join her husband, and in late
September she was on her way to Cleves when Francis learned that the
emperor had won "a decisive victory" over the duke. William had been
forced to sign a "capitulation" under the terms of which "he surrendered
his lands to Charles V, receiving some of them back as a fief of the Holy
Roman Empire, renounced the French alliance, and promised to return to
the Catholic faith."[74]

Despite his defeat and his supposed renunciation of France, William of
Cleves pressed Francis to send Jeanne, his "lawfully wedded wife," to him,
but the changed circumstances meant that the Cleves alliance was no longer
so useful for the French king. In a letter to her brother, Marguerite wrote
that she would "rather see her [daughter] dead than in the hands of a man
who has done you such a bad turn." Jeanne herself formally renounced her
marriage in a document signed on 11 October 1544; this was followed by
a ceremony at the cathedral of Tours on 5 April 1545. The pope finally
agreed to annul the match on 12 October 1545.

Jeanne was once again an available pawn to be played by the king of
Navarre and the king of France. By 1547, when her marriage was again a
source of conflict between kings, Francis I had been succeeded by his son
Henry II. The new French king arranged a marriage for his cousin with
Antoine de Bourbon, duke of Vendôme, while her father continued to try
to arrange an imperial alliance for her. The king of France prevailed once
more, this time with the complete agreement of Jeanne. Her marriage with
the duke of Vendôme was celebrated on 20 October 1548.

Jeanne spent the next few years as, in Roelker's terms, "a soldier's wife."

War with the empire had been resumed, and Antoine de Bourbon spent most of the time at court or in battle. Jeanne spent some time with her mother, and then, despite Marguerite's failing health, left to follow her husband. A series of final letters between Jeanne of Navarre and Marguerite of Angoulême survives, and although Marguerite wrote that she wanted above all to see her daughter "with these two eyes . . . before I die," Jeanne did not return to her mother. Marguerite of Angoulême died in December of 1549.[75]

Henry d'Albret, meanwhile, continued his efforts to win back Haute Navarre from Spain; after his wife's death, he attempted to regain his lost territories by proposing a marriage for himself with Charles V's niece, who, he suggested, should bring to him Spanish Navarre as her dowry. He, in turn, would make sure that a son born of this marriage would inherit the title of king of Navarre—he was thus willing to disinherit his daughter in order to regain for himself the territories his mother had lost. But his efforts failed, and September of 1551 Jeanne of Navarre gave birth to a son whom she named Henry, after her father.

The young prince died in August of 1553, not quite two years old, and Jeanne seems to have blamed Aymée de Lafayette, her own old governess to whom she had entrusted the rearing of her son, for the child's death.[76] By early June she was pregnant again, and both her husband and her father were with her in December when the baby's birth was imminent. Tradition has it that Henry d'Albret showed Jeanne his will, "fully made out in her favor," prior to the child's birth. He promised to give it to her on two conditions:

first, that while giving birth, she sing a song popular in the region, invoking the aid of the Virgin . . . , and second, that the child be a son, born without a cry, "so that you will not present me with a crying child or a complaining mother."

Jeanne complied with both conditions, and Henry, the future king of Navarre and of France, was born on 14 December.[77]

When her father died in May 1555, Jeanne d'Albret became queen regnant of Navarre, sovereign of Béarn, Soule, and Basse Navarre. She also held a score of French fiefdoms; to those inherited from her mother she added Foix and Albret, among others, from her father. Her husband joined her in Béarn, where they held funeral services for Henry d'Albret and called the Estates into session. Only "after long altercation," did the parliament agree to recognize Antoine of Bourbon, duke of Vendôme as joint sovereign with his wife—they were persuaded only after Jeanne asserted that "if she, who was their Queen and sovereign lady, regarded him as her lord, they should do the same, because the husband is lord of the person and property of his wife."[78]

The new queen of Navarre would come to regret her assertion, but for the moment she and her husband enjoyed their welcome as they progressed through their territories. Together they faced the Emperor Charles V and Henry II of France, both of whom were suspicious of the new monarchs' intentions in Navarre. Within months, Antoine had begun to follow in his father-in-law's footsteps, opening secret negotiations with Charles V in an attempt to regain lost Navarrese territories. His efforts seemed at first to suggest success, but they dragged on, and by 1559, larger events had overtaken his efforts: Spain and France entered into negotiations to end their long years of conflict. Under the circumstances, neither the French nor the Spanish were inclined to focus on the unresolved issue of Navarre. In the same year, Jeanne of Navarre gave birth to a daughter, Catherine of Bourbon.[79]

In Paris for the marriage of Mary Stuart and the dauphin Francis, son of Henry II and Catherine de' Medici, the king and queen of Navarre attended a Calvinist service. For his part, Antoine seems to have regarded his involvement in religious reform as "a vehicle for his ambition"; after his first flirtation with the reform movement, he later rejected Calvinism and persecuted adherents of the new religion. Jeanne, however, underwent a conversion on Christmas Day 1560. In the memoirs she later commanded to be written for her, the so-called *Memoirs of Jeanne d'Albret* (*Mémoires de Jeanne d'Albret*), her conversion and her "differences" with her husband are described in a first-person account:

> Since 1560 everyone knows that it pleased God by His grace to rescue me from idolatry, to which I had been too long given, and to receive me in His church. Since then, by the same grace, He has allowed me to persevere. . . . Even during the lifetime of my husband, the late King (who, withdrawing from his first zeal, put a thorn not in my foot but in my heart . . .) neither favor nor hardship turned me to the right or to the left. . . . I have always followed the straight path.[80]

Our purpose here is not to trace the bloody history of reform in France, nor even to detail Jeanne's participation in the religious turmoil of the period. As Henry II was succeeded on the thrones by his three sons, first Francis II (1559–1560), then Charles IX (1560–1574), and finally Henry III (1574–1589), France was engulfed in political and religious conflict, brought to an end only in 1589, when Jeanne's son Henry of Navarre became King Henry IV of France.[81]

But the queen of Navarre did not live to see her son gain the throne of France. She spent the twelve years of her life between her conversion in

1560 and her death in 1572 defending herself, her faith, her kingdom, and her son.

Immediately after her conversion, Jeanne had returned to Béarn, but in 1561 she travelled once more to the French court, apparently intending to involve herself actively in politics. She may well have had ambitions larger than defending her own interests, however, since it was reported to Philip II of Spain that she had promised her husband "the crown of a great kingdom, in three months" if he would declare himself for the faith she had espoused.[82] But in 1562, apparently with an eye to the French regency rather than an ear to his wife's suggestions she could make him the king of France, Antoine of Bourbon publically denounced the Calvinist movement and official tolerance. He even attempted to "reconvert" his wife, whose reaction is summarized in a contemporary account:

> The Queen of Navarre, a very wise and virtuous princess, tried to soften her husband . . . in vain . . . with tears and prayers . . . moving everyone to pity her. When the Queen Mother [Catherine de' Medici] tried to persuade her to accommodate her husband, she finally replied that, rather than ever go to Mass, if she held her kingdom and her son in her hand, she would throw them both to the bottom of the sea. This was the reason they then left her in peace on this matter.[83]

Antoine refused to allow Jeanne to attend Calvinist services, and contemporary accounts indicate he threatened to seek a divorce from her on the grounds of heresy. Unable to force her to give in, he finally removed her son from her household and ordered her back to Béarn.[84]

A series of civil wars engulfed France, one after the other, between 1562 and 1589; Jeanne was to witness three of them. The first commenced in April 1562, and Jeanne's goal was what Roelker identifies as "a policy of disengagement"; she focused on her own possessions and strengthening her control of them.[85] This prudent course of "strategic neutrality" carried her through to the end of the conflict nearly a year later, in March 1563. While defending her kingdom, she lost a husband; commanding the siege of Rouen in September, Antoine de Bourbon was shot in the shoulder. He died on 17 November 1562. Jeanne did not comment on her loss of her husband in the *Memoirs* she had composed on her behalf; in the first-person narration of the work, "she" said, "I shall restrain myself from saying anything more about the disadvantages of all kinds this brought about for me and my son."[86]

Whatever her personal feelings, Jeanne now regained some measure of control over her son; Henry was to remain at the French court for four more years, but as his mother Jeanne could appoint his governors and make sure that his tutors reflected her religious views. He was the primary subject of a letter she addressed to Catherine de' Medici in February or March of 1563. Jeanne credited God with having given her "the grace" to "purge" herself of "avarice and ambition"; since she was "removed from these two vices," and since she had "an open heart," she indicated to Catherine that she had "special plans . . . to conserve the honor, authority, and grandeur" of her son. In her "affliction," Jeanne acknowledged that she could not carry out these plans without Catherine de' Medici's "favor and good grace." In what she characterized as her "long and wearisome letter" she outlined her concerns for her son; she wanted to assure that he would "succeed to his father's honors and estates" without being "shamed" or having them wasted.[87]

In the four years that followed the first civil war, Jeanne dedicated herself to ensuring the autonomy of her possessions and regaining possession of her son. She considered Philip II's offer of a marriage to one of his sons, which would have threatened her independence as well as her efforts to reform religion in Navarre. Rather than reject it outright, she temporized. "I am thirty-four years old," she said, adding, "It is customary for a widowed princess to wait a year before she remarries. I might change my mind between now and the end of the year." "In the meantime," she wished to continue to be "good neighbors" with Spain. In response, Philip II noted, "This is quite too much of a woman to have as a daughter-in-law." He would rather "destroy her and treat her as such an evil woman deserves."[88]

A papal attack on the queen of Navarre was launched by Pius IV in 1563. In response to a letter of "friendly advice" that threatened condemnation and suggested she was ruining her son, she wrote, "As to the reformation . . . in religion, which I have begun . . . , I am earnestly resolved, by the grace of God, to continue . . . throughout my land of Béarn." As for her son, "instead of lessening" his "heritage," she insisted that she would "increase it by the means appropriate to a true Christian."[89] Her reply did not convince the pope, who on 28 September condemned her for heresy and summoned her to Rome to appear before the Inquisition. If she failed, she faced excommunication.

Catherine de' Medici came to Jeanne's defense on this occasion, though in December of 1563 Pius IV carried through on his threat to excommunicate Jeanne. Faced with rebellion in Navarre, an imperial plot against her, and Catherine's pressure on her, Jeanne was forced to leave Béarn to join the French court, then on a tour of the kingdom. She met up with the travelling court in June of 1564. From the moment of her arrival she sought permission to return to her own territories with her son; instead, she was ordered to take up residence in Vendôme, a fief of France rather than an independent principality, where she was a duchess, not a queen regnant. Her son remained behind.

When the French court finally returned to Paris in May 1566 after its two-year progress throughout the country, Jeanne also returned to the city, where she spent the next eight months. When rebellion threatened in Béarn, she finally convinced Catherine de' Medici to let her return home, arguing that her thirteen-year-old son needed to be introduced to his subjects and his future domain. Mother and son left Paris in January 1567, but a letter from the Spanish ambassador reveals that while Jeanne had convinced Catherine, she had not convinced everyone. "I have it on absolutely reliable authority that she seeks only to fool the King and his mother," he reported.[90] The ambassador's intelligence was correct; Jeanne had no intention of sending her son back to court.

But Jeanne's return to Navarre was not an easy one. Against the backdrop of the second and third religious wars in France, the queen of Navarre faced three organized rebellions in quick succession, between the spring of 1567 and the summer of 1569.[91] Despite resistance, she remained dedicated to religious reform. She was, as well, determined to assure the independence of her kingdom, defending it against both France and Spain in order to preserve it for her son. After one Huguenot defeat, a contemporary chronicler described her appearance "on horseback" before her Protestant forces, whom she revived with her "high heart and lofty resolute spirit": "When I, the Queen, hope still, is it for you to fear?" she is said to have cried, reproaching her troops for their "despair," that "shameful failing of weak natures."[92]

By the fall of 1569, efforts were underway in France to end the third religious war, which finally concluded in August of 1570. To secure the fragile peace between Protestants and Catholics, Catherine de' Medici proposed a marriage between her daughter, the Catholic Marguerite of Valois, and Jeanne of Navarre's son, the Protestant Henry of Navarre. Once more Jeanne delayed, first by putting off a decision, then by putting off Catherine's summons to court. But when the Queen Mother produced the "ultimate weapon"—a charge that Jeanne's first marriage to William of Cleves invalidated her later marriage to Antoine of Bourbon, and that Henry was, therefore, illegitimate—Jeanne prepared once more to travel to the French court.

However unwilling, the queen of Navarre ultimately agreed to the marriage proposed by Catherine de' Medici, and it might be said that these two women together worked out a "ladies' peace" to rival the treaty negotiated by their foremother Louise of Savoy. The two queens met first in February 1572. After weeks of negotiating, the marriage contract was finally agreed to and signed on 11 April. On 4 June, waiting for her son to join her in Paris, Jeanne of Navarre fell ill. She did not live to see her son renounce her faith, convert to Catholicism, and become king of France. She five days later, on 9 June.[93]

Like the other women in our study, the queen of Navarre was widely criticized by her contemporaries. Vilified by Catholics and excommunicated by the pope, she was described by the Florentine ambassador as having a "temper" that was "very eccentric" (*molto fantastico*). It required "both skill and patience to reach her and to pin her down." "She changes often and eludes you every minute," he complained, continuing, "In the end, she hopes to manage everything her own way."[94] In Jeanne's defense, the Huguenot historian Agrippa d'Aubigny provided a more positive judgment of the queen, but even in his defense we see how Jeanne challenged conventional notions of female behavior. While praising her, d'Aubigny wrote that she had "of woman, only the sex, with a soul given to things that rather became men"—that is, "an intelligence at home in great affairs, and a courage invincible in adversity."[95]

Jeanne seems not only to have faced squarely the difficulties of a woman in her position but to have dismissed them as difficulties. In the memoirs of her life she had written for her, "she" addressed the supposed "imbecility" of women in general and herself in particular: "I will not stoop to refute [the argument that women are imbeciles]," she was presented as having said, "but if I wished to undertake the defense of my sex, I could find plenty of examples." The passage in the *Memoirs* concluded, "[T]hese people [who say so] deserve only pity . . . for their ignorance."[96]

Jeanne ruled Navarre as queen regent from 1555 until her death in 1572, a unique moment in history, for—much to John Knox's dismay—a great deal of western Europe was in one way or another under the "monstrous regiment" of women. Among Jeanne's contemporaries were Mary Stuart, queen of Scotland and her mother Marie of Guise, regent of Scotland. England was ruled by two queens regnant in succession, Mary and then Elizabeth Tudor. In Spain Juana of Castile died in the very year of Jeanne's accession, but Juana's niece Margaret of Parma followed Juana's daughter Mary of Austria as regent of the Netherlands. And in France, Jeanne's great adversary and advocate Catherine de' Medici—like Anne of France and Louise of Savoy before her—was regent of France.

We have encountered Catherine—then Caterina—before, briefly touching on her early life.[97] As we have seen, her marriage to Henry of Orléans, younger son of Francis I, represented part of the French king's ongoing effort to consolidate his gains in Italy. In 1517, after his victory at Marignano, Francis I had negotiated a treaty with the Medici pope Leo X. As part of this agreement, Francis awarded Leo's nephew Lorenzo de' Medici both the duchy of Urbino and a bride. "I intend to help you with all my power," the French king promised, adding, "I also wish to marry you off to some beautiful and good lady of noble birth and of my kin, so that the love which I bear you may grow and be strengthened."[98] Accordingly, Lorenzo de' Medici was married to Madeleine de la Tour d'Auvergne, a princess of the royal blood.[99] After a lavish wedding in April 1518 at Amboise, Madeleine travelled to Italy, arriving in Florence in September. A year later, on 13 April 1519, she gave birth to a daughter, Caterina. She did not live long after her baby's birth, however; Caterina's mother died just two weeks later, on 28 April. Days later, on 4 May, Caterina's father died as well.

We have already learned something of the young Caterina's early life in Italy; we will pick up her story in 1533 when Francis I once more sought an Italian alliance. Accordingly, he arranged for the marriage of his younger son Henry to Caterina de' Medici. The two fourteen-year-olds were married by the pope on 28 October, and Caterina, now Catherine, spent the next period of her life at the court of Francis I. Her life took an unexpected turn, however, when the *dauphin*, Francis, died unexpectedly in 1536. Henry became the heir apparent, and Catherine, now *dauphine*, found herself in a precarious position: she had been married for three years and had failed to produce any children.

Nor would she become pregnant for some time. Meanwhile, the French king seems to have considered the possibility that his son should be divorced from a wife who had failed to provide an heir. A report of the Venetian ambassador, written several years after the event, seems to give a reliable account of the situation:

> Lorenzo Contarini . . . reported that Francis and Henri had both decided on a divorce. Catherine allegedly told the king that she owed him so much that she would not stand in his way: she was ready to enter a nunnery or to become the companion of the lady who would be fortunate enough to wed her husband. Francis was apparently so moved by Catherine's gesture that he promised never to banish her.[100]

Catherine's "gesture" and the French king's response are particularly interesting, since the question of her divorce arose so soon after Henry VIII's own "Great Matter"—the English king had finally divorced himself from Catherine of Aragon in 1534, his repudiated wife dying in 1536. As R. J. Knecht notes in his biography of Catherine de' Medici, the young wife "could not be certain that reason of state would not oblige Francis or his son to set her aside." Her "best safeguard," Knecht concludes, "was to become pregnant."[101] That, of course, is easier said than done. In the meantime, Catherine de' Medici's willingness to step aside gracefully—or, at any rate, her offer to do so—can be contrasted to Catherine of Aragon's refusal to do so. By the same token, Francis I's decision *not* to insist on a divorce can be contrasted to Henry VIII's insistence that he *must* have one.

The *dauphine* was further humiliated when her husband's mistress gave birth to an illegitimate child in 1537, thus proving that the "fault" in conception was hers and not Henry's. But, given time, she was eventually successful. Her first child, a son named Francis, was born in January 1544; his birth was followed, in rapid succession, by Elizabeth (1545), Claude (1547), Louis (1549), Charles-Maximilien (1550), Edouard-Alexandre (later Henry, 1551), Marguerite (1553), Hercule (later Francis of Anjou, 1555), and twin daughters, Jeanne and Victoire (1556). Having fulfilled her duties as a woman at last, Catherine de' Medici remained in the background throughout the remaining years of her father-in-law's reign and, after her husband succeeded to the throne as Henry II in 1547, throughout her years as queen consort, though she was briefly appointed regent in 1548 when the king travelled to Italy and then in 1552, when Henry was at the siege of Metz. On this occasion, she resisted her husband's effort to curtail her authority by referring to the powers granted to his grandmother Louise of Savoy when *she* was regent.

Despite these brief regencies, Catherine de' Medici was dominated at the royal court by the king's mistress, Diane de Poitiers, who, as Knecht notes, "exercised considerable political influence" throughout Henry's reign.[102] Even so, at least one contemporary saw the queen's potential. The Venetian ambassador noted, "She is not beautiful, but she possesses extraordinary wisdom and prudence; there is no doubt that she would be adept at governing, even though she is neither consulted nor considered to the extent that she deserves to be."[103] When Henry II died in 1559, at the age of forty, the fifteen-year-old *dauphin* succeeded to his father's throne as Francis II, and his young wife, Mary Stuart, already queen of Scotland, became queen of France. Henry II's mistress was banished from the court, but his queen was denied an opportunity to realize whatever potential skill at governing she might possess. Now Queen Mother, Catherine de' Medici was relegated to the background once more; any influence she might have expected to exert as "the king's mother" was denied to her by Mary Stuart's two uncles, the duke of Guise and his brother the cardinal of Lorraine, who engineered what Knecht describes as a coup d'état immediately following Henry II's death.

Although related to French royalty, the Guise family itself represented the duchy of Lorraine, still part of the Holy Roman Empire. Thus the duke of Guise and his brother were regarded with suspicion and resentment as "aliens and usurpers."[104] Despite Guise control of the king and his policies, the king's mother began gradually to claim a public role for herself. In response to the "increasingly draconian legislation" designed to suppress heresy, her "pity and compassion"—if not her political insight—led her to work for some measure of conciliation with Protestant reformers, and to her influence can be credited the March 1560 edict of Amboise, which "offered amnesty to all peaceful reformers."[105] And the king's mother seems to have been "mainly responsible" for the edict of Romorantin, issued some two months later. In distinguishing between heresy and sedition, the edict "unwound" the "savage persecution" of the reformers: "Protestants were implicitly tolerated as long as they behaved discreetly."[106] In August, when she presided over the opening of an assembly gathered at Fontainebleau aimed at reform of the judicial system and of the church, she tried to steer a middle course between the contending and contentious factions.

The outbreak of civil war seemed imminent when, on 5 December, fate intervened, and Francis II died. The grieving mother appeared before the privy council the next day: "Since it has pleased God to deprive me of my elder son, I mean to submit to the Divine will and to assist and serve the King, my second son, in the feeble measure of my experience," she announced. The new king, Charles IX, was ten years old. "I have decided . . . to keep him beside me, and to rule the State as a devoted mother must do," she concluded.[107] Several days later, the Venetian ambassador reported, "In the government, the Queen Mother is considered as the one whose will is supreme in all matters; it is she who will henceforth have her hand upon the most important negotiations." He continued, "within the Council there will be no chief other than herself."[108] On 21 December, Catherine de' Medici, the king's mother, became "governor of the kingdom." In a letter to her daughter, she described her "principal aim": "to have the honour of God before my eyes in all things and to preserve my authority, not for myself, but for the conservation of this kingdom and for the good of all your brothers."[109]

In the period following her second son's accession to the throne, Catherine "continued to hope for religious compromise": "She worked for a provisional toleration of Huguenot worship and the ultimate reunion of Catholic and Calvinist by means of wide concessions in ceremonial and discipline and the mutual acceptance of doctrinal formulae."[110] Her "pragmatic" efforts resulted, first, in the Colloquy of Pouissy (September to November 1561), which aimed at religious conciliation, and then, when reconciled failed, in the March 1562 edict of January, which, granting concessions to both sides, satisfied neither and angered both. By April the first war of religion had begun.

While she sought peace, the Queen Mother, now regent of France, did not fear war. When warned away from siege of Rouen, she is said to have responded to the duke of Guise and the Constable of France, who led French forces, "My courage is as great as yours."[111] By March of 1563 she was once more able to negotiate a settlement, the peace of Amboise (March 1563). She next turned her attention to getting rid of the English troops Queen Elizabeth had sent to France in support of Huguenot forces. She openly rallied French forces, Huguenot and Catholic alike, against the English troops, who surrendered in July.

Soon after, in August 1563, Catherine had her son declared of age. Although he was only thirteen, she was wanted to have him accepted as king, recognizing that a king "commanded more authority" than a regent. She officially handed over the government of France to him. But the recognition of the king's majority had been sought at Rouen, and the *Parlement* of Paris opposed it. To gain support for her son she commenced the "grand tour" that stretched out over the course of two years, from March 1564 through May 1566. As part of this journey, she also negotiated an alliance designed to strengthen the ties between France, Spain, and the empire by arranging for a marriage between her son and Elizabeth of Austria.[112]

Throughout this period, as we have seen, religious tensions remained high. To this period, too, dates Catherine de' Medici's efforts on behalf of the queen of Navarre; in addition to shielding her from papal condemnation, Catherine met with Jeanne d'Albret in Béarn and urged the Protestant queen to tolerate Catholicism within her realm. For her part, as we have seen, Jeanne agreed to rejoin the court in Paris, then sought permission to take her son with her to her kingdom for a visit so that his future subjects could meet him. When Jeanne left France with her son, her individual act of rebellion was followed by open Huguenot rebellion in September 1567, which Catherine condemned as "infamous," the "greatest wickedness in the world," and "unmitigated treason."[113]

The second religious war was ended in March 1568, with the peace of Longjumeau, which confirmed the peace of Amboise. By August, however, it had been revoked, sparking the third religious war, which lasted until 1570, when peace was restored and the edict of Saint-Germain published. During the brief peace that followed, Charles IX's marriage to Eleanor of Austria was celebrated, and in March the king addressed the parliament of Paris, expressing his gratitude to his mother for her care of the country:

> After God . . . I am most obliged to my mother. Thanks to her tenderness towards me and my people, her application, her zeal and her prudence, the affairs of the state have been so well managed when I was too young to attend to them myself that the storms of civil war have not damaged my kingdom.[114]

In further matrimonial efforts, Catherine offered her daughter Marguerite to Jeanne of Navarre as a match for *her* son, Henry of Albret; the marriage took place on 18 August 1572. To Queen Elizabeth, she offered her third son, Henry of Anjou (the queen of England was thirty-seven, Henry seventeen), but the young duke resisted his mother's efforts to marry him off to a woman he considered "a whore"; undaunted, Catherine offered up her youngest son, the sixteen-year-old Francis, duke of Alençon. Elizabeth, as we know, took neither, but that didn't stop Catherine from hoping that the union would come about.[115]

The fragile peace that had allowed Catherine de' Medici to pursue her matrimonial schemes did not last; after the notorious St. Bartholomew's Day massacre, which took place on 24 August 1572, religious war resumed. Whether Catherine was responsible for the massacre, satisfied with its results, or worn out by the religious conflict, she turned her attention to securing the throne of Poland for her son Henry, duke of Anjou. To those who questioned her policy, she pointed out its strengths: French influence would be extended into a new kingdom, and an ally against the empire would be guaranteed.[116] She was successful in her efforts; Henry was elected king of Poland on 29 May 1573.

A year later, the new king of Poland would return to France as its king. On 30 May 1574, the twenty-three-year-old Charles IX died in his mother's arms after signing an act appointing her to act as regent of France. The next day Catherine wrote to her son, the new king, summoning him home: "I am grief stricken . . . to have witnessed such a scene and the love which he showed me at the end," she wrote. "He could not leave me and begged me to send for you in great haste and pending your return to take charge of the government and to punish the prisoners who, he knew, were the cause of all the kingdom's ills." Her only consolation was to look forward to seeing her son "here soon," as his kingdom "required." If she were to lose him too, she claimed she would have herself "buried alive" with him. She then outlined her plans for governing France until his return:

> I will keep all benefices and offices that will fall vacant. We shall tax them as there is not an *écu* left to do all the things you need to do to maintain your kingdom. Your late brother has entrusted me with that task, and I will not let you down: I will do my best to hand it over to you entire and at peace so that you should not have to work for your greatness and to allow you a little pleasure after so much worry and care. . . . The experience you have gained from your voyage [in Poland] is such that I am sure that there has never been a king as wise as you.

Since he left, she had had "only worry on top of worry"; thus, she concluded, "I believe that your return will bring me joy and contentment and that I will no longer have trouble or annoyance."[117]

But Catherine's confidence in her son's wisdom was misplaced, and her longed-for "joy and contentment" eluded her. She was to spend the remainder of her life trying to maintain peace among her children—her son the king, her son Alençon, her daughter Marguerite, and her son-in-law Henry of Navarre, who described the atmosphere of the French court in a letter to a friend:

> The court is the strangest I have ever known. . . . We are nearly always ready to cut each other's throat. We carry daggers, wear coats of mail and often a cuirass beneath a cape. . . . The king is as vulnerable as I am. . . . I am waiting for a minor battle, for they say they will kill me, and I want to be one jump ahead of them.[118]

Beyond keeping order among her children, Catherine continued to work for peace in France: as Knecht indicates, she was "extremely active politically, travelling widely across the kingdom, often enduring severe physical hardship, in order to help her son impose his authority."[119]

The situation in France remained tumultuous: The king's brother involved himself in the Dutch revolt against the Spanish, threatening to draw France into the conflict; unrest in the south of France erupted into open war; her daughter Marguerite's defiance of her husband resulted in a public scandal; and the death of the troublesome Alençon threw the country into a succession crisis.[120] With the death of Henry III's younger brother, the Protestant Henry d'Albret, king of Navarre became heir presumptive to the French throne, a prospect that revived the Guise party, which negotiated an agreement with Spain in 1584 to defend the Catholic faith in France and to exclude the Huguenot heir from the throne. The Holy League recognized the cardinal of Bourbon as heir presumptive in France. When war began again, Henry III turned to his mother.

The aging Catherine de' Medici once more negotiated for peace. She travelled to Epernay to negotiate in person with Henry of Guise, so ill she often remained in bed while she worked; added to her "usual ailments (colics, catarrh, rheumatism)" were "a persistent cought, an earache, a pain in her side and thigh, gout, toothache" and unidentified "bouts of sickness." The unyielding position of the Catholic Guises made her efforts at conciliation impossible; the resulting treaty of Nemours was, in Knecht's terms, "a humiliating capitulation by the king."[121] The sixty-seven-year-old Catherine, for her part, summed up her frustration and despair, caught between opposing forces that had no interest in compromise: "If I had a voice . . . I would please kings and popes until I had forces to command and not to obey."[122]

Meanwhile Catherine had suggested to the Huguenot Henry of Navarre that he renounce his faith in order to remove opposition to his succession. To that end, she arranged to meet with him in December 1586. In a series of encounters that extended into March of 1587, she sought to come to terms with him, but her efforts failed. In May she was off again, this time to meet once more with the Guises. In September Henry III prepared for war, leaving his mother in control of the government of Paris during his absence, but without the power and authority to act effectively on his behalf. Blamed for his failure with the forces allied against him, she wrote that her son had been taught "that he must obey God's command to love and honour his mother" but "not to give her the authority and credit" she needed to act effectively on his behalf.[123]

When her son arranged for the murder of the duke of Guise and his brother on 23 and 24 December, he announced their assassination to his mother himself. On Christmas Day she told a friar attending her that she saw her son "rushing towards his ruin"; "I am afraid he may lose his body, soul and kingdom." Although she had spent her life in the service of peace, she was blamed for what had happened. Called to her side on 1 January 1589, the cardinal of Bourbon reportedly said, "Your words, Madam, have led us all to this butchery."[124] She died on 5 January.

Like Louise of Savoy before her, and Anne of France before them both, Catherine de' Medici received both praise and condemnation in her day. The Venetian ambassador had once noted that "the blame of everything that happens is put on the Queen Mother"; no matter what she did, he observed, she was "little loved" because she was "a foreigner and an Italian."[125] On hearing of her death, a contemporary chronicler recorded the following appraisal of Catherine in his diary:

> She was seventy-one years old and well preserved for such a fat woman. She ate heartily and was not afraid of work . . . although she had to face as much as any queen in the world since the death of her husband thirty years before. . . . She was mourned by some of her servants and intimates and a little by her son the king. . . . Those closest to her believed that her life had been shortened by displeasure over her son's deed. This was due not so much to her friendship for the victims (whom she liked in the Florentine way—that is to say, in order to make use of them) but because she could see that it would benefit the king of Navarre, her son-in-law, whose ruin she had sworn to bring about by any means. His succession was what she feared most in the world. Parisians, however, believed that she had given her consent to the murder of the Guises, and . . . said that if her body were brought to Paris for burial in the magnificent sepulchre she had built for herself and her late husband, Henry, they would drag it through the streets or throw it in the river. So much for the Parisian view. In Blois, where she had been adored and revered as the court's Juno, she had no sooner passed away than she was treated with as much consideration as a dead goat.[126]

In both of these evaluations of Catherine de' Medici, we can see the seeds of what Nicola Sutherland has described as "the legend of the wicked Italian queen," which grew out of Catherine's "dual disadvantages": She had the "misfortune" of being "both a woman and of Italian paternity." (The fact that Machiavelli had dedicated *The Prince* to her father only fed fears of Catherine de' Medici's ruthless ambition.) Beginning in the seventeenth century, accounts of her life stressed her personal ambition, her treachery, her intrigues, and her weaknesses. By the nineteenth century, the "legend" of her wickedness was "complete in all its ugly, incoherent vituperation."[127] As Sutherland makes clear, such views of Catherine de' Medici have not altogether changed. Citing two eminent historians—J. E. Neale and Garrett Mattingly—she demonstrates how these views have persisted into the twentieth century.[128]

To arrive at a more accurate view of Catherine de' Medici, we need to to place the "black legend" surrounding Catherine, the "wicked Italian queen," within in the context of the treatment of women rulers, particularly those women who were foreign queens in the countries where they exercised power. When we compare Catherine de' Medici's reputation to those of women like Isabel of Bavaria, Margaret of Anjou, and Marie of Guise, for example, we can see how common such a "legend" is; while no less ugly, it is all too familiar.

Catherine herself was only too aware of these contemporary views, accepting them as a necessary consequence of her role. "I have preserved and guarded this realm from being divided into several parts," she wrote to her son, "God granted it to me that I might see it entirely obedient to yourself." Given her duty, she accepted "whatever evil or hatred" directed toward herself "this may have occasioned."[129] Even so, like her contemporary Elizabeth Tudor, Catherine de' Medici endeavored to craft an image to counter her reputation.

As queen consort Catherine de' Medici had been figured as the goddess Juno, but after her husband's death, she needed what Sheila ffolliott has called "a radically redefined role." While the unmarried English queen Elizabeth fashioned her image as the "Virgin queen," the French queen needed an image that would fit her situation: "Since her only ties to the French throne were through her deceased husband and her male children," ffolliott notes, "any imagery that would enhance her position as regent would have to be based on her status as a widowed mother." She decided to base her imagery on Artemesia, the "inconsolable widow" who "dramatically mourned the loss of her husband—the rightful monarch—and stood as an authoritative ruler in his stead." To illustrate her "indirect" rule, she was "always shown with her son, never running things on her own," but in this "marginalized position," ffolliott writes, "she is shown to exercise great power." Artemisia was an "ideal woman," perpetually mourning her lost husband, who epitomized as well the "masculine virtues of a ruler." She was thus a "perfect" image for Catherine de' Medici to deploy in her efforts to craft a public persona to counter her reputation: "Artemisia was the epitome of a nonthreatening prototype."[130]

Both Jeanne d'Albret, queen regnant of Navarre, and Catherine de' Medici, queen regent of France, thus proved themselves formidable "daughters" of Anne of France. But in the next generation, their own daughters found less room to craft for themselves a political role.

Catherine of Bourbon, Jeanne d'Albret's daughter, was as dedicated to her brother Henry of Navarre as Jeanne's mother, Marguerite of Angoulême, had been to *her* brother, Francis I. While Henry, a valuable playing piece in the game of succession, had been wrested away from the queen of Navarre and spent a considerable amount of his youth at the French court, Catherine was allowed to remain with her mother throughout her childhood. From her mother she received not only a humanist education but her Huguenot religion. After her mother's death the Protestant princess was transferred to the guardianship of Catherine de' Medici. Something of a Catholic "re-education" was attempted, but in 1576 Catherine of Bourbon was allowed to return to Béarn and, along with her brother, made a "public profession" of her Calvinist faith.

Seventeen years old, the young princess began what might have become a political career to rival her mother's if she had been given the opportunity to continue in this role. In 1577 her brother appointed her to govern Béarn in his stead, granting her the title of lieutenant-general. She exercised power for some ten months. From February until October 1582 she again served as her brother's representative, this time in Pau. In July 1583 she returned to Béarn where she remained until 1592 and occupied herself "with indefatigable zeal" governing "in the interests of her brother." Roelker notes that "she proved to be an efficient administrator and was very popular with her subjects."[131]

But Catherine's marriage proved more useful to her brother than her role as governor in Béarn. In his own political maneuvering, her brother could use Catherine's marriage to advance his cause. Consequently, he forced her to give up a love match with her cousin Charles of Bourbon and arranged her marriage to the Catholic Henry of Lorraine, duke of Bar. The marriage was delayed at first by her refusal to submit to it and then, once her agreement had been achieved, by her refusal to abjure her faith. The marriage was finally celebrated on 31 January 1599. She left for Lorraine in March, after having exerted "all her influence" to hasten the recording of the Edict of Nantes.[132] Although Henry had promised that after her marriage he would return her share of their inheritance from their mother, he did not do so.

Unlike her brother, Catherine would not renounce her mother's religion, to which she remained faithful even in Bar and despite papal excommunication. She remained equally devoted to her brother as well, her letters reflecting her powerful emotions. Right after her marriage, she "humbly begs" for his understanding and friendship, reminding him of "the obedience, affection, and faithfulness" that she had given him her entire life. She closed with "eyes full of tears," sending him "a thousand kisses." Later, suffering from a fever that has delayed her on her trip, she wrote, "I am sure you don't mind that your little sister brings herself to your attention and assures you of her undying affection and humble obedience." She continued, "O my dear king, how I miss you! I am sure my cruel pain results from having to part from you." She concluded lovingly, "Let me close this letter . . . by sending you a million kisses, my dear, wonderful king."[133] Just two months later, in June 1599, she told her brother she was "grateful" to him for providing her "a good husband." Nevertheless, her "changed" condition—her marriage—made her "no less subject" to her brother's commands. "You are my advocate and judge," she wrote, "I took the husband you gave me. Let me know that this obedience pleases you. You are able to make me happy or miserable."[134]

Aside from professions of love to her brother, Catherine's letters spoke of her desire for a child, not so much to provide her husband an heir as to present her brother a nephew "to serve him." "I love you more than myself," she wrote in August, "Command me, my King, to make you a little page." A sad note indicates her fears about her ability to become pregnant: "I fear that unless you command it yourself, he [the "little page"] will not consent to lodge in my body."[135] But there were to be no children. She spent the remaining few years of her life in Bar. She was not allowed to return to Béarn, even for a visit, although she did make two brief trips to the French court. She died in February 1604, believing herself to be pregnant. Her last words were "Save my child." Her brother the king buried her next to their mother.[136]

Catherine of Bourbon nevertheless did prove herself, in the only way she could, her mother's daughter, for nothing and no one, not even the brother to whom she was so passionately devoted, could change her religious views. Denied personal and political agency, she funneled her energy and commitment into her faith instead. Her life thus illustrates Nancy Roelker's assessment of the role religion came to play in the lives of many women like Catherine of Bourbon: "Circumstances made religion the most obvious vehicle—and the most acceptable socially—for the assertion of a woman's independence in the sixteenth century."[137]

While she lived, Jeanne of Navarre had focused all her political efforts on her son, failing to arrange a marriage for her daughter that might have insured both Catherine of Bourbon's inheritance and her independence. Catherine de' Medici, by contrast, recognized the significance of marriages for her daughters, though her care and attention did not necessarily produce more successful futures for them.

The marriage of her oldest daughter, Elizabeth of Valois, was a part of the 1559 peace of Cateau-Cambrésis. To seal the peace between their countries, the thirteen-year-old French princess was to become the third wife of the recently widowed Philip II of Spain. The marriage was celebrated on 22 June 1599. In 1566 Elizabeth gave birth to a daughter, Isabel Clara Eugenia.[138] By 1568 the young queen of Spain was dead.

The marriage of Catherine's second daughter, Claude, was celebrated just months before her older sister became the Spanish queen, and it too represented an effort at political conciliation. The young princess, not yet twelve years old, was married in January 1599 to Charles of Lorraine, son and heir of the Guise duke of Lorraine. In 1575, not yet thirty years old, Claude, duchess of Lorraine died.

A number of political marriages had been considered for Marguerite of Valois, Catherine's youngest daughter. In 1561 the Queen Mother suggested Marguerite to her son-in-law the king of Spain as a bride for his son and heir, Don Carlos, a course she was still pursuing in 1564. Immediately after the death of her daughter Elizabeth in 1568, she suggested to Philip II that he, rather than his son, marry Marguerite. When the Spanish king declined to pursue the match, she turned instead to Portugal, attempting to arrange a marriage between her third daughter and Sebastian, the young king. When *that* proposal, too, failed, she ultimately turned to Henry of Navarre. Marguerite was married to the king of Navarre in Paris on 18 August 1572, the alliance aimed at keeping the peace between Catholics and Protestants. The effort was an immediate failure, the St. Bartholomew's Day massacre taking place just five days later.

La reine Margot has gained notoriety—for her sexual relationships, for her involvement in various conspiracies and plots, for her vivid *Memoirs*. As the king of Navarre's queen consort she was a "failure"; she not only failed to produce the requisite heir for her husband, she abandoned him in 1585, took a lover, or series of lovers, and involved herself with the Guise party. Outraged, her brother Henry III condemned her and banished her to the castle of Usson in 1586. Catherine de' Medici too condemned her daughter, referring to her as "this creature," this "insufferable torment," and this "affliction" that had been sent to punish her.[139] With the help of the Guises, Marguerite regained her freedom, remaining in Auvergne.

When her marriage to Henry of Navarre was annulled in 1600, she retained her royal title. In 1605 she returned to Paris, where she lived the last ten years of her life. The sixteenth-century double standard applied to women and to men is reflected today in the *Encyclopedia Britannica*'s final comment on her "licentiousness": in Paris, "she lived in magnificent style, free to pursue her amours." And, as a afterthought, "In addition to her *Mémoires*, she wrote poems and letters."[140]

While her daughters failed to follow in their mother's political footsteps, Catherine de' Medici's granddaughters and great-granddaughters proved more successful. Elizabeth of Valois' daughter Isabel Clara Eugenia was suggested as a Catholic alternative to the succession of the religiously suspect Henry of Navarre after the death of Henry III of France. But as a woman she did not—and could not—become ruler of France. She did become regent of the Netherlands.[141] After Claude of Valois' death, Catherine de' Medici arranged for the marriage of her granddaughter Christine of Lorraine to Ferdinand, grand duke of Tuscany in 1589. Christine's two daughters, Catherine and Claudia, became, respectively, Governor of Siena and Regent of Tyrol.[142]

When *la reine Margot* agreed to the annulment of her marriage, she made way for a woman who, as a Medici, was a "daughter" of both Catherine de' Medici and of *Madame la grand*, Anne of France. Marie de' Medici was also a direct descendant of another powerful foremother, Caterina Sforza. Thus she provides a fitting end not only for our chapter on the "daughters" of Anne of France but also for our study of women and power in early modern Europe.

Like Catherine de' Medici, Marie was ridiculed in France as the descendant of rich merchants, but as with her Medici foremother, such was not entirely the case. Her father Francesco II de' Medici was undoubtedly the descendant of wealthy merchants, but he was also related to powerful cardinals and popes and succeeded his brother as grand duke of Tuscany. Marie de' Medici's mother was Joanna of Austria, the daughter of the Holy Roman Emperor Ferdinand and Anne Jagellion, queen of Hungary; through her mother, then, Marie was related to Habsburg royalty throughout Europe.[143] The young Marie was sixteen years old when she attended the burial of Catherine de' Medici in 1589, and legend has it that on this occasion her lifelong friend and companion Leonora Dori, later Leonora Galigai and later still Leonora Concini, said that there was no reason Marie should not occupy the French throne herself one day. As improbable as the prediction may have seemed, Marie did succeed her Medici cousin on the throne of France.

The childless Henry III was assassinated soon after Catherine de' Medici's death, and Henry of Navarre became Henry IV of France. The new king already had a wife, Marguerite of Valois, from whom he was estranged, and a mistress, Gabrielle d'Estrées, to whom he was devoted. Nevertheless Marie's uncle Ferdinand, grand duke of Tuscany, offered the new king his political support against the Catholic League that opposed his accession—if Henry would accept his niece as a bride. Henry IV could not afford to reject the duke's offer, but neither did he accept it. He wanted to marry his mistress; his wife, however, refused to cooperate with the annulment of their marriage unless he accepted the offered Medici alliance. In 1594 Henry IV converted to Catholicism and entered Paris; by 1599, somewhat more secure on his throne, he announced his intention of marrying Gabrielle. Within a month, however, she died in childbirth, and Marguerite agreed to release him from their marriage; by the spring of 1600 the king was negotiating with Ferdinand of Tuscany for a match with Marie. They were married by proxy on 5 October.

The forty-eight-year-old king had many illegitimate children, but Marguerite had "failed" to provide him a son, so Henry had no legitimate heir to follow him on the throne. His new bride arrived in France in November and quickly produced the requisite son. Louis, later King Louis XIII, was born on 27 September 1601. Five more children followed: Elizabeth, born in 1602; Christine, in 1606; Henry, in 1607; Gaston, in 1608; and Henrietta Maria, in 1609.[144]

While fruitful, the marriage of Henry IV and Marie de' Medici was not easy, but despite their frequent and public quarrels, it was not the disaster that so many historians claim.[145] But successful or not, it did not last forever. On 14 May 1610 Henry IV was assassinated.

Just the day before the king's death, Marie de' Medici had been crowned queen of France in a splendid ceremony. Despite his original "command" that his queen "not meddle in affairs of state," the coronation ceremony had taken place so that Marie's position as regent of France could be strengthened while the king undertook a military campaign in the Netherlands. Within two hours of her husband's assassination, Marie placed her children under guard to safeguard their security, secured the streets around the Louvre palace, and appeared before the *Parlement* of Paris to have her regency acknowledged.[146]

In conducting herself as queen regent, Marie decided to model herself on her predecessor and cousin Catherine de' Medici; she aimed for conciliation and appeasement. "Her task," as A. Lloyd Moote defines it, was "avoiding internal turmoil and external danger." Her "success in achieving those twin aims must, in the immediate setting, be considered a major achievement."[147] After the rivalries and tensions that had culminated in her husband's assassination, the queen's regency was at first welcomed by opposing factions and began peacefully. Marie herself approached her new role as regent with a measure of confidence and optimism; "I can call myself very fortunate and quite consoled because of the good order and great tranquillity that begin to be seen in the affairs of this realm" she wrote to her sister three months after her husband's death.[148] But her optimism proved to be ill-founded.

Unlike her model, Marie was not a success as regent. Religious unrest continued to be a problem, and relationships with foreign powers were uneasy. To complicate matters further, her relationship with her son the king was tense. Resentful of the humiliations she had endured during her husband's life, she abandoned his counselors and friends, turning for support to her Italian courtiers, to Rome, and to her Habsburg relatives.[149] For her principal advisor she looked to her friend Leonora's husband Concino Concini, whom she arranged to have appointed *maréchal* of France, an appointment that "conferred [on him] the second-highest military honor in France."[150] Unlike Henry IV, Louis XIII had been raised a Catholic, like Marie herself; to defuse religious tensions, Marie acted to "curb inflammatory rhetoric" on both sides of the relgious debate and "republished the agreement of Nantes in 1612, 1614, and twice in 1615." Among the most serious problems Marie faced was the external danger posed by Habsburg aggression. Accordingly, she "placed all her hopes" on the Franco–Spanish pact negotiated in 1612. To appease the increasingly rebellious nobility, Marie offered a number of concessions, but, as Louis' biographer Elizabeth Marvick notes, this "policy of appeasement" was "costly," and in spite of her efforts, "public tranquillity continued to be disturbed by dissatisfied lords."[151]

In 1614 Louis XIII was fourteen years old, the age at which he could be proclaimed an adult, capable of ruling without a regent. Marie, under increasing pressure, was forced to summon a meeting of the Estates General. On 2 October Louis' majority was declared; during the ceremony marking the occasion, he announced his intention to assume his role as king:

> Gentlemen, having arrived at the age of majority . . . I intend to govern my realm by good counsel, with piety and justice. I expect from all my subjects the obedience and respect that are due the sovereign power and royal authority which God has placed in my hands.

But "he" did not intend to rule alone. He noted with gratitude the role his mother had played as regent in the preceding years and concluded with a request to her that she "continue" to "govern and command" as she had "heretofore."[152]

Gaining some recognition during the 1614–1615 meetings of the Estates was Armand de Richelieu, then bishop of Luçon. By the summer of 1615 Marie's pro-Spanish policy came to fruition with a double marriage: Her thirteen-year-old daughter Elizabeth was married to the ten-year-old Philip, son and heir of Philip III of Spain, while Louis XIII was married to the thirteen-year-old Anne of Austria, Philip's older sister. Although these alliances represented a personal success for the regent, they only increased the disaffection of the nobility, and despite a truce agreement reached in 1616, the resulting conflict culminated in the assassination of Concini on 24 April 1617. The next day, the fifteen-year-old Louis turned on his mother. He exiled her to the chateau of Blois: "Madame," he is quoted as saying to her, "I wish to relieve you now of the fatigue of state business." He continued:

> It is time for me to take this burden from you for I do not intend to allow anyone else to do so. But I shall always treat you with the respect due to a mother. You will hear from me at Blois. *Adieu, madame*. Do not cease to love me and you will find me a good son.

Marie responded: "Sire, I regret not having acted, as regent, in accordance with your wishes. But I did my best, and I beg you to consider me in future your humble and obedient mother and servant."[153]

Interestingly, Louis' harsh treatment of his mother and her friend Leonora Concini, who was tried for witchcraft and executed, encouraged support for the queen. After she was denied permission to attend the marriage of her daughter Christine to Victor Amadeus, heir to the duke of Savoy, in February 1619, her "rescue"—or escape—was arranged. With the aid of Richelieu, she travelled to Provence and raised a rebellion against her son. The king gathered an army to proceed against his mother, preparing for the first of the so-called Wars of the Mother and Son. Mother and son were reconciled, and by the terms of the treaty of Angoulême, signed on 30 April, he assigned her the governorship of Anjou.[154]

By 1620, mother and son were once more at odds, and the second "War of the Mother and Son" commenced. This time the king was determined not to surrender to his mother. Accordingly, he went to war against his mother's army, which he defeated. With a "face-saving acknowledgment" that "she had taken up arms only out of fear of being oppressed by the royal government," Marie signed the treaty of Angers in August. Within six weeks "the king's mother" had been restored to her son's good graces and rejoined his privy council.[155]

In thanks to Richelieu, she arranged for his appointment as cardinal, and in 1624 Cardinal Richeliu also joined the king's council. Marie's restoration was so complete that in 1621 and 1622, while her son was engaged in a fight against the Huguenots, she often travelled with him. The king, for his part, turned increasingly to his mother for advice. "There was only one person who seemed cautious and sensible" to him, according to Tapié:

The queen mother had lost none of her ambition of desire for power, but now she strove to avoid any upheaval. She confined herself to telling Louis XIII that his realm was badly governed, that his ministers were no longer achieving anything notable, that they were especially negligent in their conduct of foreign policy, and that in consequence French prestige was on the wane all over Europe.

But such "insight" was not her own, Tapié asserts; she was, in "reality," simply "obediently reciting something that she had been taught," in this case the advice of Richelieu.[156]

Whatever the ultimate source of Marie's advice to her son, Louis nevertheless relied on her, appointing her as regent of France in 1627–28, when he joined his forces at the siege of La Rochelle, and again in 1629, when he was in Savoy.[157] But when Richelieu advised the king to pursue a course of conciliation with the Huguenots and with Protestant Europe to balance Habsburg influence, Marie turned against her former adviser. On 10 November 1630, she demanded that her son dismiss Richelieu. She believed Louis would honor her demand, but she was wrong. Instead, her supporters were eliminated; by February 1631 she was exiled again, "escorted" to Compiègne. Louis seems to have considered sending her back to Florence; instead he allowed her to "escape" to Brussels. Her son "declared her a rebel against his authority, outlawed her person, and sequestrated her property."[158]

Although her nephew Ferdinand II of Tuscany offered her asylum in Florence, Marie de' Medici refused. In June 1633 she was in Ghent and ill; Richelieu sent her a note of sympathy, which she rejected, but by February of 1634 she wrote him to ask him to ask for a reconciliation. When he answered, he advised her to go to Tuscany.[159] Her younger son Gaston, whom she seems to have encouraged to think of gaining the throne of France for himself, had followed her to the Netherlands, but by 1635 he had reconciled to his brother and returned to France. Marie repeatedly asked Louis to allow her to return to Paris as well.

When French troops threatened to invade the Netherlands in 1638, the exiled Marie de' Medici fled to England, where her daughter Henrietta Maria was queen, married to Charles I, and where the former queen consort and queen regent of France was decidedly unwelcome. Again Marie wrote to Richelieu: "I have forgotten the past. I only want to be friends with you. I should be so happy if you would deign to grant me the great favour of my return to France."[160] Marie seems also to have been considering yet another regency, rumors of which reached Richelieu, but her efforts at reconciliation came to nothing.

Meanwhile, England had been plunged into its own internal difficulties, and the increasingly unpopular king found that the presence of his Catholic mother-in-law only added to his problems. Attacked in parliament, she was finally forced to leave England in 1641, but where she would go was problematic. Her predicament is described by Cleugh: "England had rejected her. France declined to receive her. Even King Philip IV of Spain [her son-in-law] now refused to allow her to settle in . . . the Netherlands. Her pride would not allow her to return to Tuscany as a rejected Queen and mother."[161] She was eventually allowed to travel to Cologne, where she died on 3 July 1642.

Marie's role as "the king's mother" offered her access to power, particularly since Louis seems to have been his mother's son in many ways. Jean Héroard, Louis' physician, noted the prince's resemblance to his mother in a number of remarkable ways. In addition to his striking physical resemblance to his Habsburg relations, he shared his mother's musical and artistic interests and sensibilities. Héroard admired and appreciated his charge's mother. "The constance and firmness of the queen was marvelous and incredible," he remarked on the day she gave birth to the prince. With his "overriding passion for assuring the dauphin's future," Héroard "allied himself" with the queen in her "recurrent struggles with the king." "Nevertheless," Louis' biography Elizabeth Marvick notes,

> that Héroard appreciated her talents and character and nurtured some of her attributes in Louis accentuated a dilemma: despite her fortitude in adversity and even danger, Marie could not be a model for her son. Only males could serve to exemplify the qualities the prince required to fulfill the norms for kingly conduct in love, statecraft, and war.[162]

And yet, as we have seen, a king's mother could provide a powerful "model" for her son, one whose influence and authority were both appreciated and indispensible, as Louise of Savoy's relationship with Francis I makes clear. I would argue that Marie de' Medici's failures as a model lie not so much with her sex as with her foreignness. Like her predecessor Catherine de' Medici, the Italian Marie was isolated at the French court, viewed with a mixture of suspicion (of her "Medicean cunning") and ridicule (as a "fat banker's daughter"). In a court known for its sexual freedoms, the indisputably chaste Marie was rumored to be engaged in her own adulteries and condemned for them. Criticized for her coldness to others, her "most extraordinary" friendship with Leonora Concini was suspect, one contemporary going so far as to describe the queen as being "in love" with her lifelong friend and companion.[163]

Historians have been equally condemnatory. Like Jeanne of Navarre and Marguerite of Angoulême before her, Marie's inability to "express warm feelings" for her children is widely noted, yet she is criticized for her "warm feelings" for and strong allegiance to her Medici and Habsburg family connections.[164] While Henry IV was careless of his appearance and "famous for his strong smell," Marie is berated for her extravagance as "the most splendidly dressed woman of her time"; her "ruling passion" is "the display of outward magnificence."[165]

"Marie de' Medici," in fact, seems almost to have been constructed by many historians in opposition to her husband. The king is admired for his activity, his "inability to remain still."[166] Marie, by contrast, is "sedentary." Henry is short; Marie's size thus becomes an issue. Her "bovine features, heavy body, and general lack of animation" displeased her husband, Cleugh notes. Marie's "reticence" must be judged "humourless" in contrast to the "casual jocularity" of the king.[167] While Henry is "endowed with remarkable mental abilities," his wife is judged for her "lack of common sense" or her "limited intellect."[168] Henry is legendary for his "quickness of mind"; the rapidity with which he conducted business and moved from one matter to another, is, therefore, judged to be a strength. For Marie, on the other hand, rapid shifts in attention are negative; she "never acquired a long attention span for affairs of state, and . . . was easily diverted."[169] Arranging marital alliances is politics for a king; for Marie it is a "mania."[170]

Like Catherine de' Medici, Marie was only too well aware of the way she was regarded. In 1617, looking back at the seventeen years she had spent in France, she commented that "she had never had any peace in France, no more in the time of her husband than afterward."[171]

She might equally well have made this remark in 1631 as she left France, never to return.

CHAPTER SIX

THE END OF AN ERA

The state of monarchy is the supremest thing upon earth, for kings are not only God's lieutenants upon earth and sit upon God's throne, but even by God himself they are called Gods, . . . and so their power after a certain relation compared to the divine power. Kings are also compared to fathers of families, for a king is truly parens patriae, *the politique father of his people.*

—King James I of England, "A Speech to the Lord and Commons of the Parliament," 1609[1]

The fire of the gynecocracy debate, ignited by the events of the late 1550s, continued to burn unabated even after the execution of Mary Stuart in 1587, the death of Catherine de' Medici in 1589, and the succession of James VI of Scotland to the throne of England in 1603. By the time Marie de' Medici became regent of France in 1610, the development of patriarchal political theory had changed the terms of the debate, equating a king's rule with God's rule and kingship with fatherhood. In such an equation, there was no place for women to exercise sovereignty.

This formulation of political authority began as the sixteenth century drew to a close. In his *Six Books of the Republic*, published in 1576, the French lawyer and political philosopher Jean Bodin drew an analogy between the family and the state, beginning with definitions. "A family is the right government of many subjects or persons . . . under the rule and command of one and the same head of the family," he wrote, while "the commonwealth is a lawful government of many families and of those things which unto them in common belongeth with a puissant sovereignty." Thus "the manner of the government of a house or family" is the "true model" for the "government of the commonweal."[2] As the "right and power to command" the family is given by God to the father, so, by extension, the "right and power to command" the state is granted by God to the king. The "law of God" ordains that the woman should be "subject" to the man not only "in every particular man's house and family" but "in the government of kingdoms and empires."[3]

While other theorists used the metaphor to support different conclusions, their arguments did not prevail.[4] Bodin's *Six Books of the Republic* was translated into English by Richard Knolles in 1606. By mid-century the family analogy was carried even further by Sir Robert Filmer; in his *Patriarchia* he argued that a king inherited his absolute authority from Adam.[5] In France these ideas would find their fullest expression in Bishop Jacques Bossuet's *Statecraft Drawn from the Very Words of Holy Scripture*, written at about the time Filmer's *Patriarchia* was published.[6]

With this change in the terms of the political debate about sovereignty, I will draw my study of female rulers to a close. Such arguments did not, of course, keep women from acting as regents or from becoming queens regnant, but the circumstances that led to the number of women exercising political authority in the sixteenth century were unparalleled in the seventeenth. It seems more than coincidental that when Elizabeth Tudor finally named her successor just before her death in 1603, she chose not one of the female claimants to her throne but a male, James VI of Scotland, who became James I of England and whose own views of his sovereignty, quoted at the outset of this chapter, reflect growing notions of "patriarchia." As the century progressed, Christina would become queen of Sweden, then abdicate her throne; Marie de' Medici's daughter-in-law Anne of Austria would become regent of France for her son Louis XIV; and Mary II would become queen regnant of England in name, if not in fact. But the ranks of the "monstrous regiment" that had ruled from Portugal in the west to Poland in the east and from Scotland in the north to the city-states of Italy in the south were noticeably thinned, and the power of those few queens and regents who remained was sharply reduced.[7]

In undertaking this project, I thought of my work as an exploration rather than a resolution, a beginning rather than an ending. I expected the unexpected. Even so, I am surprised by what my research has revealed. As I wrote in my introduction, I was at first afraid that I would find too few women to make the book I wanted to write a real possibility. Then I found too many women who ruled, so many, in fact, that this project took on a life (and length) of its own, becoming a "monstrous regiment" in way I had not intended. In the end, I could include only the names of some of the women I found.[8] Their stories remain to be told, and I am sure that many more women will be added to this company.

And I did not expect to find that the political circumstances that incensed John Knox and so many of his contemporaries were not unprecedented.

Despite their outrage, the series of "dynastic accidents" that led to the "monstrous regiment" of Mary Tudor, Marie of Guise, and Mary Stuart was a repetition of an earlier political moment when, as Marjorie Chibnall notes, "Three daughters of kings, all near contemporaries, who stood in the direct line of succession, forced the problem [of female succession] into the open."[9] The whole sixteenth-century gynecocracy debate in fact repeats the opposition to Urraca of Castile and León, Melisende of Jerusalem, and Matilda of England. The arguments that were marshalled for and against female rule by Knox and his contemporaries had been iterated and reiterated in the twelfth. Even the specific terms of the later war of words were echoes of the earlier dispute. Mary Tudor and Mary Stuart were both compared to Jezebel, as were Matilda and Queen Urraca. Less obviously, the more obscure example of the daughters of Zelophehad was also cited with some frequency in the sixteenth century, just as it had been in the twelfth.[10]

Our tendency to focus on one historical period or one historical figure obscures such precedents and parallels. Elizabeth Tudor's rather remarkable decision to remain unmarried, to become the "Virgin Queen," for example, is not unprecedented; recognizing those precedents increases, rather than decreases, the significance of her deployment of that image. Similarly, the practice of discrediting a woman—Juana *la Beltraneja*, Juana *la Loca*, Arbella Stuart, "cracked in the brain," to name only three examples—by labelling her illegitimate or crazy so that she could be removed as a political threat is also notable. So, too, is the removal of an "inconvenient" queen. Henry VIII's divorce of Catherine of Aragon can—and should—be viewed in relationship to less well known examples. We can assess Catherine's resistance, for example, by noting Jeanne of France's submission, and we can perhaps understand Catherine's passivity in light of her sister-in-law Margaret Tudor's activity; we can even see why Catherine de' Medici might have been so agreeable when the possibility of divorce was raised by her father-in-law. The vilification of the "wicked" foreign queen is another motif that recurs with striking frequency: Isabel of Bavaria in France, Margaret of Anjou in England, Marie of Guise in Scotland, Margaret Tudor in Scotland, Catherine de' Medici in France, and Renée of France in Ferrara are only a few of the many examples.

The tendency to examine women in isolation has led historians to label a woman "obsessive" or "neurotic" when she expressed her love for her son; both Margaret Beaufort and Louise of Savoy have been so diagnosed. But if a mother doesn't express such devotion, she is unnatural, even monstrous, as Caterina Sforza, Jeanne of Navarre, and Marie de' Medici have variously been labelled. Similarly, if a sister expressed deep devotion to her brother, her attachment must be incestuous; the reputations of both Lucrezia Borgia and Marguerite of Angoulême have suffered because of their "unnatural" love for their brothers. But if we resist the tendency to focus on women in isolation, we may come to very different conclusions about the nature and purpose of women's language. In her study of three powerful women at the court of Philip III, for example, Magdalena Sánchez analyzes "the language of familial affection and devotion" among Habsburg women. Such language is neither neurotic nor obsessive nor the reflection of incestuous desire, but "a political language" with a carefully calculated purpose:

> [I]t served to make the petitions, requests, or opinions of the women acceptable to their male relatives. The frequent references to affection and devotion worked to soften the opinions that the women were expressing and to reassure male relatives that women were merely speaking out because of affection and familial concern.[11]

A broader perspective, like the one Sáchez adopts, allows us to see such patterns more clearly.

Yet even as we broaden our focus, we are reminded anew of the old double standard, and not just in terms of sexual freedom. Whether it is Caterina Sforza refusing to negotiate for her hostage children, Louise of Savoy trying to acquire Bourbon lands, or Catherine de' Medici devising elaborate plans for her daughters' marriages, the action is interpreted in gendered ways, as unfeeling, unnatural, or unreasonable. For their male contemporaries, the personal is understood in political terms; for women, on the other hand, the political is still too often dismissed as just personal.

Sometimes the double standard means that women are still written out of the picture. No history of the early modern period fails to mention Henry IV and the 1589 edict of Nantes, for example. We must not "underestimate the novelty of such a religious settlement," a recent college textbook reminds us; "for the first time in Western Europe a political system . . . accepted the existence of two different religious creeds in one state."[12] But, while not "underestimating" the edict, we shouldn't overestimate its singularity. We must not "underestimate" Catherine de' Medici's earlier efforts, the 1560 edicts of Amboise and Romorantin, the 1561 Colloquy of Poissy, and the 1562 edict of January, all of which were aimed at ending religious persecution and establishing religious toleration. Nor should we overlook the achievement of Isabella Jagellion in 1558; as Roland Bainton notes, she should be recognized as "the first ruler to issue an edict of universal toleration."[13]

Finally, by considering the lives of women, we can see how their experiences counter the dominant narrative of the early modern period. The rise of the nation–state has "always held pride of political place in accounts of the fifteenth and sixteenth centuries," as one recently published history notes.[14] In the conventional narrative of history, then, the early modern period is about *drawing* boundaries. But as we can see here, the experience for royal women runs counter to that narrative. For them, the early modern period is still a time of *crossing* boundaries. Their husbands and brothers do, of course, cross boundaries when they go to war, but when Henry VIII and Francis I met not on field of battle but on the Field of the Cloth of Gold, their peacetime encounter was a momentous occasion, the meeting celebrated in its own day and remarked on in our own. Meanwhile, their contemporary Margaret of Austria quietly travelled from Burgundy to France, then returned to Burgundy before being dispatched to Spain, and headed back to Burgundy once more before leaving for Savoy. After Margaret left Savoy, she established herself in the Netherlands, from which she travelled to Cambrai to negotiate the "Ladies Peace" with Louise of Savoy. She is only one of many remarkable women who criss-crossed the emerging national boundaries of the states of western Europe: Anne Boleyn, educated in the Netherlands and France before returning to England; Marguerite of Angoulême, journeying from France to Spain to secure her brother's release from captivity; Renée of France, travelling to Ferrara for her marriage and returning "home" decades later; and the unfortunate Marie de' Medici, leaving Florence to become queen of France, acting as regent of France, then living out her days an exile.

Since the experiences of women often run counter to the experiences of their male counterparts, I set out to construct a *counter-narrative* here. But as I worked on this project, I discovered that the counter-narrative to traditional political history already exists. As I wrote, I not only found more queens and regents than I thought I would, but I also found a surprising number of nineteenth- and early twentieth-century historians and biographers who had written extensively about women and their political roles. The impressive body of work by scholars like Pier Desiderio Pasolini, Jane de Iongh, and Julia Cartwright, to name only three, raises questions about when and why women and their stories were written out of the historical narrative. As we continue our work today on the process of recovering women's history, it is also important for us to reclaim the work of those scholars who have preceded us.

Another counter-narrative to conventional history exists as well. The lives of the women I have written about here are the source of a considerable amount of historical fiction. While I complained in my introduction that "I had learned almost nothing" about female rulers in textbooks "or from the pages of the histories and biographies I had read on my own throughout the years," I discovered that many women have found an alternative view of European history in the pages of historical novels. Although the queens who inhabit the pages of these novels are invariably beautiful and "tempestuous" (and the focus of their stories is usually romantic), we shouldn't overlook such counter-narratives or view with condescension the novels of writers like Eleanor Hibbert, who wrote under the pseudonym Jean Plaidy.[15] In their dedication to women's lives and experiences, they too deserve a place in our appreciation of "the monstrous regiment of women."

NOTES

In the notes that follow, I hope to meet the needs of a variety of readers. I have included not only specific references for quotations and citations but also references to secondary works that have influenced my thinking in critical ways. The notes also provide additional references for those readers who may want to read more widely. At times, they take the form of brief explanatory or background essays that I hope will be of use to some readers.

Introduction

1. John Knox, *The First Blast of the Trumpet against the Monstrous Regiment of Women* (Geneva, 1558), sig. 9 (text modernized). Knox's "blast" is included in David Laing, ed., *The Works of John Knox* (Edinburgh, 1855), vol. 4, 363-420 (the quotation cited appears on p. 373).

   I have used many different sources in this study, including early printed books, like Knox's, and original letters and documents printed in seventeenth-, eighteenth-, and nineteenth-century editions. In order to make the documents more accessible for readers, I have on occasion standardized the spelling and punctuation of the quotations that appear in the text; where I have modernized the text, I have so indicated in the notes.

2. After Knox, among the more notable entries in the lengthy debate about female rulers are John Gilby, *An Admonition to England and Scotland to Call Them to Repentance* (Geneva, 1558); Christopher Goodman, *How Superior Powers Ought to be Obeyed of Their Subjects . . .* (Geneva, 1558); Richard Bertie, "These answers were made by Mr. Richard Bertie, husband to the lady Catherine Duchess of Suffolk against the book of John Knox, 1558," British Library MS Additional 48043 (Yelverton MS 48), fols. 1-9; John Aylmer, *An Harbor for Faithful and True Subjects against the Late Blown Blast Concerning the Government of Women . . .* (London, 1559); John Leslie, *Defense of the Honour of . . . Marie Queen of Scots* (London, 1569); Henry Howard, "A Dutifull Defence of the Lawfull Regiment of Women," British Library MS Lansdowne 813; Jean

Bodin, *Six Livres de la République* (Paris, 1576); David Chambers, *Discours de la légitime succession des femmes aux possessions de leurs parents; & du gouvernement des princesses aux empires & royaumes* (Paris, 1579); Thomas Smith, *De Republica Anglorum: The Manner of Government or Policy of the Realm of England . . .* (London, 1583); John Case, *Sphaera Civitatis* (Oxford, 1588); Denis Godefroy, *Praxis civilis et antiquis et recentioribus authoribus Germanis, Italis, Gallis, Hispanis, Belgis et Aliis* (Frankfurt, 1591); Pierre Grégoire, *De Republica* (Frankfurt, 1597); Richard Knolles, *The Six Books of a Commonwealth* (London, 1606), a translation of Bodin; Giovanni Stefano Menochi, *Institutiones politicae e sacris scripturis depromptae* (Lyons, 1625); Robert Filmer, *Patriarchia* (London, 1680); and Bishop Jacques Bossuet, *Politique tirée des propres paroles de l'Écriture Sainte* (probably written about 1680, but published Paris, 1709).

Analysis of the "gynecocracy debate" has appeared regularly: James E. Phillips, Jr., "The Background of Spenser's Attitude Toward Women Rulers," *The Huntington Library Quarterly*, 5 (1941), 5-32; Mortimer Levine, *The Early Elizabethan Succession Question, 1558-1568* (Stanford, California, 1966); Paula Louise Scalingi, "The Scepter or the Distaff: The Question of Female Sovereignty, 1516-1607," *The Historian*, 41 (1978), 59-75; Levine, "The Place of Women in Tudor Government," in *Tudor Rule and Revolution: Essays for G.R. Elton from his American Friends*, ed. Delloyd J. Guth and John W. McKenna (Cambridge, 1982), 109-23; Retha M. Warnicke, *Women of the English Renaissance and Reformation* (Westport, Connecticut, 1983), 47-66 (Chapter 4: "Queens Regnant and the Royal Supremacy, 1525-1587"); Constance Jordan, "Woman's Rule in Sixteenth-Century British Political Thought," *Renaissance Quarterly*, 40 (1987), 421-51; Patricia-Ann Lee, " 'Bodye Politique to Governe': Aylmer, Knox and the Debate on Queenship," *The Historian*, 52 (1990), 242-61; Robert M. Healey, "Waiting for Deborah: John Knox and Four Ruling Queens," *The Sixteenth Century Journal*, 25 (1994), 371-86; Susan Felch, "The Rhetoric of Biblical Authority: John Knox and the Question of Women," *The Sixteenth Century Journal*, 26 (1995), 805-22; and Judith M. Richards, " 'To Promote a Woman to Beare Rule': Talking of Queens in Mid-Tudor England," *The Sixteenth Century Journal*, 28 (1997), 101-21. The most extended analysis of the gynecocracy debate in England is Amanda Shephard, *Gender and Authority in Sixteenth-Century England: The Knox Debate* (Keele, Staffordshire, England, 1994).

3. The term "early modern" is a slippery one. I use it here to include the period from the late fifteenth through the mid-seventeenth centuries: while incorporating as many earlier precedents for women rulers as I can, I have included as "early modern" those women who may have been born in the late fifteenth century but who lived into the sixteenth and those who might have lived into the seventeenth but who were born in the sixteenth. This corresponds to the "long sixteenth century," a term coined by Fernand Braudel and referred to throughout the *Handbook of European History, 1400-1600: Late Middle Ages, Renaissance, and Reformation*, ed. Thomas A. Brady Jr., Heido A. Oberman, and James D. Tracy, 2 vols. (Grand Rapids, Michigan, 1994); on the significance of this period, see "Introduction: Renaissance and Reformation, Late Middle Ages and Early Modern Era," vol. 1, xii-xxii.

There is a great deal of fluidity in the periods we label "medieval" and "early modern," however, and scholarly works reflect this. Merry Wiesner, *Women and Gender in Early Modern Europe* (Cambridge, 1993), identifies the period 1500-1750 as "early modern" (3), while Natalie Zeamon Davis and Arlette Farge mark out "the sixteenth through eighteenth centuries" in their introduction ("Women as Historical Actors," p. 1) to *Renaissance and Enlightenment Paradoxes*, vol. 3 of *A History of Women* (Cambridge, Massachusetts, 1993). In her essay "Women in the Renaissance" in the newest edition of *Becoming Visible: Women in European History*, 3rd ed. (New York, 1998), 153-73, Carole Levin focuses on the period from 1350 to 1600 (she also addresses the question of whether to use the term "Renaissance" or "early modern," the phrase I have chosen). As further examples of this fluidity in periodization, an essay on Louise of Savoy (d. 1531) is included in *Medieval Queenship* (New York, 1993, 117-41), edited by John Carmi Parsons, while an essay on Christine de Pizan (d. c. 1434) appears in *Political Rhetoric, Power, and Renaissance Women* (Albany, New York, 1995), edited by Carole Levin and Patricia A. Sullivan.

4. The phrase is used by Wiesner in her discussion of "Gender and Political Power" in *Women and Gender in Early Modern Europe*, 241.

5. According to Arin Woolf, "Apart from France, with her interpretation of the Salic Law to exclude female succession, and the Empire, with its elected rulers who were always male, all other European kingdoms had the possibility of installing a reigning queen—not very often, but nonetheless in a considerable number of cases" ("Reigning Queens in Medieval Europe: When, Where and Why," in *Medieval Queenship*, 169). Woolf calculates that, between 1100 and 1600, some 20 women reigned as queens in their own right (Woolf excludes women of lesser rank and those who acted as regents for husbands and sons in his count).

6. René de la Croix, duc de Castries, *The Lives of the Kings and Queens of France*, trans. Anne Dobell (New York, 1979).

7. Victor-L. Tapié, *The Rise and Fall of the Habsburg Monarchy*, trans. Stephen Hardman (New York, 1971).

8. For genealogical tables noting only the sons of Edward III, see sources as diverse as J.D. Mackie, *The Oxford History of England*, vol. 7: *The Earlier Tudors, 1485-1558* (Oxford, 1952); Charles Ross, *Edward IV* (Berkeley, California, 1974); and Michael Hicks, *Who's Who in British History*, vol. 3: *Who's Who in Late Medieval England (1272-1485)* (London, 1991). Even the venerable *Encyclopedia Britannica* lists only "5 daughters"—underneath "2 sons died young" (15th ed., vol. 9, 501).

9. Victor-L. Tapié, *France in the Age of Louix XIII and Richelieu*, trans. D. Lockie (Cambridge, 1974; rpt. New York, 1984).

10. G. F. Young, *The Medici*, vol. 2 (New York, 1909).

11. With a nod to Natalie Zemon Davis, "Women on Top," in *Society and Culture in Early Modern France: Eight Essays* (Stanford, 1975), 124-51.

12. My reconception of the biographical essays in this volume has been informed by Gerda Lerner's chapter "Female Clusters, Female Networks, Social Spaces," in her *Women and History*, vol. 2: *The Creation of Feminist Consciousness: From the Middle Ages to Eighteen-seventy* (New York, 1993), 220-46.

13. Studies focusing on women and queenship are now appearing with some frequency. See, for example, Louise Olga Fradenburg, ed., *Women and Sover-*

eignty (Edinburgh, 1992); Parsons, *Medieval Queenship*; Levin and Sullivan, *Political Rhetoric, Power, and Renaissance Women*; and Anne J. Duggan, ed., *Queens and Queenship in Medieval Europe* (Woodbridge, Suffolk, 1997).

Chapter 1

1. Isabella's address to Ferdinand on the subject of the Castilian succession is quoted by Nancy Rubin, *Isabella of Castile, the First Renaissance Queen* (New York, 1991), 131.

   Margaret Beaufort's letter to her son is printed by Anne Crawford, ed., *Letters of the Queens of England, 1100-1547* (Stroud, England, 1994), 149.

   Caterina Sforza's letter to her uncle Ludovico Sforza is printed by Pier Desiderio Pasolini, *Caterina Sforza* (Rome, 1893), vol. 3, 303 (my translation).

   Anne of France's instructions—*enseignements*—for her daughter Suzanne of Bourbon are printed by A. M. Chazaud, ed., *Les Enseignements d'Anne de France, duchesse de Bourbonnois et d'Auvergne a sa fille Susanne de Bourbon . . .* (Moulins, France, 1878), 20 (my translation).

2. In this account, I rely on two standard histories of Spain: Rafael Altamira, *A History of Spain from the Beginnings to the Present Day*, trans. Muna Lee (London, 1949; rpt. New York, 1962); and J. N. Hillgarth, *The Spanish Kingdoms, 1250-1516*, vol. 2: *1410-1516: Castilian Hegemony* (Oxford, 1973).

   In addition to these general political histories, I have used two recent biographies of Isabella: Nancy Rubin, *Isabella of Castile: The First Renaissance Queen* (New York, 1991); and Peggy K. Liss, *Isabel the Queen* (Oxford, 1992). These two works offer extensive bibliographies, including primary sources (letters, documents, chronicles) as well as secondary material referring interested readers to additional sources.

   Blanche of Navarre (1424–64), Enrique's first wife, was the oldest daughter of Blanche, queen of Navarre and her husband Juan II of Aragon. The younger Blanche was married to Enrique in 1440, but in 1453 their childlessness was explained by the claim that the marriage had never been consummated, Enrique's "bewitchment" blamed on his wife. After the death of her brother Charles of Viana in 1461, Blanche should have inherited the throne of Navarre; instead, in order to further his own political ends, her father arranged with Louis XI of France that the Navarrese crown would be given to Blanche's younger sister, Eleanor, and her husband, Gaston of Foix. In 1463 Juan signed an agreement with the French king: "This treaty was ratified by Juan's surrender of his elder daughter, Blanche, . . . to prison and rapid death at the hands of Gaston and his wife" (Hillgarth, 63).

3. Quoted by Rubin, 32.
4. The phrase "confusions of Castile" comes from Hillgarth, 301.
5. Altamira, 110.
6. Detailed information about Urraca, *Infanta* of Castile and León, is found in *Enciclopedia Universal Ilustrada Europeo-Americana* (Madrid, 1908-30), *s.v.*, an invaluable source for all of the women mentioned here.
7. See Bernard F. Reilly, *The Kingdom of León-Castilla under Queen Urraca: 1109-1126* (Princeton, 1982), 352.

Alfonso VI also had an illegitimate daughter, Teresa of Castile (1080-1130), Urraca's half-sister. She was married to Henry of Burgundy, who was given the county of Portugal; following his death in 1112, Teresa served as regent for their son Alfonso Enriquez. Teresa's interests in the kingdom of Castile and León threatened Urraca throughout the period of Urraca's rule. Alfonso Enriquez wrested control of Portugal from his mother in 1128, becoming the first king of an independent Portugal in 1143.

8. Perhaps in acknowledgment of his mother's abilities as queen regnant, Alfonso VII gave his sister Sancha the title of queen and a place on the throne at his side. Energetic and discreet, she was consulted with frequency by her brother. Sancha died shortly before Alfonso; if she had lived, she might have advised Alfonso VII against a decision that once again divided Castile and León.

In addition to his sons Sancho and Ferdinand, Alfonso had an illegitimate daughter named Urraca; she was married to the king of Navarre in 1146. Following her husband's death, *this* Urraca, queen of Navarre, was named by her father as the governor of Asturias. Meanwhile, Ferdinand II of León married yet another Urraca, Urraca of Portugal, about the year 1160. The two were eventually separated because they were related within the prohibited degree of consanguinity, but not before a son, who would become Alfonso IX of León, was born. Before their separation, Urraca of Portugal was said to have played a significant role in her husband's government.

9. Eleanor of England (1161-1214), mother of Berenguela and Blanca, was the second daughter of Eleanor of Aquitaine and Henry II of England; Theresa M. Vann indicates that Eleanor had "played a significant role in the political and cultural development of late-twelfth century Castile" ("The Theory and Practice of Medieval Castilian Queenship," in *Queens, Regents and Potentates*, ed. Theresa M. Vann [Dallas, Texas, 1993], 125). Contemporary records and witnesses could not sort out which of Eleanor's daughters was the elder. Blanca [or Blanche] was queen of France, wife of Louis VIII; her role as regent of France is discussed later in this chapter.

10. Both Altamira and Hillgarth make brief references to Sancha, Urraca, and Berenguela (also known as "Berengaria"); more detailed entries for these queens are found in the *Enciclopedia Universal Ilustrada Europeo-Americana*.

Although these are the most commonly noted precedents, earlier examples could be cited: Ermesinda (d. 757) inherited León and Asturias from her father, Pelayo, her husband becoming King Alfonso I; Ermesinda's daughter Adosina (mid eighth century) seems to have claimed León and Asturias after her brother, Fruela, was assassinated; Elvira, queen of Navarre (eleventh century), succeeded in the county of Castile, transmitting it to her son, who became its first king as Ferdinand I (see Roger Collins, "Queens-Dowager and Queens-Regent in Tenth-Century León and Navarre" in *Medieval Queenship*, ed. John Carmi Parsons [New York, 1993], 79-92).

11. *Las Siete Partidas*, trans. Samuel Parsons Scott (Chicago, 1931), Partida II, Title XV, Law II.

12. Quoted by Rubin, 53.

13. Quoted by Liss, 68.

14. These proposed marriages represented a nightmare of interrelationships. Ini-

tially, papal dispensation for the marriage of Princess Juana to her uncle was granted.

For the complicated relationships, see Chapter 2, Table 1.

15. Quoted by Rubin, 78-79.

    Ferdinand of Aragon was the son of Juan II, whose first marriage had been to Queen Blanche of Navarre; his children by that marriage were Charles of Viana, the younger Blanche of Navarre, and Eleanor (see n. 2). Juan II's second marriage was to Juana Enriquez, Ferdinand's mother. Juana Enriquez was said to have poisoned Charles of Viana (he died of tuberculosis) so that Ferdinand, instead of Charles, would succeed Juan as king of Aragon.

16. Rubin, 124.

17. The ceremony is described by Frasier, *The Warrior Queens*, 185-86. Ferdinand is quoted by Rubin, 129, and Gonzalez by Marvin Lunenfeld, "Isabella I of Castile and the Company of Women in Power," *Historical Reflections*, 4 (1977), 213-14.

18. Quoted by Liss, 104.

19. Quoted by Rubin, 129.

20. Quoted by Rubin, 131.

21. Aragonese custom did not formally exclude women from the throne, but it gave preference to her husband when a woman inherited. The most notable example of such preference is the case of Petronilla of Aragon (c. 1135-c. 1173). When Alfonso I of Aragon died in 1134, his brother Ramiro II followed him as king. The "monk king" had left his monastery to follow his brother on the throne, and he married Agnes of Poitiers (or a woman named Matilda—sources vary). A daughter, Petronilla, was born, and Ramiro abdicated the throne in her favor, returning to his monastery. The one-year-old queen was betrothed to Ramon Berenguer IV, count of Barcelona, who became the effective ruler of Aragon for Petronilla, though he did not assume the title of king but of "Prince of Aragon."

    Although it is often assumed that Petronilla played no part in governing Aragon, William Clay Stalls notes that she was "one of the pivotal figures in the political history of twelfth-century Iberia" and suggests that "she enjoyed her rule over Aragon separately from Ramon." In 1152, in an ironic demonstration of this "substantial authority," she signed a will that excluded women from the throne; see Stalls, "Queenship and the Royal Patrimony in Twelfth-Century Iberia: the Example of Petronilla of Aragon" in Vann, 49-61. (See also E. L. Miron, *The Queens of Aragon: Their Lives and Times* [New York, 1913], 62-71.)

    When Pedro IV of Aragon (r. 1336-d. 1387) attempted to have his daughter Constanza recognized as his heir, she was rejected by the *Cortes* in favor of Jaime, Pedro's brother. Those who opposed Constanza's rule cited Petronilla's will as the basis of their opposition.

22. Rubin, 131.

23. Liss, 105, and Rubin, 131.

24. Altamira, 263. The motto is variously cited and interpreted—Rubin translates it (in her version it is "*Tanto monta, monta tanto, Fernando como Isabel, Isabel como Fernando*") as "One is equal to the other, Ferdinand as much as Isabella, Isabella as much as Ferdinand," 132.

25. Altamira, 263. On Isabella as co-regent in Aragon, see Lunenfeld, 216.
26. Quoted by Rubin, 137-38.
27. Quoted in part by Rubin, 140-41, and in part by Liss, 116-17.
28. Rubin, 175.

   An interesting rumor about Princess Juana circulated after Isabella's death in 1504 when it was said that, in an effort to secure the Castilian succession for himself, Ferdinand planned to marry *la Beltraneja*. In 1505, English envoys in Spain reported that "many in these parts rejoiced at this [Ferdinand's plan to marry Juana]." See Hillgarth, 595.

29. The two "views" of Isabel of Portugal are those of Rubin, 26, and Liss, 14.
30. Quoted by Hillgarth, 314.
31. Liss, 14. Isabel de Barcelos was the granddaughter of King João of Portugal— her father was one of the king's illegitimate sons. She married her uncle, son of Philippa of Lancaster, queen of Portugal, and King João; see n 34.
32. Quoted by Hillgarth, 246. Maria of Castile (1401-1458) was the daughter of Catherine of Lancaster and Enrique III of Castile; see below. She functioned as governor of Aragon for her husband from 1434 until her death.
33. Maria of Castile's marriage to Alfonso of Aragon had been matched by her brother Juan's marriage to Alfonso's sister, also named Maria. Maria of Aragon (1403-1445) was King Juan II's first wife and mother of Enrique IV. At times the two Marias met, queen of Aragon and queen of Castile, to negotiate on behalf of their respective husbands, their abilities recognized by contemporary judgment that "if the queen of Castile were king, there would be peace and well-being in the realm" (Liss, 16). See also Miron, 286-306.
34. Gerda Lerner, *Women and History*, vol. 2: *The Creation of a Feminist Consciousness: From the Middle Ages to Eighteen-seventy* (New York, 1993), 227-29.

   Not to be overlooked in this network of influence is the figure of Isabella's paternal grandmother, Catherine of Lancaster, queen of Castile (1372-1418). Catherine was the granddaughter of King Pedro I of Castile. When Pedro was deposed and murdered in 1369, his unmarried daughters Constance and Isabel fled to England. There Constance married John of Gaunt and Isabel married Edmund of Langley. John of Gaunt and Constance of Castile declared themselves to be king and queen of Spain, which Gaunt invaded in 1386. His invasion failed, but his daughter Catherine of Lancaster's marriage to Enrique III in 1386 was negotiated to help settle the civil war between two branches of the Castilian royal family. Catherine's son Juan II was Isabella's father, her daughter Maria of Castile (n. 32) Isabella's aunt. After Enrique III's death in 1406, when Juan was two years old, the dowager queen Catherine functioned as co-regent for her son until her death in 1418. Her regency was spent preserving Juan's interests against those of his uncle, who aimed to seize the Castilian throne for himself.

   As an interesting note on how closely interrelated these royal women are, Philippa of Lancaster, who was the mother-in-law of Isabel de Barcelos, was Catherine of Lancaster's half-sister. John of Gaunt's first wife, Blanche of Lancaster, was Philippa's mother; Catherine was his daughter by Constance of Castile, his second wife.

35. Queen and Governor of Aragon, Maria of Castile (see n. 32) was Ferdinand's aunt, married to Alfonso I, brother of Ferdinand's father Juan II.

36. On this see n. 15.

    For Juana Enriquez (1425-68), daughter of the Admiral of Castile, see Hillgarth, 274-96. A more dated view is found in Miron, 307-24.

37. Jaime Vicens Vives, *Historia crítica de la vida y reinado Fernando II de Aragón* (Zaragoza, 1962), 503-05.

38. Quoted by Hillgarth, 352.

    See also Ramon Menendez Pidal, "The Significance of the Reign of Isabella the Catholic, According to her Contemporaries," in *Spain in the Fifteenth Century, 1369-1516: Essays and Extracts by Historians of Spain,* ed. Roger Highfield and trans. Frances M. Lopez-Morillas (New York, 1972), 380-403.

39. Rubin, 222.

40. Quoted by Pidal, 395.

41. Liss, 68.

42. Quoted by Liss, 106.

43. Quoted by Hillgarth, 363.

44. Of importance in understanding Isabella's shaping of her role as queen is Lunenfeld, "Isabella of Castile and the Company of Women of Power," 207-29. The quotation is from 219. See also Elizabeth A. Lehfeldt, "Ruling Sexuality: The Political Legitimacy of Isabel of Castile," *Renaissance Quarterly,* 53 (2000), 31-56.

45. For what follows I rely on standard histories of the period: J. D. Mackie, *The Oxford History of England,* vol. 7: *The Earlier Tudors, 1485-1558* (Oxford, 1952); G. R. Elton, *The New History of England,* vol. 3: *Reform and Reformation: England, 1509-1558* (Cambridge, 1983); John Guy, *Tudor England* (Oxford, 1986).

    In addition to these general political histories, I have used two recent biographies of Margaret Beaufort: Linda Simon, *Of Virtue Rare: Margaret Beaufort, Matriarch of the House of Tudor* (Boston, 1982); and Michael K. Jones and Malcolm G. Underwood, *The King's Mother: Lady Margaret Beaufort, Countess of Richmond and Derby* (Cambridge, 1992).

46. The origins of this bloody contest can be traced back to the fourteenth century, when Edward III's queen, Philippa of Hainault, gave birth to twelve children, seven sons and five daughters. Four of the royal daughters survived infancy. Joan of the Tower died at age thirteen, while Margaret of Calais, married to the earl of Pembroke, died without children. The two remaining daughters, Isabella and Mary, were married abroad. By contrast, the five sons who survived infancy grew to adulthood in England, and all of them had children. The eldest and heir to the throne, Edward of Woodstock, died a year before his father, in 1376, but he left a son and heir, Richard. When Edward III died, his ten-year-old grandson inherited the throne and became Richard II. His minority was supervised by his uncles, four royal dukes: Lionel of Antwerp, duke of Clarence; John of Gaunt, duke of Lancaster; Edmund of Langley, duke of York; and Thomas of Woodstock, duke of Gloucester.

    Richard finally threw off the regency of his powerful uncles, but he proved to be a feckless, ineffectual ruler. Eventually he was deposed by his cousin, Henry Bolingbroke, who assumed the throne as Henry IV. Following his 1399 usurpation, the English crown passed smoothly from father to son, as Henry IV was succeeded by his son, Henry V, who was succeeded by his son, Henry

VI. But when Henry VI proved to be another ineffectual ruler—incapacitated by periodic bouts of insanity—a political crisis became a civil war that resulted in a succession crisis.

The Lancastrians—Henry VI and his supporters—claimed the throne by "right" of inheritance, from son to father back to Henry IV, son of John of Gaunt, duke of Lancaster. But Gaunt had been Edward III's *third* surviving son; when Henry Bolingbroke deposed his cousin and claimed the title of king for himself, he had bypassed the descendants of Edward III's *second* son, Lionel, whose heir had been a daughter, named Philippa. Opposed to the Lancastrians were the descendants of Edward III's *fourth* son, Edmund, duke of York. This branch of Edward III's family had allied itself with Lionel's descendants: Edmund of York's son Richard had married Anne Mortimer, Philippa's granddaughter. Their son, Richard of York, thus argued that his claim to the throne superseded that of the incapacitated king.

The Lancastrian kings Henry IV, Henry V, and Henry VI are the descendants of John of Gaunt by his first wife, Blanche of Lancaster; the Beauforts, however, descended from Gaunt's third wife, Katherine Swynford. On the legitimacy of the Beauforts, see below.

47. The first scholarly biography of Matilda in English is Marjorie Chibnall's *The Empress Matilda: Queen Consort, Queen Mother and Lady of the English* (Oxford, 1991).

Chibnall's biography begins with reference to Matilda's early twelfth-century contemporaries: "Three daughters of kings, all near contemporaries who stood in direct line of succession, forced the problem [of female succession] into the open" (1). These contemporaries were Urraca of Castile and León, whose story we have heard, and Melisende of Jerusalem, whose story is told in n. 48.

48. Geoffrey of Anjou is related by marriage to Melisende, the only heir of Baldwin II of Jerusalem. To ensure her throne, King Baldwin married his daughter to Fulk of Anjou, Geoffrey's father, in 1129. Baldwin seems to have intended Fulk to rule Jerusalem jointly with Melisende, but Fulk had difficulties securing his recognition as joint ruler; see Chibnall, 56 and 60.

49. Stephen was Matilda's cousin. He was the son of Henry I's sister Adela, who had married Stephen of Blois; interestingly, his claim to the English throne came through the female line.

50. Chibnall, 158.

51. Quoted by Chibnall, 62.

52. Quoted by Chibnall, 63.

53. Christopher Tyerman, *Who's Who in Early Medieval England* (London, 1996), 133.

While attributing Matilda's failings in 1141 to her "arrogance and tactless demands for money," the *Encyclopedia Britannica*, 15th ed., does note her "steadying influence over Henry II's continental dominions" from her retirement in 1144 until her death.

54. See Cary J. Nederman and N. Elaine Lawson, "The Frivolities of Courtiers Follow the Footprints of Women: Public Women and the Crisis of Virility in John of Salisbury," in *Ambiguous Realities: Women in the Middle Ages and the Renaissance*, ed. Carole Levin and Jeannie Watson (Detroit, Michigan, 1987),

85; and Lois Huneycutt, "Female Succession and the Language of Power in the Writing of Twelfth-Century Churchmen" in John Carmi Parsons, *Medieval Queenship* (New York, 1991), 189-201.

55. The chapters of *Policraticus* devoted to political theory are found in *The Statesman's Book of John of Salisbury, Being the Fourth, Fifth, and Sixth Books, and Selections from the Seventh and Eighth Books, of the Policraticus*, trans. and ed. John Dickinson (New York, 1963), 246-48.

56. For an excellent overview of various legal efforts to resolve questions of succession in England, see Mortimer Levine, *Tudor Dynastic Problems, 1460-1571* (New York, 1973).

57. Levine, *Tudor Dynastic Problems*, discusses the very complicated succession question in 1485, 33-34.

In 1485 Margaret was the next *English* descendant of John of Gaunt, but there were direct descendants of the duke in Portugal and Castile—Philippa of Lancaster, daughter of John of Gaunt and his first wife Blanche, had married Joaõ of Portugal. As Levine writes, "If primogeniture was the determinant and an alien was eligible [to inherit the English throne], that claim belonged to John II of Portugal" (33-34). There were also direct descendants in Castile; Catherine of Lancaster, daughter of John of Gaunt and his second wife Constance of Castile, had, as we have seen (n. 34), married Enrique III of Spain—her grandchildren included Enrique IV and Isabella of Castile.

58. Levine, 35.

59. Quoted by Levine, 34.

60. Elizabeth of York (1466-1503) was the eldest surviving child of Edward IV and Elizabeth Woodville.

61. Merry Wiesner notes the important distinction between "political authority," that is, "power which is formally recognized and legitimated," and "power," that is, "the ability to shape political events." While women were often denied authority, they often wielded considerable power. See her *Women and Gender in Early Modern Europe* (Cambridge, 1993), 240.

62. Simon, 16-17.

63. Jones and Underwood, 38 (they make the same point on p. 25).

Edmund and Jasper Tudor were Henry VI's half-brothers. The king's mother, Henry V's widowed queen Catherine of Valois, married Owen Tudor; Edmund and Jasper were her sons by this second marriage.

64. Stanley stood to gain from the marriage as well; as Jones and Underwood note, "For Stanley the marriage with Margaret Beaufort expanded his territorial influence" (59).

65. Desmond Seward, *The Wars of the Roses, Through the Lives of Five Men and Women of the Fifteenth Century* (New York, 1995), 274.

66. The conspiracy is detailed by Simon, 70-75, and by Jones and Underwood, 62-65. See also Seward, 274-84.

67. Charles Ross, *Richard III* (Berkeley, California, 1981), 210. These instructions to Stanley are recorded by Polydore Vergil.

68. On the designation, see Jones and Underwood, 66.

69. Quoted by Seward, 327.

Although their marriage seems to have been a successful one personally as well as politically, Henry's queen never achieved a place equivalent to his mother's. In her biography of the queen, Nancy Lenz Harvey writes, "The story of Elizabeth of York reveals a life of reaction rather than action" (xiii); see *Elizabeth of York: The Mother of Henry VIII* (New York, 1973). Chapters define her as "daughter to the king," "niece to the king," "consort to the king," and "mother to the king."

According to Charles T. Wood, "Elizabeth of York's greatest strength was her greatest problem":

> [T]he queenship of Elizabeth of York teaches . . . lessons about women and sovereignty, lessons which suggest that if a woman wanted to have influence and to exercise genuine power, then it was far better not to have any legitimate claim to them. Such claims were dangerous and a clear threat to male hegemony. Few males could ever have accepted them comfortably, least of all a man whose own rights were as dubious as those of Henry Tudor.

See his "The First Two Queens Elizabeth, 1464-1503," in *Women and Sovereignty*, ed. Louise O. Fradenburg, 129.

70. Alison Plowden, *Tudor Women* (1979; rpt. Gloucestershire, England, 1998), 17–21; and Simon, 100–1.
71. Jones and Underwood, 73–74, 91–92.
72. Jones and Underwood, 75, 79–81. On Margaret of York, duchess of Burgundy, see Chapter 2.
73. Jones and Underwood, 87–89.
74. Jones and Underwood, 83–85.
75. Jones and Underwood, 91–92.
76. Seward, 332.
77. Jones and Underwood, 83, 92.
78. Jones and Underwood, 94.
79. Two of Margaret Beaufort's letters to her son are printed in Mary Ann Everett Wood, *Letters of Royal and Illustrious Ladies of Great Britain* . . . (London, 1846), vol. 3, 116–20; they are reprinted by Crawford, 149–51. The unique quality of the expressions of affection in these letters can be judged by comparing them to the letters of Joan of Navarre, wife of Henry IV, to her son, for example (printed by Wood, vol. 1, 89–91), or to those of Catherine of Aragon, written to her father and mother (printed by Wood, vol. 3, 128–54). Barbara J. Harris notes, "No other mother's letters from the period compare to Lady Margaret's"; see "Property, Power, and Personal Relations: Elite Mothers and Sons in Yorkist and Early Tudor England," *Signs: Journal of Women in Culture and Society*, 15 (1990), 620.

    Henry VII's letters to his mother are quoted by Seward, 33, Jones and Underwood, 74, and Crawford, 145. As an interesting note, Seward—notable for his careful treatment of Margaret Beaufort's political involvement and her significance in the Wars of the Roses—calls Margaret's "affection" for her son "obsessive, even neurotic" (330). Harris, too, judges Margaret's language "effusive, almost romantic" (620).
80. Seward, 326.
81. Crawford, 146.
82. Jones and Underwood, 71.
83. Jones and Underwood, 69–70.

84. Jones and Underwood, 86. For examples of the letters combining "By the king's mother" with the signature "Margaret R.," see Crawford. About the designation, Mary Ann Everett Wood writes, "The signature of 'Margaret R.' was always adopted by the Countess, to shew, we presume, that if she were not a queen she thought that she ought to have been" (116-17).

85. On Margaret Beauchamp (fl. 1440s), see Simon, 1-5, and Jones and Underwood, 28-34.

    In addition to her guardianship, Margaret Beauchamp oversaw her daughter's education, which was, in Simon's words, "an unusual education for a female at the time" (3). Although she did not receive the Greek and Latin study she requested, Margaret Beaufort's studies went beyond the religious instruction and "obligatory skill of needlework" that marked the usual training for girls—the kind of education that her contemporary, Isabella of Castile, had received.

86. Quoted by Christine Weightman, *Margaret of York, Duchess of Burgundy, 1446-1503* (New York, 1989), 16.

    Cecily Neville, duchess of York (1415-1495) was mother to Edward IV, Richard III, and Margaret of York.

87. Simon, 47; Jones and Underwood, 79-70.

88. Anne Crawford, "The King's Burden? Consequences of Royal Marriage in Fifteenth-century England," in *Patronage, the Crown and the Provinces in Later Medieval England*, ed. Ralph A. Griffiths (Atlantic Highlands, New Jersey, 1981), 38.

89. Charles T. Wood, "The First Two Queens Elizabeth," 126.

90. Wood, 127-28.

91. Quoted by Wood, 128.

92. Crawford, 53.

93. Wood, 128.

94. Quoted by Simon, 27.

95. For the effect of Edward of Lancaster's birth on Margaret of Anjou, see Keith Dockray, "The Origins of the Wars of the Roses," in A. J. Pollard, ed., *The Wars of the Roses* (New York, 1995), 86.

96. Quoted by Simon, 28.

97. For these views of Margaret of Anjou (1430-1482), see Patricia-Ann Lee, "Reflections of Power: Margaret of Anjou and the Dark Side of Queenship," *Renaissance Quarterly*, 39 (1986), 183-217, especially 193 to end; see also Simon, 27-28.

    The range of Margaret of Anjou's activities during the Wars of the Roses can be seen in her correspondence. Mary Anne Everett Wood prints one letter and a summary of her wardrobe accounts, vol. 1, 95-99; Crawford reprints this letter (129) along with five others (125-28). A wider range of letters by and about her is contained in Joseph Stevenson, ed., *Letters and Papers Illustrative of the Wars of the English in France During the Reign of Henry the Sixth, King of England* (London, 1861), vols. 1 and 2.

98. J. J. Bagley, *Margaret of Anjou, Queen of England* (London, [1948]), 26.

99. Isabelle of Lorraine (fl. c. 1420s-1440s), the wife of René of Anjou, was daughter and heiress of Charles, duke of Lorraine. When her husband was held captive, Isabella assumed the title of Queen of the Two Sicilies, proceeding to Italy, defending her husband's interests there, and proclaiming him King of the Two Sicilies.

100. Yolande of Aragon (1380–c. 1430s), the wife of Louis II of Anjou, functioned for fifteen years as regent of Anjou for her son Louis III. For a full-length biography, see Jehanne d'Orliac, *Yolande d'Anjou, la reine des quatre royaumes* (Paris, 1933).

101. While discussing the political roles of Isabelle of Lorraine and Yolande of Aragon (24–29), Bagley also notes the influence on Margaret of Anjou of her maternal grandmother, Margaret of Bavaria (fl. 1410s–30s), in whose care she was left while her mother recruited an army for her husband.

102. Margaret Beaufort would have been well aware of Matilda from the works of the Lancastrian propagandist Sir John Fortescue (c. 1385–c. 1479), if not from other sources.

Fortescue, a jurist and legal theorist, produced a series of arguments defending Lancastrian and refuting Yorkist titles to the crown, including *Defense of the House of Lancaster* and *Of the Title of the House of York*. Citing "diverse chronicles and parliaments," Fortescue argued that a hereditary claim to the throne could not be made through a woman. Because the Yorkists claimed the throne through the female line—through Philippa and Anne Mortimer—their claim was a false one. For a discussion of these two works, see Veikko Litzen, *A War of Roses and Lilies: The Theme of Succession in Sir John Fortescue's Works* (Helsinki, 1971), especially pp. 17–26. For the text of *Of the Title*, see Thomas Fortescue, lord Clermont, *The Works of Sir John Fortescue, Chief Justice of England and Lord Chancellor to King Henry the Sixth* [London, 1869], vol. 2, 497–502.)

Fortescue's most extensive treatment of the question of female sovereignty is in his *On the Law of Nature*. In this treatise, a deceased king's daughter, grandson, and brother, each claiming the throne, argue their cases before a judge empaneled to "clear up . . . the minds of men darkened by their ignorance." The judge's "sentence," preceded by a long summary of divine, natural, and human law, is absolutely clear:

> [W]e, having with mature deliberation listened to their allegations and replies, and also to the reasons and arguments which they have framed . . . , most clearly discovered and arrived at the undoubting conviction that a woman is not capable of holding a kingdom which is subject to no superior, and that her son, therefore, cannot by any law of nature succeed in right of his mother to such a kingdom; we, I say, adjudge, arbitrate, and by this our final sentence decree, that the brother aforesaid hath the right to the kingdom and in the kingdom in dispute, by title of succession as heir of the deceased king, his late brother. . . . And we absolutely exclude therefrom the daughter and grandson aforesaid, and declare them to be devoid and destitute of all right and title to the same.

(The argument in *On the Law of Nature* is in *Works*, vol. 1, 250–333; the judgment is found on p. 331.)

Fortescue's partisanship in the Lancastrian-Yorkist civil wars may well have dictated his position on the subject of female sovereignty. Both his *Defense* and *Of the Title* were written from his exile in Scotland with Henry VI's queen, Margaret of Anjou. Captured in 1471 after the Lancastrian defeat at Tewkesbury, he not only survived but eventually served on the council of the Yorkist king Edward IV. As part of his reconciliation with his former enemies, he repudiated his political writings.

In his arguments about women and succession, Fortescue took particular care with the example of Matilda. Noting that "rights are not similar in the case of royalty and of private possession," Fortescue worked through the succession crisis of the twelfth century. In his analysis, Henry I is succeeded not by his daughter, because women are excluded from rule, nor by his grandson, Matilda's son, because she cannot "transfer more right to another person than is known to belong" to her, but, correctly, by Stephen. Stephen's claim is valid not because he is Henry's sister's son, but because he is proclaimed king. Similarly, after Stephen's death, Henry II succeeds not because he is Matilda's son and not because Stephen's son is dead, but because he has been accepted as king; in Fortescue's view, he has succeeded "not by right of succession but by authority of parliament" (see Veikko, 18).

During the War of the Roses, conflicting Lancastrian and Yorkist claims were strenuously argued in an extensive propaganda war. See Alison Allan, "Yorkist Propaganda: Pedigree, Prophecy, and the 'British history' in the Reign of Edward IV," in *Patronage, Pedigree and Power in Later Medieval England*, ed. Charles Ross (Totowa, New Jersey, 1979), 171–92; and Charles Ross, "Rumour, Propaganda and Popular Opinion During the Wars of the Roses," in *Patronage, the Crown and the Provinces in Later Medieval England*, ed. Ralph A. Griffiths (Atlantic Highlands, New Jersey, 1981), 15–32.

103. Rosemary Horrox, "Personalities and Politics," in Pollard, 103. About Warwick as "kingmaker" Sir Thomas More wrote: "he made kings and put down kings almost at his pleasure, and not impossible to have attained it himself, if he had not reckoned it a greater thing to make a king than to be a king"; see *More's history of King Richard III*, ed. J. Rawson Lumby (Cambridge, 1883), 62–63.

Karen Lindsey makes the same comparison between Warwick and Margaret Beaufort in her *Divorced, Beheaded, Survived: A Feminist Reinterpretation of the Wives of Henry VIII* (Reading, Massachusetts, 1995), 3; since both works were published in the same year, I do not mean to imply that Horrox's is the source of the idea, but I rely on her insights and analysis here.

104. The only full-length biography of Caterina Sforza in English is Ernst Breisach, *Caterina Sforza: A Renaissance Virago* (Chicago, 1967).

The definitive study of Caterina Sforza remains Pier Desiderio Pasolini's three-volume *Caterina Sforza* (Rome, 1893); following two volumes of biography, Pasolini prints an extensive collection (vol. 3) of primary-source documents. An additional volume of documents appeared later: Pasolini, *Caterina Sforza: Nuovi Documenti* (Bologna, 1897).

In English, Caterina's story is briefly told in Lacy Collison-Morley's *The Story of the Sforzas* (New York, 1934) and, more recently, Antonia Fraser's *The Warrior Queens*; these accounts rely either on Pasolini or on Breisach.

For what follows here, I have followed Pasolini's more detailed narrative of Caterina's life except where noted, and I have consulted primary source documents wherever possible; for critical and analytical reflections, I have referred to Breisach.

105. Pasolini, *Nuovi Documenti*, 98 (my translation).

106. Pasolini, *Caterina Sforza*, vol. 1, 40 (my translation). Although "adopted" by Bona of Savoy, Caterina maintained a lifelong relationship with her natural mother, Lucrezia Landriani, and with Giampietro Landriana, Lucrezia's husband. Pasolini indicates (vol. 2, 347) that Lucrezia resided at Caterina's court from 1488 until 1499; after Caterina's retirement to Florence in 1501, Lucrezia again joined her daughter, at least for some time. Pasolini prints no letters between Caterina and Lucrezia, but a letter to Caterina dated as late as 17 August 1507, from an unknown writer, contains news of her mother.

107. Breisach, 23.

108. Breisach, 36.

109. Breisach, 63; Pasolini, vol. 1, 133 (my translation). The period is covered by Pasolini, vol. 1, 125-44.

110. Reports about Caterina's entrance into the castle are included in Stefano Guidotti's letter to the marquis of Mantua, 14 August 1484 (Pasolini, *Nuovi Documenti*, 87-89), and in Guidantonio Vespucci's letter to Lorenzo de' Medici, 15 August 1484 (Pasolini, vol. 3, 99).

111. Quoted by Pasolini, vol. 1, 150 (my translation).

112. For Caterina's comparison of her capacities to her father's, see Vespucci's letter to Lorenzo de' Medici, 18 August 1484 (Pasolini, vol. 3, 100 [my translation]).

113. Breisach, 73.

114. Pasolini, vol. 1, 181-88. The distance is, very roughly, ten miles.

115. Pasolini, vol. 1, 189-92 (my translation).

116. Pasolini, vol. 1, 217-18 (my translation).

117. Pasolini prints several contemporary letters and several passages from chronicles that describe Girolamo's assassination and Caterina's defense of the fortress of Ravaldino (vol. 3, 107-15, and *Nuovi Documenti*, 97-99).

118. Machiavelli's account in his *Discourses on Livy* was written in 1513; I have used the edition of Havey C. Mansfield and Nathan Tarcov (Chicago, 1996), XIII.6.18 (the story is retold by Machiavelli in his 1525 *Florentine Histories*, VIII.34; an abbreviated version appears as well in *The Prince*, see n. 153).

On Machiavelli's version of this incident, see also John Freccero, "Medusa and the Madonna of Forlì," in *Machiavelli and the Discourse of Literature*, ed. Albert Russell Ascoli and Victoria Kahn (Ithaca, New York, 1993), 161-78, and Julia L. Hairston, "Skirting the Issue: Machiavelli's Caterina Sforza," *Renaissance Quarterly*, 53 (2000), 687-712.

119. See Pasolini, vol. 1, 228 (my translation).

120. Quoted by Breisach, 112.

121. Quoted by Pasolini, vol. 1, 264-66 (my translation).

122. The punishment of the conspirators is described by Pasolini (vol. 1, 287-313) in a chapter called "*La Vendetta*."

123. After Caterina imprisoned Cobelli, he became her constant critic; see Pasolini vol. 1, 318. Ludovico Sforza's reference to Caterina's "disorderly" life is made in a letter of 11 September 1489; printed in Pasolini, vol. 3, 147. For the pope's judgment, see Pasolini, vol. 2, 131. For Breisach's remarks, see his *Caterina Sforza*, 120-28.

124. Pasolini, vol. 3, 138-47.

125. On Caterina's affair with Ordelaffi, see Breisach, 129-31.

126. For Frasier's remark, see her *Warrior Queens*, 197.

Caterina's letter to the duke of Ferrara is printed by Pasolini, vol. 3, 155 (Breisach translation).

127. The event is described in Pasolini, vol. 1, 322-24. The governor of Imola's letter is printed by Pasolini, vol. 3, 155.

Tommaso's removal, however it was effected, was temporary; he was eventually married to Bianca Landriani, Caterina's half-sister. By 1493 he was governor of Imola and by 1495 he had become governor of Forlì.

128. The reports by one Bello da Castrocaro were sent to the Florentine commissioner Puccio Pucci, who forwarded them to Piero de' Medici; Pasolini, vol. 3, 181-95 (my translation).

129. Pasolini, vol. 1, 360-84. Sources disagree about whether Caterina and Giacomo Feo were actually married; Pasolini accepts the secret marriage as valid, while Breisach judges such a marriage "highly unlikely" (307 n. 83). What is certain is that during the period of her relationship with Giacomo, Caterina gave birth to another child, a son named Bernardino (b. c. 1490), later renamed Carlo.

Correspondence about the assassination and Caterina's punishment of the conspirators is printed by Pasolini, vol. 3, 229-30.

130. Pasolini vol. 3, 257 (my translation).

131. Pasolini vol. 3, 262-63 (my translation). The report is contained in a letter of the Milanese ambassador in Venice, 19 December 1496.

132. The series of letters are date from 10 October 1496 through 23 January 1497; Pasolini vol. 3, 257-88 (my translation).

133. Since no record exists, the exact date of the marriage is unknown, but it most likely took place at some point in late 1497 or 1498. Breisach (324 n. 126) discusses various theories about when the marriage occurred. The child born to Caterina and Giovanni de' Medici was named Lodovico. His name was later changed to Giovanni, and he is known popularly as Giovanni delle Bande Nere; see Chapter 4.

134. For the conflict, see Pasolini, vol. 2, 3-29. Caterina's letter to Ludovico Sforza, dated 24 August 1498, is printed by Pasolini, vol. 3, 304 (Breisach translation).

135. Pasolini, vol. 2, 131. On the events preceding Caterina's condemnation, see vol. 2, 111-43. For a brief account of the political situation in Italy, see T. A. Morris, *Europe and England in the Sixteenth Century* (New York, 1998), 144-45; and John A. Marino, "The Italian States in the 'Long Sixteenth Century,'" in Thomas J. Brady, Jr., et al., eds., *Handbook of European History, 1400-1600: Late Middle Ages, Renaissance, and Reformation*, vol. 1: *Structures and Assertions* (Leiden, 1994), 331-61.

136. On Machiavelli's legation to Caterina, see Pasolini, vol. 2, 90-110. Pasolini includes here extracts from seven letters Machiavelli dispatched from Forlì to Florence.

137. Caterina's letters about guardianship of her son are printed by Pasolini, vol. 3, 399-401.

138. The flight of Ludovico, Louis XII's entry in Milan, and Caterina's delegation to Rome are in Pasolini, vol. 2, 115-23. The letter accusing the Florentines and the papal brief are printed by Pasolini, vol. 3, 406-7; the chronicler Bernardi's account of the attempted poisoning of the pope is on pp. 408-10.

139. Pasolini, vol. 2, 134-50.

140. Caterina's defiance is quoted by Breisach, 220.

141. Those inside Ravaldino with Caterina are named in a list of prisoners printed by Pasolini, vol. 2, 157-58. They included two half brothers, Alessandro and Galeazzo Sforza, along with "another Sforza" whose name was unknown; a poet named Marullo, described as a *constantinopolitano*; Giovanni da Casale, described as Caterina's "pretended lover"; and Girolamo Riario's "natural son," Scipione.

142. Caterina's 26 December "debate" with Cesare is printed by Pasolini, vol. 2, 177-80 (my translation).

143. The siege and fall of the fortress of Ravaldino are described by Pasolini, vol. 2, 130-203; the events are also narrated impressively by Breisach, 228-33.

144. Breisach, 233.

145. Quoted by Pasolini, vol. 2, 205 (my translation).

146. Quoted by Breisach, 233. For Caterina's capture, rape, and imprisonment, see Pasolini, vol. 2, 204-47.

147. Letters to and from Caterina's sons are printed by Pasolini, vol. 3, 446-51, 454-55.

   Alexander VI's letter to the Signory of Florence, dated 13 July 1501, is printed by Pasolini, vol. 3, 456 (my translation).

148. Caterina's last years are narrated by Pasolini, vol. 2, 305-40.

149. There were many Italian precedents for Caterina. The kingdom of Naples had had two queens regnant, Joanna I (1329-1382) and Joanna II (1371-1435).

   In Sicily, Isabelle of Lorraine (fl. 1420s-1440s) had assumed the title of the Queen of the Two Sicilies and had asserted her husband's right to rule there, functioning as his regent while he was imprisoned (she was Margaret of Anjou's mother; see n. 99). Juana of Aragon (m. 1477-d. 1517), daughter of Juan of Aragon, also served as regent in Sicily; she married Ferrante I of Naples, serving as his regent in Sicily after his death in 1494.

   Anne of Lusignan (c. 1420s-1460s) married Louis, duke of Savoy. She was not, strictly speaking, regent of Savoy, but after 1439 Louis left governing responsibilities to her. She is the mother of both Charlotte of Savoy, queen of France, and Bona of Savoy, duchess of Milan—Caterina Sforza's stepmother (see below). Blanche of Montferrat (fl. 1430s-1490s) married Charles I of Savoy in 1485; she was regent of Savoy for her son, Charles II, born in 1488.

   In Urbino, Battista Sforza (1446-1472) was the second wife of Federigo da Montefeltro; she served as his regent during his absences. Eleanor of Aragon (1455-1493) was the regent of Ferrara for her husband, Ercole d'Este. She was the mother of Isabella d'Este; see Chapter 4.

150. On Bianca Maria Visconti (1424-1468), see Pasolini, vol. 1, 20-27.

151. Quoted by Julia Cartwright, *Beatrice d'Este* (1890; 8th ed. New York, 1920), 18.

152. Pasolini, vol. 1, 40-41.

153. For Machiavelli's references to Caterina Sforza, see *The Prince*, Chapters 3 and 20; the reference to Joanna II is in Chapter 12. Machiavelli refers to Caterina as well in his *Discourses on Livy*, as we have seen; see n. 118.

   On Machiavelli's view of Caterina, John Freccero goes even further:

   We cannot attribute to Machiavelli an anachronistically enlightened view of women in society any more than we can credit him with a democratic spirit; yet it is undeniable that he saw in Caterina Italy's only hope, in the absence of a prince. ("Medusa and the Madonna," 178)

On women's inheritance of titles and their succession in Italy, see Charles Mistruzzi, "La Succession nobilaire en Italie dans le drois et dans l'histoire, in Ida Auda-Gioanet, *Une Randonée à travers l'histoire d'Orient (les Comnènes et les Anges)* (Rome, 1953), 107-19.

154. For a brief account of the period, see Bernard Chevalier, "France from Charles VII to Henry IV," in *Handbook of European History*, vol. 1, 369-401. An extended account is John S. C. Bridge, *A History of France from the Death of Louis XI*, 5 vols. (New York, 1921).

155. There is no full-length biography of Anne of France in English. For what follows I rely on Jehanne d'Orliac, *Anne de Beaujeu, Roi de France* (Paris, 1926; Louis XI's judgment of his daughter is quoted on p. 48, my translation); Marc Chombart de Lauwe, *Anne de Beaujeu: ou la passion du pouvoir* (Paris, 1957); Bridge, vol. 1, *passim* (the quotation about Anne's care to "disguise her power" is on p. 34); and J. H. M. Salmon, "The Regent and the Duchess: Anne de Beaujeu and Anne de Bretagne," *History Today*, 16 (1960), 341-48. References to Anne of France occur throughout René de Maulde La Clavière, *The Women of the Renaissance: A Study of Feminism*, trans. Georbe Herbert Ely (New York, 1901); he argues that she was the "virtual ruler of France" for the first eight years of her brother's reign (25 n). For a somewhat dated but still very useful work addressed specifically to Anne of France as ruler, see P. Pélicier, *Le Gouvernement de la dame de Beaujeu* (Chartres, 1882).

Louis XI did not have to far to find women who could confirm his faith in his daughter's abilities. His grandmother was Isabel of Bavaria, regent of France for her husband (see p. 59 and n. 177). His maternal grandmother was Yolande of Aragon, duchess of Anjou and regent of Anjou for her husband René (see n. 100). His sister Yolande of Valois (1434-1478) married Amadeus of Savoy in 1452; after her husband's death in 1472, she was regent of Savoy for her son, Philibert.

156. The events following Louis XI's death are narrated by d'Orliac, 65-76.

157. Quoted by d'Orliac, 76 (my translation).

Charlotte of Savoy (1439-1483) was the sister of Bona of Savoy, Caterina Sforza's adopted mother. For Bona of Savoy, see pp. 39 and 51-52.

158. For the meeting of the Estates General, see Bridge, vol. 1, 54-102. Jean Masselin, an official of the church, left an eyewitness journal account of events that provides the basis of Bridge's narration.

159. Quoted by d'Orliac, 79 (my translation).

160. Quoted by d'Orliac, 82 (my translation).

161. Events are narrated by Bridge, vol. 1, 122-26.

162. Bridge, vol. 1, 125.

163. For Louis' activities in Brittany, see Bridge, vol. 1, 101-32.

Anne of Brittany (1477-1514) was the daughter of Francis II, duke of Brittany and his second wife, Marguerite de Foix; she was the sole surviving child of Francis and thus heiress to Brittany. See Salmon and the highly romanticized but useful biography of Mildred Allen Butler, *Twice Queen of France: Anne of Brittany* (New York, 1967). Also useful is the older biography by Louisa Stuart Costello, *Memoirs of Anne, Duchess of Brittany, Twice Queen of*

France (London, 1855). A new biography in French has recently appeared, Geroges Minois, *Anne de Bretagne* (Paris, 1999).

For Margaret of Austria, see Chapter 2.

164. D'Orliac, 87.

165. On the events of the "Mad War," see Bridge, vol. 1, 132-219.

166. Quoted by d'Orliac, 103 (my translation).

167. See d'Orliac, 97-99 (my translation).

168. D'Orliac, 97 (my translation).

Though she has been accused of rapacity, enriching herself by securing the Bourbon inheritance, Bridge concludes, "the striking thing is, not that she took what she did, but that she took so little" (vol. 1, 246).

169. André Poulet, "Capetian Women and the Regency: The Genesis of a Vocation," in John Carmi Parsons, ed., *Medieval Queenship* (New York, 1993), 103-4. See also Marion F. Facinger, "A Study of Medieval Queenship: Capetian France, 987-1237," *Studies in Medieval and Renaissance History*, 5 (1968), 3-47. The thirteen Capetian kings ruled France from the reign of Hugh Capet (elected king in 987) through Charles IV (d. 1328). On earlier and informal arrangements granting women power, see Janet L. Nelson, "Women at the Court of Charlemagne: A Case of Monstrous Regiment?" in Parsons, 43-61.

170. On the development of Salic law, see: John Milton Potter, "The Development and Significance of the Salic Law of the French," *English Historical Review*, 52 (1937), 235-53; Ralph E. Giesey, "The Juristic Basis of the Dynastic Right to the French Throne," *Transactions of the American Philosophical Society*, n.s. 51 (1961), 3-47; and Fanny Cosandey, "De lance en quenouille. La place de la reigne dans l'État moderne (14e-17e siecles)," *Annales*, 52 (1997), 799-820.

The reference is to the *Lex Salica*, the law code of the Salian Franks, issued (c. 507-11) during the reign of Clovis and reissued by Charlemagne and his successors. It included a chapter declaring that daughters could not inherit land. The exclusion of women from the throne was not addressed in Salic law, nor did this exclusion become an issue for centuries.

From the time of Hugh Capet (d. 1328) until Philip IV (d. 1314), each king of France left behind a son to succeed him. When Louis X died in 1316, he was survived by a daughter, Jeanne, who had been born in 1308, and by his second wife, Clemence, then pregnant. A posthumously born son survived only a few days, precipitating a succession crisis. Should the crown fall to Jeanne of France, as Louis' sole surviving heir, or should it pass to the king's brother, Philip of Poitiers, his closest male heir? Although there was no law to prevent her inheritance, Jeanne did not succeed her father. Instead, Philip became king of France. The rules by which he did so, as historian Fanny Cosandey notes, "remain uncertain"; what is certain is that on 13 March 1317, Jeanne "abdicated" all claims to the throne of France and her uncle became Philip V (Cosandey, 801).

Such a turn of events was not inevitable. Louis X had earlier acted to protect the rights of women to inherit from their fathers. In response to a petition from this same Philip, in fact, requesting that his own daughter's inheritance "might be secured," Louis X had acceded to his brother's request:

reason and natural law instruct us that in default of male heirs females should inherit and have succession to the goods and possessions of the fathers of whom they are procreated and descended in legal marriage, the same as do the males. (Quoted by Potter, 237)

"Considerations of legality had . . . little immediate practical importance in the settlement actually reached in 1316 and 1317," however:

Philip V made good his possession of the throne in part because of division and lack of steadfastness amongst his opponents, in part by bribery, in part by the consent of an assembly of notables. . . . The lawyers said little. (Potter, 237)

However it was arrived at, the decision itself was clear and direct: "Women do not succeed to the throne of France." When Philip V died in 1322, he was survived only by his daughter Margaret, whose inheritance rights he had earlier tried to assure. He was, therefore, succeeded by another brother, Charles. When Charles IV died in 1328, he too had failed to produce a male heir—the last Capetian king was survived only by a daughter, Blanche. In England, however, there was a direct male claimant to the French throne, Edward III: the son of Isabella of France—wife of Edward II of England and sister of Louis X, Philip V, and Charles IV, all kings of France. To preserve the independent French monarchy, it was necessary to turn to a collateral line, the Valois, and to justify the exclusion of daughters of France and of male issue of those daughters from the throne. The result was the formulation, over the course of the next hundred years, of the "Salic law" denying female inheritance.

In the sixteenth century, Claude de Seyssel (c. 1450-1520) became one of Louis XII's councillors after his accession to the throne of France. Seysel's *Monarchy of France* was published in 1515. His discussion of the Salic law occurs in a chapter entitled "How It Is Well That the Realm Passes by Masculine Succession," 48-49. As a further justification for male succession, he continues,

When the succession goes from male to male, the heir is always certain and is of the same blood as those who formerly ruled, so the subjects have the very same love and reverence for him as for his predecessors. Even though he be related only distantly and the dead king have daughters, yet without deviation or scruple the people turn to him as soon as the other has ceased to be, and there is no disturbance of difficulty. (49)

See Claude de Seyssel, *The Monarchy of France*, ed. Donald R. Kelley, trans. J.H. Hexter (New Haven, Connecticut, 1981).

171. On the developing law of regency, see Cosandey, 803-810; on the preference for a woman to serve as regent, see pp. 810-15.

172. For what follows I rely primarily on Poulet, 108-15.

173. Poulet, 108; see also Facinger, 8-9. Adele of Champagne (1145-1206) was queen of France for twenty years, dowager queen for twenty-six.

On the earliest Capetian queens, Facinger singles out Adelaide of Aquitaine (c. 960s-1006), wife of Hugh Capet, and Constance of Arles, wife of Robert II, Adelaide's son. During his lifetime, Hugh designated his wife as his "partner in governing"; the king, his queen, and their son Robert "shared the monarchy" for the last nine years of Hugh's reign, from 987, when Robert II became co-king. When Robert II succeeded his father in 996, "the dowager Adelaide dominated the court": "Robert was accustomed to his mother's participation in governing, and Adelaide was used to sharing the duties and prerogatives of a monarch." A "seasoned and experienced" queen, Adelaide provided "a needed stability" to the early years of her son's reign. After her death, Robert II's third wife, Constance of Arles (986-1032) "continued to function and to dominate the court and the king in the same manner as had Robert's mother": she advised the king, shared in judicial proceedings, and participated in the Council of Orléans (1022); see Facinger, 24-25.

174. Poulet, 110. On this "model of mothers and of regents," see the discussion of Blanche of Castile (Chapter 15) in Alphonse Dantier, *Les Femmes dans la societé chrétienne* (Paris, 1879). See also n. 9.

175. Poulet, 112.

176. Poulet, 112-114.

177. Rachel Gibbons, "Isabeau of Bavaria, Queen of France (1385-1422): The Creation of an Historical Villainess," *Transactions of the Royal Historical Society*, 6th ser., 6 (1996), 54. For recent biographies, see Jean Verdon, *Isabeau de Bavière* (Paris, 1981) and Jean Markale, *Isabeau de Bavière* (Paris, 1982).

178. Gibbons, 55-57.

179. Pierre de Bourdeille, abbey of Brantôme (c. 1540-1614) spent his childhood at the court of Marguerite of Valois, queen of Navarre, where his mother and grandmother belonged to the royal household. His "The Book of the Ladies" was published under the title of *Vies des dames illustres* ("Lives of Illustrious Ladies"); I have used the translation by Katharine Prescott Wormeley, *Illustrious Dames of the Court of Valois Kings* (New York, 1912). The biographical portrait of Anne of France is on pp. 216-220.

180. Unfortunately, as Pélicier notes, most (*la plupart*) of Anne of France's letters have been lost, and the remaining few throw "little light" on her political role (198-99).

181. D'Orliac, 123; see also Poulet, 115. D'Orliac claims Anne of France resumed her role as regent, though de Lauwe indicates that Charles designated Pierre de Beaujeu officially to act as regent (343-44). See also Costello, 193-97.
     On Charles VIII's reign during the years 1493-1498, see vol. 2 of Bridge's five-volume history. On his Italian campaign, see above, p. 47.

182. D'Orliac, 146. On Jeanne de France, *la reine sacrifeé*, see de Lauwe, 361-83; on her divorce from Louis XII, see Bridge, *A History of France*, vol. 3: *Reign of Louis XII, 1498-1507*, 8-14.

183. On Louis' Italian campaign, see 47-48, and Chevalier. Louis XII's reign is narrated in vols. 3 and 4 of Bridge's five-volume history.

184. Valentina Visconti (c. 1408) was the daughter of Giangaleazzo Visconti and Isabel of Valois (1348-1372), the daughter of King John II of France. She was married to Louis, duke of Orléans in 1388; by the terms of her marriage contract, she brought him a right of succession to the duchy of Milan should the Visconti male line fail.

185. De Lauwe, 398 (my translation); see also D'Orliac, 163-65. Pierre de Beaujeu had opposed the marriage of his daughter to Charles de Montpensier, preferring instead a match with the duke of Alençon.
     Before venturing into Italy Louis had allied himself to papal interests. In order to secure Alexander VI's approval of the annulment of his marriage, he

arranged for the marriage of Charlotte d'Albret (1482-1514), daughter of Alain d'Albret (his old rival for the hand of Anne of Brittany) to the pope's son. Cesare Borgia arrived in France on 18 December 1498. Louis' marriage to Anne of Brittany took place on 7 January 1499. Charlotte d'Albret was married to Cesare Borgia on 10 May 1499. Shortly after the marriage, Cesare left France. Charlotte remained in France, however, a kind of hostage for her husband's compliance with the terms of his agreement with Louis. She never saw him again. A daughter, Louise Borgia, was born in 1500.

186. Francis of Angoulême was a direct descendant, like Louis XII, of Louis of Orléans and Valentina Visconti. Louis was the grandson of their older son, Charles, duke of Orléans, while Francis was the great-grandson of their younger son John, count of Angoulême. When Claude of France was married to Francis of Angoulême, the long-desired union of Brittany with France was complete. On Francis' mother Louise of Savoy, see Chapter 5.

187. *Les Enseignements d'Anne de France . . . a sa fille Susanne de Bourgon* was printed in the sixteenth century in Lyon (n.d.); I have used here the edition of A.-M. Chazaud (Moulins, 1878). Chazaud indicates (x) that *Les enseignements* was printed "at the request" of Suzanne de Bourbon, "without doubt with the consent of her mother"; thus it would have been printed before Anne of France's death in 1522.

188. "Niccolò Machiavelli to His Magnificence Lorenzo de' Medici," in *The Prince*, ed. and trans. David Wootton (Indianapolis, 1995), 5.

189. *Les enseignements*, 2-4. All quotations from this work are my own translations.

For a brief discussion of Anne's work, see Constance Jordan, *Renaissance Feminism: Literary Texts and Political Models* (Ithaca, New York, 1990), 98-99.

190. *Les enseignements*, 16-17, 20-23, 78.

191. D'Orliac, 230 (my translation).

192. *Les enseignements*, 50-51.

193. For further details of queens in these regions, see Armin Wolf, "Reigning Queens in Medieval Europe: When, Where, and Why," in *Medieval Queenship*, ed. John Carmi Parsons, 169-88.

194. Anne of France seemed to recognize her status as a "queen who might have been." A seventeenth-century chronicler reported that, after her brother's dead, she "thought for a moment to claim the crown for herself, saying that 'she was the first among the descendants of the kings of France'" (de Lauwe, 357 n. 1).

Chapter 2

1. Mary of Austria's letter to her brother, written at the end of August 1555, is abstracted in *Calendar of Letters, Despatches and State Papers Relating to the Negotiations Between England and Spain, Preserved in the Archives at Vienna, Simancas, Besançon, Brussels, Madrid and Lisle*, ed. Royall Tyler (London, 1954), XIII, 242; hereafter referred to as *Calendar of State Papers, Spanish*.

For Mary of Austria and the women mentioned in this chapter, see Table 1.

2. The independent kingdom of Portugal had been formed in the twelfth century; see Chapter 1, n. 7.

3. Blanche of Navarre (1386-1441) was the queen regnant of Navarre; Juan II of Aragon was her king-consort, their children Charles of Viana, Blanche of Navarre, and Eleanor of Navarre. As we saw in Chapter 1, Isabella's half-brother Enrique had first married, then repudiated, the younger Blanche. After the death of the Navarrese queen regnant, Juan II then married Juana Enriquez, Ferdinand of Aragon's mother. To secure support from King Louis XI of France, Juan II had arranged for the crown of Navarre to pass to his daughter Eleanor and her husband Gaston IV of Foix; see Chapter 1, n. 2.

4. Parts of Navarre remained independent until Henry of Navarre joined them to France; see Chapter 5.

5. Three chapters in *The Handbook of European History, 1400-1600*, vol. 1: *Late Middle Ages, Renaissance, and Reformation* (Grand Rapids, Michigan, 1994), survey the Habsburg lands in the early modern period: see Volker Press, "The Habsburg Lands: The Holy Roman Empire, 1400-1555"; Henry Kamen, "The Habsburg Lands: Iberia"; and Hugo de Schepper, "The Burgundian-Habsburg Netherlands."

6. See Chapter 1.

7. On the education of Isabella's daughters, see Garrett Mattingly, *Catherine of Aragon* (New York, 1941), 7-10; see also Amarie Dennis, *See the Darkness: The Story of Juana la Loca* (Madrid, 1953), 15-17.

   On the education of Prince Juan, see Nancy Rubin, *Isabella of Castile* (New York, 1992), 220-21, 272, and 304-05.

8. Marvin Lunenfeld, "Isabella I of Castile and the Company of Women in Power," *Historical Reflections*, 4 (1977), 222.

9. Quoted by Rubin, 304.

10. On this see Rubin, 361-66.

11. Having married two of Isabella's daughters in succession, Manuel of Portugal would marry yet another of her descendants, a niece this time. After Maria's death in 1517, he married Eleanor, the oldest daughter of Maria's sister Juana.

12. The letter from Ferdinand and Isabella announcing their intentions is quoted by Rubin, 349.

13. On Philip, see Rubin, 369-70; on Juana, see Mary M. Luke, *Catherine the Queen* (New York, 1967), 21-22. The contemporary views of Juana are quoted by Hillgarth, *The Spanish Kingdoms, 1250-1516*, vol. 2: *1410-1516, Castilian Hegemony* (Oxford, 1978), 589.

14. For what follows, I rely on Hillgarth, 587-90; Rubin, 397-98; Dennis, 81-85.

15. For what follows, see Hillgarth, 589-91.

16. For what follows, see Dennis, 108-13.

17. Ferdinand's letter is quoted on pp. 112-13. I also rely on the detailed account of A. S. Martin Hume, *Queens of Old Spain* (New York, 1906), 141-206. A brief account appears in Hillgarth, 592-603. See also Ludwig Pfandl, *Juana la Loca: Su Vida, Su Tiempo, Su Culpa* (Buenos Aires, 1937; 8th ed., Madrid, 1945), 198.

18. Quoted by Hume, 144 (capitalization and punctuation modernized).

19. Hume, 150.

20. For what follows, including quotations from Philip and Ferdinand's agreement, see Hume, 160-61.

21. The Spanish ambassador and the Admiral of Castile are quoted by Dennis, 147.

22. These contemporary views are quoted by Hume, 171 n. 2, and Hillgarth, 597.

23. Lunenfeld, 209.

24. S. B. Chrimes, *Henry VII* (London, 1972; rpt. London 1987), 292 and n 5.

25. Maria of Portugal (c. 1310s-1350s) was abandoned and imprisoned by her husband Alfonso XI of Castile. Blanche of Bourbon (1338-1361) was married to Pedro I of Castile in 1352. He repudiated her the day after their marriage, and she remained imprisoned until her death. Eleanor Telles (c. 1350s-1386) was the wife of Ferdinand I of Portugal. She was regent of Portugal for her daughter Beatrice, who was to inherit her father's throne, but because of her "cruelties," Eleanor was overthrown, exiled in Castile, and ultimately imprisoned. (Beatrice, who had married the king of Castile, fought to retain the crown of Portugal, but she never succeeded because of the desire of the Portuguese nobility to remain independent.) Beatrice of Castile (1353-1368) was the oldest daughter of Pedro I of Castile (by his mistress Maria of Padilla); she was was forced to renounce her claim to the throne of Castile and enter a convent at Tordesillas.

   As an interesting note to Juana's later life, during the 1519-21 revolt against Charles in Spain, rebels captured Tordesillas and Queen Juana (Dennis, 219-39). In explaining her ignorance of the affairs of Castile, Juana said simply, "For fifteen years I have not been told the truth nor have I been well treated" (Dennis, 222). She welcomed the rebels and for more than four months was installed as queen. See Ellen Tremayne, *The First Governess of the Netherlands, Margaret of Austria* (London, 1908), 184.

26. Dennis, 140, 156, 171.

27. "Burgundy" had been formed in the fourteenth century when John II of France (d. 1364) presented the duchy of Burgundy to his son Philip the Bold (d. 1404). Philip's wife Margaret, daughter of the count of Flanders, brought to her marriage the dowry of several Flemish provinces, including Artois, Flanders, and Franche Comté. Philip the Good, her grandson (d. 1467), purchased Namur and Luxemburg; later Brabant, Limberg, Holland, Zeeland, and West Friesland, among others, were incorporated. Charles the Bold added Guelderland and Zutphen. The seventeen autonomous provinces of the Low Countries were roughly divided between the German-speaking north and a French-speaking south, these linguistic differences reflecting their political divisions and allegiances. Charles the Bold hoped to meld his diverse Burgundian possessions into one united and unified kingdom.

28. On Margaret of York's mother, Cecily Neville, see Chapter 1.

   Noting that the life of Margaret of York (1446-1503) "has attracted much more attention in Belgium than it has in England" and that in English history her life "has been confined to a few brief appearances" in biographes of her brothers and of King Henry VII, Christine Weightman has produced the first full-length biography of Margaret in English: *Margaret of York, Duchess of Burgundy, 1446-1503* (Stroud, Gloucestershire, England, 1989; rpt. New York, 1993). The list of Margaret's titles appears on p. 61.

   Margaret was the third wife of Charles, duke of Burgundy. Charles had first been married to Catherine of Valois (1428-1446), the oldest daughter of Mary of Anjou and Charles VII of France (see Chapter 1). His second wife was Isabelle of Bourbon (fl. 1430s-1465), daughter of Agnes of Burgundy and

Charles, duke of Bourbon; Isabelle gave birth to Charles's only child, his daughter and heir Mary of Burgundy (1457–1482).

29. Weightman, 51.

Isabel of Portugal (1397–1471) was the daughter of Philippa of Lancaster, the granddaughter of Blanche of Lancaster and John of Gaunt (see Chapter 1, n. 34). Philippa married the king of Portugal; Isabel, their daughter, married Philip of Burgundy in 1430.

30. Weightman, 63.

31. Weightman, 77–79.

32. Weightman, 115.

33. Weightman, 127.

During her brothers' reigns as kings of England, Margaret played an important role in Anglo-Burgundian politics; she was equally important as an adversary during the reign of Henry Tudor as Henry VII. We come back to Margaret of York in Chapter 3, discussing her involvement in English politics.

34. Weightman, 152.

35. Quoted by Weightman, 187.

36. For a biography of Margaret of Austria in English, see Jane de Iongh, *Margaret of Austria, Regent of the Netherlands*, trans. M. D. Herter Norton (New York, 1953), a clear and readable narrative, if undocumented and somewhat romanticized. Tremayne's older *The First Governess of the Netherlands, Margaret of Austria* is an excellent and carefully documented work focusing principally on Margaret's later years as regent. (Margaret of Austria is sometimes referred to as Margaret of Savoy, a reference to her title after her third marriage.)

Many of Margaret's letters are abstracted in *Calendar of State Papers, Spanish*.

37. de Iongh, 58.

38. Margaret's household and routine are described by de Iongh, 63–67. Her companions at Amboise are noted by Tremayne, 4. For Louise of Savoy, see Chapter 5.

39. de Iongh, 74–76. See also Chapter 1.

40. de Iongh, 79.

41. Quoted by Tremayne, 1.

42. Bianca Maria Sforza was the daughter of Bona of Savoy and Giangaleazzo Sforza; she was, thus, Caterina Sforza's half-sister; see Chapter 1 and Chapter 4.

43. The verse is quoted and translated by de Iongh, 94. In other accounts, Margaret has her epitaph and money tied into her waistband.

44. Rubin, 360; Dennis, 44.

45. Rubin, 361.

46. Peter Martyr and Isabella are quoted by Dennis, 45.

47. Quoted by Rubin, 364.

48. Rubin, 364; de Iongh, 103.

49. de Iongh, 111–12.

50. de Iongh, 118–19.

51. de Iongh, 120–21.

52. Quoted and translated by Tremayne, 46.

53. On this see Tremayne, 50–51.

54. Quoted by Tremayne, 62–63.

55. Quoted by de Iong, 137-38.

56. Andrew Wheatcroft, *The Habsburgs: Embodying Empire* (London, 1996), 123-25.

57. See Hugo de Schepper, "The Burgundian-Habsburg Netherlands."

58. Quoted by de Iongh, 143 (my translation).

59. Quoted by de Iongh, 152.

60. Quoted by Tremayne, 92-93; the meetings in Cambrai are discussed on pp. 90-95.

61. de Iongh, 155.

62. For all these quotations, see Tremayne, 112-14.

63. Isabel of Austria (1501-1526) was married by proxy on 11 June 1514 to Christian II, a man twenty-two years her senior. Since she was just thirteen she remained in the Netherlands for another year. When she was finally sent to her husband, she found that he was dominated by two women, his mistress and her mother, Siegebritte Willems, whom de Iongh describes as "the real ruler of Scandinavia" (173). Isabel was isolated from court, and her first-born son was raised by Siegebritte. In 1523 Christian's subjects rebelled and he was deposed. Isabel fled to Mechelen with her husband, taking refuge there with Margaret of Austria. She died there in 1526, at the age of twenty-five. Margaret of Austria refused to let Christian II leave Mechelen with his children, his son and heir John and two daughters, Dorothea and Christina. She "bought" them by offering him a yearly payment and kept them to raise.

   Mary of Austria, queen of Bohemia and Hungary (1505-1558), is discussed later in this chapter.

   Ferdinand of Austria's marriage to Anne of Bohemia (b. 1502?) took place on 5 May 1521.

   See Paula Sutter Fichtner, "Dynastic Marriage in Sixteenth-Century Habsburg Diplomacy and Statecraft: An Interdisciplinary Approach," *American Historical Review*, 81 (1976), 243-65.

64. Quoted by Tremayne, 121-29.

65. Quoted by Tremayne, 147-48.

66. Quoted by de Iongh, 193.

67. Quoted by Tremayne, 148-49 (punctuation modernized).

68. Quoted by Tremayne, 161 (punctuation modernized).

69. On Manuel of Portugal's first two marriages, see Chapter 1, 17, and above, 70-71. His third marriage did not last long; the old king died in 1523. He was succeeded by his son and heir Joaõ III, who in 1518 married Eleanor's sister Catalina.

70. On the imperial election, see de Iongh, 211-17.

71. Quoted by Tremayne, 253-54 (capitalization and punctuation modernized).

72. Quoted by Tremayne, 258.

73. Quoted by de Iongh, 251 (capitalization and punctuation modernized).

74. Contemporary chroniclers, in particular Peter Martyr, despised Ferdinand's second marriage, recording scurrilous stories about an aphrodisiac of herbs and bull's hormones that Germaine prepared for her aging husband—instead of restoring his virility, the potion "brought on a state of weakness and despair" (Dennis, 191) and resulted in Ferdinand's death; see also Hillgarth, 595 and 601.

75. Germaine's brother Gaston (1489-1512) is not to be confused with an earlier Gaston of Foix, the father of Catherine of Foix, who was queen of Navarre at the time of Germaine's marriage (see n. 3). Germaine and her brother, the younger Gaston, were the Navarrese queen's cousins, children of her father's younger brother. The twenty-three-year-old Gaston died fighting on 11 April 1512 in Italy.

76. For a well-documented biography, see Jane de Iongh, *Mary of Hungary, Second Regent of the Netherlands*, trans. M. D. Herter Norton (New York, 1958). As can be seen from the title of de Iongh's biography, Mary of Austria is often referred to as Mary of Hungary, and sometimes she appears as Mary of Savoy. Also very useful is David P. Daniel, "Piety, Politics, and Perversion: Noblewomen in Reformation Hungary," in *Women in Reformation and Counter-Reformation Europe: Public and Private Worlds*, ed. Sherrin Marshall (Bloomington, Indiana, 1989), 68-88.

77. de Iongh, *Mary of Hungary*, 36-45.

78. Peter G. Bietenholz, ed., *Contemporaries of Erasmus: A Biographical Register of the Renaissance and Reformation* (Toronto, 1989), vol. 2, 400.

79. The comment of Erasmus' friend is quoted by de Iongh, *Mary of Hungary*, 93. The letter from Guidoto, the Venetian ambassador, is quoted in *Calendar of State Papers and Manuscripts, Relating to English Affairs, Existing in the Archives and Collections of Venice and in Other Libraries of Northern Italy*, ed. Rawdon Brown (London, 1877), VI.1, 32 n.

   The English humanist Roger Ascham recorded a criticism of Mary as well: "she is a Virago and is never so well as when she is flinging about on horseback and hunting all the night long" (quoted by Daniel, 70).

80. Quoted by de Iongh, *Mary of Hungary*, 105.

81. Quoted by de Iongh, *Mary of Hungary*, 107.

82. de Iongh, *Mary of Hungary*, 119.

83. Quoted by de Iongh, *Mary of Hungary*, 126, 132, 135.

84. de Iongh, *Mary of Hungary*, 142-51.

85. James V of Scotland married Madeleine of France; after her early death he married Marie of Guise; see Chapter 5.

86. Quoted by de Iongh, *Mary of Hungary*, 168-69 (capitalization and punctuation modernized).

87. After the duke of Milan's death, Christina of Denmark (b. 1522) remained with her aunt for several years. She finally married Francis I of Lorraine in 1541; after her husband's death in 1545, she served as regent of Lorraine for her son, Charles III.

89. de Iongh, *Mary of Hungary*, 226.

88. In addition to de Iongh's biography, Mary of Austria's activities as regent are summarized in the *Contemporaries of Erasmus* (vol. 2, 399-401), quoted here. See also Daniel R. Doyle, "The Sinews of Habsburg Governance in the Sixteenth Century: Mary of Hungary and Political Patronage," *Sixteenth Century Journal* 31 (2000), 349-60.

90. Mary's letter is abstracted in the *Calendar of State Papers, Spanish*, as indicated in n. 1. It is also quoted by de Iongh, 202 (capitalization and punctuation modernized).

91. Mary's lengthy letter is quoted by de Iongh, *Mary of Hungary*, 263-66 (capitalization and punctuation modernized).

92. Quoted by de Iongh, as noted.
93. Quoted by de Iongh, as noted.
94. de Iongh, *Mary of Hungary*, 280-88.
95. de Iongh, *Mary of Hungary*, 202-03.
   Beyond her defiance of gender roles, Mary was, as Daniel notes, "the hated importer of 'foreign ways'" (70).
96. Wheatcroft, 123.
97. Information on Isabel of Portugal (1503-1539) is available primarily in biographies of her husband and her son. For the information here I rely on Henry Kamen, *Philip of Spain* (New Haven, Connecticut, 1997), 2-3.
98. Wheatcroft, 125.
99. The interrelationships are complicated. Catalina, queen of Portugal, was Juana of Castile's youngest daughter—Charles V's sister and, thus, Juana of Spain's aunt.
100. *Calendar of State Papers, Spanish*, XII, 181-95.
101. Kamen, 56, 65, 70, 73, 87.
102. Kamen, 73, 80.
103. Kamen, 89, 134.
104. Kamen, 202-03. Philip II's fourth wife, as noted here, was Anne of Austria (1549-80)—his niece, the daughter of his sister Maria and Maximilian II. About the complicated interrelationships among the Habsburgs, Wheatcroft writes:

> The impact of . . . Spanish fixation with blood and race on the Habsburgs remains conjectural. But their marriage patterns in the century and a half of the "Madrid-Vienna axis" are unique in the history of western Europe. "Happy Austria marries"; and it is a matter of record that the Habsburgs had gained their patchwork of lands by marriage alliances and inheritance rather than by war. This focus on marriage and alliance underestimates the intense military activity undertaken, especially in Italy, to sustain and consolidate their holdings. It also, wrongly, suggests that other families did not use marriage in the same way to cement or consolidate political alliances. But what distinguished the Habsburgs' marriage strategy, especially after the death of Charles V, was its inventiveness and capacity to adapt to new circumstances. No other royal house had developed so coherent a notion of "the power of the blood."

Wheatcroft notes that Habsburg marriages, "replicating the same incestuous patterns generation after generation," have long been considered a "genetic disaster." But he notes that their "unusual and distinctive marriage patterns" reflected their ideas that "to marry 'in,' conserving the blood, was good," while "to marry 'out' could lead to disaster, both economic and political" (Wheatcroft, 165).
105. Kamen, 35, 196, 257.
106. Philip left Spain in January 1585 and returned at the end of the year; Kamen, 257.
107. Kamen, 2, 75.
108. Edward Grierson, *The Fatal Inheritance: Philip II and the Spanish Netherlands* (London, 1969), 51. Grierson devotes a whole chapter to Margaret of Parma's regency, 51-85.

109. M. J. Rodriguez-Salgado, "The Court of Philip II of Spain," in *Princes, Patronage, and the Nobility: The Court at the Beginning of the Modern Age, c. 1450-1650*, ed. Ronald G. Asch and Adolf M. Birke (Oxford, 1991), 205.

110. Kamen, 155, 207, 261.

111. Kamen, 298-99.
      Philip had earlier suggested Isabel as the Catholic heir to the throne of England in 1587 after the execution of Mary Stuart.

112. Kamen, 305-6.

113. Philip III's wife, Margaret of Austria (1584-1611), was a second cousin; her mother, Maria of Bavaria, accompanied Margaret to Spain. The empress, Maria of Austria (1528-1603), was the daughter of Charles V and Philip II's sister. Margaret of the Cross (1567-1633) was Maria of Austria's daughter. See Magdalena S. Sánchez, *The Empress, the Queen, and the Nun: Women and Power at the Court of Philip III of Spain* (Baltimore, Maryland, 1998), 4-5.

Chapter 3

1. Margaret Tudor's letter is printed by Mary Anne Everett Wood, ed., *Letters of Royal and Illustrious Ladies of Great Britain from the Commencement of the Twelfth Century to the Close of the Reign of Queen Mary* (London, 1846), vol. 1, 232-35.
   On Margaret Tudor and the women in this chapter, see Table 2.

2. Alison Weir, *The Six Wives of Henry VIII* (New York, 1991); Antonia Fraser, *The Wives of Henry VIII* (New York, 1993); David Loades, *Henry VIII and His Queens* (Stroud, Gloucestershire, 1994; rpt. 1997); Karen Lindsey, *Divorced, Beheaded, Survived: A Feminist Reinterpretation of the Wives of Henry VIII* (Reading, Massachusetts, 1995).

3. Loades, "Preface" (n.p.). Loades's book was originally and more accurately published under the title of *The Politics of Marriage: Henry VIII and His Queens*.

4. Garrett Mattingly, *Catherine of Aragon* (New York, 1941; rpt. for the Book-of-the-Month Club, 1990). In his 1982 essay "The Place of Women in Tudor Government," Mortimer Levine alludes to Mattingly's biography of Catherine, concluding that "there is no need to go on with a story that has been well told by a master" (in *Tudor Rule and Revolution: Essays for G. R. Elton from his American Friends*, ed. Delloyd J. Guth and John W. McKenna [Cambridge, 1982], 116); Mattingly's work remains the primary source for virtually all the later accounts of Catherine's life (see those named in n. 2, above, and n. 5, below, for example).

5. Quoted by Mary Luke, *Catherine, the Queen* (New York, 1967), 57.

6. Mattingly, 115. Margaret Beaufort had not opposed Catherine's marriage to Prince Arthur; she participated fully in court ceremonies welcoming the Spanish princess, was said to have wept at the marriage ceremony, and gave a banquet in honor of the future queen.

7. Quoted by Weir, 49. Margaret Beaufort ultimately participated in Henry VIII's marriage to Catherine; see Chapter 1, 32.

8. Catherine's letters from this period, quoted here, are printed by Wood, vol. 1, 120-43 (capitalization and punctuation modernized). Her correspondence also appears in the *Letters and Papers, Foreign and Domestic, of the Reign of Henry*

VIII, 1509-1547, ed. J.S. Brewer et al. (London, 1862-1932), hereafter referred to as *Letters and Papers*, and in the *Calender of Letters, Documents and State Papers Relating to the Negotiations between England and Spain Preserved in the Archives at Simancas and Elsewhere*, ed. G. A. Bergenroth et al. (London, 1862-1965), hereafter referred to as *Calendar of State Papers, Spanish*.

9. It was at this point that Henry VII met Juana of Castile, whom he seems later to have considered making his second wife despite claims of her "madness"; see Chapter 2.

10. Catherine became the Spanish ambassador at the English court in 1507. For examples of her diplomatic reports to Ferdinand, see the two letters printed by Wood, vol. 1, 143-54, quoted here (capitalization and punctuation modernized).

11. The new king's doubts were reported to Ferdinand by Guitier Gomez de Fuensalida, who served as Spanish ambassador in 1508-9; Mattingly, 118.

12. Wood, vol. 1, 159 (capitalization and punctuation modernized).

13. Mattingly, 129-35.

14. Loades, 18.

    Catherine's letters to her father, written while she was his ambassador, are printed by F. A. Mumby, *The Youth of Henry VIII* (London, 1913); Luke cites many of Mumby's texts, 84-116.

15. Wood, vol. 1, 157-61 (capitalization and punctuation modernized).

16. Quoted by Luke, 129.

17. Loades, 23.

18. Catherine's letter to Thomas Wolsey is quoted by Fraser, 66.

19. Mattingly, 162.

20. Quoted by Mattingly, 164.

21. Loades, 24.

22. See Betty Behrens, "A Note on Henry VIII's Divorce Project of 1514," *Bulletin of the Institute of Historical Research*, 11 (1934), 163. The theory that the king was seeking to divorce Catherine is accepted by some historians (see Loades, 23, as only one example) and disputed by others (while acknowledging it, Mattingly calls it "gossip," 169). For a brief review of the positions, see see J. J. Scarisbrick, *Henry VIII* (Berkeley, 1968), 55 and 151.

23. In 1523 the Spanish humanist Juan Luis Vives was commissioned to devise a program of instruction for the princess. See Juan Luis Vives, *The Education of a Christian Woman: A Sixteenth-Century Manual*, ed. and trans. Charles Fantazzi (Chicago, 2000).

24. Loades, 34-35.

25. The comment comes from a letter by Giovanni Batista Sangi to the Bishop of Capua, quoted by Loades, 35.

26. Mattingly, 229-30.

27. Mattingly, 229-30; Loades, 36.

28. For the chronology and political analysis of the divorce, see Scarisbrick, 147-228. Of particular note is his chapter on the canon law of the divorce, 163-97. Mattingly devotes "Part III" of his biography of Catherine, fully one half of the book, to the divorce (233-435), while Mary Luke's biography of Catherine of Aragon is completely swamped by the relationship between Henry and Anne ("His days were long and at night he dreamed of Anne in his

arms. And always in the background was the nagging possibility he might lose her to someone else," 312); see pp. 261-432.

29. Loades, 48.

30. Enrique IV of Castile was Isabella of Castile's half-brother. His first wife, Blanche of Navarre (1424-64), was returned to Navarre in disgrace; on her ultimate fate, see Chapter 1, n. 2. Enrique's second queen eventually gave him a daughter, the unfortunate Juana *la Beltraneja*.

31. Louis XI had married his daughter Jeanne of France to Louis of Orléans; in 1498, when Louis succeeded to the throne as Louis XII, he divorced Jeanne and married Anne of Brittany, the widow of Charles VIII. See Chapter 1.

   On René of Lorraine (1451-1508) and his divorce, see Rosalind K. Marshall, *Mary of Guise* (London, 1977), 15.

32. The phrase describing the marriage of Suffolk and Mary Tudor is from Rosemary O'Day, *The Longman Companion to the Tudor Age* (London, 1995), 175. About Suffolk's marital situation, Mattingly writes that he "succeeded" with "the ladies"; he "had married—more or less—three of them, and his domestic entanglements in 1514 were of a fascinating complexity" (172). See Perry, 110-14.

   Margaret Tudor's divorce is discussed later in this chapter.

33. Much of Catherine's correspondence between 1527 and 1534, when Henry married Anne Boleyn, is abstracted in the *Calendar of State Papers, Spanish*, vols. 4 and 5, quoted by Mattingly, 347-87. Further details of affairs in England are relayed in the diplomatic reports of Eustace Chapuys, imperial ambassador; see *Letters and Papers*, vols. 4.3-7. Curiously, while Wood prints widely the correspondence between Catherine of Aragon and her father, she prints none of Catherine's letters relative to the struggle over the divorce.

34. Quoted by Loades, 61.

35. Quoted by Mattingly, 405.

36. Quoted by Mattingly, 429-30.

   In an interesting parallel to her mother, Catherine of Aragon is noted for her needlework; throughout the struggle over the divorce, she continued to sew Henry's shirts herself, just as her mother Isabella had done for Ferdinand (see Chapter 1).

37. Eric Ives, *Anne Boleyn* (Oxford, 1986); and Retha Warnicke, *The Rise and Fall of Anne Boleyn: Family Politics at the Court of Henry VIII* (Cambridge, 1989). Ives focuses much of his study on "Anne the Queen": on her political, cultural, and religious activities (pp. 256-331).

   Early biographies of Anne Boleyn range from the defense written by George Wyatt (1554-1624), *The Life of Queen Anne Boleigne*, to the definitive but somewhat dated *Anne Boleyn: A Chapter of English History, 1527-1536* (2 vols.), published by Paul Friedmann (London, 1884). More recent and somewhat more romanticized biographies include those written by Marie Louise Bruce, *Anne Boleyn* (London, 1972); Hester Chapman, *Anne Boleyn* (London, 1974); and Carolly Erickson, *Mistress Anne* (New York, 1984).

38. Ives, 23-35. On Margaret of Austria, see Chapter 2.

39. Ives, 36.

40. For Louise of Savoy, see Chapters 2 and 5.

41. Loades, 70, 89.

42. Quoted by Loades, 150.
43. See, for example, Susan E. James, *Kateryn Parr: The Making of a Queen* (London, 1999), who argues that Catherine Parr's advice led to Mary Tudor's restoration in the line of succession and that Parr's regency was important for Elizabeth I's understanding of "power politics."

   Also useful is Minna F. Weinstein, "Queen's Power: The Case of Katherine Parr," *History Today*, 26 (1976), 788-95. Weinstein discusses Catherine's mother, Lady Maud Parr, who was one of Catherine of Aragon's ladies-in-waiting (789); her daughter was educated at the royal school she herself would later reform during her regency (789, 791-94).

   In his recent *Elizabeth: The Struggle for the Throne* (New York, 2001), David Starkey devotes a chapter (35-41) to Catherine Parr, including useful analysis of her regency.
44. Henry VIII's sisters have received far less attention than his wives, but two dual biographies have been written, most recently Maria Perry's, *Sisters to the King: The Tumultuous Lives of Henry VIII's Sisters—Margaret of Scotland and Mary of France* (London, 1998), which is a chronological account of the lives of Margaret and Mary Tudor. An earlier dual biography by Hester Chapman, published in England as *The Sisters of Henry VIII* (London, 1969) and in the United States as *The Thistle and the Rose* (New York, 1969), focuses first on Margaret, then on Mary. For Margaret Tudor alone, see Patricia Hill Buchanan, *Margaret Tudor, Queen of Scots* (Edinburgh, 1985). I have relied on all three accounts of Margaret Tudor's life.
45. Chapman, 26 and 21.

   On Margaret Tudor's education, see Buchanan, 10-11.
46. For Margaret of York, duchess of Burgundy, see Chapter 2.
47. Chapman, 25.
48. Quoted by Perry, 10.
49. Quoted by Chapman, 25.
50. See Chapter 1.
51. Perry, 22-24. For an analysis of the "link between marriage and sovereignty" that focuses on Margaret Tudor's marriage, see Louise Olga Fradenburg, "Sovereign Love: The Wedding of Margaret Tudor and James IV of Scotland," in *Women and Sovereignty*, ed. Louise Olga Fradenburg, vol. 7 of *Cosmos: The Yearbook of the Traditional Cosmology Society* (Edinburgh, 1992), 78-100.
52. Perry, 45.
53. Quoted by Chapman, 59.
54. Perry, 62-63.
55. Margaret's letter is quoted in part by Buchanan, 67, by Perry, 63-64, and by Chapman, 64.

   Buchanan notes that Margaret's spelling was "wildly erratic" and that her handwriting was "atrocious, baffling not only later scholars but even her own contemporaries." Her syntax is also extremely difficult, her run-on sentences and mixed constructions a writing instructor's nightmare. In quoting from her letters, I have tried to make grammatical sense using ellipses and brackets.
56. Quoted by Chapman, 66.

   On Anne of Brittany, twice queen of France, see Chapters 1 and 3.
57. Quoted by Chapman, 66.

58. Quoted by Buchanan, 70.
59. Quoted by Buchanan, 83.
60. Perry, 71-72.
61. Quoted by Chapman, 76.
62. Perry, 72-73.
63. Quoted by Chapman, 80.
64. Buchanan, 86-87, Chapman, 81, and Perry, 75.
65. Quoted by Perry, 76.
66. Quoted by Perry, 79.
67. For Margaret of Anjou, wife of Henry VI, see Chapter 1.
68. Chapman, 81. On Margaret Tudor's marriage, see Fradenburg, 80-81.
69. Chapman, 88.
70. Margaret's letter describing the events from September through November, quoted here and in the paragraphs that follow, is printed by Wood, vol. 1, 166-69 (capitalization and punctuation modernized).
71. Margaret's letter, quoted here and in the paragraphs that follow, is printed by Wood, vol. 1, 208-10 (capitalization and punctuation modernized).
72. Henry is quoted by Perry, 120.
73. The eyewitness account is quoted by Buchanan, 99. For Perry's assessment, see p. 122.
74. Quoted by Perry, 123.
75. Wood, vol. 1, 211-13 (capitalization and punctuation modernized).
76. Wood, vol. 1, 215-16 (capitalization and punctuation modernized).
77. Printed by Wood, vol. 1, 215-216 (capitalization and punctuation modernized).
78. Printed by Wood, vol. 1, 217-18, and quoted in the following paragraphs (capitalization and punctuation modernized).
79. Chapman indicates that Margaret was told about her son's death on 28 December (103), while Perry says she learned of it "in January or February" (130).
80. The Venetian ambassador in England reported home frequently on Margaret's situation, for example; his letters are cited by Perry, 132.
81. Wood, vol. 1, 227 (capitalization and punctuation modernized).
82. Wood, vol. 1, 232-35 (capitalization and punctuation modernized). This is the letter quoted at the outset of this chapter.
83. Quoted by Perry, 158.
84. Wood, vol. 1, 298-305 (capitalization and punctuation modernized).
85. Margaret's letter is printed by Wood, vol. 1, 245-52 (capitalization and punctuation modernized). A letter of 1523 outlining her relationship with the Scots lords is also printed by Wood, vol. 1, 298-305.
86. Quoted by Perry, 164.
87. Margaret's letter quoted here and in the paragraphs that follow is printed by Wood, vol. 1, 322-28 (capitalization and punctuation modernized).
88. Chapman, 130-31; Perry, 165-66.
89. Quoted by Chapman, 142-43.
90. Chapman, 149.
    Margaret Erskine, later Margaret Douglas of Lochleven, had been James V's mistress before her marriage, and their son was born in 1533. Margaret Erskine did not become Lady Margaret Douglas until 1536.

91. Diplomatic reports describing Margaret are printed by Wood, vol. 2, 276.

92. Marie of Guise was the daughter of the duke of Guise and Antoinette of Bourbon. She had been married before, to the duke of Longueville, to whom she had given one son (a second boy had been born after his father's death, but this second child had died). Marie had been widowed just a month before James's wife Madeleine died. On Marie of Guise, see Chapter 1 and later in this chapter.

93. Antonia Fraser, *Mary Queen of Scots* (New York, 1969), 5.

94. Joan Beaufort (fl. 1410-1450) is mentioned by Chapman, 77.

95. Mary of Guelders (1433-1463) was the daughter of Arnold, duke of Guelders. In addition to three sons, James III, Alexander, and John, she had two daughters, Mary and Margaret. Her daughter Mary was married to James Hamilton; for descendants of Mary Stewart and James Hamilton, see n. 102. Mary of Guelders was also the aunt of Philippa of Guelders; see p. 121.

96. Fraser, 60.

    Marie of Guise's daughter Mary Stuart, the new queen of Scotland, had meanwhile been sent to France in 1548, where she was initially placed in the care of her grandmother, Antoinette of Bourbon (d. 1583); the daughter of Francis, count of Vendôme and Marie of Luxembourg, she had married Claude, duke of Guise, and had given birth to twelve children, Marie among them. The mother of a "remarkable brood," Antoinette of Bourbon, duchess of Guise was, as Fraser describes her, "in herself, a remarkable woman":

    > She exhibited considerable administrative talent, which she handed on to her daughter Mary of Guise—not only at domestic economy, a subject at which she was considered to excel, but in the running of the vast and increasing Guise dominions. (37-38)

    Antoinette of Bourbon was in frequent correspondence with her daughter about her granddaughter; she acted as Marie of Guise's representative in the marriage negotiations in France, for example (Marshall, *Mary of Guise*, 215-16). For letters to the regent of Scotland from her mother about Mary Stuart, see Marguerite Wood, ed., *Foreign Correspondence with Marie de Lorraine [Guise], queen of Scotland, from the Originals in the Balcarres Papers, 1537-1548* (Edinburgh, 1923).

97. The duke of Guise's advice to his sister is quoted by Fraser, 99. Fraser's assessment of Marie of Guise's accomplishments are from the same source. Marie of Guise's own evaluation of the task she faced is quoted by Marshall, 210.

    On Marie of Guise's regency, see also E. Marianne H. M'Kerlie, *Mary of Guise-Lorraine, Queen of Scotland* (Edinburgh, 1931), esp. 165-256.

98. For the view of her family and for the quotation about Marie of Guise's "queenly" mind and "heart of a man of war," see Fraser, 99.

    For Knox's view of Marie of Guise, see Fraser, 99, as only one example. John Lesley and Raphael Holinshed are quoted by Marshall, 263-64.

99. The literature on Lady Jane Grey, whom Levin describes as "the darling of Victorians," is large, but Levin's article is an important note to more recent biographers who, as she indicates, "have continued to accept the conventional notion of Lady Jane Grey as a weak, powerless victim of political intrigue"; see her "Lady Jane Grey: Protestant Queen and Martyr," in *Silent But for the*

Word: Tudor Women as Patrons, Translators, and Writers of Religious Works, ed. Margaret P. Hannay (Kent, Ohio, 1985), 92-106, 272-74. See Levin's notes for biographical works on Grey and for texts and criticism of Grey's writings.

100. Henry VIII's younger sister Mary Tudor (1495-1533) was married first to Louis XII of France, as we have seen, then to Charles Brandon, duke of Suffolk. Her son Henry, earl of Lincoln died in 1534. Her older daughter Frances Brandon (1517-1559) married Henry Grey, second marquis of Dorset. Frances's daughters were Jane (1537-1554), wife of Guildford Dudley and the "nine days" queen, executed in 1554; Catherine (1540-1568), wife of Edward Seymour, earl of Hertford; and Mary (1545-1578), wife of Thomas Keys. Frances Brandon's younger daughter Eleanor married Henry Clifford, earl of Cumberland; she gave birth to a daughter, Lady Margaret Clifford. On this see Mortimer Levine, *Tudor Dynastic Problems, 1460-1571* (London, 1973), and his *The Early Elizabeth Succession Question, 1558-1568* (Stanford, California, 1966).

　　All three succession acts passed in Henry VIII's reign (1534, 1536, and 1543) are printed by J. R. Tanner, *Tudor Constitutional Documents, A.D. 1485-1603, with an Historical Commentary* (Cambridge, 1951), 382-88, 389-95, and 397-400.

101. We have already discussed the descendants of Henry VIII's older sister Margaret, but we will review them here. Margaret Tudor (1489-1541) had one surviving child by her first husband James IV of Scotland, James V (1512-1542); Margaret Douglas (1515-1578) was her child by her second husband, Archibald Douglas, earl of Angus. This daughter spent much of her life at Henry VIII's court and eventually married Matthew Stewart, earl of Lennox. On this, see Table 2.

102. King James II of Scotland had two children, a son and a daughter. Mary Stuart (1542-1587) claimed her title as queen through this royal Stewart line, directly from James II, through his son James III, through his son James IV, through her father, James V.

　　The Hamilton and Lennox Stewart claims came not from this royal Stewart line but from James II's daughter, Mary. Mary, sister of James III, had married James, lord Hamilton. Her son, James Hamilton, was the first earl of Arran, from whom James Hamilton, second earl of Arran inherited both his title and his claim to the throne. The second earl of Arran had, as we have seen, been made regent of Scotland for Mary immediately following James V's death, but he had been discredited and replaced by Marie of Guise, the queen's mother, in 1554. The Lennox Stewart claims also originated with Mary, sister of James III: In addition to her son by Hamilton, Mary had a daughter as well, Elizabeth Hamilton. Elizabeth Hamilton married Matthew Stewart, second earl of Lennox. Her grandson Matthew Stewart, the fourth earl of Lennox, married Margaret Douglas, daughter of Margaret Tudor and her second husband, Archibald, earl of Angus. Their son was Henry Stuart, lord Darnley, born in 1546.

　　On Arbella, see Sara Jayne Steen, ed., *The Letters of Lady Arbella Stuart* (Oxford, 1994), 14. Arbella's biography has been written numerous times; early efforts, cited by Steen, include an account in Louisa Stuart Costello's *Memoirs of Eminent Englishwomen* (London, 1844); Elizabeth Cooper's *The Life and*

Letters of Lady Arabella Stuart, Including Numerous Original and Unpublished Documents, 2 vols. (London, 1866); E[mily] T[ennyson] Bradley's *Life of the Lady Arabella Stuart*, 2 vols. (London, 1889); and B[lanche] C[hristabel] Hardy's *Arbella Stuart: A Biography* (London, 1913). Among more recent biographies noted by Steen are P[hyllis] M[argaret] Handover's *Arbella Stuart: Royal Lady of Hardwick and Cousin to King James* (London, 1957); and David N. Duran's *Arbella Stuart: A Rival to the Queen* (London, 1978).

As Steen notes, even these later writers have reflected "assumptions about women" that "are no longer those of a growing community of scholars"; I have thus relied here on Steen's extended account of Arbella Stuart's life ("Introduction," 1-105) as well as on her edition of Stuart's letters. In her introduction, Steen indicates that "Stuart's letters are presented with her original spelling, punctuation, capitalization, and word division" (108); in order to make Arbella's letters as accessible as possible for a contemporary reader, I have modernized quotations from these letters, as noted.

103. For all this, see Steen, 17-18. Arbella Stuart was eleven when Mary Stuart was executed in 1587.
104. Steen, 19.
105. Steen, 19.
106. Steen, 19-22.
107. The Venetian ambassador reported that, in assuming precedence as a princess, Arbella had said it was "the very lowest place that could possibly be given her"; quoted by Steen, 21. Arbella herself alludes to the rumors about Essex in her letter of 9 March 1602/3, quoted here (from p. 162, text modernized) and printed in full by Steen, 158-75.
108. Steen, 27.
109. Arbella's letter of January 1602/3 is quoted by Steen, 124-26 (text modernized).
110. Arbella's message to the earl of Hertford, which outlined the plan she had devised, is printed by Steen, 120-22.
111. Arbella's letter is printed by Steen, 122 (text modernized).
112. Steen, 33.
113. Arbella's letter to Queen Elizabeth is printed by Steen, 124-26 (text modernized).
114. Arbella's letter to Henry Brounker, 9 March 1602/3, is printed by Steen, 158-75 (text modernized).
115. Arbella's letter to William Seymour is printed by Steen, 241-42 (text modernized).
116. Arbella's letter to King James, from December 1610, is printed by Steen, 252-55 (text modernized).
117. Steen, 67.
118. The description is Steen's, 68.
119. Steen, 101. According to Steen, William Seymour later married Frances Devereux, the daughter of the earl of Essex; he named his first-born daughter Arbella (101).
120. Quoted by Steen, 82 and 85.
121. Steen, 83.
122. Steen, 97.

123. Steen, 105.
124. Margaret Tudor chose her second and third hubands for herself; we can see the same pattern in the life of Lady Margaret Douglas, her daughter. Henry VIII had at first planned to use his niece's marriage to his advantage, suggesting her as a bride for the duke of Angoulême, but in 1536 the young woman engaged herself secretly to Thomas Howard, perhaps even marrying him. When their relationship was discovered, the two were both imprisoned in the Tower. Howard was declared guilty of treason for "treating for marriage with one of royal blood without the King's consent." In the successions act of 1536, Margaret Tudor's descendants were precluded from inheriting the throne; Margaret Douglas herself was branded "illegitimate." She was eventually released from the Tower and restored to royal favor, but Howard died of an illness in 1537, still imprisoned. After a second such incident landed Lady Margaret in the Tower once again, Henry married her off to Matthew Stewart, earl of Lennox, an English sympathizer. Still, Margaret Douglas continued the tendency to make politically imprudent marital arrangements. She incurred Queen Elizabeth's displeasure twice, imprisoned when her oldest son Darnley was married Mary Stuart and again when her youngest married Elizabeth Cavendish.

    On the other side of the family, Mary Tudor's marriage to Charles Brandon was a secret one. Her granddaughter Catherine Grey, Jane Grey's younger sister, followed a similar path. Her first marriage, to the son of Lord Pembroke, was dissolved. In late 1560 she secretly married Edward Seymour, earl of Hertford. Obviously pregnant, Catherine was forced to admit to the marriage in 1561, and both she and her husband were sent to the Tower. There she gave birth to a son, Edward Seymour; Queen Elizabeth had Catherine's marriage declared invalid in May 1562, but a second son, Thomas, was born to the pair in February 1563. Both of their sons were officially determined to be illegitimate. The oldest of Edward Seymour's sons, another Edward, was the young man to whom Arbella sent her proposal of marriage in 1602; the younger, William, was the man whom she secretly married in 1610.

    (Of course the most inept of Margaret Beaufort's descendants, at least in the marriage market, was Henry VIII.)
125. *Statutes of the Realm*, 122-24.
126. Quoted by Constance Jordan, "Woman's Rule in Sixteenth-Century British Political Thought," *Renaissance Quarterly*, 40 (1987), 426-29. For a thorough analysis of Mary Tudor's reign, see David Loades, *The Reign of Mary Tudor: Politics, Government, and Religion in England, 1553-1558* (London, 1979).
127. Carolly Erickson, *Bloody Mary: The Life of Mary Tudor* (New York, 1978), 303-4.

    For an analysis of the political relationship between Mary and Philip, see especially David Loades, *Mary Tudor: A Life* (Oxford, 1989), 223-73.

    As an additional note on Tudor marriage patterns, Henry VIII's fourth queen was Anne of Cleves, the only other foreign bride among the women he married; after her divorce from Henry, she decided not to return to Cleves, where another dynastic marriage would almost surely have been arranged for her. Instead, she remained in England and unmarried for the rest of her life. See Mary Saaler, *Anne of Cleves, Fourth Wife of Henry VIII* (London, 1995),

94-100. In her excellent *The Marrying of Anne of Cleves: Royal Protocol in Early Modern Europe* (Cambridge, 2000), Retha M. Warnicke analyzes political and dynastic strategies of royal marriages.

128. As selected examples of an extensive literature, see Frances A. Yates, *Astraea: The Imperial Theme in the Sixteenth Century* (London, 1975), particularly her section on "the triumph of chastity"; Carole Levin, "Power, Politics, and Sexuality: Images of Elizabeth I," in *The Politics of Gender in Early Modern Europe*, ed. Jean R. Brink et al. (Kirksville, Missouri, 1989); and Helen Hackett, *Virgin Mother, Maiden Queen: Elizabeth I and the Cult of the Virgin Mary* (New York, 1995), which contains a thorough and recent bibliography.

129. Janet L. Nelson, "Women at the Court of Charlemagne: A Case of Monstrous Regiment?" in *Medieval Queenship*, ed. John Carmi Parsons (New York, 1993), 59.

130. Parsons, "Family, Sex, and Power: The Rhythms of Medieval Queenship" in *Medieval Queenship*, 7.

131. See Roger Collins, "Queens-Dowager and Queens-Regent in Tenth-Century León and Navarre" in *Medieval Queenship*, 80, 85.

132. Pauline Stafford, "The Portrayal of Royal Women in England, Mid-Tenth to Mid-Twelfth Centuries," in *Medieval Queenship*, 155.

133. Quoted by Jo Ann Kay McNamara, *Sisters in Arms: Catholic Nuns through Two Millenia* (Cambridge, Massachusetts, 1996), 197-98.

134. Margaret L. King, *Women of the Renaissance* (Chicago, 1991), 159. King includes an interesting analysis of Elizabeth's construction of her role as a female ruler: She was a "master builder of her public image" who presented herself in a number of images, including "Astraea, Deborah, Diana"; see 158-59. (King erroneously states that Elizabeth "was the only woman to hold sovereign power during the Renaissance" [59].)

135. Much has been written about Elizabeth's Tilbury speech; for a recent analysis see Janet M. Green, " 'I My Self': Queen Elizabeth's Oration at Tilbury Camp," *The Sixteenth Century Journal*, 28 (1997), 421-45. Green appends the two versions of the speech to her essay (443-45); I have quoted from Green's text here.

On the speech itself, and the lines quoted here, see also Carole Levin, *The Heart and Stomach of a King: Elizabeth I and the Politics of Sex and Power* (Philadelphia, Pennsylvania, 1994).

136. Patricia-Ann Lee, " 'A Bodye Politique to Governe': Aylmer, Knox and the Debate on Queenship," *The Historian*, 52 (1990), 261.

One further note here. Jane Dormer might be considered a "daughter" both of Isabella of Castile and Margaret Beaufort. The daughter of Mary Sidney and Sir William Dormer, Jane Dormer was one of Mary Tudor's personal attendants and closest friends. After the queen's death, she married one of Philip II's advisors, Gómez Suárez de Figueroa, who became duke of Feria. The Spanish king was said to be "too much under the influence of the duke of Feria . . . and his English wife" (Henry Kamen, *Philip of Spain* [New Haven, 1997], 132). As duchess of Feria, Jane Dormer became, later in her life, "a candidate for the governor-generalship of the Netherlands" (Starkey, *Elizabeth*, 197).

137. Allison Heisch, "Queen Elizabeth I: Parliamentary Rhetoric and the Exercise of Power," *Signs: Journal of Women in Culture and Society*, 1 (1975), 33.

138. Quoted by Heisch, 33.

On Elizabeth's rhetoric, see also Starkey; Anne Somerset, *Elizabeth I* (New York, 1991), 58-60; and Susan Frye, *Elizabeth I: The Competition for Representation* (Oxford, 1993), 39.

Chapter 4

1. Isabella d'Este's letter to her husband Francesco Gonzaga is quoted by Julia Cartwright, *Isabella d'Este, Marchioness of Mantua, 1474-1539: A Study of the Renaissance* (1903; rpt. New York, 1926), vol. 1, 117-18 (capitalization and punctuation modernized).

   On Isabella d'Este and the women mentioned in this chapter, see Table 3.

2. On the succession of women to titles in Italy, see Charles Mistruzzi de Frisinga, "La Succession nobilaire féminine en Italie dans le drois et dans l'histoire," in Ida Auda-Gioanet, *Une Randonnée à travels l'histoire d'Orient (Les Comnènes et les Anges)* (Rome, 1953), 107-19.

3. On his way to the Holy Land, Richard I of England had conquered Cyprus in 1191 and had given it to Guy of Lusignan, the dispossessed "king" of Jerusalem. It remained under Lusignan control from that time. Carlotta of Lusignan (c. 1440s-1487) was Giovanni III's only legitimate child; her half-brother Giacomo was Giovanni's illegitimate child. Carlotta had married John of Portugal; after his death she then married Louis of Savoy.

   As a reminder of the close relationships among the women we are examining here, Carlotta's second husband, Louis of Savoy, was her cousin, the second son of Anne of Lusignan and Louis, duke of Savoy; Anne of Lusignan was the mother of both Charlotte of Savoy, wife of Louis XI of France and of Bona of Savoy, wife of Galeazzo Maria Sforza and regent of Milan (see Chapter 1).

4. For a biographical essay on Caterina Cornaro (1454-1510), see Marian Andrews (pseud. Christopher Hare), *The Most Illustrious Ladies of the Italian Renaissance* (New York, 1904), 187-203. For a full-length biography, see Marcel Brion, *Catherine Cornaro, reine de Chypre* (Paris, 1945).

5. The phrase "her throne was on a volcano" comes from an unidentified biographer quoted by Andrews, 193; on the situation in Cyprus following Giacomo's death, see pp. 192-93.

6. Quoted by Andrews, 195.

7. Quoted by Andrews, 196.

8. Andrews's phrase is from p. 196; the Venetian ambassador is quoted on the same page.

   Caterina's rival for the throne of Cyprus, Carlotta of Lusignan, had died in 1487.

9. Andrews, 200.

10. The widely quoted description of Isabella comes from her contemporary Niccolo da Correggio.

    Eleanora of Aragon (1455-1493) was the daughter of Ferdinand I of Naples and his first wife, Isabella of Taranto (also called Isabella of Clermont). In 1477 she travelled with her children to her father's court on the occasion of his second marriage, to Juana of Aragon (d. 1517), Ferdinand of Aragon's sister. After Ferdinand of Naples' death in 1494, Juana was regent of Sicily. See Luciano Chiappini, *Eleanora d'Aragon, prima Duchessa di Ferrara* (Rivigo, 1956); and Werner L. Gundersheimer, "Women, Learning and Power: Eleanora of Aragon and the Court of Ferrara" in *Beyond Their Sex: Learned Women of the European Past*, ed. Patricia Labalme (New York, 1984), 43-65.

As the daughter of the king of Naples, Eleanora's marriage to Ercole d'Este "conferred prestige" on Ferrara and "enhanced the social status" of her husband; her descent also "gave her an unusually strong hand in dealing with her spouse and her new subjects," Gundersheimer notes (46). She often acted as regent of Ferrara for her husband; when war broke out in 1477 while Eleanora was in Naples, for example, she returned home to govern Ferrara during his absence (Julia Cartwright, *Beatrice d'Este, duchess of Milan (1475-1497): A Study of the Renaissance* [1899; rpt. New York, 1920], 6). Gundersheimer assesses her role in Ferrara:

> [I]t was she who often served as the final arbiter of political and diplomatic decisions. Many of her letters seek retroactive approval from the duke for some action she had to take during his frequent expeditions on military campaigns or, more commonly, pleasure trips outside the city. For long periods it was Eleonora, not Ercole, who knew and coped with the details of day-to-day events. When Eleonora died, her reputation for competence, and Ercole's for a studied indifference to duty, were so extreme that her father is reported to have said, "Now the strongest bastion against the French is expunged." (52-53)

The literature on Eleanora's daughter Isabella d'Este is rather extensive (see *Women in Western European History: A Select Chronological, Geographical, and Topical Bibliography from Antiquity to the French Revolution*, ed. Linda Frey et al. [Westport, Connecticut, 1982]), and includes a fairly recent biography in English, Edith Patterson Meyer's *First Lady of the Renaissance: A Biography of Isabella d'Este* (Boston, 1970). Much superior, however, is Cartwright's earlier two-volume biography, cited in n. 1.

11. Quoted by Cartwright, vol. 1, 105 (capitalization and punctuation modernized).

> On the geographical and political significance of Mantua, see Meyer, 18-19:
> The marquisate was still technically under the protection of the head of the Holy Roman Empire, who had been its overlord in centuries long past . . . but . . . Mantua was practically independent. For security she relied on her small military force, her strong natural situation, diplomatic alliances, and her importance as a buffer between the rival city-states of Milan and Venice. Yet not so long before, Venice had seized some Mantuan land only a few miles northeast of the city, and no Mantuan felt really secure about the Republic, even though their marquis was its captain-general.

And in the west, "Milan was another possible danger."

In the spring of 1493, Isabella's sister Beatrice also assumed a role of some political significance, appearing as her husband's "ambassador and spokeswoman" before the Venetian senate; on this see Cartwright, *Beatrice d'Este*, 185-204.

12. Cartwright, *Isabella d'Este*, vol. 1, 116-17; the letter quoted at the outset of this chapter dates from this period.

On Charles VIII's invasion of Italy and his claim to Naples, see Chapter 1.

13. Meyer, 46.

On Isabella d'Este's education and humanist scholars at the court of Ferrara, see Cartwright, vol. 1, 9-13. She continued her studies in Mantua and throughout her life; see Cartwright, *passim*.

14. Quoted by Cartwright, vol. 1, 136 (capitalization and punctuation modernized).

15. Cartwright, vol. 1, 145-50.

16. See Chapter 1.

17. Cartwright, vol. 1, 178-79.

On Caterina Sforza and Cesare Borgia, see Chapter 1.

18. Cartwright, vol. 1, 227-28 and 243-53.

Isabella d'Este eventually gave birth to nine children: Leonora (1493), who married Francesco de Rovere, duke of Urbino; Margherita (who died shortly after her birth in 1496); Federico (1500-1540), first duke of Mantua; Livia (1501-1508); Ippolita (1503-80), who became a nun; Ercole (1505-1565), who became a cardinal; Ferrante (1507-1557), who married Isabella di Capua; another Livia, who became a nun as "Paula" (1508-1569); and another daughter named Margherita, who also died as an infant.

On Cesare Borgia's marriage to Charlotte d'Albret and the birth of their daughter, see Chapter 1.

19. Quoted by Cartwright, vol. 1, 236-37 (capitalization and punctuation modernized).

20. Pius III, elected after Alexander's death, died within a month of his election. His successor, Julius II, demanded return of the papal cities of Romagna, and Cesare was arrested. He surrendered the cities to Julius and fled to Naples, where he was imprisoned and sent to Spain. He escaped in 1506 and sought out his brother-in-law in Navarre, where he was killed in 1507.

21. Cartwright, vol. 1, 306.

22. Quoted by Cartwright, vol. 2, 41-42 (capitalization and punctuation modernized).

23. Quoted by Cartwright, vol. 2, 49 (capitalization and punctuation modernized).

24. Quoted by Cartwright, vol. 2, 56 (capitalization and punctuation modernized).

25. On the continued war in Italy and the so-called Congress of Mantua, see Cartwright, vol. 2, 69 (on Isabella d'Este's role, see pp. 65-66).

At this conference, Isabella's nephew, Maximilian Sforza, the son of Lodovico and Beatrice d'Este, was declared duke of Milan; after his father's fall, he had been raised by Bianca Maria Sforza, the wife of the Emperor Maximilian; see pp. 165-66 and below, n. 45.

26. Meyer, 225.

27. Meyer, 234.

28. Meyer, 246. Francesco was Maximilian's younger brother, who succeeded after Maximilian's death. On the meetings in Bologna, see Cartwright, vol. 2, 286-322.

29. Cartwright, vol. 2, 336 and 344.
30. The theme of incest between brother and sister will be repeated; it plays a part in negative views of Marguerite of Angoulême, for example (see Chapter 5).

    The notorious Lucrezia Borgia (1480-1519) has been the focus of many biographical studies, including the two-volume work by William Gilbert, *Lucrezia Borgia, Duchess of Ferrara* (London, 1869); see *Women in Western European History* for a bibliography of works about her.

    I have relied here on the recent *The Borgias* by Ivan Cloulas, trans. Gilda Roberts (New York, 1989). A delightful defense of Lucrezia Borgia is found in M. Beresford Ryley's *Queens of the Renaissance* (Boston, 1907), 150-201.

    Lucrezia spent much of her girlhood in the household of Adriana del Mila (fl. 1500), her father's cousin. There Lucrezia was noted for her abilities in language (in 1512 a contemporary indicated she "speaks Spanish, Greek, Italian, and French, and a little and very correctly Latin"; she also "composes poems in all these languages," Beresford, 155). There she was joined by Giulia Farnese (1475-1500s), who married Adriana's son Orso Orsini in 1489 and became Lucrezia's companion and friend. But Giulia became Pope Alexander VI's mistress; much shock and dismay about Alexander VI's domestic arrangements have been expressed by Lucrezia's biographers—and much speculation about how such irregularities contributed to Lucrezia's "moral failings."
31. Giovanni Sforza was the illegitimate son of Costanzo Sforza; he succeeded his father as lord of Pesaro; see Chapter 1. Caterina Sforza's grandfather was Francesco Sforza; Francesco Sforza's brother was Alessandro, Giovanni's grandfather.
32. Cloulas, 88.
33. Cloulas, 141.
34. Cloulas, 141.
35. A mysterious *Infans Romanus*, named Giovanni, appeared in 1501, and this child is often claimed to be Lucrezia's illegitimate child, the boy's father variously named as a young Spanish man named Pedro Caldes, as Lucrezia's father Alexander VI, or as Lucrezia's brother Cesare. Cloulas concludes that the father was Caldes (142-44), but there is little evidence, as Cloulas acknowledges, to support the conclusion that Giovanni was Lucrezia's child at all, and nothing beyond contemporary scandal and anti-Borgia propaganda to suggest that the child was born out of an incestuous relationship with her father or her brother (Cloulas, 145-46).
36. Cloulas, 164.
37. Cloulas, 180.
38. Cloulas, 195-96.
39. Quoted by Cloulas, 207.
40. Cartwright, *Isabella d'Este*, vol. 1, 115-16.
41. Bianca Maria Sforza (1472-1510) was Caterina Sforza's half-sister, the daughter of Galeazzo Maria Sforza and Bona of Savoy (c. 1488-1505); Caterina Sforza was Galeazzo Maria's illegitimate child (on all this see Chapter 1).
42. On all this, see Chapters 1 and 2.
43. Much information about Bianca Maria is contained in Cartwright's biography of Ludovico Sforza's wife, Beatrice d'Este; Bianca Maria's wedding, for

example, is described in great detail, *Beatrice d'Este*, 208-20. See also the biographical essay in Andrews, *The Most Illustrious Ladies of the Italian Renaissance*, 135-50.

44. Cartwright, *Beatrice d'Este*, 219.
45. When Bianca Maria died in 1510, Ludovico's sons "lost their best friend" (*Beatrice d'Este*, 377). They remained in Innsbruck, but in 1512 Pope Julius II and Maximilian expelled the French from Milan and reinstated the Sforzas, placing Maximilian Sforza on the ducal throne. When Francis I invaded and defeated the Italians at Marignano, Maximilian was forced to abdicate and spent the rest of his life "in honorable captivity," in France. Francesco, meanwhile, retired to the Tyrol after the victory of Francis I; in 1521 Pope Leo X and Charles V opposed the French in Italy, and Francesco Sforza, in turn, became duke of Milan. He was driven from Milan three years later, but after the battle of Pavia, having "won the love of all his subjects," he was restored. Thereafter he entered into a period of conflict with Charles V, opposing imperial influence in Italy. Francesco was deposed again, eventually reconciling with Charles V, who restored him once more in 1530. He married Charles V's niece, Christina of Denmark, in 1534 (see Chapter 2). He died in 1535, "the last of the Sforzas" (*Beatrice d'Este*, 377-78).
46. Lucrezia de' Medici (1470-c. 1540) was the oldest child of Clarice Orsini and Lorenzo de' Medici ("the Magnificent"); see Yvonne Maguire, *The Women of the Medici* (New York, 1927), 173-76. We will encounter her and her daughter Maria Salviati again, later in this chapter.

    On Lucrezia de' Medici's relationship to Caterina Sforza: Lucrezia was the great granddaughter of Cosimo de' Medici (1389-1464); Caterina Sforza's husband Giovanni de' Medici was the grandson of Cosmo's younger brother Lorenzo (1395-1440).
47. Maguire, 174.
48. The only child of Caterina Sforza and Giovanni de' Medici, Giovanni di Giovanni, "the Invincible," was born in 1498. He was sent away from Forlì to Florence by Caterina Sforza the next year, as she was about to be besieged; she rejoined her son in Florence after her release from Rome, and as a boy he "was entirely trained" by her. For a biographical chapter on Giovanni delle Bande Nere, see G. F. Young, *The Medici* (New York, 1933), 534-50.
49. James Cleugh, *The Medici: A Tale of Fifteen Generations* (New York, 1975), 239.
50. Bona Sforza (1494-1557) was the daughter of Caterina Sforza's half-brother Giangaleazzo and his wife Isabella of Aragon (1472-1524), who was herself a Sforza, the daughter of Ippolita Sforza (1442-1480s) and Alfonso of Aragon, king of Naples. There is no full-length biography of Bona Sforza in English, but biographical essays are included in Roland H. Bainton, *Women of the Reformation from Spain to Scandinavia* (Minneapolis, Minnesota, 1977), 135-55; and Peter G. Bietenholz, ed., *Contemporaries of Erasmus: A Biographical Register of the Renaissance and Reformation*, vol. 1 (Toronto, 1985), *s.v.* Both of these sources concentrate on Bona's religious rather than political contributions, however; Bainton's notes refer to a four-volume biography of Bona in Polish, Wladyslaw Pociecha's *Królowa Bona*, 4 vols. (Poznan, 1949). On Bona of Savoy, regent of Milan and Bona Sforza's grandmother, see Chapter 1.
51. On the alliance between the Holy Roman Emperor Maximilian and Ludovico

Sforza, Bona's powerful great uncle who had made himself duke of Milan in her brother's stead, see Chapter 1.

Sigismund's first wife had been Barbara of Hungary, the daughter of Stephen Zápolya; they were married in 1512, and after three years of marriage—and having given birth to at least two daughters—she died.

52. Bainton, 140.

53. Bainton, 140.

54. Bona's oldest child, Isabella (b. 1519), was married to John Zápolya, king of Hungary in 1539 (see pp. 174–76). Sophia (b. 1522) was married to Henry II of Braunschweig. Anna (b. 1523) was married to Stephen Báthory, prince of Transylvania, who was elected as king of Poland in 1575, succeeding Sigismund Augustus, Anna's brother. Catherine (b. 1526) was married to John III, king of Sweden; Catherine's son Sigismund Vasa succeeded Stephen Báthory as king of Poland in 1587 (he was recognized as king of Sweden in 1592). Bona's youngest son, Olbracht (b. 1527), died immediately after his birth.

55. Bainton, 143–44.

56. Marceli Kosman, quoted by Bainton, 145.

As an interesting note, the *Encyclopedia Brittanica* (15th ed.) entry on Sigismund I makes no reference to Bona Sforza's role in Poland other than mentioning her marriage to the king.

57. Sigismund Augustus (b. 1520) had married previously; his first wife was a bride chosen by Bona for political reasons.

58. Bainton, 151. After Barbara Radziwill's death in 1551, Sigismund married his first wife's sister, Catherine, in 1553.

59. Quoted by Bainton, 151.

60. Bainton, 150–51.

61. Renée of France (1510–1574) was the younger sister of Claude of France; after the death of their father Louis XII of France, Claude's husband succeeded to the throne as Francis I; see Chapter 5.

No full-length biography in English of Renée exists, but a biography in German and a three-volume biography in Italian appeared in the nineteenth century; see *Women in Western European History*, *s.v.* A biographical essay is included in M. Beresford Ryley, *Queens of the Renaissance*, 251–303; her life is also detailed by Andrews, *Men and Women of the Italian Reformation*, especially 120–35. Brantôme includes a brief portrait of Renée in his *Illustrious Dames of the Court of the Valois Kings*, trans. Katharine Prescott Wormeley (New York, 1912), 220–23.

62. Ryley, 259–60.

But contrast Brantôme's view: ". . . if Madame Renée was clever, intelligent, wise, and virtuous, she was also so kind and understood the subjects of her husband so well that I never knew any one in Ferrara who was not content or failed to say all the good in the world of her" (221).

63. Renée shared her Protestant interests with her sister-in-law Marguerite of Angoulême (see Chapter 5), who sent Marot and other Huguenots to Renée for protection.

64. Quoted by Ryley, 294.

65. Quoted by Ryley, 299.

66. Quoted by Andrews, 129.

    Francis of Guise married Renée of France's daughter Anne d'Este (before 1536-1607); after his death, Anne married Jacques, duke of Nemours, who also opposed reformed religion (he was the son of Philippe of Savoy, Louise of Savoy's younger brother). She died in 1607.

67. Reported by Andrews, 132.

68. Andrews, 132-33.

    Renée's second daughter, Lucrezia d'Este, was married in 1571, at the age of thirty-five, to Francesco Maria of Urbino, fifteen years her junior. After two years they separated, and she returned to Ferrara. Renée's youngest daughter, Leonora, never married.

69. Quoted by Andrews, 134-35.

70. Andrews, *Men and Women of the Italian Reformation*, 62. As the daughter of Maddalena de' Medici, Caterina Cibo was thus related to Caterina Sforza by marriage.

71. For a biographical essay of Caterina Cibo (1501-1557), see Roland H. Bainton, *Women of the Reformation in Germany and Italy* (Minneapolis, Minnesota, 1971), 187-98; the entry on Caterina Cibo in the *Contemporaries of Erasmus* (*s.v.*) lists Bainton as its source. A biographical essay is also contained in Andrews, *Men and Women of the Italian Reformation*, 59-72.

72. In 1528 Caterina undertook to protect the Capuchins and, evidently about the same time, became interested in reformed religion; see Bainton.

73. A contemporary account, quoted without attribution by Andrews, 63.

74. Quoted by Andrews, 64.

75. None of the sources I have used has provided specific information about the date that Caterina Cibo left Camerino. Andrews, who focuses more on the narrative of her life, says only that Caterina's daughter was married in 1534 and that "soon after this" her mother "resigned the government of the city" (64). Bainton devotes relatively little attention to Caterina's life, focusing primarily on her relationship with the Capuchins and on her relationship with Bernardino Ochino, general of the Capuchins after 1534. Bainton mentions that, defecting to Geneva in 1542, Ochino spent time with Caterina in Florence; thus we may assume that she left Camerino for Florence before that time. The entry in the *Contemporaries of Erasmus* (vol. 1, 304) is quite confused on the date. According to the entry, "After Paul III deposed her in 1545 she spent the last twenty-two years of her life in Florence"—but she died in 1557, so it may be that "1545" is a typographical error for "1535."

    The Capuchin Bernardino Ochino "made her a principal speaker" in his *Seven Dialogues* (*Contemporaries of Erasmus*). About these dialogues Roland Bainton notes that "they have the air of authentic conversations" (192); he quotes at length from the first and the seventh (192-95) as well as from two letters written to her by Marco Antonio Flaminio, who seems to have become something of a "spiritual adviser" (195-97). Andrews quotes briefly from the first, second, fourth, and seventh dialogues (67-72) and briefly summarizes the remaining three.

    About the last fifteen years of Caterina Cibo's life virtually nothing is known, other than that her residence in Florence seems to have been a literary and religious center. She was falsely rumored to have married Cardinal Ippolito d'Este, who resigned his cardinalate (*Contemporaries of Erasmus*). Ten years after her death she was arraigned for heresy by the Inquisition.

76. Caterina Sforza's third husband was, as we have seen, Giovanni de' Medici, descended from the younger brother of Cosimo de' Medici, while Caterina de' Medici's father descended from Cosimo himself.

   On Madeleine de la Tour d'Auvergne, see Chapter 5, n. 99. As yet one more indication of how the lives of women are intertwined, Madeleine's sister Anne was married to John Stuart, duke of Albany—who was to play such a big part in the life of Margaret Tudor; see Chapter 3.

   For biographies of Catherine de' Medici (1519-1589), see Chapter 5, n. 97.

77. Mark Strage, *Women of Power: The Life and Times of Catherine de' Medici* (New York, 1976), 9.

78. In the most recent biography of Catherine de' Medici, R. J. Knecht traces the early years of her life (8-10), but focuses primarily on larger historical events and male members of the Medici family, including her great-uncles, Pope Leo X and Pope Clement VII.

79. James Cleugh, *The Medici: A Tale of Fifteen Generations* (New York, 1975), 238. Alfonsina Orsini (1472-1519) was the daughter of Roberto Orsini.

80. Theodore K. Rabb, *Renaissance Lives: Portraits of an Age* (New York, 1993), 128.

81. Clarice de' Medici (1493-1528) was Alfonsina Orsini's daughter and the sister of Lorenzo di Piero. In 1508 she had married Filippo Strozzi. A brief biographical essay is found in G. F. Young, *The Medici* (New York, 1933), 334-40.

82. Clarice is quoted by Rabb, 127. The contemporary assessment of her is quoted by Young, 338.

83. Knecht, 11.

84. Quoted by Young, 391.

85. Isabella Jagellion (or Jagiellon) was the oldest of Bona Sforza's children, born in 1519.

   I am aware of no biographies of Isabella Jagellion in English; I have relied here on Roland Bainton's essay in *Women of the Reformation from Spain to Scandinavia*, 217-29, and on David P. Daniel, "Piety, Politics, and Perversion: Noblewomen in Reformation Hungary" in *Women in Reformation and Counter-Reformation Europe: Public and Private Worlds*, ed. Sherrin Marshall (Bloomington, Indiana, 1989), 68-88.

   The description of Isabella is from Daniel, 76.

86. As part of Habsburg expansion into Hungary, Emperor Ferdinand I had married Anne of Bohemia, the sister of Louis Jagellion, king of Hungary, in 1520; Louis had, in turn, married Mary of Austria. Louis died without an heir in 1526, and Mary worked to secure her brother's election as king of Hungary in his wife's right. (On this, see Chapter 2.) One faction of the Hungarian nobility elected John Zápolya king in 1526, while another elected Ferdinand king in 1527. They fought for the next ten years, until the agreement worked out in the 1538 treaty of Varda.

87. Quoted by Bainton, 219-20.

88. Daniel, 77.

89. Bainton, 221-23.
90. Daniel, 78.
91. Daniel, 78-79.
92. Quoted by Bainton, 226.
93. Daniel, 80.

Daniel notes one further woman who exercised considerable power in Hungary, Elizabeth Báthory (1560-1613), the "Blood Countess." Her family had holdings throughout Hungary and Transylvania. In 1575 she was married to Francis Nádasdy; for his service to the Habsburgs he was named Palatine of Hungary. The two had three children who survived childhood, for whom "illustrious marriages were arranged." Thus "by birth and through her own marriage as well as those of her children, Elizabeth was related to many of the major families in Hungary" (81). While Francis was absent, Elizabeth governed for him "with military efficiency and discipline" (81). After her husband's death in July 1604 the countess took complete control of his estates and commenced a series of tortures and murders. She was judged by her contemporaries "a wild beast in a woman's guise." Despite rumors of her atrocities, Elizabeth's powerful connections protected her for a time, but in 1610 she was indicted as a mass murderer. If she were tried and convicted, her family's property would be confiscated; thus a secret deal was arranged. Rather than undergoing a trial, she was imprisoned until her death in 1614. "The inheritance of her family, which she had threatened by her actions, had been secured by her kinsmen," Daniel writes, "even if at the expense of an equitable and full execution of the law":

> But, after all, Elizabeth was a noblewoman, and, no matter how famous or infamous, pious or perverse, noblewomen performed one fundamental, one essential function in sixteenth-century society: they were the vessels, the agents by which dynastic capital was transmitted from generation to generation. (83)

Aside from Daniel's account of her life (80-83), no biography of Elizabeth Báthory in English exists. The most accessible version of her life is the fictional *The Blood Countess* by Andrei Codrescu (New York, 1995).

94. As a descendant of the house of Valois, Margaret of France (1523-1574) was also a "daughter" of Anne of France (see Chapter 1).

For the details of Margaret's life I have relied on Winifred Stephens, *Margaret of France, Duchess of Savoy, 1523-1574* (New York, 1902). A brief portrait is found in Brantôme's *Illustrious Dames of the Court of the Valois Kings*, 224-29.
95. Quoted by Stephens, 145.

On the close relationship between Catherine de' Medici and her sister-in-law, see Knecht, 20-21.
96. Charles III of Savoy was married to Beatrice of Portugal, sister of Isabel of Portugal; she was "so masterful" that "she was said to possess nothing of a woman save the sex" (Stephens, 158).
97. On all this see Stephens, 174-89, and Knecht, 54-58.
98. Stephens, 233.
99. Quoted by Stephens, 233.
100. Margaret's "idolisation" of her son and her "coddling" of him are described by Stephens, 240-41.

Again we see something of the dilemma of royal and noble women. If, like Margaret Beaufort (Chapter 1) or Louise of Savoy (Chapter 5), they are devoted to their children, their relationship is somehow suspect. If, on the other hand, they do not devote themselves to their children, like Caterina Sforza, refusing to surrender to the conspirators who hold her children hostage (Chapter 1), or like Marguerite of Angoulême and Jeanne of Navarre (Chapter 5), they are monstrous.

101. Stephens, 248.
102. Stephens, 135-36; Stephens devotes an entire chapter to the nine years (1550-1559) of Margaret's rule of Berry (135-44), which she never visited again after her marriage.
103. Stephens, 255; the contemporary is quoted by Stephens, 255.
104. Stephens, 242.
105. Stephens, 292-93.
106. Margaret's last letter is printed in full by Stephens, 302-3.

Chapter 5

1. Louise of Savoy's words come from her journal, printed by Samuel Guichenon, "Journal de Louise de Savoye, duchesse d'Angoulesme, d'Anjou et de Valois, mere du grand Roy François premier . . . ," in *Histoire genealogique de la royal maison de Sauoye* (Lyons, 1660), vol. 2, 457-64, my translation.

   The earliest entry in the journal is dated 1459, the last 1522, about which time Louise apparently compiled the entire document. The journal is organized by month rather than by year; for example, Louise notes all the significant events of January before moving on to February. The monthly listings are not always chronological, either by year or by date within the month. Louise begins her January entries, for example, with a note about an incident that occurred on 25 January when her son Francis of Angoulême was seven, then she moves on to record the entry I have quoted here, then indicates that Anne of Brittany was born on 26 January "1576" [*sic*] and that on 11 January (no year specified) Anne gave birth to a son who died (this boy "was not able to prevent the elevation of my Caesar," Louise writes, because he failed to live; see n. 16).

   On the journal, see Henri Hauser, "Le 'Journal' de Louise de Savoie," *Revue historique*, 86 (1904), 280-303. No modern edition of the journal has been made, and while some of entries have been translated, appearing in books and articles on Louise, no complete English translation is available. Three nineteenth-century French versions exist, but they have proven to be more inaccessible than the original seventeenth-century text by Guichenon; for those nineteenth-century editions, see John F. Freeman, "Louise of Savoy: A Case of Maternal Opportunism," *Sixteenth Century Journal*, 3 (1972), 78 n. 5.
2. On the Salic law prohibiting women from inheriting the throne of France, see Chapter 1, n. 170.
3. On this see Table 4.

   There is one full-length biography of Louise of Savoy in English, Dorothy M. Mayer's *The Great Regent, Louise of Savoy, 1476-1531* (New York, 1966), which I have relied on here, despite the fact that it is somewhat romanticized.

It is also undocumented, as is Paule Henry-Bordeaux's *Louise de Savoie, régente et roi de France* (Paris, 1954). These and earlier biographies are analyzed by Freeman, 77-98, who concludes that the "opinion of V. L. Bourrilly (1903) still stands, that the biography of Louise of Savoy is yet to be written" (81).

While very helpful, Freeman's own essay is by now also dated. The most useful recent analysis of Louise of Savoy as regent is Elizabeth McCartney's "The King's Mother and Royal Prerogative in Early-Sixteenth-Century France," in *Medieval Queenship*, ed. John Carmi Parsons (New York, 1993), 117-41.

Additional valuable information about Louise—as well as some of more dubious value—is found in biographies of her son; see, for example, the early *Francis the First* by Francis Hackett (New York, 1937) and the more recent *Francis I* by R. J. Knecht (Cambridge, 1982).

4. The split in the Valois family derives from Charles V (1338-1380). His older son, representing the royal line, was Charles VI (1368-1422), succeeded by his son Charles VII (1403-1461), succeeded by his son Louis XI, who was in turn succeeded by *his* son, Charles VIII, the younger brother of Anne of France (see Chapter 1). Charles V's younger son was Louis, duke of Orléans, from whom derive the Valois-Orléans and Valois-Angoulême branches of the Valois family tree. Louis' children included an older son, Charles of Orléans (who was Louis of Orléans' father); a younger son Jean, count of Angoulême (who was Charles of Angoulême's father); and a daughter, Marguerite, who married Richard of Brittany (her granddaughter was Anne of Brittany).

   On Louis of Orléans, later Louis XII, see Chapter 1.

   In arranging for the marriage of Louise of Savoy and Charles of Angoulême, Louis XI prevented Charles from marrying Mary of Burgundy: "The result of such a marriage could have been an alliance between the house of Burgundy and a branch of the house of Orléans against the French monarchy" (Freeman, 82). On Mary of Burgundy, see Chapter 2.

5. Freeman, 82; Mayer 11. Freeman indicates that "home management" and "Christian morality" are topics "included" in the *enseignements* Anne of France later prepared for her daughter, but he refers only to the first two pages of her book. Her instructions to her daughter encompass many topics; for a discussion of Anne of France's advice to her daughter, see Chapter 1.

   When she was sent to France, Margaret of Austria was just three years old. On her life as "the little queen" and her education by Anne of France, see Chapter 2. Margaret of Austria would later marry Philibert of Savoy, Louise's brother; see Chapter 2.

   For Louise of Savoy's contact with Margaret of Austria, see Mayer, who speculates (without citing any evidence) that Louise would have been jealous of Margaret, "bitterly" feeling the difference in their stations (8).

6. Knecht, 1; on this see also Chapter 1. Various motives are ascribed to Anne of France for insisting on the marriage her father had arranged for Charles of Angoulême; Elizabeth McCartney, citing numerous early biographers, indicates that Anne "supported the marriage to assure that Louise (her orphaned niece) would be provided for by the aging count" (118).

7. This may account for some of the differing dates for Louise's marriage. In an overheated but generously detailed chapter, for example, Millicent Garrett Fawcett (cited on the title page of her book only as "Mrs. Henry Fawcett")

indicates that Louise of Savoy's marriage took place in 1491 (*Five Famous French Women* [London, 1905], 54), a date also given by the *Annotated Index of Medieval Women*, ed. Anne Echols and Marty Williams (New York, 1992).

8. There are several contradictory accounts of Charles of Angoulême's household and personal relationships. Knecht, for example, who seems to rely on a nineteenth-century biography of Francis I for his information, indicates that Louise's husband had two mistresses in his household, Antoinette de Polignac and Jeanne Comte. Their children were, respectively, Jeanne and Madeleine [de Polignac] and Souveraine [Comte]. By contrast, Hackett (his biography of Francis I is undocumented), Mayer, and Freeman (relying on René de Maulde la Clavière, *Louise de Savoie et François Ier trente ans de jeunesse [1485-1515]* [Paris, 1895]) claim that Jeanne de Polignac was Charles's mistress and that by her the count had one daughter, Jeanne, later countess of Bar. Thus the details are too muddled to be absolutely clear, but the majority opinion seems to be that the name of Charles's mistress was Jeanne de Polignac.

9. For Louise's note on the birth of her "peace-loving Caesar," see her *Journal*, 461 (my translation).

   On the relationship between wife and mistress, see Mayer, 11-13, 25. On Jeanne's nursing of Francis, see Freeman, 83. On the marriages Louise arranges for her husband's illegitimate children, see Mayer, 66, for example.

10. Mayer, 24; Knecht, 3; Freeman, 84-85.

11. *Journal*, 457 (my translation). The incident occurred when Francis was about seven years old, thus about 1501 or 1502.

12. Freeman, 85-86; Knecht, 3-4. On Louise of Savoy's education of her children, see Freeman, 84-85, and Knecht, 4-5.

13. McCartney, 119.

14. *Journal*, 461 (my translation).

15. *Journal*, 457 (my translation).

16. *Journal*, 457 (my translation); see also n 1.

17. Francis is quoted by Knecht, 10.

   Louise's view of Louis XII is recorded in her *Journal*, 462 (my translation). On Mary Tudor, see Chapter 3.

18. Just as Ferdinand's marriage to Germaine de Foix was said to have killed him (Chapter 2), Louis XII's sexual exploits with his young bride were said to have resulted in his death. The young queen of France, for her part, was said to have deliberately worn out the old king so she could free herself from an unwanted political marriage.

19. McCartney, 126.

   In an interesting note, Hackett indicates that the Venetian ambassador in France reported that, in addition to Louise of Savoy, Anne of France also exerted considerable influence over the new king (146; Hackett's "quoted" words of the ambassador are not documented, however).

20. Quoted by Mayer, 80.

21. Quoted by Mayer, 82.

22. Quoted by Mayer, 85-86.

23. McCartney, 126.

   On French interests in Italy, and in particular on its claims to the duchy of Milan, see Chapter 1.

24. Hackett, 150-175; Knecht, 41; Freeman, 77, 92-93.

25. Mayer, 80-90.

26. Knecht, 42; McCartney, 126-27.

27. *Journal*, 460 (my translation).

One further entry alludes to the difficulty she encounters in her regencies. Just as the journal ends, Louise writes, "In the years 1515, [1]516, [1]517, [1]518, [1]519, [1]520, [1]521, & [1]522, without any way of making provision, my son and I were continually robbed by men of finance" (*Journal*, 646).

28. *Journal*, 460, 461, 462, 464 (my translations).

29. Quoted by Knecht, 87.

On Louise's role, see Mayer, 99-100.

30. Quoted by J. J. Scarisbrick, *Henry VIII* (Berkeley, California, 1968), 85.

31. Quoted by Scarisbrick, 92.

32. Fawcett, 104-7.

33. Knecht, 151. Freeman (79 n 8) quotes the diplomatic report Knecht refers to, illustrating the quality of the "evidence" of Louise of Savoy's feelings: Louis de Praet wrote to Charles V from London on 7 May 1523 and said that *Henry VIII* had reportedly said "there is no misunderstanding between [Montpensier] and the king, except, perhaps, on account of his refusal to marry Louise of Savoy, who is very much in love with him."

34. Mayer, 145, 153-58.

35. Freeman, 93-94; McCartney, 133.

In his account of the conflict, Bernard Chevalier notes only that Francis I "exploited unjustly a claim of inheritance of the duke of Bourbon" and was "led . . . to confiscate the Bourbonnais and the Auvergne"; see his "France from Charles VII to Henry IV," in *Handbook of European History, 1400-1600: Late Middle Ages, Renaissance, and Reformation*, vol. 1: *Structures and Assertions*, ed. Thomas A. Brady, Jr., et al. (Grand Rapids, Michigan, 1994), 379.

36. McCartney, 131.

37. Francis I's letter is printed by Mayer, 192.

Louise's letter to Francis is quoted in part by Mayer, 193; a different version is printed by Fawcett, 109. Louise of Savoy's journal does not contain any entries after 1522.

38. Knecht, 176; Louise's second regency is discussed in a complete chapter, 176-91.

See also Mayer's chapter on the "great regency," 194-219.

39. Freeman, 94; Fawcett, 109. See also Mayer, 196.

40. McCartney, 132; see also Mayer, 198-208. Knecht discusses this as well, 179.

41. Knecht, 179.

42. Mayer, 199.

43. Francis's wife Claude had died in 1524.

44. Knecht, 189; see also Freeman, 95.

45. On Margaret of Austria's role in negotiating the so-called Ladies' Peace, see Chapter 2. (See also the extended account in Mayer, 249-76.)

46. Freeman, 97.

Francis's letter is quoted by Mayer, 285.

47. Quoted by Freeman, 80.

48. Freeman, 81, quoting (without citation) Mayer, 290.

49. Mayer, 48.
50. On Caterina Sforza's actions when her children are held hostage, see Chapter 1.

    The harsh conditions of the French princes' imprisonment are described by Mayer, 277-78. Louise protested their situation, but Knecht (216) suggests her complaints may be "exaggerating." Nevertheless, reports about the boys' imprisonment seemed serious enough to prompt Margaret of Austria to write to her nephew Charles V, requesting that their conditions be improved (Mayer, 278).

51. Mayer, 145, quoting two early French historians, Louis-Marie Prudhomme (*Les Crimes des reines de France*, 1791) and Jules Michelet (*Histoire de France au XVI siècle*, 1855).

52. Again, the tendency to view women in isolation obscures the similarities between them. Earlier we noted (Chapter 1, n. 79) that some historians judged Margaret Beaufort's expressions of love for her son to be "obsessive, even neurotic," or "effusive, almost romantic," the same kinds of judgments, in fact, that are made about Louise's references to her son as her "love," her "lord," and her "Caesar."

53. A two-volume biography of Marguerite in French, Pierrre Jourda's *Marguerite d'Angoulême* (Paris, 1930), is the most complete version of her life; it is among the sources used by Nancy Lyman Roelker, *Queen of Navarre: Jeanne d'Albret, 1528-1572* (Cambridge, Massachusetts, 1968), whose more accessible work I have relied on here.

    Pierre de Bourdeille, abbey of Brantôme (c. 1540-1614), included an admiring sketch of Marguerite in his "Lives of Illustrious Ladies" (*Vies des dames illustres*); I have used the translation by Katharine Prescott Wormeley, *Illustrious Dames of the Court of Valois Kings* (New York, 1912), 234-43.

    Many advantageous marriages were suggested for Marguerite. Louis XII tried to arrange a marriage for her with Arthur of England and, failing that, with Arthur's younger brother, the future Henry VIII, but Henry VII refused both offers—some years later he suggested that he might marry her himself. Marguerite was said to have refused this alliance, insisting on a French marriage (for a brief treatment, see Knecht, 87).

    In addition to her political role, Marguerite is known for her interest in religious reform and for her writing. For a concise summary of her religious views, along with a bibliography for further reference, see *Contemporaries of Erasmus: A Biographical Register of the Renaissance and Reformation*, vol. 2 (Toronto, 1986). For a concise view of her writing, with further references, see *The Feminist Companion to Literature in English: Women Writers from the Middle Ages to the Present* (New Haven, Connecticut, 1990). Her *Heptameron*, a collection of stories similar to Boccaccio's *Decameron*, is available in a Penguin paperback edition, trans. P. A. Chilton (1984). Marguerite's mother, too, wrote some poetry; on this see Freeman, 85. Mayer quotes a *rondeau* written by Louise during the period of Francis's captivity, translated in a note, 145-46.

54. Jourda, translated and quoted by Roelker, 2.

    An exceptional new article has appeared just as *The Monstrous Regiment* went to press: Leah Middlebrook, "'Tout Mon Office': Body Politics and Family

Dynamics in the Verse and Epîtres of Marguerite de Navarre," *Renaissance Quarterly* 54 (2001), 1108-41.

55. Knecht, for example, notes that the story is a "legend," throughly "repudiated" by Jourda (86 n. 15), but nonetheless includes the "allegation" in his biography of Francis I.

56. The reference to Marguerite as a heroine comes from Jourda, translated and quoted by Roelker, 2.

For a brief treatment of Marguerite's journey to Spain, see Knecht, 187-88. Francis's statement of "obligation and love" comes from Brantôme, 238. The phrase "virtual queen of France" comes from Fawcett, 76.

57. Claude (1499-1524) was Anne of Brittany's older daughter and heir; her marriage to Francis meant that the duchy of Brittany lost the independence Anne had struggled throughout her life to ensure (see Chapter 1).

On Renée of France (1510-74), see Chapter 4.

58. On Elizabeth of York and Henry Tudor's claim to the throne, see Chapter 1.

59. On one of these children, Margaret of France (1523-1574), see Chapter 4.

60. On the kingdom of Navarre and Catherine of Foix's possessions, see Roelker, 5 and 254-61, and Chapter 1.

61. Marguerite was without question devoted to her brother's children. When Francis's children were returned to France in July 1530, she said that their return was the greatest joy of her life. Later in that month, in a letter to her brother, she wrote that "you say . . . your children are also mine, and I do not disclaim the honor, because I love them more than those I have borne" (quoted by Roelker, 11). Such statements may of course be read as evidence of whether—or how much—Marguerite loved her daughter; they may also be read as reflections of Marguerite's careful negotiations of family politics and the political moment.

62. Roelker, 18.

63. Roelker, 18-30.

Roelker discusses Aymée de Lafayette, 20-23, who appears as the character of Longarine in Marguerite's *Heptameron*.

64. On Jeanne's education, see Roelker, 31-34.

65. Roelker, 34-35.

66. Roelker, 36.

67. Quoted by Roelker, 36-37.

68. Charles de Ste. Marthe's funeral oration for Marguerite is translated and quoted by Roelker, 44-45.

69. For this and what follows, see Roelker, 46-59.

William of Cleves was the brother of Anne of Cleves, who had just become the fourth wife of Henry VIII of England.

70. Roelker quotes extensively from the report of the Spanish spy Juan Martinez Descurra, who quotes Marguerite's proposal that Jeanne publicly protest her proposed marriage in these words:

> I here protest before you that I do not wish, that I have no desire to marry the Duke of Cleves, and, as of now, I swear that I will never be his wife. If by chance . . . I should promise to be his wife it would be because I fear that the King will otherwise do harm to my father the King. I make this protest in your presence so that you will be my

witnesses. I sign this written protest and I beg you to sign it as witnesses. (48-49)

Descurra also reports, in the form of a dramatic dialogue, the supposed confrontation between Jeanne and her uncle, the French king (49-51).

71. The protest is quoted in full by Roelker, 54.

72. This is Brantôme's view of the ceremony, 237.

73. Jeanne's historian Bordenave is quoted by Roelker, 56.

The circumstances of Jeanne's marriage—the variety of opinion about and interpretations of her parents' motives and her own—are thoroughly analyzed by Roelker, 56-59.

74. Roelker, 62.

75. The letters are summarized and quoted by Roelker, 81-86. Criticized for ignoring her daughter, Marguerite is also criticized when she doesn't. While she notes Jourda's claim that Marguerite's letters "speak from the heart," Roelker concludes that Marguerite's letters to Jeanne are "stylized"; they "lack intimacy," 87.

76. Roelker, 89, 95.

77. Roelker, 99. A third son, who died in infancy, was born in February 1555.

78. Quoted by Roelker, 107.

79. On the political events of 1559, see Roelker, 118-19.

Roelker fails to note the birth of Catherine (1559-1600), except in an aside, and writes little of her, except for a few brief paragraphs at the end of her work (410-16), most of this detailing the struggle between Catherine and her brother over her marriage. Catherine Bourbon is the subject of a biographical essay in Roland H. Bainton, *Women of the Reformation in France and England* (Minneapolis, Minnesota, 1973), 75-81, which begins only with her marriage at age eighteen. A brief biographical introduction precedes Raymond Ritter's *Lettres et poésies de Catherine de Bourbon* (Paris, 1927), v-x. As an interesting note, Catherine of Bourbon's name is mentioned only twice in David Buisseret's biography of her brother, *Henry IV* (London, 1984).

80. Quoted by Roelker, 126; the "evolution of the religious posture" of Jeanne and her husband are analyzed by Roelker, 120-54.

The *Mémoirs de Jeanne d'Albret* was written in 1568, intended to justify her rebellion against the crown; Roelker notes it was "written at her command" by a member of her household; it is edited by A. de Ruble, *Mémoires et poésies de Jeanne d'Albret* (Paris, 1893).

81. The events are neatly summarized by Chevalier, 391-94.

82. The diplomatic report of Perrenot de Chantonay, Philip II of Spain's ambassador in France, is quoted by Roelker, 176.

83. Quoted by Roelker, 180.

84. Roelker, 183.

Jeanne's seven-year-old son Henry had accompanied her to the French court in 1560, and when she was ordered to leave, she had to leave him behind. Unable to reconvert his wife, Antoine dismissed his son's Protestant tutor and placed Henry in the care of a Catholic one. The boy was forced to abjure his Protestant faith in a formal ceremony on 1 June 1562. On all this see Buisseret, 4-5.

85. Roelker, 187.

86. Quoted by Roelker, 201.
87. Quoted by Roelker, 204-6.
88. Quoted by Roelker, 217.
89. Quoted by Roelker, 218-19.
90. On this period, see Roelker, 238-42.
    The Spanish ambassador's letter is quoted on pp. 241-42.
91. About these rebellions, Roelker notes, "Even a general account of them would require a book in itself" (278). Following Roelker, I omit any extended discussion of them here.
92. Quoted by Fawcett, 230-31.
93. The marriage negotiations are detailed by Roelker, 354-83.
94. Giovanni Maria Petrucci, quoted by Roelker, 363.
95. Quoted by Fawcett, 232.
96. The *Mémoirs*, quoted by Roelker, 421.
97. On Catherine de' Medici's early life in Italy, see Chapter 4. In addition to the sources cited there, see Hector de la Ferrière and Baguenault de Puchesse, eds., *Lettres de Catherine de Médicis*, 10 vols. (Paris, 1880-1909). For a brief discussion of the available biographies, see the bibliograhical essay in R. J. Knecht's *Catherine de Medici* (London, 1998), whose work I have relied on here.
98. Quoted by R. J. Knecht, *Catherine de' Medici*, 6.
99. Madeleine de la Tour d'Auvergne (1501-19) was the daughter of Jean III de la Tour and of Jeanne de Bourbon-Vendôme; on her royal connections, see Knecht, *Catherine de' Medici*, 7.
100. Contarini's report is summarized by Knecht, *Catherine de' Medici*, 30.
101. Knecht, *Catherine de' Medici*, 30.
102. Diane de Poitiers (1499-1566) apparently became Henry's mistress in 1538, when she was thirty-eight and he was nineteen. On her influence at court during Henry II's reign, see Knecht, *Catherine de' Medici*, 37-41. Several biographies exist; see Knecht, *Catherine de' Medici*, 281.
103. Lorenzo Contarini, Venetian ambassador to the French court, is quoted by Mark Strage, *Women of Power: The Life and Times of Catherine de' Medici* (New York, 1976), 84.
104. The Guises were descended from Claude, duke of Guise, and his wife Antoinette of Bourbon—the sister of Antoine of Bourbon, king of Navarre; on this see Knecht, 61 and genealogical table, 308.
     Retha Warnicke summarizes the status of the duke of Lorraine in her *The Marrying of Anne of Cleves: Royal Protocol in Tudor England* (Cambridge, 2000): "Nominally, as Lorraine's duke, he was a feudatory of the empire, but in reality he acted as an independent prince. Technically, Lorraine owed allegiance to France as well as to the empire, since he did homage for the duchy of Bar to both, one-half to France and the other half to the emperor" (53).
105. Knecht, *Catherine de' Medici*, 71.
106. On all this, see Knecht, *Catherine de' Medici*, 63-72.
107. Catherine's statement to the council is quoted by Strage, 112.
108. Giovanni Michieli, the Venetian ambassador to France in 1560, is quoted by Strage, 113.
109. Quoted by Knecht, *Catherine de' Medici*, 73.
110. Knecht, *Catherine de' Medici*, 84.

111. Quoted by Knecht, *Catherine de' Medici*, 90.

112. On the king's majority, see Knecht, *Catherine de' Medici*, 96-100; on the grand tour, see 101-10.

Elizabeth of Austria (1554-92) was the daughter of the Holy Roman Emperor Maximilian II. Already marriage had been used in an effort to secure the alliance between Spain and France; Elizabeth of Valois, Catherine's oldest daughter, had married Phillip II of Spain in 1559. She died in 1568, and the widowed Spanish king married Anne of Austria, Elizabeth of Austria's older sister.

On Catherine de' Medici's "matrimonial strategy," see Knecht, *Catherine de' Medici*, 134-36 and 138-41.

113. Quoted by Knecht, *Catherine de' Medici*, 115.

114. Quoted by Knecht, *Catherine de' Medici*, 139.

115. On this see Knecht, *Catherine de' Medici*, 140-41.

116. Knecht, *Catherine de' Medici*, 168.

117. Quoted by Knecht, *Catherine de' Medici*, 172-73.

118. Quoted by Knecht, *Catherine de' Medici*, 181.

119. Knecht, *Catherine de' Medici*, 191.

120. On all this see Knecht, *Catherine de' Medici*, 191-219.

121. On all this see Knecht, *Catherine de' Medici*, 248-55; the quotation is found on 251.

122. Quoted by Knecht, *Catherine de' Medici*, 253.

123. Quoted by Knecht, *Catherine de' Medici*, 255-64.

124. Catherine and the cardinal are quoted by Knecht, *Catherine de' Medici*, 267.

125. Giovanni Michieli, Venetian ambassador in France, is quoted by Strage, 207.

126. The diarist Pierre de L'Estoile is quoted by Knecht, *Catherine de' Medici*, 268-69.

127. Nicola M. Sutherland, "Catherine de Medici: The Legend of the Wicked Italian Queen," in her *Princes, Politics and Religion, 1547-1589* (London, 1984), 237-48.

128. Sutherland, 243-44. Sutherland refers to J. E. Neale, *The Age of Catherine de Medici* (London, 1943); and Garrett Mattingly, *The Defeat of the Spanish Armada* (London, 1959).

129. Quoted by Strage, 235.

130. Sheila ffolliott, "Catherine de' Medici as Artemisia: Figuring the Powerful Widow," in *Rewriting the Renaissance: The Discourses of Sexual Difference in Early Modern Europe* (Chicago, 1986), 227-41; the quotations are from 230 and 241.

Artemesia II (d. c. 350 B.C.E.) was the wife of King Mausolus of Caria; she ruled independently for three years after his death and built a tomb for her husband called the Maosoleum, one of the Seven Wonders of the World.

See also Katherine Crawford, "Catherine de Médicis and the Performance of Political Motherhood," *Sixteenth Century Journal*, 31 (2000), 643-73, and Susan Broomhall, " 'In my opinion': Charlotte de Minut and Female Political Discussion in Print in Sixteenth-Century France," *Sixteenth Century Journal*, 31 (2000), 25-46.

131. The most information about Catherine of Bourbon's political role comes from Ritter, and it is just one brief paragraph (v-vi). The phrases quoted from Ritter are my own translation.

Roelker's conclusion is found on 411. The same point is made by Bainton: "For a decade she [Catherine of Bourbon] was the governor of an area to which she gave an excellent administration" (75).

One letter from Catherine of Bourbon survives from the first period of her governership of Béarn, printed by Ritter, 8, though its contents are personal. Two letters survive from the months she was in Pau. Letters from her later regency in Béarn are concerned primarily with finances and military funding (14-110).

132. Ritter, ix (my translation).

133. Catherine's letters are printed by Ritter, 147-49 (quotations from the first letter are my translation; the second letter is translated by Bainton, 78).

134. Ritter, 159-60 (translated by Bainton, 79).

135. Ritter, 166-67 (translated by Roelker, 416).

136. See Bainton, 80-81.

137. Roelker, 416.

138. The Spanish king's second wife, Queen Mary of England, died in 1558; see Chapter 3.

Brantôme includes a chapter on Elizabeth of Valois, 137-51.

For Isabel Clara Eugenia, see Chapter 2.

139. Quoted by Knecht, 254.

The literature on Marguerite of Valois, queen of Navarre (1553-1615), is fairly extensive; see the bibliography compiled by Linda Frey et al., *Women in Western European History: A Select Chronological, Geographical, and Topical Bibliography, from Antiquity to the French Revolution* (Westport, Connecticut), 1982, 402-3.

Brantôme includes a lengthy portrait of Marguerite, 152-93, which contains Catherine's very positive view of her daughter. It also includes a lengthy discussion of Salic law and the inheritance of the crown by women. Brantôme quotes a conversation between Catherine de' Medici and a "silly" lady of the court, who suggests that, if the king of France were to die, Marguerite might inherit the crown. According to Brantôme, Catherine replies:

> If by the abolition of the Salic law, the kingdom should come to my daughter in her own right, as other kingdoms have fallen to the distaff, certainly my daughter is as capable of reigning, or more so, as most men and kings whom I have known; and I think that her reign would be a fine one, equal to that of the king her grandfather and that of the king her father, for she has a great mind and great virtues for doing that thing. (168)

According to Brantôme, Catherine regarded the Salic "law" as "an abuse," something "old dreamers and chroniclers had written down," "not just, and, consequently, . . . violable." She goes on to give a historical account of the development of this "law" and a long list of women, including regents, who had ruled successfully (contrasting them with the "infinitude of conceited, silly, tyrannical, foolish, do-nothing, idiotic, and crazy kings," 173). She concludes:

> If, therefore, foreign ladies (except Madame de Bourbon [Anne of France], who was daughter of France) were capable of governing France so well, why should not our own ladies do as much, having good zeal and affection, they being born here and suckled here, and the matter touching them so closely? . . . I should like to know in what

> our last kings have surpassed our last three daughters of France, Elisabeth, Claude, and Marguerite; and whether if the latter had come to be queens of France they would not have governed it . . . as well as their brothers. (174)

140. *Encyclopedia Britannica*, 15th edition, *s.v.*
      For her memoirs, see L. Lalanne, ed., *Mémoires de Marguerite de Valois* (Paris, 1842).

141. For Isabel Clara Eugenia, see Chapter 2.

142. For Christine of Lorraine (1565-1636) and her daughters Catherine (1593-1629) and Claudia (1604-1648), see Table 3.

143. Marie de' Medici (1573-1642) and Caterina de' Medici were cousins, both descendants of Lorenzo de' Medici and Clarice Orsini (1453-1587); see Table 3.

   Several nineteenth-century biographies of Marie de' Medici in French and Italian exist, as well as two more recent treatments: Francoise de Kermina, *Marie de Medicis: Reine, regente et rebelle* (Paris, 1979); and Salvo Mastellone, *Le Reggenza di Maria di Medici* (Messina-Florence, 1962). No full-length biography in English is available. Information about her is most readily accessible in biographies of her husband, of her son, and of her political advisor Cardinal Richelieu. I have relied here on Buisseret and Victor-L. Tapié, *France in the Age of Louis XIII and Richelieu*, trans. D. McN. Lockie (Cambridge, 1974); A. Lloyd Moote, *Louis XIII, the Just* (Berkeley, California, 1989); and Elizabeth Wirth Marvick, *Louis XIII: The Making of a King* (New Haven, Connecticut, 1986). A biographical profile of Marie de' Medici is also included in James Cleugh, *The Medici: A Tale of Fifteen Generations* (New York, 1975), 314-30.

   For a fairly brief bibliography see *Women in Western European History*, 498; more sources for Marie's life are to be found in the histories by Tapié, Bousseret, and Marvick.

144. Among Marie de' Medici's daughters, Elizabeth (1602-1644) became queen of Spain, married to Philip IV; Christine (1606-1663) married Victor Amadeus of Savoy and eventually became regent of Savoy; Henrietta Maria (1609-1669) became queen of England, married to Charles I.

145. Cleugh, for example, paints a devastating portrait, as does Marvick. The king's sexual appetite was "omnivorous, insatiable, and fruitful," and he insisted that his queen not only tolerate but acknowledge and accommodate his mistresses and their children. While "liberal with his affections," the king was "tight with money." Marie, by contrast, was "extravagant with money but had little spontaneous affection to give." She, for her part, was "stout, stiff, stubborn, and proud," "suspicious, sensitive to slights, and persistent in harboring resentment." While she was generally dignified and correct in her behavior, "she was occasionally unable to control outbursts of rage" directed at her husband, "whom she came to blame bitterly for humiliating her by flaunting his many affairs" (7-9). But for a more positive and ultimately considered view, see, for example, Tapié, 48-49, and Moote, 23 and 28-29.

146. Henry is quoted by Bousseret, 108.
      On Marie's actions immediately following her husband's assassination, see Moote, 40-42. Her regency is discussed on pp. 39-60. See also Tapié, 48-88.

Contrast Moote's version of events with that found in Cleugh, however, who indicates that following right after her husband's death, Marie secluded herself in the Louvre for forty days, only beginning to assert her authority when she emerged (320-21).

147. Marie's immediate "task" is defined by Moote, 44.

148. Marie is quoted by Marvick, 121.

149. Marvick, 122-44.

150. Marvick, 144.

151. Moote, 47 and 48, and Marvick, 150.

152. Quoted by Marvick, 154.

153. Quoted by Cleugh, 325.

Marie de' Medici's friend Leonora, Concini's wife, was tried for witchcraft, convicted, and executed.

154. See Tapié, 107, and Moote, 109-111.

155. Moote, 112-13. See also Tapié, 116-17.

156. Tapié, 126-27.

157. Tapié, 184-97, and Moote, 168.

158. Cleugh, 328-29. See also Tapié, 238-41, and Moote, 170-71.

159. Cleugh, 329.

160. Quoted by Cleugh, 330.

161. Cleugh, 330.

162. Marvick, 82.

On Louis' resemblance to his mother and his rather fraught relationship with his father, see Marvick, 78-90.

163. Matteo Botti's contemporary description is quoted by Marvick, 122.

164. The phrase describing her coldness to her children is from Marvick, 122.

Marie's supposed distance from her children is considered and discounted by Moote, 27.

165. The description of Henry IV comes from Cleugh, 317, and Bousseret, 88; the description of Marie is from Cleugh, 318 and 316.

166. Bousseret, 180.

167. Cleugh, 318.

168. Bousseret, 182; Cleugh, 121.

169. Bousseret, 180; Marvick, 123.

170. Marvick, 124, quoting Berthold Zeller, *Marie de Médicis et Villeroy* (Paris, 1897), 149.

Marie de' Medici was unable to construct an influential public image, despite the efforts of Peter Paul Rubens, who painted a series of twenty-four allegorical paintings executed for her:

Rubens did not impress the French with his overly theatrical style. The Spanish Netherlander's historical tableaux for Marie reveal a dutiful heir looking up adoringly at his mother as his father hands over authority, and a boy king holding on for dear life in a storm-tossed boat. These representations were not entirely convincing either as history or as psychology. (Moote, 264-65)

See also Beverly Heisner, "Marie de Medici: Self-promotion through Art," *Feminist Art Journal* 6 (1977), 21-26.

171. Quoted by Tapié, 240.

Chapter 6

1. King James VI [of Scotland] and I [of England], "A Speech to the Lords and Commons of the Parliament at Whitehall, on Wednesday the 21 of March, Anno 1609" in *Political Writings*, ed. Johann P. Sommerville (Cambridge, 1994), 181.

2. Jean Bodin, *Six Books of the Republic*, trans. Richard Knolles, *The Sixe Bookes of a Commonweale, Written by I. Bodin . . . out of the French and Latine Copies, done into English, by Richard Knolles* (London, 1606), 8 (text modernized).

   Bodin's use of the analogy of the family was not a new formulation. As Gordon J. Schochet writes, "The relationship between the family and society as a whole—and between familial and political authority—is one of the leit-motives of social and political theory," originating as early as Plato and Aristotle. Yet, as Schochet notes, "It was not until the seventeenth century that familial reasoning was used as a direct justification of political obligation." See his *Patriarchalism in Political Thought: The Authoritarian Family and Political Speculation and Attitudes Especially in Seventeenth-Century England* (New York, 1975), 18-19. Schochet traces the development of patriarchal political thought "From Plato to Bodin and Althusius," 18-36.

   Similarly, Merry E. Wiesener identifies in Bodin's *Six Books of the Republic* "what would become in the seventeenth century the most frequently cited reason against [female rule]:

   > that the state was like a household, and just as in a household the husband/father has authority and power over all others, so in the state a male monarch should always rule. (*Women and Gender in Early Modern Europe* [Cambridge, 1993], 243)

   Also very useful in tracing "the analogy of the family" that is "so marked a feature of the political debate of the sixteenth and seventeenth centuries" is R. W. K. Hinton, "Husbands, Fathers and Conquerors," *Political Studies*, 15 (1967), 291-300, and 16 (1968), 55-67:

   > As the Church was the bride of Christ and bishops were married to their sees, so kings were to be married to their commonwealths. As the father loved the son and the son honoured and obeyed the father, so kings and commonwealths were to be understood as comprising a single family. (*Political Studies*, 15, 291)

3. Bodin, 746 (text modernized).

4. See Sir Thomas Smith, *De Republica Anglorum: The Manner of Government or Policy of the Realm of England . . .* (London, 1583) and John Case, *Sphaera Civitatis* (Oxford, 1588).

   In his *De Republica Anglorum*, Smith identified the family as the "the first sort of beginning" of society. The husband and the wife together have "care of the family," but each has a particular role, "either of them excelling other in wit and wisdom to conduct those things which appertain to their office"; "the man," for example, is "to get, to travel abroad, to defend," while "the wife" is "to save that which is gotten, to tarry at home, to distribute that which commeth of the husband's labor" (sig. C2v, text modernized).

   Since nature has "made" women "to keep home and to nourish their family and children," they are meant neither "to meddle with matters abroad, nor to bear office in a city or commonwealth, no more than children and infants." "We do reject women" in such affairs, Smith wrote. But, while "rejecting" women in general from public affairs, he did allow for the exception in the larger commonwealth when "authority is annexed to the blood and progeny, as the crown, a duchy, or an earldom, for there the blood is respected, not the age nor the sex":

> Whereby an absolute queen, an absolute duchess, or countess—those I call absolute which have the name, not by being married to a king, duke, or earl, but by having the true, right, and next succes[sion] in the dignity, and upon whom by right of the blood that title is descended—those I say have the same authority although they be women or children in that kingdom, duchy, or earldom as they should have had if they had been men of full age.

In such a case, Smith argued, the "right and honor of the blood" and the "quietness and surety of the realm" are more to be considered than "the tender age as yet impotent to rule" or the "sex not accustomed otherwise to intermeddle with public affairs" (sig. D1v, text modernized).

A similar argument was made by Case in *Sphaera Civitatis*. He refuted the claim that women were by nature imperfect, demonstrating that the "logic" that led to such a conclusion was faulty. "All that is imperfect by nature is monstrous," he began. He then continued the syllogism: "all women are imperfect by nature; therefore all women are monstrous." But such a proof was, he said, "ridiculous" (*Sphaera Civitatis*, 18-19). Having demonstrated the folly of such an argument, he then turned to the claim that men were meant to command while women were meant to obey. While acknowledging that women in general were not suited to command, he allowed for the "command" of an exceptional woman:

> Nature often makes woman shrewd, hard work makes her learned, upbringing makes her pious, and experience makes her wise. What, therefore, prevents women from playing a full part in public affairs? If one is born free, why should she obey? If one is heiress to a kingdom, why should she not reign? (Case, quoted and translated by Ian Maclean, *The Renaissance Notion of Woman: A Study in the Fortunes of Scholasticism and Medical Science in European Intellectual Life* [Cambridge, 1980], 61)

Although he used the analogy of the family in his discussion of the state, Case argued that such a comparison was limited, because the family was different from the state. A woman was to be subservient to her husband but not to all men, he pointed out, and further qualified the family analogy by noting that a female sovereign was different from a married woman (Case, 85-89).

5. Robert Filmer, *Patriarchia: Or the Natural Power of Kings* (London 1680). Filmer's work was probably written during 1648-53. According to Filmer, the king "claims not his power as a donative from the people," but from God, "from whom he receives his royal charter of an universal father" (22); the king's authority "is the only right and natural authority of a supreme father" (23).

6. Jacques Bossuet, *Politique tirée des propres paroles de l'Écriture-Sainte* (Paris, 1706), but probably written about 1680.

7. I don't mean to imply that changing political theories are themselves the *cause* of the reduced ranks of women rulers; rather, such theories both reflect and, in their turn, shape larger social developments in the early modern period, including legal, religious, and economic changes. Seeing *when* a change occurred is always easier than understanding *why* a change occurred. Accounting for such changes remains outside the scope of my study here.

8. Among the women I have only listed are Catalina of Spain (1507-77), regent of Portugal; Catalina of Spain (1567-97), duchess of Savoy and regent of the Netherlands; Christina of Denmark (b. 1522), duchess of Milan, then duchess and regent of Burgundy; and Christine, duchess of Lorraine (1565-1636), whose older daughter Catherine (1593-1629) became the governor of Siena and whose younger daughter Claudia (1604-48) became regent of Tyrol.

9. Marjorie Chibnall, *The Empress Matilda: Queen Consort, Queen Mother and Lady of the English* (Oxford, 1991), 1.

10. See Chibnall, especially 64-87, and Bernard F. Reilly, *The Kingdom of León-Castilla under Queen Urraca, 1109-1126* (Princeton, 1982), 47, for a discussion of the twelfth-century arguments against rule by women and the specific examples like Jezebel and the daughters of Zelophehad.

    John Knox uses the example of Jezebel (1 and 2 Kings), as do those who follow him in their denunciations of rule by women. He also referred to the less obvious example of the daughters of Zelophehad (Numbers 27:1-11), which had been suggested as offering a biblical precedent for female rulers. In the Old Testament story, the daughters of Zelophehad appealed to Moses after the death of their father. Zelophehad left no sons; why, his daughters ask, should the name of their father be lost because he had no sons? They ask that their father's possessions be left to them. Moses takes their request to God, who deems that, when a man leaves no male heir, the inheritance should pass to his daughters. Knox replied that it is not only lawful that women have their inheritance, but that justice requires it. But he adds that "to bear rule or authority over man can never be right nor inheritance to woman." Authority—and, by extension, office—are not possessions that can be inherited. For his arguments using such specific examples, see *The First Blast of the Trumpet against the Monstrous Regiment of Women* (Geneva, 1558), sigs. 39-53v (also available in David Laing, ed., *The Works of John Knox* [Edinburgh, 1855], IV:402-17). These specific examples are repeated by those who defend women rulers and by those who, like Knox, oppose them.

11. Magdalena S. Sánchez, *The Empress, the Queen, and the Nun: Women and Power at the Court of Philip III of Spain* (Baltimore, Maryland, 1998), 130-36; the quotation is on 132-33.

12. The quotation is from T. A. Morris, *Europe and England in the Sixteenth Century* (New York, 1998), 344. Similar assessments can be found in standard college texts like Robert E. Lerner et al., *Western Civilizations: Their History and Their Culture*, 13th ed. (New York, 1998); Donald Kagan, et al., *The Western Heritage*, 7th ed. (New York, 2000); and Jackson J. Spielvogel, *Western Civilization: A Brief History to 1715*, 2nd ed. (New York, 2002).

13. Roland H. Bainton, *Women of the Reformation from Spain to Scandinavia* (Minneapolis, Minnesota, 1977), 226.

14. Thomas A. Brady, Jr., Heido A. Oberman, and James D. Tracy, eds., *Handbook of European History, 1400-1600*, vol. 1: *Late Middle Ages, Renaissance, and Reformation: Structures and Assertions* (Grand Rapids, Michigan, 1994), xix. See also Morris, 5-6).

15. For Eleanor Hibbert (1906-93), see the entry in Joanne Shattock, *The Oxford Guide to British Women Writers* (Oxford, 1993), 211-12: "These [her novels] were usually based on an historical . . . female figure, narrated by a female observer, often royal, and designed to instruct as well as entertain." Many readers have supplemented whatever conventional political history they learned in the classroom with Plaidy's historical narratives; she produced nearly ninety of them, "at the rate of two a year," and they "appeared annually in the list of the top 100 library titles (borrowed at least 300,000 times)."

SELECT BIBLIOGRAPHY

Full bibliographical references for all of the sources used in this book appear in the notes. This select bibliography is intended to provide readers with general works on women and political power that will lead them to further titles. Secondary works that address particular issues or individual figures are included in the notes.

Reference Works

Bietenholz, Peter G., ed. *Contemporaries of Erasmus*. 3 vols. Toronto: University of Toronto Press, 1985-87.

Echols, Anne, and Marty Williams. *An Annotated Index of Medieval Women*. New York: Markus Wiener Publishing, 1992.

Frey, Linda, Marsha Frey, and Joanne Schneider. *Women in Western European History: A Select Chronological, Geographical, and Topical Bibliography from Antiquity to the French Revolution*. Westport, Connecticut: Greenwood Press, 1982.

Gibson, Peter. *The Concise Guide to Kings & Queens: A Thousand Years of European Monarchy*. New York: Dorset Press, 1985.

Jackson, Guida M. *Women Who Ruled*. Oxford: ABC Clio, 1990.

Tauté, Anne. *Kings & Queens of Europe: A Genealogical Chart of the Royal Houses of Great Britain and Europe*. Chapel Hill: University of North Carolina Press, 1989.

Secondary Sources

Amussen, Susan D. "Gender, Family and the Social Order, 1560-1725." In *Order and Disorder in Early Modern England*, ed. Anthony Fletcher and John Stevenson, 196-217. Cambridge, U.K.: Cambridge University Press, 1985.

————. *An Ordered Society: Gender and Class in Early Modern England*. Oxford: Blackwell, 1988.

Anderson, Bonnie S., and Judith P. Zinsser. *A History of Their Own: Women in Europe from Prehistory to the Present.* Vol. 1. London: Penguin Books, 1988.

Axton, Marie. "The Influence of Edmund Plowden's Succession Treatise." *The Huntington Library Quarterly,* 37 (1974), 209-26.

——————. *The Queen's Two Bodies: Drama and the Elizabethan Succession.* London: Royal Historical Society, 1977.

Bainton, Roland. *Women of the Reformation from Spain to Scandinavia.* Minneapolis: Augsburg Publishing House, 1977.

——————. *Women of the Reformation in France and England.* Minneapolis: Augsburg Publishing House, 1973.

——————. *Women of the Reformation in Germany and Italy.* Minneapolis: Augsburg Publishing House, 1971.

Beard, Mary R. *Woman as Force in History: A Study in Traditions and Realities.* 1946. Reprint. New York: Octagon Books, 1976.

Benson, Pamela J. *The Invention of the Renaissance Woman: The Challenge of Female Independence in the Literature and Thought of Italy and England.* University Park: the Pennsylvania State University Press, 1992.

Bornstein, Diane. *The Feminist Controversy of the Renaissance.* Delmar, New York: Scholars' Facsimiles and Reprints, 1980.

Brady, Thomas A., et al. *Handbook of European History, 1400-1600: Late Middle Ages, Renaissance, and Reformation.* Vol. 1: *Structures and Assertions.* Grand Rapids, Michigan: William B. Eerdmans Publishing Company, 1996.

Bridenthal, Renate, and Claudia Koonz, eds. *Becoming Visible: Women in European History.* 1977. 2nd ed. Boston: Houghton Mifflin Company, 1987.

Bridenthal, Renate, Susan Mosher Stuard, and Mary E. Wiesner, *Becoming Visible: Women in European History.* 3rd ed. Boston: Houghton Mifflin Company, 1998.

Brink, Jean R., Allison P. Condert, and Maryanne C. Horowitz. *The Politics of Gender in Early Modern Europe.* Kirksville, Missouri: Sixteenth Century Journal Publishers, 1989.

Carlton, C. "The Widow's Tale: Male Myths and Female Reality in Sixteenth and Seventeenth Century England." *Albion,* 10 (1978), 118-29.

Church, William F. *Constitutional Thought in Sixteenth-Century France: A Study in the Evolution of Ideas.* New York: Octagon Books, 1969.

Coole, Diana. "Re-reading Political Theory from a Woman's Perspective." *Political Studies,* 39 (1986), 129-48.

Davis, Natalie Zemon. "Women on Top." In *Society and Culture in Early Modern France: Eight Essays,* 124-51. Stanford, California: Stanford University Press, 1975.

Davis, Natalie Zemon, and Arlette Farge, eds. *Renaissance and Enlightenment Paradoxes.* Vol. 3 of *A History of Women in the West.* Cambridge, Massachusetts: Harvard University Press, 1993.

Duggan, Anne J., ed. *Queens and Queenship in Medieval Europe.* Woodbridge, Suffolk, England: Boydell Press, 1997.

Elshtain, Jean Bethke. *Public Man, Private Woman.* Princeton, New Jersey: Princeton University Press, 1981.

Erler, Mary, and Maryanne Kowaleski, eds. *Women and Power in the Middle Ages.* Athens: The University of Georgia Press, 1988.

Fahy, Conor. "Three Early Renaissance Treatises on Women." *Italian Studies*, 2 (1951), 30-55.

Farrell, Kirby, Elizabeth H. Hageman, and Arthur F. Kinney. *Women in the Renaissance: Selections from English Literary Renaissance.* Amherst: University of Massachusetts Press, 1988.

Felch, Susan M. "The Rhetoric of Biblical Authority: John Knox and the Question of Women." *The Sixteenth Century Journal*, 26 (1995), 805-22.

Ferguson, Margaret W. "Lady Honor Lisle's Networks of Influence." In *Women and Power in the Middle Ages*, ed. Mary Erler and Maryanne Kowaleski, 188-212. Athens: the University of Georgia Press, 1988.

Ferguson, Margaret W., et. al. *Rewriting the Renaissance: The Discourses of Sexual Difference in Early Modern Europe.* Chicago: University of Chicago Press, 1986.

Fichtner, Paula S. "Dynastic Marriage in Sixteenth-Century Habsburg Diplomacy and Statecraft: A Dynastic Approach." *American Historical Review*, 81 (1976), 243-65.

Fleischer, Manfred P. "'Are Women Human?'—The Debate of 1595 Between Valens Acidalius and Simon Gediccus." *The Sixteenth Century Journal*, 12 (1981), 107-20.

Fradenburg, Louise O., ed. *Women and Sovereignty.* Vol. 7 of *Cosmos: The Yearbook of the Traditional Cosmology Society.* Edinburgh: Edinburgh University Press, 1992.

Fraser, Antonia. *The Warrior Queens.* New York: Alfred A. Knopf, 1989.

Gibbons, Rachel. "Medieval Queenship: An Overview." *Reading Medieval Studies*, 21 (1995), 97-107.

Giesey, Ralph E. "The Juristic Basis of Dynastic Right to the French Throne." *Transactions of the American Philosophical Society*, N.S. 51.5 (1961), 3-47.

Grafton, Anthony, and Lisa Jardine. *From Humanism to the Humanities: Education and the Liberal Arts in Fifteenth- and Sixteenth-Century Europe.* Cambridge, Massachusetts: Harvard University Press, 1986.

Greaves, Richard L. *Theology and Revolution in the Scottish Reformation: Studies in the Thought of John Knox.* Grand Rapids, Michigan: Christian University Press, 1980.

————. "John Knox's Theology of Political Government." *The Sixteenth Century Journal*, 19 (1988), 529-40.

Greco, Norma, and Ronaele Novotny. "Bibliography of Women in the English Renaissance." *University of Michigan Papers in Women's Studies*, 1 (1974), 30-57.

Hanawalt, Barbara. *The Ties That Bound: Peasant Families in Medieval England.* New York: Oxford University Press, 1986.

Hanawalt, Barbara, ed. *Women and Work in Pre-Industrial Europe.* Bloomington: Indiana University Press, 1986.

Haney, Sarah. *Les droits des femmes et la loi salique.* Paris: Indigo & Côte-femmes, 1994.

Hanmer, Jalna, and Mary Maynard. *Women, Violence, and Social Control.* Atlantic Highlands, New Jersey: Humanities Press, 1987.

Hannay, Margaret P. *Silent But for the Word: Tudor Women as Patrons, Translators, and Writers of Religious Works.* Kent, Ohio: Kent State University Press, 1985.

Harris, Barbara. "Women and Politics in Early Tudor England." *The Historical Journal*, 33 (1990), 259-81.

Harris, Barbara, and JoAnn McNamara, eds. *Women and the Structure of Society.* Durham, North Carolina: Duke University Press, 1984.

Healey, Robert M. "Waiting for Deborah: John Knox and Four Ruling Queens." *The Sixteenth Century Journal*, 25 (1994), 371-97.

Henderson, Katherine, and Barbara F. McManees. *Half Humankind: Contexts and Texts of the Controversy about Women in England, 1540-1640*. Urbana: University of Illinois Press, 1985.

Herlihy, David. "Did Women Have a Renaissance? A Reconsideration." *Medievalia et Humanistica*, n.s., 13 (1985), 1-22.

Hinton, R.W.K. "Husbands, Fathers and Conquerors." *Political Studies*, 15 (1967), 291-30, and 16 (1968), 55-68.

Hogrefe, Pearl. "Legal Rights of Tudor Women and the Circumvention by Men and Women." *The Sixteenth Century Journal*, 3 (1972), 97-105.

——————. *Tudor Women: Commoners and Queens*. Ames: Iowa State University Press, 1975.

——————. *Women of Action in Tudor England*. Ames: Iowa State University Press, 1977.

Hopkins, Lisa. *Women Who Would Be Kings: Female Rulers of the Sixteenth Century*. London: Vision Press, 1991.

Hufton, Olwen. "Women in History: Early Modern Europe." *Past and Present*, 101 (1983), 125-41.

Hull, Suzanne W. *Chaste, Silent, & Obedient: English Books for Women, 1475-1640*. San Marino, California: Huntingon Library Press, 1982.

Jankowski, Theodora A. "Women in Early Modern England: Privileges and Restraints." In *Women in Power in the Early Modern Drama*, 22-53. Urbana: University of Illinois Press, 1992.

Jordan, Constance. *Renaissance Feminism: Literary Texts and Political Models*. Ithaca, New York: Cornell University Press, 1990.

——————. "Women's Rule in Sixteenth-Century British Political Thought." *Renaissance Quarterly*, 40 (1987), 421-66.

Kantorowicz, Ernst. *The King's Two Bodies: A Study in Mediaeval Political Theory*. Princeton, 1959.

Kelly-Gadol, Joan. Did Women Have a Renaissance?" In *Becoming Visible*, 2nd ed., 175-201. Rpt. in Joan Kelly, *Women, History, and Theory*, 19-50. Chicago: University of Chicago Press, 1984.

Kelso, Ruth. *Doctrine for the Lady of the Renaissance*. Urbana: University of Illinois Press, 1956.

Kettering, Sharon. "The Patronage Power of Early Modern French Noblewomen." *Historical Journal*, 32 (1989), 817-41.

King, Margaret L. "Thwarted Ambitions: Six Learned Women of the Italian Renaissance." *Soundings*, 59 (1976), 280-304.

——————. *Women of the Renaissance*. Chicago: University of Chicago Press, 1991.

Kinnear, Mary. *Daughters of Time: Women in the Western Tradition*. Ann Arbor: University of Michigan Press, 1982.

Klapisch-Zuber, Christiane. *Women, Family, and Ritual in Renaissance Italy*. Trans. Lydia G. Cochrane. Chicago: University of Chicago Press, 1985.

Klein, Joan Larsen, ed. *Daughters, Wives, and Widows: Writings by Men about Women and Marriage in England, 1500-1640*. Urbana: University of Illinois Press, 1992.

LaBalme, Patricia H. *Beyond Their Sex: Learned Women of the European Past*. New York: New York University Press, 1980.

Lamphere, Louise. "Strategies, Cooperation, and Conflict among Women in Domestic Groups." In *Woman, Culture, and Society*, ed. Michelle Zimbalist

Rosaldo and Louise Lamphere, 97-112. Stanford, California: Stanford University Press, 1974.

Laslett, Peter, and Richard Wall. *Household and Family in Past Time.* Cambridge, U.K.: Cambridge University Press, 1972.

Lerner, Gerda. *The Majority Finds Its Past: Placing Women in History.* New York: Oxford University Press, 1979.

—————. *Women and History.* Vol. 1: *The Creation of Patriarchy.* New York: Oxford University Press, 1986.

—————. *Women and History.* Vol. 2: *The Creation of Feminist Consciousness: From the Middle Ages to Eighteen-seventy.* New York: Oxford University Press, 1993.

Levin, Carole. "John Foxe and the Responsibilities of Queenship." In *Women in the Middle Ages and the Renaissance,* ed. Mary Beth Rose, 113-33. Syracuse, New York: Syracuse University Press, 1986.

—————. "Queens and Claimants: Political Insecurity in Sixteenth-Century England." In *Gender, Ideology, and Action: Historical Perspectives on Women's Public Lives,* ed. Janet Sharistanian, 41-66. Bloomington, Indiana: Greenwood Press, 1986.

Levin, Carole, and Jeannie Watson. *Ambiguous Realities: Women in the Middle Ages and the Renaissance.* Detroit, Michigan: Wayne State University Press, 1987.

Levin, Carole, and Patricia A. Sullivan. *Political Rhetoric, Power, and Renaissance Women.* Albany: State University of New York Press, 1995.

Levine, Mortimer. *The Early Elizabethan Succession Question.* Stanford, California: Stanford University Press, 1966.

—————. "The Place of Women in Tudor Government." In *Tudor Rule and Tudor Revolution: Essays for G.R. Elton from His American Friends,* ed. Delloyd J. Guth and John McKenna, 109-23. Cambridge, U.K.: Cambridge University Press, 1982.

Litzen, Veikko. *A War of Roses and Lilies: The Theme of Succession in Sir John Fortescue's Works.* Helsinki: Suomalrinen Tiedeakatemia, 1971.

Lucas, Angela M. *Women in the Middle Ages: Religion, Marriage, and Letters.* New York: St. Martin's Press, 1983.

Maclean, Ian. *The Renaissance Notion of Woman: A Study in the Fortunes of Scholasticism and Medical Science in European Intellectual Life.* 1980. Reprint. Cambridge, U.K.: Cambridge University Press, 1988.

—————. *Woman Triumphant: Feminism in French Literature, 1610-1652.* Oxford: Clarendon Press, 1977.

Martines, Lauro. "A Way of Looking at Women in Renaissance Florence." *Journal of Medieval and Renaissance Studies,* 4 (1974), 15-28.

de Maulde la Claviere, R. *The Women of the Renaissance: A Study of Feminism.* Trans. George Herbert Ely. London: Putnam, 1905.

Morris, Terence A. *Europe and England in the Sixteenth Century.* New York: Routledge, 1998.

O'Faolain, Julia, and Lauro Martines, eds. *Not in God's Image: Women in History.* New York: Harper & Row, 1973.

Okin, Susan Moller. *Women in Western Political Thought.* Princeton, New Jersey: Princeton University Press, 1979.

Orlin, Lena Cowen. *Private Matters and Public Culture in Post-Reformation England.* Ithaca, New York: Cornell University Press, 1994.

Ozment, Steven. *When Fathers Ruled: Family Life in Reformation Europe*. Cambridge, Massachusetts: Harvard University Press, 1983.

Parsons, John C., ed. *Medieval Queenship*. New York: St. Martin's Press, 1998.

Perrot, Michelle, ed. *Writing Women's History*. Trans. Felicia Pheasant. Oxford: Blackwell, 1984.

Phillips, James E. "The Background of Spenser's Attitude Toward Women Rulers." *The Huntington Library Quarterly*, 5 (1941), 5-32.

———. "The Woman Ruler in Spenser's *Faerie Queene*." *The Huntington Library Quarterly*, 5 (1941), 211-34.

Pitkin, Hanna Fenichel. *Fortune Is a Woman: Gender and Politics in the Thought of Niccolò Machiavelli*. Berkeley: University of California Press, 1984.

Plowden, Alison. *Tudor Women: Queens and Commoners*. New York: Atheneum, 1979.

Potter, John Milton. "The Development and Significance of the Salic Law of the French." *English Historical Review*, 52 (1937), 235-53.

Prior, Mary, *Women in English Society, 1500-1800*. London: Routledge, 1985.

Richards, Judith. "'To Promote a Woman to Beare Rule': Talking of Queens in Mid-Tudor England." *The Sixteenth Century Journal*, 28 (1997), 101-21.

Rose, Mary Beth, ed. *Women in the Middle Ages and the Renaissance: Literary and Historical Perspectives*. Syracuse, New York: Syracuse University Press, 1986.

Rosenthal, Joel T. "Aristocratic Widows in Fifteenth-Century England." In *Women and the Structure of Society*, ed. Barbara J. Harris and JoAnn K. McNamara, 36-47. Durham, North Carolina: Duke University Press, 1984.

Saxonhouse, Arlene W. *Women in the History of Political Thought: Ancient Greece to Machiavelli*. New York: Praeger, 1985.

Scalingi, Paula L. "The Scepter or the Distaff: The Question about Female Sovereignty, 1516-1607." *The Historian*, 41 (1978), 59-75.

Schochet, Gordon. *Patriarchalism in Political Thought*. New York: Basic Books, 1975.

Shephard, Amanda. *Gender and Authority in Sixteenth-Century England*. Keele, U.K.: Keele University Press, 1994.

———. "Henry Howard and the Lawful Regiment of Women." *History of Political Thought*, 12 (1991), 589-603.

Shepherd, Simon, ed. *The Women's Sharp Revenge: Five Women's Pamphlets from the Renaissance*. New York: St. Martin's Press, 1975.

Sutherland, N.M. *Princes, Politics and Religion 1547-1589*. London: Hambledon Press, 1984.

Travitsky, Betty S. "Placing Women in the English Renaissance." In *The Renaissance Englishwoman in Print: Counterbalancing the Canon*, ed. Anne M. Haselkorn and Betty S. Travitsky, 3-41. Amherst: University of Massachusetts Press, 1990.

———, ed. *The Paradise of Women: Writings by Englishwomen of the Renaissance*. London: Greenwood Press, 1981.

Travitsky, Betty S., and Adele F. Seeff, ed. *Attending to Women in Early Modern England*. Newark, New Jersey: Associated University Press, 1994.

Trexler, Richard. *Public Life in Renaissance Florence*. Ithaca, New York, Cornell University Press, 1980.

Warnicke, Retha M. "Private and Public: The Boundaries of Women's Lives in Early Stuart England." In *Privileging Gender in Early Modern England*, ed. Jean R. Brink, 123-40. Kirksville, Missouri: Sixteenth Century Journal Publishers, 1993.

—————. *Women of the English Renaissance and Reformation*. Westport, Connecticut: Greenwood Press, 1983.

Weinstein, Minna F. "Reconstructing Our Past: Reflections on Tudor Women." *International Journal of Women's Studies*, 1 (1978), 133-40.

Wiesner, Merry E. *Women and Gender in Early Modern Europe*. Cambridge: Cambridge University Press, 1993.

—————. *Women in the Sixteenth Century: A Bibliography*. St. Louis: Center for Reformation Research, 1983.

—————. *Working Women in Renaissance Germany*. New Brunswick, New Jersey: Rutgers University Press, 1986.

Wyntries, Sherrin Marshall. "Women in the Reformation Era." In Bridenthal, *Becoming Visible*, 165-91.

Yost, John. "The Value of Married Life for the Social Order in the Early English Renaissance." *Societas*,6 (1976),25-39.

Index